German Winter Nights

Studies in German Literature, Linguistics, and Culture

Edited by James Hardin
(*South Carolina*)

Johann Beer

German Winter Nights

Translated by John Russell

With an
introduction by
James Hardin

CAMDEN HOUSE

English translation of Johann Beer's *Teutsche Winternächte*,
first published in German in 1682.

Translation © 1998 John R. Russell

First published 1998
Camden House
Drawer 2025
Columbia, SC 29202–2025 USA

Camden House is an imprint of Boydell & Brewer Inc.
PO Box 41026, Rochester, NY 14604–4126 USA
and of Boydell & Brewer Limited
PO Box 9, Woodbridge, Suffolk IP12 3DF, UK

ISBN: 1–57113–195–7

Library of Congress Cataloging-in-Publication Data

Beer, Johann, 1655-1700.
    [Teutsche Winternächte. English]
    German winter nights / Johann Beer; translated by John Russell,
and with an introduction by James Hardin.
        p.   cm. – (Studies in German literature, linguistics, and
culture)
    ISBN 1–57113–195–7 (alk. paper)
    I. Russell, John Raymond. II. Hardin, James N. III. Title.
IV. Series: Studies in German literature, linguistics, and culture
(Unnumbered)
PT1707.B15T4813   1998
833'.5—dc21   98-39707
                                                      CIP

This publication is printed on acid-free paper.
Printed in the United States of America

Acknowledgments

I again would like to thank two persons for having been of special help to me with this text: Professor James Hardin, my editor, for having suggested it as a worthy candidate for translation and nursing it through to publication, and Professor Gerda Jordan for having offered so many suggestions for improving the penultimate version thereof. Having themselves co-translated the *Summer Tales* (Zürich and New York: Lang, 1984), the sequel Beer announces at the end of this book, they are uniquely qualified to understand the problems I encountered.

The text used was Richard Alewyn's edition of Beer's *Teutsche Winter-Nächte* (Frankfurt am Main: Insel Verlag, 1963). The material in most of the footnotes was also derived from this edition.

Title page of first edition of Teutsche Winternächte, 1682.

Introduction

Johann Beer was one of the most remarkable figures of seventeenth-century German letters, a man who had risen from poverty in a provincial Austrian village to a respected position as court musician and composer. He was only incidentally, and relatively briefly, a writer. In fact until 1932, when his identity as author of over twenty prose satires was established by Richard Alewyn and Hans F. Menck,[1] he was not even mentioned in German literary histories. His "novels," or prose satires, were written under a variety of pseudonyms, none of which had been identified with his musical and theoretical works that appeared under his name. His prose fiction stands in the tradition of the Spanish and French picaresque novel, but was clearly most influenced by the "Simplician" writings of Johann Jakob Christoffel von Grimmelshausen. He is generally regarded as the most talented successor to that giant figure, and his two "Willenhag" novels,[2] *Die teutschen Winter-Nächte* and *Die kurzweiligen Sommer-Täge*, are among the few German works of the period that are still enjoyable reading today. With the publication of a historical-critical edition of his fictional works, he has finally entered the German canon.[3] The discovery of his handwritten and illustrated diary in 1963 in Erfurt[4] was a notable event in the history of German Baroque literature; there is no other diary of this kind, from this period, in existence. As dry and laconic as most of the diary is, it is invaluable as a measure of the man's ceaseless activity, of his interests in things and events. It reveals little of Beer the thinker or husband, but much of the public man. It is also unique in that it reports, in Beer's own hand, the shooting accident that led to his premature death.

Johann Beer was born 28 February 1655 in the village of St. Georgen, Austria, the seventh of fifteen children, most of whom died in childbirth.

---

[1] Richard Alewyn, *Johann Beer: Studien zum Roman des 17. Jahrhunderts.* (Leipzig: Mayer & Müller, 1932); H. F. Menck, *Der Musiker im Roman: Ein Beitrag zur Geschichte der vorromantischen Erzählungsliteratur* Heidelberg: Winter, 1931).

[2] Named for the protagonist of the second of the two novels.

[3] Edited by Hans-Gert Roloff and Ferdinand von Ingen, and published by Peter Lang. This edition will include a carefully edited version of the diary, which was preserved on microfilm.

[4] The diary was sent to the city archive in Weissenfels, where Adolf Schmiedecke transcribed most of it and provided notes and a list of names (though incomplete) for the apparatus. The diary was reported missing in the 1980s.

His father was an innkeeper (the inn today bears a plaque identifying it as Beer's birthplace), probably strapped for funds, since he sent his son for a time to live with his aunt. Later, at the age of five (based on information in Beer's diary), he appears to have been cared for by his grandmother. The Beer family was Protestant, but the young Beer, who early on displayed what must have been a remarkable musical talent, was educated in the famous Benedictine monastery at Lambach, attending school there "in order to study music," as we read in the diary. He remained there for three years, then went on to Cloister Reichersperg am Inn where he continued to study music and in 1669 went to the Latin school in Passau at the expense of a (Catholic?) friend of the family. At this point Johann's parents made the decision to leave Catholic Austria for Regensburg, Germany, then a predominantly Protestant city, and in 1670 the fifteen-year-old joined them there. Just as the beautiful rolling countryside around St. Georgen was deeply rooted in Beer (it recurs in many of his novels), so too the variegated life in Regensburg was to be an unforgettable experience. This was a city filled with churches, patrician homes, nunneries, with a variety of Romanesque, Gothic and Baroque architecture, set picturesquely on the Danube River. The city retains much of its romantic appearance even today. The Imperial Diet, which met in Regensburg from 1663 until 1806, brought a large number of ambassadors and their retinues from all over Europe. Their pomp and costume, their exotic (for Beer) languages and dress, all this rich material remained in Beer's remembrance of the place and plays a role in his novels.

Music played a much more significant role in city life in those days than today, as it naturally did in church and other religious ceremonies, so that a young man with musical talent might well be in demand and make a good career for himself. This is precisely what Beer, doubtless an excellent self-promoter, did. He was admitted, almost certainly owing to his musical abilities, to the Regensburg Gymnasium Poeticum, a venerable and demanding school with a strong curriculum in Latin, mathematics, philosophy and music. Beer attended the Gymnasium from 1670–76, receiving board and tuition in return for musical services (singing at funerals and the like), and it was here that he must have developed his outrageous penchant for pranks and storytelling that was to serve him in good stead as a comic writer. There is, in fact, an obscure record relating to one of Beer's pranks played on one of the teachers at the Gymnasium, and this same teacher appears as the butt of a joke in one of his earliest novels. He also learned to play stringed instruments and, according to his diary, wrote three (brief) Latin comedies. These have been lost, but a number of funeral poems, some set to music, have survived this earliest literary period in his life.

Aside from his solid musical training, the most important aspect of the Regensburg years was the emergence of Beer's storytelling. He must have been a spellbinder. Drawing on personal experience, what he had heard in his father's inn, and on the reading of German chapbooks and tales of adventure, Beer at night told long, extemporaneous tales to his fellow students. The latter must have been especially appreciative after long days of study, music rehearsals, sweeping up, clock winding, running errands, and doing other tedious chores that lends a decidedly Dickensian cast to our picture of their lives.

The diary tells us little of his last two years at the Gymnasium Poeticum. We learn that Beer took an oral examination (the record of which still exists) at the courthouse, and that on the basis of this he was awarded a stipend to study at the university in Leipzig. He went to Leipzig in 1676 but spent only a few months in the university. From autobiographical passages in his novels one may surmise that he was lonely and unhappy and that he did not devote himself to his studies. In fact he began writing his comic "inventions" in which numerous passages satirize the neo-scholastic rhetorical and logical exercises that in Beer's view had little pedagogical value. If the academic world does not come off well in Beer's novels and satires, if students in his works typically have become addled rather than enlightened through their studies, it may have to do both with the pedantic mode of teaching in Regensburg and in Leipzig. The distance of the academic world from experience was anathema to the young, imaginative, budding writer and composer.

In the seventeenth century, city and court were in active competition for the talents of musicians and artists, and Beer took advantage of these conflicting forces. His musical gifts became known, and he was offered a position in the court orchestra of Duke August of Saxony-Weissenfels in October 1676. In 1669 the orchestra had consisted of some nineteen musicians; it was now enlarged on order of the duke because he was competing with the court of the Elector of Saxony in Dresden, no easy undertaking, for the Dresden orchestra was considered by some to be the most accomplished musical ensemble in Europe. Since the prestige of the court was linked to the quality of its orchestra, the social status of court musicians had risen in the course of the century. This heightened reputation was not shared by city musicians in that period, who were generally organized in guilds. Acceptance of a court post therefore had advantages, both in regard to pay and social status,[5] and after some negotiation, Beer opted for the court, and that is where he remained the rest of his life.

In the period 1677 to 1685 Beer wrote most of his twenty-one fictional works. The works vary immensely. The first was *Der Symplicianische Welt-Kucker oder Abenbtheuerliche Jan Rebhu*, a long picaresque novel in four parts that showed the strong influence of the now deceased Grimmelshausen. The work apparently sold well by the

---

[5] See on this and on the musical situation in general Arno Werner, *Städtische und fürstliche Musikpflege in Weissenfels* (Leipzig: Breitkopf & Härtel, 1911), 65.

standards of the time[6] and Beer wrote other works apace, likely driven by eager publishers and by his need for money. The other novels (a term I will use somewhat loosely here) are a disparate mix: picaresque adventure novels, to some extent influenced by the *Amadís* books so popular throughout Europe in the sixteenth and seventeenth centuries, that were at the same time parodies of this outgrown form; of somewhat bitter, misogynistic satires; and of a later, more serious form, that of the "political novel," a form invented by the German writer and educator Christian Weise (1642–1708). This sub-genre of the novel, which flourished in the 1670s and 1680s in Germany, sought to inculcate a new philosophy of education for the upper and upper middle classes, one based on a rational, empirical, practical grasp of the world. The popularity of these rapidly written, rapidly printed books illustrates the increasing popularity of the home-grown novel in the late seventeenth century.

On 17 June 1679 Beer married Rosina Bremer, daughter of the deceased owner of the Black Bear Inn in Halle. Beer, ever a busy man, was now author, musician, composer, owner of an inn, and as of 22 March 1680, father. Ten more children followed, but only six survived their father. There were other important developments: the death on 4 June 1680 of the duke of Saxony-Weissenfels brought about a long-planned relocation of the court, under his son and successor, Johann Adolf I, from Halle to Weissenfels. Weissenfels was then a provincial village[7] but August had begun years before his death to develop a court and school there. The move was a major event for the town, because it was now populated by a group of relatively sophisticated and well-educated men. One cannot help but wonder if they did not come to this village with considerable reluctance. Beer reports in his diary making the trip in December 1680 in "unbelievably cold weather." Once at the court the freespirit writer quickly acclimated himself to the usually more decorous manner of the court, and by 1685 had ceased to write the comic novels for which we know him best now. In that year he was named concertmaster of the Weissenfels orchestra. He became a friend and confidant of Duke Johann Adolf and took on substantial responsibilities at court, including the writing of occasional poetry, singing, writing of plays or masques. He later became the court librarian, and was second in rank musically only to the conductor and prominent composer, Johann Philipp Krieger (died 1726).

With all his new responsibilities, and in spite of the dour religiosity that pervades his diary, Beer apparently remained an ebullient man. Erdmann Neumeister, who wrote what is in effect one of the first histories of German literature, noted in his Latin survey Beer's predilection

---

[6] Based on the several editions and continuations. Printings of 1000 copies were fairly common in this period, probably limited by guild law to the advantage of typesetters.

[7] Population 1663: ca 800 according to Alewyn, p. 49.

for the pun, for the jest.[8] Beer himself wrote that he was glad of two things: that he was born in the Christian faith and that he had an optimistic frame of mind.[9] There is considerable evidence in the diary that he and the young duke and their entourage enjoyed late night parties and storytelling. But official duties were very time-consuming as well, and one can imagine an unending series of "gigs" these musicians had to perform. Beer writes:

> Today you've got to go with the court there, tomorrow to another place, it makes no difference whether it's night or day, and doesn't matter whether it's raining or the sun is shining [. . .]. Today one has to go to the church, tomorrow to [perform at] the banquet table, the day after tomorrow to the theater.[10]

The picture is not exaggerated: there were trips to Leipzig, Gotha, Jena, not inconsiderable distances (and on bad roads) in those days. The musical offerings were by no means trivial: Alewyn calculated that between 1679 and 1720 at least seventy-six different operas were performed at the court in Weissenfels. Beer himself wrote an opera, or at least the libretto for one, *Die keusche Susanne* (The Chaste Susanne).[11] Music remained at the center of Beer's life, and this central activity is also reflected in his novels, particularly in the novel printed here. His musical propensities and training are revealed in his language, which is replete with musical metaphors, used even in the most banal situations, such as descriptions of animal sounds and the like.[12] He also inserted musical theory into the novels — Beer was perhaps more talented as a theoretician than performer — and made veiled, often uncomplimentary remarks about other composers and musicians throughout his writings. He used the novels to emphasize the social and musical distinctions between well-trained professional musicians at court and the vagrant musicians or *Bier-Fiedler* who were apparently present in considerable number in the late seventeenth century. He hoped to justify, even glorify, the role of music at court and in church, for he saw the reputa-

---

[8] Neumeister, *Specimen Dissertationis [...] de Poëtis Germancicis* (Leipzig, 1695).

[9] In his polemic *Ursus murmurat*, attacking rector Vockerodt for his severe and restrictive view of the role of music. Page A4^r

[10] Quoted from Beer's *Musicalische Discurse* (Nuremberg: Monath, 1719), 18-19.

[11] See Alewyn, *Beer*, 53-53. See also Manfred Lischka's bibliography of Beer's musical works which corrects some errors in Alewyn: *Daphnis* 9, Heft 3 (1980), 557-96.

[12] See Heinz Krause on the musical aspect of Beer's writings: *Johann Beer 1655-1700: Zur Musikauffassung im 17. Jahrhundert* (Saalfeld, 1935 [printed Diss. U. of Leipzig].

tion of "respectable" musicians being sullied by these itinerant amateurs and charlatans.

I earlier mentioned the unique significance of Beer's diary. Its discovery in 1963 was a bit of a disappointment (as Alewyn admits in his introduction to the printed version) since it says nothing about his novels, nothing directly at any rate, and reveals little about his feelings about friends or his wife, or about life at court, nothing about his relationship with his publishers, his thoughts on his own writings, or everyday life in Weissenfels. There are references to court dress and decorum (one dresses in the "Spanish" model on Holy Days), to an address or debate by Christian Thomasius, the famous philosopher, but lacking are Beer's reactions to these events. His own family gets short shrift; the diary limits itself to dates of birth, baptism, and death of children and relatives. Much more space is devoted to executions, robberies, "supernatural" events, the tragic aspects of everyday life, especially their grisly side. In this Beer's interests seem to correspond to the Zeitgeist of the period.

It is an oddity of German cultural history that Beer should have set down, on his death-bed, the events that led to his death. During a shooting contest near Weissenfels on 28 July 1700, the musket of a certain Captain Barth fired accidentally, the ball striking first an organist and then Beer. Beer lived several days and reported the incident in his diary. He died on 6 August and was buried on the eighth, at the age of forty-five. He was survived by his wife and six children. The funeral was held in Weissenfels, and in accordance with the custom of the time, the funeral sermon was printed together with poems written by friends and colleagues.[13]

German Winter Nights

The *German Winter Night*s and *Summer Days* constitute Beer's most ambitious works. In length, complexity, and in skill of characterization they are superior to the other Beer novels. Their episodic structure, the elements of adventure, knightly combat, despicable villains and the like reveal the influences of the *Amadís* novels and of the courtly chapbooks; their portrayal of charlatans, cheats, crooks, criminals, other lower social types and their colorful language shows clearly the influence of the picaresque novel. But beyond that, the books – which must be considered a single work, even though the figures of the second

---

[13] The organist, Garthoff, survived and was still alive in 1726. See Jacob Adlung, *Anleitung zu der musikalischen Gelahrtheit* (Erfurt: Bach, 1785), footnote p. 99. The sermon at the funeral was given by Johann Christoph Stange, professor of rhetoric at the Weissenfels gymnasium. A copy exists in the Nationale Forschungs- und Gedenkstätten der klassischen deutschen Literatur, Weimar.

novel have different names than those of the first — are fascinating chronicles about everyday rural life, about farming, accounting, husbandry, but also about youthful pranks, and abound with a delightful student humor that tells us more about the age than history books and archival materials. The plot of the works is not original, but the treatment of relationships is extremely interesting, particularly those between close friends and between men and women. There are many passages in the novels that contradict the prevailing scholarly attitude that people of the seventeenth century had not yet attained the sensibility to appreciate and foster close friendships, and there are other passages that bring to light a rather hard relationship between men and women.

The action of the novel will not be discussed here in detail, as I don't want to ruin the story for the reader, but I must give away the fact that there is a happy ending of sorts. The novel's plot, which, following Grimmelshausen, demonstrates that the nature of life is constant change, that man is the plaything of fate. And nothing could be clearer to the hero, Zendorio, who finds his life at the end of the novel, when he has fought for, sought and lost the love of his beloved Caspia, to be a perfect illustration of how fickle fate can be. He resolves, like Simplicissimus, to become a hermit (a favorite figure in Beer's novels) and sets up a hut in the forest. But he learns from hunters that Caspia is not dead (a relative with the same name had died), that in fact she is to be married to a certain Faustus because she thinks Zendorio is dead. Zendorio appears at the marriage banquet, Faustus leaves, and there is a happy reconciliation, much celebration and story telling.

In the latter part of the novel scenes of parlor games and story telling take up a good portion of the book and are interesting as intimate pictures of the daily life of the privileged classes. Zendorio is now a landed owner of a sizable estate; his duties are serious and he attends to them accordingly, treating his tenants fairly and tending his financial matters with prudence. In short, this section of the novel has departed entirely from the picaresque happenings for the earlier chapters. The novel ends with a massive tying up of loose ends and with several weddings (somewhat in the manner of the much more elevated courtly novel). But in spite of his new, responsible ways (his wife Caspia has just had a child), Zendorio and his old friends at the conclusion of the work allow a feast to turn into a debauch, and they all return to their respective castles, determined to change their ways.

The "sequel," *Sommer-Täge*, reintroduces figures of the first novel under different names. The story telling, adventures, love affairs, tricks, and occasional violence of the first Willenhag novel are continued here. The narrator has fallen in love with Lisel, and he marries her after his first wife, suddenly aged, dies. Wolffgang (the narrator of the second work) soon regrets the marriage, because she is an overbearing lazy glutton, similar to the female figures of Beer's antifeminist novels, but she too dies. Wolffgang increasingly turns away from life and contemplates eternity, often donning the costume of a hermit. He meditates and reads religious tracts, eventually becoming an object of curiosity. The various figures who populated the first novel gradually revert to type or die, one rejecting the falsity of the court, another becoming an ascetic, another living happily with his wife, and the narrator turning more and more inward. The picaresque novel turns into a contemplation of how one lives one's entire life — a remarkable achievement for a self-made writer who was only twenty-seven when the novels appeared.

Characterization obviously plays a secondary role to plot in the Willenhag novels. Figures are "typed" according to social class. There are two basic groups of characters: the country nobility, and the peasants or poor wandering figures such as musicians, soldiers, and students. The representatives of the latter group generally work for a time at a castle and then continue their wanderings. But within each social group many figures are so similar as almost to be interchangeable: one thinks, for instance, of the recurring foul-mouthed female servants. The range of personalities is therefore limited; Beer's imaginativeness lies more in the manipulation of events, in the variation on similar themes, than in delineation of character. His creation of complex links among figures coming from the most disparate backgrounds, his emphasis on incident, are the primary characteristics of the Willenhag novels. Another, also demonstrating Beer's preoccupation with event, is the technique of delayed revelation.With all his attention to intricate connections among his figures Beer was careless — perhaps deliberately — in the treatment of time and the ages of his characters. The span of the action in the two novels is about forty-two years altogether, but exact dates and numbers are rarely given. Willenhag is presumably around sixty-two at the conclusion of the *Sommer-Tage*, which would mean that Krachwedel is ninety-one. At this point we learn that the old warrior has a four-year-old son. When Sophia, Wolffgang's first wife, dies, she is seventy-two, an age that is out of kilter with her husband's, which is about fifty. It is difficult to say whether Beer merely overlooked these inconsistencies or was twitting his audience.

Beer provides few precise dates, but there are references to historical events that allow us to determine within a year or two the dates of certain episodes. For instance, in the *Winternächte* Isidoro's mother mentions the battle of Wittstock, which took place on 4 October 1632, and says that since the battle about thirty-two years have passed. She therefore must be speaking in 1664 or 1665. And in the *Sommer-Täge*, at the age of eighty to ninety, Krachwedel tells of the battle of Stadtlohn, allowing us to place the time of that portion of the novel in the 1680s. It is clear that Beer was not intent on precisely dating the events, but that he set the action roughly in a time corresponding to his own. With some exceptions, such as Krachwedel, the figures are therefore about a generation younger than Simplicissimus.

As in Beer's "courtly" novel, *Der Verliebte Oestereicher*, actual place names occur, and many of these are found in the Attergau, as Alewyn has pointed out, although some are invented. The locations of the noblemen's castles and their distance from one another are not precisely described. In short, the geographical picture is somewhat cloudier than Alewyn found it. The one detailed topographical description, one particularly singled out by Alewyn as an example of the specificity and realism of the novels, describes in glowing colors a region – upper Austria – unrelated to the main action of the novels. In other words, it appears rather unmotivated and is surely to be chalked up to Beer's local patriotism. Our author is interested in the portrayal of events, not of topography. He evokes a landscape that vaguely suggests the Attergau, his birthplace, yet Zendorio says his castle is not far from the Rhine! In this work, space is a means to an end, a fictional, arbitrary landscape.

Other themes and motifs of the novel might be discussed at considerable length: Beer's fascination with sin, remorse, and repentance; his realistic descriptive technique; his pragmatic view of life as typically expressed by Ludwig, who says:

> For definitions don't mean much to me, and it's far more useful to me to know how and when to plow the field, to sow the grain, to cut the hay, shake the apple trees, to fatten the pigs, wean the calves, to fell wood, to manage the servants, than it would be if I were a highfalutin Ph. D.

But I think it best, in view of Beer's clear preference for the useful and practical, to avoid further scholarly speculation, and to turn instead to this wonderfully inventive, ingenious translation by Professor John Russell. I think Beer would be delighted to know that Russell and he must have been kindred spirits, as John was able not only to render the difficult prose, but even the farcical poetry.

James Hardin
July 1998

Important Works About Beer

Biography

Johann Beer: Sein Leben, von ihm selbst erzählt, ed. by Adolf Schmiedecke (Göttingen: Vandenhoeck & Ruprecht, 1965.

Bibliographies

Gerhard Dünnhaupt, "Johann Beer" in Dünnhaupt's *Personalbibliographie zu den Drucken des Barock*. (6 vols, 2nd ed. Stuttgart: Hiersemann, 1990).

James Hardin, *Johann Beer. Eine beschreibende Bibliographie*. (Munich: Francke, 1983). Bibliographien zur deutschen Barockliteratur, Vol. 2.

References

Richard Alewyn, Johan Beer. Studien zum Roman des 17. Jahrhunderts. (Leipzig: Mayer & Müller, 1932).

Robert Paul Tyler Aylett, "Alewyn Revisited: Realism in Grimmelshausen and Beer." *Daphnis* 19 (1990): 81–104.

Aylett. "Violence in Johann Beer's *Willenhag* Novels." *Daphnis* 16 (1987): 423–439.

Jörg Jochen Berns, "Reflex und Reflexion der oberösterreichischen Bauernaufstände im Werk Johann Beers." In: *Die österreichische Literatur. Ihr Profil von den Anfängen im Mittelalter bis ins 18. Jahrhundert (1050–1750)*. Edited by Herbert Zeman. (Graz: Akademische Druck- und Verlaggesellschaft, 1986), 1149–1179.

Berns, ed. *Simpliciana: Schriften der Grimmelshausen-Gesellschaft* 13 (1991) [papers given at the Colloquium *Johann Beer & Grimmelshausen. Deutsche Prosasatire an der Wende vomn 17. zum 18. Jahrhundert*, 3.–7 Oct. 1990. Contains:

Jaumann, Herbert. Satire zwischen Moral, Recht und Kritik.

Knight, Kenneth. Grimmelshausen, Beer und die politische Satire.

Jacobsen, Roswitha. Johann Beer in Weissenfels.

Breuer, Dieter. "Lindigkeit." Zur affektpsychologischen Neubegründung satirischen Erzählens in Johann Beers Doppelroman."

Neuber, Wolfgang. "Regionalismus und biographisches Erzählmodell in Beers Willenhag-Dilogie."

Gurtner, Kuno. "'Bald droben, bald drunten, bald gar verschwunden.' Bilder der Gesellschaft im Werk Johann Beers."

Ingen, Ferdinand van. "Spielformen der 'satirischen Schreibart.'"

Kremer, Manfred. "Wirklichkeitsnähe in der Barockliteratur."

Eilert, Hildegard. "Essen und Politik in Johann Beers *Der politische Bratenwender.*"

Kiesant, Knut. "Die Bauern-Oper. Zur Literatursatire bei Johann Beer."

Battafarano, Italo Michele. "Literarische Skatalogie als Therapie literarischer Melancholie: Johann Beers *Der berühmte Narren-Spital.*"

Hesselmann, Peter. "Zur Tradition der Narrensatire im 17. Jahrhundert: Text und Bild in den B- und C-Auflagen des Narrenspitals von Johann Beer."

Locher, Elmar. "Dimensionen der 'Kurtzweil' in Johann Beers Narren-Spital."

Höpel, Ingrid. "Der Autor in der Spinnstube."

Lam-Bär, Elisabeth and Hesselmann, Peter. "*Die Klag der Soldaten.* Ein unveröffentlichtes Vokalwerk Johann Beers."

Busch, Walter. "Poetischer Experimentalismus und artistische Form."

Kühlmann, Wilhelm. "'Syllogismus practicus.' Antithese und Dialektik in Grimmelshausens *Satyrischem Pilgram.*

Gaede, Friedrich. "Barocke Transzendentalpoesie? Grimmelshausen aus der Sicht der Bärnhäuter- und Philistersatire Clemens Brentanos."

Berns, Jörg Jochen. "Policey und Satire im 16. und 17. Jahrhundert."

Martin Bircher, "Neue Quellen zu Johannes Beers Biographie." *Zeitschrift für deutsches Alterum und deutsche Literatur* 100 (1971): 230–42.

Friedrich Gerhardt, *Geschichte der Stadt Weissenfels a. S.* Weissenfels: R. Schirdewahn, 1907.

Gerhardt, *Schloß und Schloß-Kirche zu Weissenfels.* Weissenfels: Max Lehmstedt, 1898.

Kuno Gurtner, "'Ich agiere eine Comedia'. Theaterszenen in den Romanen Johann Beers." *Simpliciana* 11 (1989): 115–127.

Dieter Guzen, "Johann Beer." In: *Deutsche Dichter des 17. Jahrhunderts. Ihr Leben und Werk.* Edited by Harald Steinhagen and Benno von Wiese. (Berlin: E. Schmidt, 1984), 772–797.

Fritz Habeck, "Der verliebte Österreicher oder Johannes Beer." In: Fritz Habeck *In eigenem Auftrag.* (Graz und Wien: Stiasny Verlag, 1963), 115–23.

James Hardin, "Johann Beers Parodie Printz Adimantus." In: Akten des V. Internationalen Germanisten-Kongresses Cambridge 1975. (Bern: H. Lang, 1976), 82–89.

Hardin, *Johann Beer*. (Boston: Twayne Publishers, 1983). Twayne's World Author Series, 689.

Hardin, "A Note on Johann Beer's *Der verkehrte Staats-Mann*." *Daphnis: Zeitschrift für Mittlere Deutsche Literatur* 4, 2 (1975): 202-4.

Hardin, "Johann Beer's *Der politische Feuermäuer-Kehrer* [. . .]," *Modern Language Notes* 96 (1981), 488-502.

Hardin, "Descriptive Bibliography and the Works of Johann Beer," *Wolfenütteler Barock-Nachrichten* 4, Heft 1 (1977), 2-6.

Ilse Hartl, "Die Rittergeschichten Johannes Beers." Diss., Vienna, 1947.

Urs Herzog, *Der deutsche Roman des 17. Jahrhunderts: Eine Einführung.* (Stuttgart: Kohlhammer, 1976).

Arnold Hirsch, "Barockroman und Aufklärungsroman." *Etudes Germaniques* 9 (1954): 97-111.

Hirsch, *Bürgertum und Barock im deutschen Roman*. Frankfurt am Main, 1934. 2d. ed., edited by H. Singer, Cologne and Graz: Böhlau, 1957.

Giles R Hoyt,. "Bild und Funktion des Volkes im deutschen und französischen Roman des späten 17. Jahrhunderts." In: *Literatur und Volk im 17. Jahrhundert. Probleme populärer Kultur in Deutschland*. Edited by Wolfgang Brückner, Dieter Breuer and Peter Blickle. (Wiesbaden: Harrassowitz, 1985), 301-316.

Roswitha Jacobsen, ed. Weißenfels als Ort literarischer und künstlerischer Kultur im Barockzeitalter. Vorträge eines interdisziplinären Kolloquiums vom 8.-10. Oktober 1992 in Weißenfels, Sachsen/Anhalt. Amsterdam and Atlanta: Rodopi, 1994.

K. G. Knight, "The Novels of Johann Beer (1655-1700)." *Modern Language Review* 56 (1962): 194-211.

Jörg Krämer, Johann Beers Romane. Poetologie, immanente Poetik und Rezeption "niederer" Texte im späten 17. Jahrhundert. Frankfurt am Main, Bern, New York, Paris: Peter Lang, 1991.

Heinz Krause, *Johann Beer 1655-1700: Zur Musikauffassung im 17. Jahrhundert*. Diss., Leipzig, 1935. Saalfeld: Günthers Buchdruckerei, 1935.

Helmut Krause, *Feder kontra Degen. Zur literarischen Vermittlung des bürgerlichen Weltbildes im Werk Johannes Riemers*. (Berlin: Hofgarten Verlag, 1979).

Manfred Kremer, "Der Kantor im Werke Johann Beers." *Modern Language Notes* 88 (1973): 1023-29.

Kremer, "'Nicht allein von denen Liebes-Geschichten . . .' Anmerkungen zu Johann Beers *Der verliebte Europaeer*." *Daphnis* 13 (1984): 205-216.

Kremer, "Johannes Beers *Bruder Blaumantel*." *Neophilogus* 51 (1967): 3.

Kremer, "Vom Pikaro zum Landadligen: Johann Beers *Jucundus Jucundissimus*." In: *Der deutsche Schelmenroman im europäischen Kontext. Rezeption, Interpretation, Bibliographie*. Edited by Gerhart Hoffmeister. (Amsterdam: Rodopi, 1987), 29-48.

Manfred Lischka, "Johann Beers Lebensbeschreibung — ein Tagebuch?" *Wolfenbüttler Barocknachrichten* 22, 1 (1985): 15-19.

Johann Mattheson, Grundlage einer Ehrenpforte, woran der tüchtigsten Capellmeister, Componisten, Musikgelehrte, Tonkünstler etc. Leben, Wercke, Verdienste etc. erscheinen sollen. Hamburg, 1740. Reprint Berlin: Leo Liepmannssohn, 1910.

Volker Meid, *Der deutsche Barockroman.* (Stuttgart: Metzler, 1974). Sammlung Metzler vol. 128.

Jörg-Jochen Müller, *Studien zu den Willenhag-Romanen Johann Beers.* (Marburg: N. G. Elwert, 1965). Marburger Beiträge zur Germanistik 9.

Hans Pörnbacher, "Johann Beer." In: *Deutsche Dichter. Leben und Werk deutschsprachiger Autoren.* Vol. 2. Edited by Gunter E. Grimm and Frank Rainer Max. (Stuttgart: Reclam, 1988), 409-427.

Andreas Solbach, "Transgression als Verletzung des decorum bei Christian Weise, J. J. Chr. v. Grimmelshausen und in Johann Beers *Narrenspital.*" In *Writing on the Line.* Edited by Lynne Tatlock. (Amsterdam: Rodopi, 1991), 33-60.

Johann Christoph Stange, *Das unversehene, aber doch Seelige Ende [. . .] Herren Johann Bährs.* (Sermon on occasion of Beer's death.) Weissenfels: Brühls Wittbe, 1700.

Rolf Tarot, "Grimmelshausens Realismus." In: *Rezeption und Produktion zwischen 1570 und 1730. Festschrift für Günther Weydt zum 65. Geburtstag.* Edited by Wolfdietrich Rasch, Hans Geulen, and Klaus Haberkamm. (Bern and München: Francke, 1972), 233-65.

Lynne Tatlock, "Fact and the Appearance of Factuality in the Novels of Johann Beer." In: *Literatur und Kosmos. Innen- und Außenwelten in der deutschen Literatur des 15. bis 17. Jahrhunderts.* Edited by Gerhild Scholz Williams and Lynne Tatlock. (Amsterdam: Rodopi, 1986), 345-373.

Hans Hartmut Weil, "The Conception of Friendship in German Baroque Literature." *German Life and Letters* 13 (1959-1960): 106-15.

Arno Werner, *Städtische und fürstliche Musikpflege in Weissenfels bis zum Ende des 18. Jahrhunderts.* Leipzig: Breitkopf & Härtel, 1911.

Werner, "Johann Beer." In: *Die Musik in Geschichte und Gegenwart: Allgemeine Enzyklopädie der Musik.* Kassel: Bärenreiter, 1949-51, vol. 1, cols. 1506-8.

Günther Weydt, "Der deutsche Roman von der Renaissance { . . .} bis zu Goethes Tod." In: *Deutsche Philologie im Aufriß* 2d ed. Edited by W. Stammler. Berlin: Erich Schmidt, 1960, 2: cols. 1217-1356; on Beer, cols. 1257-59.

Hildegard E. Wichert, *Johann Balthasar Schupp and the Baroque Satire in Germany.* (New York: King's Crown Press, 1952).

Remarks on the Translation

Translating this work proved to be a pleasure because it succeeds so well in its desire to be humorous. It is particularly pleasant for a translator when treating verse that is not meant to be understood as the baring of the poet's soul. But it was often less than pleasant because of the three centuries linguistic change has had to affect the language of the original. Although one can find a meaning for almost all of the German words, one can't be sure that the various dictionaries have recorded the one intended by the author. I will readily confess that at a number of points I had to be content with an educated guess.

I also may well have missed more than a pun or two, of which there are many in Beer. In the belief that footnotes are better used in a critical edition than for showing a translator's erudition, I did not footnote a number of gratuitous puns contained in names. A joke explained is a dead joke.

Another problem arose in that this work is picaresque. Even though Beer moved the genre out of the lowest classes and into noble circles, most of his characters still seek to be hip, and there are a great many loan words rendered obscure by the author's hearing of the word or his rendering of it in an era when orthography was capricious at best and usually guided by vagaries of dialect. The German edition used contains a very helpful list of such words, but it is far from complete, and a question mark is frequently the only definition supplied.

Since education was still very much a mark of distinction in the Baroque, there is much Latin here, not only to make fun of those parading their knowledge of it, but also for its own sake. In footnoting it, I followed the decisions of the German edition. The first patch of Latin occurs in the guide to writing poetry, where its simplicity should pose few problems for the reader. A second is the list of Latin commonplaces, which would have generated a footnote for each, often extended to explain a pun as with the first one where Latin *parvus* is read as German *barfuß*. Once again, a joke explained . . . . Otherwise Latin passages of any difficulty are footnoted when not translated or explained by the author.

Finally, no attempt was made to determine a modern equivalent for the many various coins. Their German capitalization was retained for the few occasions where it might not have been clear that a coin was being talked about.

J. R. R.

Zendorio a Zendorio's

German Winter Nights

or the complete and memorable
description of his life story which
contains all manner of coincidences and
strange happenings, curious love stories,
and remarkable events of some nobility
and other private persons.
Written in detail not only with all sorts
of circumstances and conversations, but also
larded here and there with
valid moral teachings
for all lovers of diverting writings,
of whatever estate or condition
they may be,
composed for special entertainment
yet not without gain
therefrom and recently described
by the author himself,
subsequently translated for the benefit
of the reading public, and published
adorned by pretty engravings.
Printed in 1682.

Preface

Before we proceed to this work, it is necessary for the reader to know that this entire project resembles a satire more than a history. The kind reader thus has the freedom to judge it as he wishes, even if he is first amicably asked by me, as translator, to let the virtues noted in it serve him as a road guide and the castigated vices as a detestation on the paths a man of the world walks daily.

Having said that, I must explain my attitude further and freely admit that now a disgrace, now some other affair ascribed to this person or that was not described to prejudice the standing or person of anyone, whoever he might be. For with regard to the original, it was originally written some sixty years ago in the office of a noble castle and was preserved there in secret for whatever reason down to the present time. Thus, one can forget the whole matter, and if one person or another should find himself insulted in it, he must know that it is not this book which is responsible for that, but his own mistakes he has committed. Hence such a book is like a painter who draws a face on the wall with charcoal; if a stranger comes up by chance and completely resembles this face, then everyone knows that the source of the likeness is not the painter but the person who resembles the face.

That is principally why I here assert that one should explain and interpret everything for the best. Although all the material is treated in a thoroughly satirical manner, only the vices are punished and not the people burdened by them and not the people who are shown a better way, for which the original author of this book is in no way to be scolded, but much rather to be praised. Like a gardener tearing out weeds, he sets good plants in their place.

The value of such writings and the moral lessons arising from them will always remain in high regard among those who are capable of making a distinction between good and evil. For what is more appropriate for a modest spirit than loving that which is good and hating evil? This brings fame and honor, and, most importantly, it sets the conscience in contented peace, which is a treasure that cannot be expressed by words.

And who does not see that joy of the heart arises from that? A person who loves virtue is free of worries, happy in spirit, and whatever he endures, he endures with pleasure. *Dulce jugum amor est.*[14] This love of virtue diminishes all human misfortunes, no matter how evilly they may be conceived.

Also the greatest part of temporal and, indeed, eternal honor is concerned with one's following good and hating evil. Between the two there is no other step in attaining either honor or disgrace. Good for him

---

[14] "Love is a sweet yoke."

who steps to the first where his feet will not slip. He will be not only loved, but praised everywhere, and his honor will bind him a wreath whose leaves will not dry up in all eternity.

And what do those who cultivate uncleanliness ultimately have from it? Disgrace, abuse, derision, and mockery are their eternal reward, and when they have pursued their vices long enough, they are regarded with great and painful contempt by all persons. Also, in such a sinful life there is no pleasure but much rather a burden when the conscience begins to preach about all these acts we have committed in such a disgraceful way. One defames honor through this and denigrates one's good name, and ultimately everything that is useful for our edification is lost and ruined.

Whoever desires an example of each of these should read through this text where he will find a sufficient number of all these virtues and vices that may apply to him for better or worse. In such a manner the reader will, as it were, be humorously instructed in what serves for his own good and through unfamiliar images catch sight of his own figure, for better or worse.

If I had known a better way of writing than this, I would have adopted such and applied this effort to a different work, but I have been led to such from a definite hope of the great profit that will result therefrom for the person who doesn't grab merely the shell, but the substance which lies hidden within. Many a person stumbles on a stone that contains more gold than his entire wealth; because he doesn't know how to extract the gold from it, he passes it by as an unthinking person and instead snatches a nut from the ground that perhaps was dropped by a woman selling fruit. Therefore, books of this sort must be read with precise attention so that one doesn't pick up feces instead of gold and instead of pearls pebbles, which only make one's feet sore.

May the preceding instruction serve the kind reader so that he doesn't read this text from another viewpoint than it was written. Then he will in no way lack the profit he can expect from fleeing the rejected vices and from pursuing the praised virtues following my desire to serve him.

The Author to His Book

I've written just for those who are in sin residing
    Just as their very deeds have said that I must do.
It's only criminals who get a proper hiding;
    As payment for misdeeds, it is their proper due.
But on the other hand, you children of the noble,
    Upon your honor great I wish to heap no blame;
I know you always keep both pure and out of trouble,
    And one can't sing enough about your well-earned fame.
Although I have ascribed a vice to such a person
    Who is the offshoot of a noble family tree,
A Judas in a church the pious does not worsen;
    One finds the fairest gold amid the nasty scree.
Nor have I sought to cast on you a word indicting,
    You ladies whose renown exceeds that of the stars;
To earn your favor dear, my pen is only writing
    To show the world just those who bear cruel vices' scars.
The evil and the good do always live together,
    I do but show who's good and who's the wicked one.
And if you now accept the thoughts I'd have you gather,
    My ultimate desire will find its goal is won.
I do not show a soul how he should do his sinning,
    And for a crime like that a man would surely pay.
The world, in any case, at godless things is grinning;
    It takes a watchful man to not be led astray.
I simply write to show how people time were passing
    When I became a man and entered in my prime.
Though now and then we laugh at foolishness surpassing,
    We can escape the wiles of vanity in time.
A bitter medicine is often mixed with honey
    So that our stomachs won't a fearful time begin;
A painted brow will draw a kiss both sweet and sunny
    Although beneath the paint one finds but putrid skin.
And so, my book, are you with many pranks well larded;
    You bring within your hold your very precious gift.
I've sent you like a ship into the sea, unguarded,
    Where love and loyalty and virtue are adrift.

Where people tend to sail towards disgraceful sinning,
    That's where I'm sending you, my little book so weak.
I'll pay no heed if now you're criticism winning
    Because I know quite well how enemies will speak.
Whoever pleases all must soon become a fool,
    He'll have enough to do to satisfy his neighbors.

But since I want to make intelligence my rule,
    It follows that I can't delight all with my labors.
Proud Jupiter himself was granted no such favor,
    The rabble were not pleased by all that he was doing.
So heed not, little book, how people may you savor,
    Somewhere within our world a storm is always brewing.
My pregnant quill gave birth to you mid great mischance,
    I went to work on you on many a darkest night;
Thus have you lost all trace of any elegance
    Because the dark can't bear a thing that's shining bright.

You friends, who always give me comfort and all joy
    Accept now this my book, your servant it shall be.
I don't know what to give you other than this toy
    In which I you can see and you in turn see me.
I often do recall those hours we spent together
    When we could join as one in happiness divine;
The lute's now out of tune, that time is gone forever,
    For darkness always comes behind the bright sunshine.
One friend lives to the west, another to the morning,
    One on a mountain high, and one down mid the floods,
We're now quite full of cheer, and now we're filled with
    mourning;
    We mortals do remain the plaything of the gods.
So go now, book, to friends to whom I cannot turn
    And say that I still live quite filled with energy
And also tell them that my life will brightly burn
    Until I bid farewell to earthly vanity.

Book One

Chapter One. Zendorio's Prison at Veronia's Castle

If your conscience is quite clear,
Then you've nothing more to fear.

It was around midnight and I found myself alone outside the castle in which up till now I had been imprisoned with a thousand worries and dejected spirits. I was surprised at my unexpected situation, on the one hand, and, on the other, by the note that had been sent to me in prison by a countess. But not as much by all that as by the great care and loyalty of the huntsman who had exerted himself to the utmost to free me of my chains. With the dark and moonless night serving as an excellent protective cloak to hide my identity, the huntsman hastened with me out of the village, and because we were going all out, we didn't have much time to converse, no matter how much I desired to get to the bottom of things. I had now reached the highroad and the huntsman urged me to hasten on quickly so that I wouldn't be returned to my chains through my halting and then find things worse than before. With that he sped back and left me standing on the road and quite puzzled, filled with a desire and eagerness to know the causes for my having been put in this prison.

I had a good hundred thousand futile fancies, but none of them served in this matter, for through them I increased my perplexity much rather than reducing it and because of this I was easily compelled to believe that my tarrying might entail no little danger. Therefore, I began to run as fast as my legs could carry me, which had gradually been affected and scraped by the irons. In this manner I passed a good part of the remaining night so that at daybreak I found that I, indeed, had gone completely astray and didn't know in what region I was wandering around at that time.

My limbs were rather tired, partly on account of the heavy irons put on them earlier, partly also from my rapid and sustained flight. Therefore, I hastened to a nearby village to rest there for a bit and to inquire about the proper road. I obtained quite easily what I desired and after I had rested in the village, the peasants directed me over the top of a hill where I was assured of reaching a way to where the road ran that I was familiar with.

As I progressed, I was continually surprised at my fate and could in no way or manner drive the thoughts from my head until finally I saw a noble estate before me which was designed and built exquisitely in the traditional style. In my estimation I was still a good half hour from there; therefore, I pulled out my testimonial in order to go to that place to beg for some food with it. This custom tends to be a common practice among beginning students with which they promote themselves from place to place. Thus I directed my way to the castle and because beggars don't tend to avoid anything, it didn't concern me greatly that I had parted from the highroad by a mile or two.

After a short while I reached the place and whipped out my testimonial to commend myself as highly as possible to the gatekeeper so that for my purpose I could produce the most stately words and put them in his mouth so that he could announce me to the nobleman. But I found the fellow in a quite different mood, and because he, at that time, had to distribute bread to the village beggars, it can be that he didn't want to let himself be detained or confused in his official duties. With an unpleasant face he said to me that the lord of this castle had died six years ago and the noblewoman it did possess was traveling overland at the time.

When I saw I had sailed past this island for naught, I reversed my way, especially since the gatekeeper had called after me needlessly that one was not obliged to give alms to one so well-dressed. Instead I should sell my cowled coat and from it buy a bit of bread, that would be better for the stomach than sour grapes. I wasn't going to concern myself greatly about what that base-minded red-beard said, especially since by nature I was inclined to laugh at foolish jokes that could neither hurt nor disadvantage me. Therefore I kept walking away from the castle and stuck the testimonial back into my pocket.

"Sir, sir, sir, hallo, sir, signor, monsieur!" called a young nobleman who was standing completely undressed at a window above the gate, and when I looked around, he meant me. He gestured at me at least twenty times with his head and waved his hand for all he was worth. I removed my hat, made a bow, and hastened back to the gate, where I asked what he desired. "By Jove, sir, *par dieu*!" said the nobleman, "the devil take me, what is the gentleman doing?" I was not a little astonished at this speech and regarded the creature as properly insane. At this he disappeared from the window, and being of the opinion this was from vexation, I was about to leave when this young member of the nobility came down to me and led me up a long stairway. I went along, and since I had gotten into a messy confusion anyway, I was not afraid to get further involved in such events. We came into a rather narrow chamber where he had his library. There he received me very politely and said that never in all his life had such a miracle happened for him as in catching sight of my person; therefore, I should be so kind as to take a seat, and he pointed me to an especially nicely embroidered easy chair. After that with his own hands he served Spanish wine and displayed all manner of politenesses toward me, at which I was truly surprised.

"Monsieur, I see from your face that unpleasant thoughts are tormenting you mightily; therefore, if you are not opposed to revealing your concerns to me, you can be assured that I will recognize such kindness as a special element of your courtliness."

"Sir," I said in reply, "the thoughts which have preoccupied me completely now hinder me in being polite. But in order that I not appear ungrateful, I find myself obliged to reveal my fate to the person who through unknown friendship has treated me not only from no obligation, but beyond that with extraordinary cordiality. This day would be too short to give my patron a report beginning with my birth and school days and because such a life is concerned only with partly amusing, partly childish, partly vain stories, I prefer to move on to telling of an affair that put me in a quite risky situation approximately five days ago.

"I am by profession a student and have studied philosophy at various universities. To this end I undertook this trip to my homeland to seek advancement there because I was given good hopes of this some years ago. I am somewhat poor in means but nonetheless of a good and honest name. My father was a sacristan there in a famous cathedral, and because I had a lively sense of humor I called myself Zendorio[15] since as a boy I helped my father light the lamps and votive candles at the altars. In such a state on my recently undertaken trip I happened at nightfall upon an inn situated by the road. I saw nothing suspicious and placed my knapsack in the bedroom to which a maid had directed me. Beside my own bed, there were three others, but I saw only one fellow sleeping in one of them. Because he had removed his clothes, he was not recognizable at all. From childhood on I've been a great fan of chatting, but because this man had already fallen into a deep sleep, I didn't want to awaken him or disturb him in his rest, and for this reason I also didn't undertake to joke with the maid, whom I otherwise would have given a good chase around the room. I fell asleep and if it weren't foolish to detain such a dashing cavalier by relating my dreams, I could spend a good hour recalling all sorts of images that appeared to me vividly then in my sleep.

"I finally awoke when it was broad daylight and since I still had a good piece to go on my way, I started to get up and get dressed. But, bless me, how much time did I waste in looking for my clothes? I looked at and under every bed but there wasn't the slightest sign much less anything else to be seen or heard of concerning my clothes, I couldn't even find my shoes; rather, I found myself in the room without my gear and stripped. I wanted to ask the stranger in the room, but from all appearances he had long since gone. But what was most surprising of all, he

---

[15] An Italianate elaboration of German *Zünder*, "lighter."

had left his clothes in the room and perhaps had put on mine instead of his. At first I believed this mistake had happened in the darkness because I've heard many hundreds of examples where even worse things have been brought about by or by means of the darkness, but unfortunately I later learned in full detail for what this deception had been planned.

"Monsieur, these very clothes I'm wearing on my body belonged to that person who put on my clothes in the room instead of these and departed with them. In the end the loss of my garb was not so almighty great; therefore, I let the innkeeper persuade me easily to throw them on my body in exchange for mine and to go on my way in them. I did so and about an hour away from the inn when, dressed like a cavalier, I came to a forest and near a spring four armed men seized me, whom I could not recognize because they were masked. They didn't say a word but hastened with me to a castle, from which I was released last night as miraculously as I had been imprisoned. They put me in a dark vault, and to all appearances it was a jail because nothing was to be seen in it save fearsome instruments. I think it was indeed a torture chamber, and so you can easily imagine the state of my spirits. As soon as they had attached a chain to my left leg, they slapped one around my waist and a ring around my neck and said I should be patient until the count returned home, and then my head would no longer be on my shoulders.

"In truth, as innocent as I knew myself to be, nonetheless I didn't feel all too well about this matter. I recalled at least a thousand pranks I had pulled in public or in secret, especially with the ladies. Thus, I always supposed that one or another might have been revealed for which I was now to receive due praise. My food consisted of poor bread and water, and the worst thing in all this was that the person in the bedroom had taken along my knapsack, in which along with some linens and a few books I had about six Taler with which I could at least get myself something better to eat in these circumstances. The jailer told me upon my arrival that the interrogation would proceed tomorrow, but I still relied on my good testimonial from the university, which I always had wrapped in my shirt, for which reason it couldn't be taken from me in the bedroom. During these scattered thoughts I reached into the pocket of my newly donned clothes and found in it a considerable packet of old Groschen and in the end I scraped together some eight Reichstaler.

"Innocence, which was my chief solace in this prison, didn't let me fall into excessive melancholy; thus, I was little concerned how things might turn out. The new day was coming on, and from strange thoughts I hadn't been able to close an eye all that night. I had nodded off for a bit toward morning, but was disturbed in my rest because I heard someone knocking. I didn't know whether it was from the door or the window; accordingly, I lay back down and because I was quite alone, I became afraid of a ghost haunting around the place, which is nothing new in prisons. I heard another, a stronger blow and when I looked around, it

4

was at the window, which was to my back. It took very little effort to open it, so I looked out and with great astonishment I saw standing on the rocks below a huntsman with a long speaking tube. Using it, he called up to me that I shouldn't grow impatient nor torment and martyr myself with useless worrying; in the deep of the coming night he intended to help me out and take me away safely.

"After these words the huntsman descended the stony cliff and quite soon was lost in the shrubbery on the hill, for the castle lies somewhat higher on this side than in the front, and the cliff seemed to me a good hundred and twenty feet high. The huntsman, however, had stood not even eighteen feet below at a point to which a person could have leaped had not the chains and the surrounding fearful heights prevented this.

"Sir, just consider what I could conclude from the huntsman's words which were Greek to me! I was supposed to be consoled by them, and he only made me more melancholy. He was supposed to enlighten me, and I only grew more confused. In a word, I didn't know how perilously people were playing with my imprisoned self. As little as I had slept on the previous night, just as little could I rest during this one until the huntsman on the next day, though somewhat earlier than previously, came to the window with his speaking tube and ordered me to open it for using his crossbow; he wanted to shoot up a letter from the countess. Wondrous chance! I was easily persuaded to do this and when I opened the window, he shot into my prison a brief note tied to a stone and took off, having assured me of certain release as soon as night had approached.

"With countless fancies I opened the letter and with unusual astonishment found its contents, which I now quote accurately, word for word: 'Sir, the misery you are suffering lowers my heart into the grave whenever from your suffering I feel my own wounds. Be assured that the huntsman will treat you honestly, but if it should fail, I entreat you once more tearfully to deny everything as long as you can and show through your deeds that a steadfast lover will not shy from enduring all torments to remain silent about that from which every misfortune can arise for his beloved. Goodby and endure your fetters patiently in the complete assurance that I will live and die — Your most faithful Veronia.'

"Such was the brief but provocative content of the note shot in by the huntsman which I had torn to pieces immediately and thrown out the window along with the stone. Then the head jailer came into my vault to fetch some chains because, he maintained, before noon he had to arrest a troop of whores across the lake and bring them back captive with him upon the orders of the regional judge. I asked him about my situation and although I offered him a generous tip, he didn't want to talk, either because he had been forbidden to or perhaps because he wasn't familiar with it. He had a good eight leg irons on his arm because he alleged that honorable company could run to twelve people, among whom an old woman was said to be the leader of the plot and its principal person. To this end he departed from me with a small boy draped in many chains and perhaps had taken the youth along with him so that the latter could perhaps one day copy his praiseworthy qualities and reproduce his well-learned trade for posterity. Meanwhile, through one of the four guards who were constantly before my jail I had arranged a good midday meal and had some thrushes roasted at the village inn because in this place I could invest my money in no other manner. Therefore, I invited them to dine with me and one of them had a pitcher of beer brought which we guzzled down in crude fashion, for such people have little regard for toasts and such courtesies. From my hospitality I had no gain other than finally eliciting from them that they were the same people who, as I've related, had seized me by the spring in the forest and brought me to this place.

"Thus did I feed those who guarded me in my chains, and just as they had arrived with no display of respect, they also departed without gratitude. Their principal consolation was they promised me that within four hours at most good company would be locked in with me so that I wouldn't be lying alone and without conversation. I had to accept this jailer's consolation against my will and wished a hundred times only to know what devil had arranged this unexpected comedy for me. I waited from one hour to the next for the interrogation, but not a word was heard and much less anything about my case until finally night approached when, according to the clear contents of the letter as well as the words of the huntsman, I was definitely to be set free.

"I acted very cleverly at that time in keeping this and that from the guards and I was all the happier, the more ignorant I was in being led around in this affair. I had consumed a little brandy; thus, a great drowsiness overcame me and I accordingly lay down on the spread-out straw although my leg irons were beginning to produce scabs because I was completely unaccustomed to wearing such bonds. The castle clock was striking midnight when I unexpectedly awoke from my dream and I was rather fearful, both of ghosts and of the huntsman who was supposed to free me from my chains; because I wasn't familiar with the slightest object or the castle itself, I halfway regarded the huntsman as half a devil, and I can't tell you what curious visions passed through my head."

Chapter Two. He Comes to Isidoro. They Discuss the Plot.

There's no one yet who's fixed a deal
That someone didn't then reveal.

The young nobleman liked this tale exceedingly and during it had drunk to me with several glasses of Spanish wine and laughed to such an extent that I had to be surprised. And when I had reached this point, he said these words to me: "Sir, your unusual story is truly a singular piece of an uncommon rarity. I am a devotee of all histories, but, sir, be so good as to go on with your story and continue it according to its circumstances. Then I'll tell you what I liked especially and how greatly it satisfied me."

At this I resumed my narration and began to continue the story with the following: "Earlier with some details I described how I passed the time in the prison until around midnight; now there's nothing left but to report in brief to my host how I escaped from it. The contents of the letter hadn't been so nonsensical at all, for after being roused I heard the same rapping at my window I had heard the two previous nights. I opened it as wide as possible and saw the huntsman with a lantern at the same spot where he had stood with the speaking tube. This time, however, he didn't talk through that instrument but spoke rather as in a normal conversation. He raised a fire ladder that was long enough to get me out of that place. As soon as it was properly positioned, he extinguished the lantern, which in any event could burn to no end save our ruin. Now he agilely climbed up to the window and we discussed our business quite quietly so that the guards lying right next to us would hear nothing; otherwise they would have spoiled our game.

"It was astonishing how artfully the huntsman swung through the window, and after freeing me of my chains with a picklock, he took me with great care to the ladder, for it would have taken but little and the two of us would have been lying below on the rocks. And although I am usually quite subject to vertigo, I had no opportunity to look down, especially since it was so pitch black that we could scarcely see one another. The huntsman went first and I followed him down so that I got out of the prison unnoticed and in total silence and helped the huntsman to return the fire ladder to the place from which he had earlier taken it.

"After this action we ran straight out of the village and although I begged him for heaven's sake to tell me what was going on, he nonetheless always replied that I should save my breath and keep running on my way, for they most surely would come after us on horseback and things might be worse than before. I didn't know one path from another and out of sheer fright took one path this way and the next one that way until I found myself quite lost in an unfamiliar region. And this same confused path has borne me before this castle which doubtless will belong to my host. This is the small cause why I have obscured my usual cheerful humor with a few sad clouds."

Then the young nobleman began to laugh frightfully. He poked himself in the sides and was about to burst from not being able to breathe. When he had done this for almost a quarter of an hour, he again sat down opposite me and said, "Monsieur, I owe you more gratitude for your story than I can pay. This castle is not my own, as you believe, but is presently occupied by my mother. I don't know what may happen some day; it's sufficient that at it I enjoy more freedom and amusement than many a big braggart.

"But in order that you know — as I promised earlier — what pleased me especially in your story and what caused me to break out in such impolite laughter, understand that the thing that satisfied me most about all this is that you were representing me in this play.

"Sir, the fellow who lay next to you in the bedroom and took your clothes away, that's me as you see me here before you, and the clothes you're wearing on your body are the same outfit I left in the bedroom for you in place of your own when I ran off before daybreak. Your knapsack is lying here beneath the stove and not even a handkerchief, much less anything else, is missing from it because in doing this I wasn't trying to commit a theft; much rather I was looking for an opportunity to remain hidden from the bailiff rabble and thus march by them unrecognized since I already had intelligence of how I was to come into their clutches. And because I knew no other way over the mountains than that one, I was compelled through taking the clothes to a great discourtesy that I'll regret for the rest of my life, especially because it was committed against a person whom I much rather should be obliged to serve because of his innate qualities. But in order to help you out of your dream and to inform you about what you could not find out from your jailers, I beg you to grant me a brief informal audience. You'll be surprised at how nicely you stumbled into the game.

"I'm called Isidoro and spent my noble childhood in a thousand delights that I'll not seek to describe here any more than you did your childhood. All that one needs to know is that by nature I've striven after nothing more than the ladies, and just as a hungry bird is easy to catch, I didn't miss an opportunity to swing myself onto a bed, however and wherever that might be, and through this lack of caution easily brought it about that everywhere it was said I was the worst gallant in the whole country. It's true that no more perfect sweet-talker was to be found than I, for I flattered now this person, now that one, and often waited on a person four whole weeks for one lousy kiss. I learned music only on this account and valued it highly solely for the reason that through it one could either make himself beloved to the lady or serve her with it. So it happened that as a student I was soon fiddling up one lane or down the next or had others fiddling. Indeed, I played the most dances before the windows of those whom I knew least or those who had at least heard of me so that I might become known and liked everywhere. In this dissolute bungling I didn't remain within the confines of my class; rather, I dressed myself as a peasant churl and in such clothing went in disguise to the villages and village inns, where I often found more diversion with the peasant girls than with many a highly regarded and trifling lady's maid who can't do anything but swing her behind back and forth like a goose. You can note how miserably I spent this period which I employed for nothing save my own ruination, and this went on until I fell in love with the countess who had the letter shot to you in the prison.

"Twelve miles from here in the forest there's a nice place where the count customarily hunts his stags. And because there's no greater devotee of hunting in the whole country, it happens that most of the time throughout the year you can find him at that very spot. From this he neglects many necessary business affairs and not only creates great inconvenience for his subjects but moreover boards certain hunting dogs with them that they must give as much to eat as would sustain a fieldhand quite easily. I myself have a lawsuit to pursue for my mother, but, to tell the truth, very little gets done in this way and I scarcely believe that a verdict will be reached within twelve years. This trial gave me the first opportunity to become acquainted with the countess Veronia and from there enter into greater familiarity. She loved small dogs; therefore, I took great pains to present her one of an unusual and rare breed that cost me twenty-four Taler. I did this under the pretense of advancing my lawsuit, but my intent was quite other than business, although at that time the count accepted it as nothing but my good esteem.

"The countess, who is a woman of incomparable beauty, didn't want to leave this present unrewarded; rather, for the dog she sent me a bag of newly minted Ducats, which I still have with me. From this time on I sought to speak to her in person, for, to tell the truth, I was so desperately in love and I believe then I would have had myself stabbed to death if I had known it would be of any pleasure to her. I could neither eat nor drink and the worst thing of all was I felt myself to be in a proper torture chamber that perhaps seemed worse than the one from which you fled last night. And this is just that castle where I so pursued my ruination and where you were imprisoned as being me.

"After I had almost been tormented to death by this love, I decided to reveal my love to her, no matter how sweetly or sourly she might gaze on me thereafter. Accordingly, upon a chance opportunity in the garden I presented her an apple in which I had secreted her a letter written on a piece of parchment. It ran roughly: 'Most charming creature! Whoever hates the one by whom he is loved is scarcely called generous. But because I believe you far surpass in generosity all creatures of your gender, I live in the pleasant hope that you will not let that person waste away in desire who without enjoying the pleasure of your reciprocated love will indeed live but always die from suffering.'

9

"Although this letter was not immediately seen by her, it aroused in her no slight aversion to me so that while still in the garden, I was undecided whether I should throw myself into the lake or hang myself in the attic of the building. I had so stamped the image of her charm upon my heart that I was of the opinion it was impossible to live without her favor being returned. I wept day and night like some old whore spreading lye in a bathhouse and ultimately avoided being seen by her, for that would have only increased my desperation. And because the countess had her residence by the lake, in the evenings I would sit in a small boat, take the lute under my arm, and sing — or have others sing — the most enamored songs I could compose, among which the following is the only one I remember completely.

> Veronia, my dear!
> I'm dying from desire
> And sailing to my end.
> Unto your will I bend
> And burn with painful fire.
> Oh, help! Is rescue near?
> Veronia, my dear!
>
> Veronia, my love!
> Do save my ship again,
> I'm stranded as you see
> And torment's killing me.
> Release me from my pain!
> Come, fairest one, and be my dove!
> Veronia, my love!
>
> Veronia, my dear!
> I'll love you all the same
> Although I'm sinking down,
> Within the fatal lake I'll drown
> And sadness is to blame.
> My rescue simply can't draw near,
> Veronia, my dear!

"Those are the only strophes I still remember from all sorts of arias and they would be quite pleasant to hear if you were acquainted with the graceful melodies with which they were delivered. Meanwhile we completed whole suites of ballets and sonatas because I spared no expense in winning her affection, no matter what it might cost. The longer I labored for her love, the less I was able to bring this about. This possessed me to such an extent that I decided to leave the place to attend to my court matters elsewhere. And in this fashion I trusted I would finally overcome myself and my emotions, because absence is the best medicine for all unclean thoughts, something I had not yet been fully able to recognize at that time because I was seeking the greatest goal and hadn't noticed how our blind arrogance is subject to wretched vanity.

"I finally mounted my horse and rode from the city so full of enamored fancies that I can't describe the state of my heart at that time. I didn't look at anyone, and it's quite possible I rode past various acquaintances whom I neither saw nor took leave of. Love had so possessed me then, I regarded everything else as less than nothing. I continually looked back on the road and sighed a good thousand times. Indeed, finally it became impossible for me to ride further; rather, I dismounted beneath a great tree to have a last look at the castle and to deliver my farewell to it. I then began a proper sermon, during which I talked to myself and to no other person.

"Be assured, sir, if I were to recite to you all the failings I introduced into my sermon, you would roar and laugh at my story even more than I did at yours. Finally I grew ashamed of the passers-by, a goodly number of whom had gradually assembled to listen to me, for I had not been aware of them, either because of my overwhelming thoughts or because I had been lying on the ground. Accordingly, I stood up and swung myself onto my horse and rode away at a gallop as quickly as the horse could run.

"In such a manner I ran up hill and down dale for all I was worth, sometimes screaming like a stable hand who has a hundred horses to control. I finally gave the horse his head to ride to wherever he wanted to take me. I conclude that at that time I was not three degrees away from true insanity because I didn't know how to find a way to escape from this passion. My steed had gone a good bit and because his reins were free, he brought me onto a completely unfamiliar road into a forest where I grew rather frightened. Not only were the trees crowded together, but also here and there were deep and rocky gullies, in which commonly robbers and other dishonest rabble tend to hide themselves. In view of this situation I somewhat returned to my senses although much too late, for I had not noticed that I had lost and left behind my hat, my gloves, and my sword among the shrubbery. Accordingly, I dismounted and because evening was coming on, I diligently sought a way out. I led the horse this way and that until it was finally night and, due to a lack of any light, the road became completely unrecognizable."

Chapter Three. Isidoro's Strange Situation in Hermit's Clothing.

Fire and brimstone vex one sore;
Love, however, even more.

"The night at hand was a true mirror of my psyche, which was completely surrounded by earthly darkness. The worst thing of all was that I heard the wild animals growling and only then thought of my great folly since I no longer had an opportunity of getting out of the forest. For the safety of my person I wanted to retreat into a tree, but because of inexperience at climbing, I had to shelve my plan, no matter how dear my life was to me. My thoughts of love rather disappeared and, in truth, I wouldn't have known what to do, had I not heard a small bell in the area. At first I imagined a cow had strayed into the forest and had such a bell hanging from its neck. From this I had reason to suspect that a farm might be close by. But when I heard the sound a second time, I found I had been wrong in my guess because it had been a much larger bell than any such cattle could have worn. I followed the sound and saw a light shimmering on a high hill, from which I concluded a hermit must be staying there. I had left my horse standing tied to a fir tree as prey for the wild animals because I was much too concerned with saving my own life. The hermit rang again and when I had completely lost my way climbing the hill, I called very loudly for help because I was afraid of no slight fall. After such a call the hermit opened his small window and I again asked him most amiably to help me out of my perplexity.

"A second bell rang, at the sound of which a young hermit came running with a lit lantern and helped me up by means of a rope because I wasn't able to move forward or backwards. He took me with him to the old man's cell, most of which was lined and decorated with tree bark and moss. There I sat down by the warm stove because I had been rather cold in the forest. I was happy at having found so safe a place for myself and I told the hermits a quite different version of how and why I had come into the forest. The had great compassion with my fate, and the young man didn't quit looking for the horse until he brought it on a cleared path over the hill and to the cell, where he shut it into a room where they had the tools they used for digging roots.

"I would have been the greatest fool on earth if I had furnished the hermits any information concerning my love; therefore, I requested to lie down and rest a bit after the frights I had survived. They then arranged a bed for me much more faithfully than blood brothers would have, and there was nothing within their poor means they wouldn't have offered me, had I had need of it.

"It is doubtless true that I found their life holier and more complete than my own; indeed, I judged them quite happy that they had never gone as far astray as had I. But in spite of this, my temptations didn't leave me with holy thoughts; rather, they dispersed them a thousandfold with their habitual poisonous manner that always seeks to kill him who is too addicted to them.

"The various and manifold complications didn't grant me sufficient peace that I could have been able to sleep for a moment, but Veronia, Veronia always remained in my head. And no matter how I wanted to drive out the thought of her, I couldn't control myself, perhaps because my intention was much too shallow and based on immoral suppositions, whereas I should have laid true virtue as their foundation.

"After an hour the young hermit took his leave and the old man also went to bed, the which heartily shocked me, for it was a funeral bier filled with moss that he produced from behind a bench. The pillow for his head was a large, hollowed-out stone in which he lay stretched out on his back, his blanket his monk's mantle which he also wore as his raincoat. He talked with me almost half an hour after he lay down and mentioned various reasons for having entered a hermitage and withdrawn from the godless world. He said the young hermit was a count who had deliberately concealed his family name. As for himself, he had already spent sixty-eight years in this frightful wilderness, where he had fed and nourished himself with roots and water and occasionally wild fruit and begged bread. Every week the young man made a collection in the villages and brought back cheese, butter, milk, bread, meat, and vegetables. So ran their household and to all appearances they were more alert and healthier than I, who from childhood on had been brought up with an exquisite cuisine.

"He casually related various events that had occurred since he first arrived in the forest, but my reflecting on my imagined love forbade me to listen to him any further because I had decided to persuade the hermit to lend me his monk's robe, clothed in which I wanted to go into the castle and in disguise to resolve things finally with the countess, however she might then judge and decide.

"With that I slumbered off for a while, but on the following day I made a deal with the old man to lend me a coat he had worn for ten years; for it I gave him enough money to enable him to get himself a new one. He retained the horse and because he said the castle in question was only a scant eight miles away from there, I promised him I would certainly return to the hermitage within twenty-four hours. With that I pulled the garment over my body and because in any case I had some wigs with me, I could suffer them to cut away my remaining hair like a monk and in such guise they directed me out of the forest to a road that led to the castle."

Chapter Four. He has to Take Flight from the Castle.

What we may think we've well concealed
Is often suddenly revealed.

"Not two hours had passed when I caught sight of the castle, for, to admit the truth, love propelled me forward twice as fast as I usually walk and especially so since I was wearing a large and coarse monk's robe, which I was not accustomed to. The castle lay on a lake, and because a boat was sailing there from a village, I paid the fare and arrived at the shore, where I wrapped my coat about me and hastened to the castle. Pretending to bring a present for the countess, I requested to see her, which I could do all the more easily because, according to the talk, her lord was still hunting. She had me admitted quite soon and as a man of the cloth I could readily be admitted to her chamber, where I began to prate about the great poverty I had to endure in the Cliff Forest, as the woods were named where I had borrowed my cowl. Therefore, I begged the countess to provide me a better dwelling; I would repay her for this through humble services and the like.

"The countess sighed and when she heard I had come from Cliff Forest, she questioned me as to whether I hadn't met a demented man in it who was supposed to be a nobleman and named Isidoro. I was startled at her mentioning this and said that, indeed, the same person had rolled back and forth on the ground like a dog but that no one knew what was wrong with him because he gave no answer to any question. At this she sighed and was silent for a long time. I could tell she bore pity for me and because I wanted to know just where I stood, I revealed myself to her quite open-heartedly, told her my condition, and requested nothing save her decision. She grew quite pale and because in her confusion she could not decide things so quickly, she said, 'Monsieur, my recent anger was not intended so maliciously. A constant lover doesn't so readily don a monk's habit. Be assured that with my attitude I simply wanted to learn whether you will be so devoted that you will visit me at great danger.'

"But while we were talking so nicely with one another, the count came from the hunt and entered the room unannounced. First he took off his hat before me and said, 'Where are you from, father? Where are you from?' My voice was quite familiar to the count; therefore, I bowed quite low, turned toward the door, and ran out of the room without answering. On my honor, it's true I never ran so fast in all my life. I let my coat, my staff, and my cowl fall behind me, and because the count couldn't decide quickly, I covered quite a way before his servants hurried after me. Easily eight or even more of them ran after me, but I had already hidden in the forest and made my way in secret to my former hermitage, where I donned my clothes and without another glance headed for this castle on my horse.

"As cold and frosty as it was at that time, I was sweating all over and I came within a hair's breadth of riding my horse to death because not a little depended on my flight. My mother was startled at my early arrival, but I told her a far different story of what had caused me to hurry so. Two days later I came again to the castle but in a different habit and a different courage than I had displayed before because the uncertainty of my former love had robbed my spirit and filled me only with irritating pain. You certainly won't be able to refrain from laughing when I tell you the manner in which the runners chased into Cliff Forest and there took the poor hermit as a captive to the castle. In her and my interest the countess had given as her principal explanation that the hermit had wanted to stab her to death. And this was actually the cause the count had had me pursued so quickly.

"When the count recognized the grey hairs of the old man, he was sorry for having caught him by mistake, asked his forgiveness, and invited him to dinner. But during the protracted meal the hermit related everything that had happened to me in the forest. I had revealed to him as little as I could and I believe if he had known my name, I would have been ruined along with the countess. But even though it remained undiscovered this time, I still couldn't escape the misfortune into which I ultimately had fallen like a bird snared in a springe."

Chapter Five. Revelation of His Love and Why Zendorio Was Imprisoned.

Misfortune loves absurdity;
It's often where it shouldn't be.

"The longer I loved Veronia, the more so, but for nothing save my own ruination. She could demonstrate no return liking for me save through friendly glances, from which I wouldn't have gotten five Groschen a year unless I had invested them with a foolish merchant. But just as a secret understanding finally tends to come into the open, so it couldn't last for long with me either, poor fellow. I had to seek an opportunity as best I could and not as I would like, for since I had nothing to do at court, I had to seek out an affair which made it seem I had something to do there although in fact it was nothing but pure idleness. To this end, I pretended I wanted to marry one of the countess's ladies although I never had had a desire to marry anyone from the court because they were either too poor or too haughty. However, through this hypocrisy I won free access and became so familiar with Veronia that she finally ended up throwing cherry stems, hazelnuts, sweets, almonds, and such things at my face. The Devil also did his work in this until I be-

15

lieved that luck had entered into an eternal alliance with me. From childhood on I was trained in cutting out apple peels and lemon rind; on account of this, in her presence I made all manner of most unusual designs and presented them to her. The girl whom I pretended to court imagined a great many things on account of me, but the poor child would have done better to cry, had she known how completely and totally I didn't want to have her. I presented her all sorts of perfumed gloves, the most elegant silk hose, beautiful armbands, elaborate chiming clocks, but I hired a lad who had to break into her armoire and steal back all the gifts. You can imagine how basely I led the young lady around by the nose, contrary to all honor and reputation and contrary to respect and propriety. It was high time that I departed from the castle; otherwise I might have done something that couldn't be spoken of without derision and disgrace.

"Such a life would have suited me quite well as a fiancée, but my mother wrote me that if I were to marry a lady of the court, she would disinherit me down to the shirt on my back because she could demonstrate with many receipts that I had wasted up to eight thousand Taler at the university. I apologized to her once again and announced to her that I thought of nothing so little as of such a marriage and that what I was up to with the ladies at court was intended for diversion and not for such a marital union. With such a resolve I placated my mother, who was usually rather stubborn, and consequently the poor creature at the castle had to let herself be fooled by me time and again. And although she incessantly asked me when we were going to get engaged, I named her one time after another and gave her so much hope that she had a dozen sacks left over if she didn't give some to her sisters.

"Finally a page caught me just as I was kissing the countess, and although I gave the boy two Taler to remain silent, he nonetheless carried the news to the count, who rode in full fury from the hunt to the castle and was resolved to run his hunting spear through my guts, for it is certain that no angrier person was to be found in the country far and wide. To my good fortune this was covertly told me by the forestry clerk, and I consequently decamped before the count caught sight of me. Subsequently I learned from a long, detailed letter how impatiently the countess complained to her husband about me. She said I had secretly attacked her from the rear and kissed her. In addition, she told other stories as well of things I had dared and thus she made herself white and me, on the contrary, blacker than India ink.

"The next week I even learned from a familiar source that I had been spotted on my journey through the mountains, and because I had renounced the proposed marriage to the lady, the count wanted to forcibly seize me and teach me a lesson as a scurrilous imposter. But as luck would have it, you came into my room at the roadside inn; otherwise I would have fallen into the hands of the lord's constables, as you can easily figure out.

"Thus, this has been the course of my fortune, and I'm keeping myself secretly hidden here in the castle. I've also ordered my people to admit no one to me save someone I've brought up here myself. And this is also the reason I'm staying in this small room; otherwise I'd entertain you in a larger and cleaner one. Forgive me meanwhile and graciously accept that it's happening to keep my person in greater safety because from here I can see far out onto the road and actually observe what comes in and out of the castle. I'm not worried in the slightest about the count and he's a long way from having me hanged, but the worst thing is, I fear he might bring charges against me at the appropriate place. But as long as he can charge me with nothing grave, people will only laugh at him. The miserable old fox wanted to secretly grab me and give me a good roughing-up in the prison, but I believe I've played a comedy that was sufficiently amusing. Forget your injuries and stay with me for as long as it suits you. My table and a poor bed are at your service, and be assured that I'm completely obliged to you."

Chapter Six. A Hard Bet. The Old Procuress Tells of a Pretty Love-Making and Thereby Helps Them Out of Their Dream.

A bird that's found in captive plight
Will use all means to gain its flight.

This story from the young nobleman was the only means of releasing me from the thoughts that had tormented me so greatly to this time. I crossed myself and had to be extremely astonished at unexpectedly being helped out of my dream at this isolated castle. For commonly those people whom we least suspect know most about our concerns, and thus the kind reader has understood and likewise emerged with me from this confusion in which I had been so entangled to the present moment.

"Highly esteemed host," I then said to the nobleman, "your hospitality is simply playing with your servants, especially when I regard myself as too lowly to repay your kindness. You needn't thank me in the slightest nor ask my pardon for my having survived something so unexpected on account of you because I have ascribed such a fate not to your person, but to miraculous luck. For if it hadn't carried me so unexpectedly to the wayhouse, you, monsieur, would never have been able to disguise yourself, but I have to laugh most of all at the letter and the huntsman. Had the countess known of the prank or would still learn of it, I believe she would be more astonished by it than we both were. Among other things you related, I'm not a little surprised at how the count went so quickly for execution. Ha, they don't hang anyone immediately, and had I known of the deception, since I'm a scamp, I would have played a prank that would have set the whole court laughing. But it's too late for that, and had things gone differently, I never would have understood the plot in such detail. There's one thing I'd still like to know: How did things turn out with the pack of whores across the lake? For after the departure of the bailiff that evening, I saw not a prisoner, much less a pack of whores, and thus don't know whether there was anything to the affair or not."

The nobleman said there was some substance to it and amid such conversation a maid, whom I took to be the chatelaine, brought up the meal he had had prepared in the meantime to go with a glass of wine. This cavalier certainly showed me every politeness and let nothing lack that would serve to attend me. Amid a very pleasant conversation we dined for three hours, and because the small room was heated due to the lingering cold, along with the warmth of the stove the fiery wine went to my head at the same time so that I almost felt dizzy.

He mentioned in passing that four weeks ago he had bet with a member of the nobility and wagered three hundred ducats that he, with the wife's permission, would go to bed with her before the year was out. The other had said that was so impossible, as impossible as mowing grass down from the sky, and the wife herself was present when the bet was made in the presence of many other cavaliers who had listened as witnesses. Because of this he asked that I show him a way of doing this, but even though I pondered it for some time, I still couldn't think of a way that the winnings from the bet could fall to him. At this time the same maid cleared the table, for the nobleman didn't want to allow many servants or other people to come in because he had come here to remain in hiding and had new clothing prepared with which he intended to travel incognito to those places where he could stay most suitably.

At this he pulled my knapsack from under the stove and showed me my shabby clothing in the adjoining chamber. I had to laugh heartily at how well they had been kept, and afterwards he led me into the courtyard after he had had the gate closed and firmly bolted. In handing over the keys, the gatekeeper reported the gardener had informed him that the old noblewoman would not be more than three hours away, for they had already risen from the table when he departed. To explain this, the nobleman commented that his mother had departed two days ago for a noble wedding, from which she would return today. The road covered some twelve miles, and in getting there she took along no one except a coachman and the gardener because the local landed gentry have more interest in good hard money than in costly affairs. After this report he gave the gatekeeper, who had sent me away from the castle so derisively, a sharp rebuke on account of me and an order to keep a sharp eye out for the lady so that she wouldn't have to wait long at the gate. Then we moved on to the courtyard room where some eleven women, partly from the village, partly from the castle, had assembled to spin their yarn and twine, for the noblewoman paid certain amounts for such work, from which she amassed a sizable amount of linen cloth. The young nobleman was an extremely amusing person and, judging by appearances, our personalities were cast in the same mold. Thus he treated me very familiarly and told me that from my presence the time had passed all the more pleasantly because otherwise he would have had to sit in boredom and low spirits.

Then we sat down at a table near the stove, and he ordered the women to tell some stories until his mother came home. "Yes, indeed," said an ugly old hag who had a hackel between her legs and was pulling tow through it, "my dear squire, I'll tell you something other than a tale." When the nobleman said she surely could and soon, she began to relate the following to our great astonishment after we were seated by a light in a corner.

"From childhood on I've heard a lot of stories but none as nice as the one I ran into yesterday. If I'm supposed to speak truly then you can easily judge from my age how I've had to feed myself in times like these. Spinning and carding won't do it alone; instead, as early as possible when I was still a girl, I learned some tricks that not everyone can do."

With that she began to laugh and went on to say, "Gentlemen, in a word: An old woman who can't pander isn't worth a moth-eaten pelt. Indeed, this trade has often brought me more in one hour than I've earned doing God knows what for a week. But yesterday I came within a hair of having hell to pay when approximately eight miles from here by the large lake at my urging some noblemen and business clerks had assembled, for whom I had provided five beautiful girls. The local judge is as hard on whores as is the hangman himself. But like they say, nothing spurs him on to such ardor more than his proud and haughty wife, who did it earlier just like whores do today. I remember well the time when I received many a Reichstaler from her for having sent her to a gallant fellow. Ha, ha, that I know quite well.

"Be that as it may, word was soon sent to the castle concerning our meeting, and before we were aware of it, our house was surrounded by many constables. We could hear the chains rattling in which we were to be locked.

"One woman among the group was exceedingly beautiful and had served the judge as a chambermaid. She was extraordinarily afraid; she begged and pleaded that I think of a way of getting her out safely and without scandal, but I lacked the best means of all, namely, the opportunity. The gallant gentlemen also didn't want to see how it would come out, but leaped at risk of life and limb through a window into a garden that the constables couldn't get into. This was impossible for the women folk, and even had it been possible, there was no one who wanted to lead the way. So we stood there in fear and consternation, for they had ordered the constables to arrest the whores as soon as they stepped through the door and to take them to the castle.

19

"After we had discussed what to do for half an hour and the noise of the chains grew louder and louder, three decided to climb out of the window from a sheet and to lower themselves gently. That worked perfectly, but the beautiful chambermaid who was really the cause of it all couldn't make up her mind because she feared falling to her death from the window because her whole body was shaking from fear. In this dangerous situation the house servant, who was an arch-knave, came to her help. He brought her some well-worn men's clothing, and what she had worn he stuffed with hay, laid it in a bed, and told the bailiffs that the others had long since fled through the garden, but that the fair chambermaid was lying in the upper room, quite ill and weak because she had been immeasurably shocked at their appearance.

"When the bailiffs grew tired of waiting, the judge ordered them to enter the house forcibly and take the remaining whores away. They did so, but the chambermaid slipped by them unnoticed and I buried myself as deep in the hay as I could.

"I can't describe how the bailiffs cursed at the house servant and they came within a hair of taking him away instead of the whores. However, he hastily quarreled with them and alleged he was going to bring to light certain stories about the judge that would disgrace him beyond belief. At that the bloodhounds had to accept things nicely and this time return home empty-handed. After their departure I returned here to the village and had a hearty private laugh at them."

During this tale I poked the nobleman and he me now with his elbow, now his foot, and when it was done we had to be surprised at how we had happened to hear such pretty stories this day. From all the circumstances this pack of whores was none other than the one of which the jailer had told me he had to catch across the lake and bring back to his jail. Thus were all my questions answered and I was surprised at the wanton slut for seeking to boast about her profession that deserved the hangman much more than her self-praise. Still, the nobleman said I should get such thoughts out of my head; that's just the way people are. Whoever could lead a pious life unto himself should reckon that as a special bliss. As we started to go on talking, we heard a clatter in the courtyard, from which we concluded that would be his elderly mother.

Chapter Seven. Isidoro Wins the Bet.

Your gold will get you beer and skittles,
You need good luck for bets and riddles.

As long as the world has existed no one was as surprised as we two when we had run with lights to the coach to receive the old woman, for instead of her there was sitting in it a quite young woman, perhaps eighteen years old. We surprised her too and after she had climbed out, she looked around everywhere in the courtyard and didn't recognize anything. "Coachman," she said, "you've driven the wrong way!"

"What?" said the coachman in reply, "I'm at my castle." Yet when he looked around, he wondered how this young lady had gotten into his coach. Whatever she might want to do, it was now well into the night and the castle lay in great solitude. Therefore, she had to remain in the place, no matter how much she wanted to turn around and drive home.

The nobleman took me to one side and whispered in my ear, "Monsieur, this is the wife of the cavalier with whom I bet I would sleep beside her at her request. Because so many a trick has been revealed to me concerning a change of clothes, I shall dress as a maid, say that I'm the chatelaine, and meanwhile see to it you introduce yourself as if you were the son in the castle. Because they took you as such in the prison, I am completely confident she will believe it because she hasn't seen me more than twice in all her life."

The matter came off perfectly, for after I had accompanied this lady into a room and promised her safe and good lodging with the assurance I would have her driven home at daybreak, she was somewhat satisfied. She said, "Monsieur, your unusual manner of attending a woman is, in truth, far more pleasant than I can say or praise. I am very sorry that through an astonishing mistake I also must disturb your polite gestures. Because chance has arranged things so, I beg to regard my impoliteness as excused. Monsieur, be assured that my husband and I will most indebtedly acknowledge your kindnesses and compensate you through other services."

With such talk from this extremely beautiful woman I escorted her into a chamber where I showed her the bed with the promise that the chatelaine was to lie with her although it was quite safe in the castle. She thanked me once again for my generosity. Meanwhile Isidoro had gotten dressed, and if I hadn't known about the deception beforehand, no one ever could have convinced me he was a man, so excellently did he know how to adapt to his costume. By nature he had a soft, effeminate voice and he asked the lady if she were satisfied that she sleep with her. To this the lady answered "Yes" in the presence of many servants and staff, and in this fashion Isidoro had already won the bet. He then positioned as many men as he could hide in the room and there wasn't a nook so small that he didn't put a fellow in it. Because I lay beside two others beneath the bed, he ordered me to leap out as soon as he had lain down with the lady and testify I and the others had seen that according to his bet he truly had lain with the woman.

With that there was an exchange of compliments, and after we lay hidden in the chamber, Isidoro lighted her in and undressed her. They both lay down in the bed and the young peeress chatted with him about nothing but the recent wedding, which tale lasted almost a full hour.

21

"Your Worship," said Isidoro, "today at this castle I had a great stroke of luck that I shan't forget for as long as live."

"How so?" said the lady of nobility. "Did you perhaps find a beloved?"

"Oh, no," answered Isidoro, "within two hours I won three hundred ducats."

"That's a lot," said the lady, "but where do you maids get so much money that you can engage in such gambling?"

"Your Worship," said Isidoro, "I wasn't gambling; rather, such money is due me from a bet I won."

"Then who lost it?" the noblewoman asked.

"Madam," Isidoro offered in reply, "your lord."

"What," she said, "my husband?"

"Yes," answered Isidoro, "your lord. Don't you know how we bet with one another that I would sleep in bed with you with your permission?"

"Heaven help me!" screamed the lady. "Are you Isidoro?"

With that she wanted to leap out of the bed, but Isidoro held her back and called, "Hello, you gentlemen who are hidden, come out so that you can witness how I was lying with the lady." For our purpose we had left the night-light burning, and as soon as Isidoro called, we crept from under the bed, over the bed, between the bed, and, in sum, from every corner, and the lady hid herself in great shame beneath the blanket. Finally she screamed out she would gladly acknowledge the three hundred ducats to be paid, if only Isidoro would just get out of the bed. After such a promise he climbed out, and the lady remained lying there, completely devastated.

The next morning quill, ink, and paper were brought to her bed in order that she write an acknowledgment of the money lost, after which she was honored with an elegant breakfast and permitted to ride home in the coach to her castle, a journey of some sixteen miles.

We knew as little as she about the mistaken identities, so we let the matter rest, however it had occurred, because we had won the money and deceived the lady brilliantly. Then we went to our earlier room because the nobleman didn't venture to stay elsewhere. There we began all sorts of conversations that were most effective for passing the time. As noon was approaching I saw in the distance on the road a coach driving toward the castle and the nobleman couldn't recognize it. It drew nearer and nearer and nearer until it finally came to the gate. Because the nobleman suspected there might be a surprise hidden in it for him, he previously had signaled by a bell to close the gate. The coachman didn't know what he should do, but in astonishment the nobleman saw his mother peering from the coach and ordering to open up.

Then the castle was opened, and the old woman greeted us both very cordially. Whispering, she asked her son who I was. He told her in reply that earlier at various universities I had been his best friend and playmate, upon whom he had been able to rely most of all in the most dangerous situations and more stories of that ilk.

She bade me come with her son to dinner, where she showed me every courtesy. "Mother," said Isidoro, "in all my days I've never encountered a farce such as happened to me last night."

"Yes, my son, nor I," she said. "Yesterday when we had risen from the table, there was a dance, at which our young cousin Pongratz put on quite a show. We watched the jumping about for some time until, indeed, it grew quite dark. We soon had the final dance, and everybody ran to their coaches like a herd of sheep. You could never have convinced me I was sitting in the wrong coach, for from within it looked just like mine. At eight this morning we entered a sunken road, and because there was no way to turn the coaches around, I was compelled to travel in this coach here and she there to her castle.

"So we drove here and there in the country from this place to that, and I have to laugh heartily when I recall how astonished the nobleman was when he assisted me out of the coach instead of his young wife. I was told he privately gave the coachman a whipping in the stall that he won't forget. On the latter's body he broke apart almost every rein he could lay his hands on, but to me he wasn't offended in the slightest; rather, he said he regarded the mistake as a special delight since he had never had the high honor of my presence at his castle. I myself was completely surprised, for I couldn't readily remember at whose home and where I was. However, I hope you treated that noble lady in a manner that will give her no cause to complain to her husband of any discourtesy shown her, for she otherwise is extremely sensitive, and feels herself insulted and mortified if you so much as look askance at her."

Chapter Eight. Quick Challenge. Dangerous Fight. The Trickery is Miraculously Discovered.

All foolish notions can deceive,
They often cause a man to grieve.

Both of us assured her we hadn't done the slightest thing with her that would have tarnished her reputation. As far as the gain from the successful wager was concerned, in times such as these one could have won it in no other way than that employed. Isidoro added that he wasn't so greatly concerned about the lady's anger; once he had his three hundred ducats in his purse, people could say and think about him whatever they wanted to. But his mother, to be sure, didn't find this prank good no matter how he tried to palliate it; rather, she was of the opinion that when the lady's husband learned of the matter, there might be hell to pay because during her lifetime several such stunts had occurred that always had had great danger as a consequence, and occasionally even death and assassination. But Isidoro kept laughing and making fun of the game until in the evening a message arrived from the nobleman that he had sent by the returning coachman.

The address was to Isidoro and upon seeing it he imagined that perhaps the three hundred ducats were enclosed. After breaking it open, he read with me the following words: "You useless creature! The Devil will turn you every way but loose when I catch up with you. Your winnings will turn to fire about your head, and I'll teach you how an arch-knave should win a bet. If my beloved had stuck a dagger in your body, she would have done better than thanking you for the insult you did her. The other lout who helped pull off the deception is included here, and you both should know that I regard you as the most miserable arch-scoundrels in the world and under the sun if you will not reasonably fight with me as I desire and demand. You knaves!"

This was the fearsome content of the letter, and unfortunately the old woman came up just as Isidoro was starting to put it in his pocket. "Give me that letter!" the mother said, "for I heard from the door that someone has challenged you to a fight. Oh, what an unending torment I must suffer from this misbegotten child! You'll bring me to the grave before my time, and I don't have an hour without worry because I always must fear that you'll still end up in the hands of the hangman!"

"Mother," answered Isidoro, "that's not good, and I hope that's not to be your maternal blessing. Here, have the letter and see if I haven't been sufficiently attacked in it. The scoundrel is angry at having to cough up the three hundred ducats and prefers to fight for them. But I swear to him that with my sword I'll have him dancing around like a trained bear. That's the way you treat rogues, so cease being impatient. This concerns my reputation; I have to fight him."

"Listen," said the mother, "it doesn't have to be, for that's not a challenge; otherwise he would have had to send it to you through one of the nobility of your rank. What does a person from the stable have to do with that?"

"Oh, noble this, noble that," said the son. "Tomorrow I'll ride before his castle and so torment the lazy lout until he comes out and slashes and stabs with me to the left and right, sideways and across, to the front and the rear, in a word, in all the ways and stances you can describe. The whole world and his handful of subjects won't be able to protect or preserve him from that."

The mother kept crying copiously but she couldn't talk her infuriated son out of his intended action. She said he should consider that he was the sole heir of her estates, but it was all not enough to still his anger; instead, on the next day he had two good horses saddled on which we rode to the castle of the man who had challenged us. On the way we agreed to taunt him one after the other. Isidoro had good hope of a victory because he said that our opponent had done nothing in the fencing-room all his life and often had been stabbed and slashed by lowly blackguards. In such conversation we came near to the castle and saw four people hacking and slashing at one another in a nearby meadow. We regarded it simply as teasing and believed fully that the nobleman was perhaps practicing parrying so that he might be all the surer in the serious fight with us. But we finally saw how serious it was all too clearly because one fellow fell over and, amid much moaning, seemed to give up the ghost. We were hurrying to decide the match or to see what it meant when a lackey came running toward us. He begged us to not go nearer, for in the bushes were lying eighteen fellows with muskets, who had been positioned there by the dueling parties to shoot down all those who would presume to disturb or hinder them in their fight.

The servant who told us this spoke German very poorly, but because he presented his matter in an unusual fashion, we decided to question him further about the event. Therefore, we inquired how and for what reasons this quarrel had arisen. "Gentlemen," said the servant, "this fight, which is now in its second year, developed in Paris when a merchant from this country, who is named Valentin Isidoro, played an especially dirty trick on my master through a bet.

"They bet one another on who could play the worst prank on the other, and because my master has a splendid estate outside the city, this Isidoro and his servant waited for him along the road, shot his horse, stripped him in an open field, put the clothes on himself, and so disguised rode in the evening to my master's castle. Since the wife couldn't recognize him because of the darkness, she lay down in the bed with him and he accordingly insisted he had won the bet and my master owed him a thousand crowns, the sum they had bet. But because he saw this joke would misfire badly, he accordingly made off in the night, and because my master almost died in fury, he decided to take a trip to Germany and catch the disgusting bird.

"Only yesterday did we meet a coachman in the nearby inn on the road leading from the castle. We asked him about Isidoro and if he had any knowledge of such a name. But he said this man was staying in the place where he was driving to. Also, because our lady solemnly swore that Isidoro had had another man with him, whom she regarded as a lackey, my master suspected the same fellow would have helped in the affair and he challenged the two of them in a letter he wrote in the castle. But something different happened last evening when, to have some fun, we rode out onto the highway with the nobleman of this castle and encountered this honest Isidoro and his servant whom he had used as a lackey back then. We looked at one another for a long time, but my master made clear his views in few words. Because the matter wouldn't suffer great delay, they agreed on the spot to meet this morning at this place. And because the merchant was accompanied, my master took one of his servants with him, and the one you saw fall to ground there is Isidoro's servant. They probably won't cease stabbing and slashing unless night or death intervenes."

How odd this news seemed to us, the reader can well imagine. We both dismounted and along with the lackey watched the fighting with unusual delight. The merchant defended himself to the best of his ability, and because they were fighting on foot, he leaped now here, now there to avoid his enemies' blows. They went at each other so that hair was flying, but the good servant crawled away on the ground like a turtle because the French cavalier's lackey had given him a good one in the side. Finally misfortune also struck the merchant, for he was so slashed and hacked here and there about his body that blood was running over his head as well as his body. The tatters of his coat and shirt were hanging from his sides like a scarecrow you put in a turnip field to scare away the deer. Finally on bended knee he begged for quarter, but, ignoring that, they gave him one more blow between the ears, from which he sank to the ground. After that the concealed soldiers and seconds hurried from the shrubbery and declared satisfaction. The two wounded men were taken to the castle, but because we were still fired up for such, Isidoro wanted to see it and ask the owner where he stood with his bet, for he was fully resolved that if he wouldn't grant him the three hundred ducats, he intended to treat him like these two, hack him to pieces, and then flee the country with me.

In such resolve we rode to the castle, where we were immediately recognized by the lady. The owner laughed heartily, and when Isidoro came into the room, on the table were lying the three hundred ducats *in specie*, which he needed only to pick up and pocket. Even more, this gentleman showed us every courtesy and was still laughing at his wife for letting herself be tricked so carelessly. And this trait in this gentleman can't be praised highly enough, because he saw that it was best to let sleeping dogs lie unless one wanted to make things worse, and a little patience accomplishes far more than sustained obstinacy. For although the French cavalier had shown himself to be highborn and had left his homeland to take revenge on the merchant, in so doing he had become the talk of the land and brought it about that his victory was not believed by all; his person, however, was regarded as the cuckold personified.

We all drank a pledge of brotherhood to one another, and they promised to help me to a good position, be it in a village or a town. In this fashion I no longer asked why I had endured such torment in the prison. Just as after sunrise one gives little or no heed to the darkness, in such a happy state I had no interest in the hours I had spent in futile worry while in custody.

Chapter Nine. Disguised as a Jew, the Gardener is Shamefully Cheated by Ludwig, a Nobleman. Ludwig Betrays Himself.

He hurts himself who picks a fight,
Disloyalty itself does bite.

The barber who treated those wounded in the duel reported of their great pain and certain conditions that gave little hope they would fully recover since the master had eighteen wounds on his body and the servant twenty-four. Meanwhile the French cavalier came marching in and thanked the owner for the courtesy he had shown and offered to a stranger in a matter not concerning himself. He spoke German very well, at which in the end we were not surprised because he told us he formerly had served almost ten years in German military service. In such fashion he departed and left behind for the owner an extremely fine watch necklace, which the Queen of France was said to have used.

After this cavalier rode off we also didn't tarry long; instead, early in the evening we rode back to our castle, where we met the weeping mother in the courtyard. Isidoro straightened her out right away by explaining the grand fraud that had been committed with the letter. She finally was satisfied, and because the sight of the three hundred ducats gave her unusual delight, she felt a desire to change money for a sizable quantity of such pieces. Quite unknown to us, she sent her gardener to the nearest city with his ass, on which he had to take in the sack of money. They arranged the matter so surreptitiously that the son didn't hear the slightest word about it, and in order that the gardener not be recognized in the city, the noblewoman dressed him as a Jew, and through that he departed from the castle quite unrecognized.

The lady had specifically ordered him to get exact information where and from what region he could get the finest pieces. He inquired about this from almost all the people he met on the road. Among others, he encountered a nobleman, who was among the very richest in the country. The latter then took the money changer with him and promised to give him the finest ducats he had within his wealth. The gardener thought he had made a miraculous find, therefore turned his ass around in the road, gently driving it behind the noble's horse, and thus they rode one after the other.

After an hour they came to the castle where the nobleman had him wait in the courtyard; he, however, in the meantime went into his treasury and counted out almost a thousand Ducats because the disguised gardener wanted to trade for this amount. The cavalier, who didn't regard it as a sin to play a Jew for the fool, took a pile of the newest Reifpfennige, and weighed them against the Ducats until they were of the same weight. He put them in two identical bags and had the Jew called in, whom he was resolved to cheat thoroughly. Upon his return the gardener swore he had done everything possible to present himself as a proper Jew; therefore, the cavalier stacked a thousand Ducats on the table, put them in the sack, and sealed it. With the help of two servants the gardener carried his heavy money up, during which work the nobleman put the other sack with the Reifpfennige in its place, and when the gardener had produced his parcel along with the agio, he loaded the exchanged bag of money onto his ass and arrived quite late at the castle gate.

We had never seen the fool in his disguise; on account of that we believed it was a Jewish money changer, of whom the whole country was full at that time. But we soon learned otherwise when the noblewoman excoriated him so woefully that we could hear it over where we were. She wept wretchedly and the disguised gardener almost tore his hair out at having been cheated so piteously. He couldn't name either the nobleman or the castle, although he said he thought he had seen it frequently. Consequently, we had no solid footing and had to come to terms patiently with this major and great loss, which from all appearances could not be made good within six years. Everyone was full of sadness and misery, for no one knew how to find a cure for this injury, no matter how much we were worried and preoccupied with it. The gardener was thrown into the prison because it was believed he had abetted in the loss, and on account of it the lady wanted to seek counsel from a lawyer concerning what should or shouldn't be done in this unanticipated case.

Three days later there came to the castle the very nobleman with whom the gardener had changed the money, but he didn't know at all that the Jew had come from this castle; otherwise, he would have kept his trap shut or earlier not committed his deception. Isidoro immediately recognized him as Monsieur Ludwig, who had once studied riding with him in Geneva and Montpellier. They had been best buddies, and because of old familiarity, Isidoro invited him to dine even though he was filled with sadness concerning the lost money. The meal was ready, but the noblewoman kept to her bed with great suffering because she couldn't stop sighing amid tears about so striking a loss. Meanwhile Ludwig was truly having fun with us at table and said to Isidoro, "Brother, do you know what happened to me three days ago with a Jew? On the road the Devil led a jabbering yid to me, who had a thousand Taler or even more in large and heavy coins. I asked him what he wanted to do with them, and he agreed to a trade for ducats." And in this manner Ludwig told the whole story just as it had happened.

"Brother," said Isidoro, "do you still have the money?"

"Sure," answered Monsieur Ludwig, "I won't have drunk it up in just three days." Then Isidoro rose from the table and brought the news to his mother, who, while still in bed, laughed so hard that one could see all her teeth because she doesn't have more than four in her mouth.

At this they had the gardener brought from the prison, who had to don his former costume and come to us at the table, at which Monsieur Ludwig turned very pale. "Sir," said the gardener, "How is the ducats, the ducats and the Gulden, the Gulden? Is she good, has she got the weight? Shalom alekha, oy, oy, bad Christian, bad Christian, is bad people, oy, oy, shalom alekha!"

"I'll be damned," Ludwig replied with great laughter. "Brother, I've betrayed myself. That's a good one, the Jew having been sent out by you."

Then we reported the entire story to him, how it had truly gone, at which he crossed himself a good twenty times. So we had caught the clever bird, and he promised the noblewoman to return the specie ducats the next day and begged her as an intelligent woman to forgive the discourtesy shown her, which was meant for the Jew and not her. He also casually promised to speak to the gardener, as becomes a cavalier, and bestow a generous tip on him for his jail time. Whether he kept it, however, I don't know, for nobles occasionally promise golden eggs, and when the time comes there's scarcely rat droppings. He also added that in all his life he had never seen so good a Jew as the gardener, who was a natural for the role. And because the deception was so nicely revealed, he promised to arrange a stately banquet as soon as possible and thereby to drink up the thousand ducats.

We all drank merrily to that, and because two blind organ-grinders were staying in our village, they had to come in with their instruments and play their noise for us. The gardener could play a little on the xylophone or straw fiddle, as it's called in Saxony; he had to perform on it to spite the Devil. Finally we loaded pistols and fired them out the window at every toast until we loaded hunting rifles and muskets that we fired the whole evening so that the neighbors were greatly annoyed. In the end we knocked over the table and benches, threw our glasses out the window, and pursued every sort of mischief we could think of, and this sort of living pleased me so well that I wouldn't have taken a lot of money to miss this party.

During the continuing tumult I decided to leave the castle the next day and make my way to my fatherland. But Isidoro called me a scoundrel if I wouldn't stay another week because he greatly enjoyed my humor. Therefore, I promised to spend the time with him but after that begged him to find me an opportunity for having a less arduous trip home. He promised me a calash and because his mother liked my company, he wanted to see if something novel and good might occur during the week.

Chapter Ten. A New Poetics.

Who rearranges part by part
Is foolish when he should be smart.

We had gotten Monsieur Ludwig so drunk that he was out of his senses. He tumbled from one side to the other until we finally got him to bed and covered with warm blankets. Had we not lacked company, we truly would have gone on the whole night, especially since we were in any case drinking worse than sailors. Finally the old lady cajoled us into going to bed, where we tore apart the quilts and pillows so that feathers were flying around the room. From this one has to see what complete fools drunken people are to destroy their own things, even though they scratch their heads at it the following day.

The next day Monsieur Ludwig set off for his castle and on that same morning sent back the ducats, which he had lost through his own mouth, along with a letter saying he would arrange the banquet as soon as possible and we should stay prepared for it. I wasn't sorry at all I had stayed, for recently Isidoro had brought some elegant maps from the city, and because I'm a great lover of the same, I examined them one after the other and in viewing the cities simultaneously recalled some knavish pranks I had pulled off in them.

His remaining library consisted principally of books on history, and since my head was aching quite a bit, I sat down with a recently published book, at which I almost laughed myself sick. The title of the same made it readily clear it was a guide for how to write the most perfect poetry in twenty-four hours. Therefore, I laid the maps aside and began to read the following lines:

The General School of Poesy
Pars prima or Part One

Poesy used to be the oldest daughter of Fritz in Cobbler's Lane who supported herself *interdum* by knitting stockings. From this comes the saying *versum contexere*, to write a verse.
But after she married a velvet weaver she gave up her *officium* and poesy now is nothing other than a whetstone, using which one can provide polish to the remaining hours.
Its *objecta circa quod* are all the things one can think of; those one can't think of are *objecta oblivionis*.
Its *accidentia* are all sorts of contributions that one receives here and there in recompense, whether these be large or small. And although nowadays many a great boaster gives only a couple of Groschen for an important poem, the *versefix* should not imag-

30

ine that his poem is criticized by this, but only that it is insufficiently rewarded.

The *subjectum* of poesy is the paper it's written on.

The *objectum* is the poet himself.

And the *medium* is the verse, be it good or bad.

After this comes the *causa principalis* and thereafter *causa minus principalis seu subordinata* and finally *causa finalis* or the final cause why I finally write or wrote the verse.

Principalis causa or the main reason for the verse is reading and writing, for this is demanded *principaliter*.

Minus principalis, seu subordinata is the day or the light; otherwise one couldn't possibly write in the darkness.

And the *causa finalis* is amusement. *Quia autem uniius rei plures possunt esse fines & modi*, let it pass that the *objectum per quod*, which is the poet, may adduce a thousand reasons why he is writing verses. I recall here most fortunately how a student who had been put in irons by the constables for a nighttime brawl, composed this verse overnight:

> Oh, Germany, great land of many wolf-dug pits,
> Between the guardroom walls this foolish student sits.

This one had the guardroom as his *causam finalem*, another poet can have something else, however it suits and pleases him.

So give everyone the freedom to act *finaliter* and to write as he wishes.

After this come the *modi figurales* and *chorales*, almost as in music. For just as all music is divided into instrumental and choral, so too is poetry. But, one might ask, what is instrumental poetry? And *respondetur*: Instrumental poetry is a way and manner of praising a person or thing honestly, and this is called *figuralismus plausibilis*.

The other *modus* is *e diametro contrar* to this one, for it is used to disgracefully defame persons or a thing, and this is called *figuralismus spurius*.

These two *figuralismi* are concerned *circa argumenta topica* and are fashioned only *probabiliter*. *Exempli gratia*: I want to praise a man *per figuralismum plausibilem* as being an honest man, so I say (the *subjectum laudis* is a bailiff):

> You, best among all men who walk the earth this day,
> Receive from City Hall your job, your clothes, your pay!

And these *figuralismi* are particularly nice to apply, as is amply shown by the preceding lines, but especially so *per negationem suppositi*, as when, for example, I say of a secret guard or gumshoe:

> You are no rogue, no thief, and not a sucker
> Although all people say you're just a mother . . . etc.

Thus these two *figuralismi* are properly laid out, and this is actually called instrumental poetry. *Camerarius Justus* calls them *optimam poesiam teutonum*, for it is rather German and can be understood by almost everyone.

Now I want to report about *poesia chorali*, which is fourfold.

The first is priestarian, the second Barbarossan, the third is planar, and the fourth Stutz-Michli.

I now want to describe all four in somewhat more detail.

Priestarian choral poetry originally comes from a priest, whence, to speak *philologice*, it derives its name. The priest was named Priester Priestly of Prestwick, Preacher in Prague. Because many pr's are to be found here, the verses must fly like an arrow and *consequenter* be read and spoken very quickly. *Exempli gratia*:

> Fly, fly, like a dart!
> He won't win who doesn't start.

This has to be delivered quick as a wink, otherwise it has no character. Such verses are also called military by some poets because they almost sound like a recruiter's drumming, as a doctor observed when near midnight he heard drumming from the guard.

The second kind, namely, the Barbarossan, applies to those who have a red or otherwise misshapen beard and is called barbaric by some *autoribus*. Can be used for a woman's birthday or name day in the following manner:

> My girlfriend's beauty does abound —
> It's worth a pile of money —
> Because a beard does not surround
> Lighthearted lips of honey.

Here the reader must not think "lighthearted is a *calumnia*" or a *formula calumniali*; no, instead it means as much as light and hearty in talking, working, sewing, kneading, and paying compliments. To interpret such verses correctly, a competent and quick spirit is needed and is actually required and demanded for such.

The third variety of the listed verses is the planar, derived from the cabinet makers, carpenters, and turners who use all sorts of planes to smooth the rough and uneven boards and to free them of wild and lumpy knots. Thus, when a poet wants to write a

verse to a coarse son of Bacchus, he must above all else see to it
and take care that on risk of life and limb he sets his quill to no
other *genus carmini* as *exempli gratia*:

> I plane away however I desire,
> I plane away by night and day.
> To smooth you, though, I don't aspire;
> A fool for all your life you'll stay.

For my part, I regard this verse as the most necessary in the
whole world.

But now comes the fourth and final type, namely, the Stutz-
Michli. These Stutz-Michli verses are composed *ex tempore*. For
instance, if when some fellow is being whipped a person composes verses to the sustained beating, such are called by the *auc-
toribus poeti* Stutz-Michli or Knipper-Dollingsch. It would be de-
sirable that the poets, and especially the *tyrones*, would exercise
diligently in this *exercitio* and occasionally test a sample at night,
during which they then could perhaps recite the following:

> Thumpety, thumpety, thumpety, thum,
> That's how the drummer plays his drum

But as soon as one has composed verses of this sort, one must
quickly and quietly escape; otherwise the watch will come and
ruin one's whole creation so that it becomes a target of derision.
It is also advisable that the author of such verses doesn't sign such
verses with his own name but keeps himself anonymous as far as
possible.

Chapter Eleven. Isidoro's *loci communes*. Dangerous Fall of a Messenger; Nice Self-Deception.

> *Whoever freely drink does swill,*
> *Quite often falls, against his will.*

It annoyed me quite heartily when Monsieur Isidoro tore the book
from my hands and called me a pedant, for I had scarcely read the
beginning of this nice composition that satisfied me greatly. I understood that its author was mercilessly lampooning the poets and completely rejected the rules through which they wanted to constrain our
youth. I was laughing heartily and no matter how much I begged for the
book, he not only wouldn't give it to me, but locked it in a cupboard,
whereby I was cut off from any further enjoyment of it. Because he saw
I was very set on reading, he threw me a small treatise in which were

recorded all manner of *loci communes* he had written down at school, such as:

parvus monachus: A discalced monk.
dominus mentitur: The gentleman is mistaken.
natura paucis contenta: Bread and cheese.
malum per accidens: A slap.
homo multorum negotiorum: A paterfamilias.
verba neutra: Those people *quæ servitum ad significant*, who would like a position, *dativum adsciscunt*, must be prepared to grease a palm.
inservio musis: I'm a servile lackey.
quo magis premitur, eo magis resurgit: A fart in the bathtub.
vita implicita erroribus: He wanted to go to the wife but came to the maid.
solus & artifices, qui facit, usus erit: A poodle.
augere aliquem honorem: To push someone down the stairs.
adoptare aliquem in filium: To drink a pledge of brotherhood with someone.
exautorare aliquem: To remove someone's pants.
rei militaris peritum esse: To be able to curse roundly and steal.
ipse sibi perniciei fuit: He's soiled his pants.
se in mare dejicere: When someone falls into a puddle of excrement.
natantem excipere: To catch a lie by its butt.
præstat honesta mors turpi vitæ: A dead louse.
cives argo atque uribus augere: To proclaim new taxes.
pecuniam numeratam ab aliquo accipere: A student who receives his allowance at the fair.
necessitas non habet legem: An IOU.
cum primis ætatis suæ comparatum: there's no great difference between the beadle and the bailiff.
in bello versari: To kill fleas.
copiæ ordinatæ consistunt: The beggars are lined up at the funeral.
magna servitate exercitui præst: A beadle.
omnia in meliorem partem: Patched trousers.
copias alicui fugare: To chase the pigs out of someone's garden.
cavete vobis: A medicine salesman.
accedere ad ignem: A burnt leg of mutton.
omnem pudorem exuit: He took off his shirt.
turpe est doctori, cum culpa redarguit ipsum: A nasty sneak.
qui proficit in literis: A professor's flunky.
et deficit in moribus: A peasant.
mali me habeo: I have no money.
aliquid ad rem conferre: To help make someone a cuckold.
in hac domo quotidie lites nascuntur: A women's hospital.
artes ad summa cacumina ascendere: The city tower watchman.
homo perversæ mentis: Pants on backwards.

jura me consilio, si potes: Tell me, how do I get to the secret chamber?

hæc res est a tuo foro aliena: You don't know shit about it.

nulla salus bello: There's nothing to drink in wartime.

cepi ursam & sex catulos eius: I got the woman who owns the Black Bear Inn and her six children.

redde quod debes: Women's talk.

res mirabilis: A brush for one's beard.

res inaudita: A rich student.

ne sutor ultra crepidam: A boundary marker.

magnas turbas dare: To have frightfully many lice.

aliquem foras extrudere: An uninvited guest.

oculos alicui effodere: To shatter someone's glasses.

magnitudine rerum gestarum aliquem nobilitare: To crown someone a cuckold.

præli signum dare: To slap someone.

de aliquo detrahere: To take the bacon from the cabbage.

addere equo calicaria: To add twelve Taler to your petition.

multa huius viri sunt: This man has many brothers-in-law.

exitu notabili concludere vitam: To spend one's whole life writing notes.

rem bene scit expiscare: He can scale the herring.

omnes superare cursu: A racehorse.

præteribo hac vice: An unfashionable thief who goes to the gallows.

nullam tibi fidem habeo: A watch-dog.

quærere fugam: To watch one's health.

admirari aliquem: A stooped dancing master.

magnum onus alicui imponere: To send someone to the gallows.

ornare aliquem honore: To tell someone to trim the candle.

merces venum exponere: A whore.

rem impatienter tulit.: He was whipped.

in amplexum amicorum venire: To end up amid the asses.

vitam componere distractiorem: To mend torn pants.

vanitatem meditari: To enjoy tobacco.

posito, non tamen concesso: To put a guard before someone's door.

artem pictoriam exercere: To smear excrement on the wall.

nulla mihi sunt vires: I have no change.

commodum reipublicæ promovere: To make sausage.

posteriora levare: When one hacks off a dog's tail.

ludere in fidibus: To light up tobacco.

esse immobili animo: To stand guard.

spem metumque deposui: A flayed sow.

mihi nulla dies sine linea: I pull a dirty trick every day.

vitam exultando consumere: A minstrel.

iam mesta quiesce quærela: A dance floor.

semper in armis: A fly swatter.

video omniuim oculos in me esse conversos: When someone's in the nuthouse.

trabit quamlibet sua voluptas: If he hadn't shouted with joy, he wouldn't have been taken to the guardhouse.

extra modum: A xylophone.

barbatos decet: A pubic louse.

cæteros omnes facilitate superare: A tailor's apprentice.

Scarcely had I read to this point when the old lady came into the room and cried, "Run, run and help!" At first I thought a fire had broken out and Isidoro, who had slept a bit on the bench, sprang up and grabbed his sword from the wall because he believed the count had sent some secret spy to the castle who was trying to take him by surprise. "Oh, dearest son," said the old noblewoman, "it's neither of the two, there's neither fire nor a traitor. Rather, I was looking out my parlor window facing the castle hill and I saw a messenger plunging down the hill head over heels. Oh, run, run and do help! The man's probably broken his neck, for he hasn't moved a muscle."

"Zendorio," Isidoro then said to me, "run swiftly, we want to come to the poor devil's help. I know only too well the situation with that miserable road, on which many an honest fellow has broken his leg. All it takes is one misstep and you're lying at the bottom. Why didn't the fool go down the hill, keeping the mill to his right, where the road's been cleared?"

"Yes, to be sure," said the noblewoman, "but that's no help, what's happened has happened. Perhaps he didn't know the situation and perhaps may even be a foreigner. Oh, do run hurriedly! My hands and feet are trembling, he's surely dead! Oh, oh, the good creature!"

We then put on two cowled coats and hastened to where she said the messenger had fallen. From all appearances the man was still alive, for he gave various indications from which one could judge he hadn't died. Then we acquired a litter and had him carried into the castle by two workers, where the old noblewoman came to his assistance with precious waters. Quite soon he felt some relief and began to talk a bit, from which one could easily tell that he was drunk, for his clothes stank from tobacco and brandy like something rotten. We inquired as best we could as to who had sent him and to where, but we could get nothing precise at all. Finally we perceived he had broken his back, for he screamed so at every turn that we could draw no other conclusion.

"Herr Zendorio," the noblewoman said to me, "see what he needs, for I don't trust myself to touch him, the man's screaming so in pain." I tried and felt him here and there, and while I was investigating, a letter fell out of his pocket, the address of which was by a female hand. Isidoro became aware of it before I did and picked it up, and because his mother had paid little or no attention, he stuck it in his pocket. We then went into our earlier room because we wanted to let the messenger rest a bit.

The coat of arms on his livery made us think that he must have been dispatched by someone of the nobility, for on it three open helmets were to be seen that we could neither recognize nor interpret. Thus we came into our former room, where we shut the door, tore open the letter, and read the following:

> Beloved friends of our hearts!
> A delightful opportunity has appeared to please you as you desire. We would, however, prefer that you leave Monsieur Christoph at home and you two come alone because we cannot approve of his foolish pranks and lack of reason in love. This messenger has with him two costumes and masks with which you can disguise yourselves and appear this evening at our estate in Peltzingen, for after the departure of our mother, we don't dare remain in the castle because we have frightfully many keepers to fear. Indeed, there are not many to be trusted at the estate, but, indeed, in the end one must avail herself of an opportunity as best as one can. Brother Emilius returned to the university; otherwise I know of nothing to fear. Take care of yourselves and do come, because we desire both of you with yearning and hope. I remain
> Your well known sisters,
S. D. L.

Chapter Twelve. The Love Story of the Three Maidens at the Country Estate of Peltzingen.

At others' cards if you do glance,
A lash across your back will dance.

"Brother," said Isidoro to me, "we can carry this off perfectly." I shuddered and offered all sorts of reasons why that couldn't be, but Isidoro was too cunning about everything and came within a whisker of persuading me. I said that although we knew the designated place, Peltzingen, we still lacked the most important thing, to wit, we didn't know the names of the young ladies. For another, we also didn't know how the two gallants spoke. "Nonsense," said Isidoro, "that's the least of our concerns. The two noblemen to whom it is addressed live only an hour and a half from here; the one is called Ignatius and the other Ruprecht. They are neither brothers nor friends, but two such arch-gallants that it would be difficult to find their equals in the whole world. Christoph, however, whom they ask to be left behind, is truly an arch-lout who heeds neither honor nor respect, but everywhere pulls off his swinish pranks and, especially with women, filthy jokes, which they have proper cause to avoid and complain about. But I believe I'm going to teach you to put your sword in another scabbard, so, brother, go quickly into the room where the messenger is lying and see how you can carry out the knapsack. Then we'll set out for Peltzingen in disguise. Although we don't know the misses' names, we can learn them from the country people, and it's enough that we saw the initials in the letter. Ruprecht talks almost like you, brother, and I think you can just soften your speech a little. But Ignatius talks somewhat more forcefully, and I'll bet you a handful of walnuts people will find little difference between me and him. Yet it's still best that we go masked, for through this means we'll reach a place we've never been before."

Isidoro had won me completely with these words, and so I brought the messenger's knapsack from the room quite safely and unnoticed. In it we found two hunter's outfits and red velvet masks, of which, according to the letter, we were to make the best possible use. As soon as we were dressed, we ordered the gatekeeper to report nothing at all of our departure because we would certainly be back in the castle this night.

If we hadn't run through the village so fast, the peasant boys might well have pelted us with lumps of manure, but we came quite soon to the fields and leaped over them like young billy goats because in that way Peltzingen was a good quarter of an hour nearer. It was already four o'clock in the afternoon when we caught sight of the village in which these three ladies were supposed to be staying. The closer we now drew, the stronger we desired to rehearse for this drama, for which no little care was demanded.

When we were only a stone's throw away from the garden, which lay beside the courtyard, we sat down and discussed everything in great detail, the most important thing being that one of us not betray the other and thus reveal ourselves. We said we would extinguish all the candles with our hats as if for a joke, for our faces did not completely match those of the two noblemen. Also our hair did not agree, which causes a major blunder in such comedies, and had the clothes and the masks not worked so well, I scarcely think we would have undertaken so dangerous an affair.

"Damn it all!" said Isidoro. "Brother Zendorio, I'm almost sorry I came here, but, be that as it may, if they see through our deception, they still won't know who we are, and if they learn it soon afterwards, it still won't be of importance because thereby they would only reveal their own complicity." I agreed with everything he said. Meanwhile, a young woman passed carrying a large bundle of hay. We asked her to whom the estate belonged and whether she didn't know who was staying there now. The woman didn't know whether she should regard us as angels or devils. And she replied that the owner was none other than Captain of Cavalry Doppel, but she didn't know whether he or anyone else was now staying there. She had seen people opening the gate to-day, and after that two fellows in long riding coats had ridden in. With that she went on her way.

At this Isidoro and I had a thousand speculations, for he knew that Captain Doppel's sisters were the most beautiful maidens in the whole country. Thus he also by chance recalled that the oldest among them was named Susanna, which agreed, to be sure, with the initial in the letter. Thus we got up and I must admit that we weren't completely happy about the affair, no matter how brave we felt.

We climbed up along the hedge to the garden and moved quite stealthfully past some hay sheds until we reached the gate. As soon as we entered it a fellow cried down from the walkway, "Close it! Close it! Close it!" In a trice someone closed the gate behind us and from every corner of the courtyard armed fellows, who were as disguised as we, charged out and beat us quite frightfully and effectively with sticks and cudgels. "You good-for-nothings," they screamed, "we'll teach you to go courting!" Amid such a drubbing we looked for ways and means to retreat from the courtyard, but all the exits were blocked. Finally we cried for help and mercy for the crowd of our opponents had thrashed us so it was pitiable. Then they shoved us out of the gate and told us to go back where we came from.

The patient reader can imagine how we then looked at one another. One of us bewailed his arm, the other his head. "Well," said Isidoro, "the Devil knows what's behind this, but do you call that a courteous invitation? Wait a minute, I'm going to find out what's going on, even if it costs me my life."

"Brother Isidoro," I said, "it's not good to hang around here. The best thing about it is no one knows us. It's Ignatius and Ruprecht who'll be made fun of, even though we took the blows. It is not at all advisable to reveal ourselves here and bring unending abuse down on our heads. Let's hurry back home or else they might serve us a dessert harder to digest than the preceding dishes. We deserved what we got. It seemed to me they would lower the boom on us."

"The Devil take you!" said Isidoro. "Am I not the perfect good-for-nothing for letting myself get beat so. Wait, the messenger's going to tell me what this is all about or I'll kill the scoundrel in the castle, if he hasn't already died."

Book Two.

Chapter One. They Learn the Facts.
Sweet Revenge.

Vengeance comes to everyone
And sometimes him who's nothing done.

We deserved this elegant feast of blows all too well since we, driven by curiosity alone, not only opened the letter illegally, but, moreover, took the messenger's knapsack, put on the clothes, and in disguise presented ourselves as other people. Therefore, we had no one to blame for this other than ourselves, who were the total cause of our blows. Now we had to laugh, now, on the other hand, wail and moan because of the pain. Each one teased the other and each thought the other had received more blows, although the one had been beaten as thoroughly as the other.

It had just struck eight in the evening when we quite covertly entered the gateroom of our castle. The noblewoman and all the others knew nothing of the earlier masquerade, and thus we had good opportunity to put the clothes and the masks into the knapsack and to reseal the letter as best we could. It all went very well, and as well as we had spirited the things away, we returned them to their previous place without anyone's having known about the deception. The messenger finally came to and because, by his own admission, he had taken the great fall when inebriated, after sobering up he didn't have such great pain because usually one doesn't feel blows received while drunk as greatly as when sober. Indeed, we regretted not having had a good drink before we went to the estate in Peltzingen, where they gave our hides a rather good tanning.

He said his only injury was a sprained back and thus he wanted to continue his trip, but out of gratitude for the courtesy shown him, he had to tell us in confidence what not one person in ten knew. We joined him on the bench where he had slowly raised himself and believed it would be some story these people pick up in their journeys. But the messenger's was of a quite different nature, and we paid all the closer attention, the more the matter concerned us.

"Your Worships," he said, "I am a messenger and live in the village of Killingen, a scant quarter hour from the village of Gertzing. A captain of horse by the name of Doppel lives there and has three sisters of unsurpassed beauty and delicacy. Now not far from here three unmarried noblemen live together in a castle and have visited the young ladies two, three, or even more times a week. The captain is quite straitlaced and has always been afraid the three noblemen might bring him disgrace, for he's caught first this one with this sister and that one with that sister alone in her room. At first he acted as if he didn't notice anything, but finally they also approached his wife, and because the captain was the jealous type, he took this amiss.

"Not long thereafter he closed the castle to them and especially to the two who had known how to play behind his back. The third, however, is not especially fond of the ladies and regards all women very scornfully, no matter how politely they treat him. This moved the captain to tolerate him before the others and to accept him, but concerning the other two he didn't want to favor the one over the other; instead he forbade them at the same time to let themselves be seen in the castle.

"This offended the sisters greatly, who nonetheless wanted to continue their trysts to assert their freedom where it seemed most purposeful. They have an old mother; however, because they are stepchildren, they pay no attention to her and instead do whatever suits and pleases them. The captain noticed this and watched out for the noblemen, but they cunningly avoided his traps at least twenty times. You can imagine how unhappy the man became; therefore, he decided on something different. He broke into his sisters' room and thought he would find the gallants there, but they had made their getaway, although he had certain news that they had been present. Finally he wrote a letter, indeed, the one I have here in my bag, imitating the handwriting of his sister Susanna so well and probably that not one person in a thousand would think it was anything but a woman's hand.

"Quite unknown to his sisters, he went with eighteen soldiers to the estate in Peltzingen, where he will await them and, judging from appearances, beat them frightfully. In this knapsack are two outfits and two masks, and the captain himself asked me to make the affair imperative and to tell the two to leave the third at home because he didn't want to see the poor devil in such trouble.

"As unhappily as I seek to cause harm to my neighbor, I had to do this against my will and liking because otherwise he threatened to fire a bullet through my body. I'm sure and convinced they'll get a proper beating of a sort they aren't expecting. The soldiers are all disguised and already this evening were awaiting their arrival with great anticipation, but on account of my accident, they've had to contain their pleasure to this point. Now I ask Your Worships quite amiably to tell me what I owe for the undeserved attention because I must get started and bring the matter to a conclusion."

At that point we could have used a clever head to advise us what was to be done. Isidoro wanted to see that the two noblemen also got beaten and also incidentally play a special joke on the captain. Finally I whispered to him that I had thought up a plan that the two of us could carry off easily. To this end we let the messenger continue on to his destination with the letter, and the reader can easily guess what we were thinking during this story and after its conclusion. But not to leave anything undone about this affair, we disguised ourselves, took six peasant fellows with us and waited in masks in a cave where the messenger had to pass by with the two noblemen.

Before we left the castle, we wrote the captain a letter as follows:

Damned Scoundrel!
We smelled your masquerade long before you put it to work. The two you beat up were peasant louts whom we sent in our place, and the messenger will be able to tell you how through our cunning things went for him on the way. We will, indeed, no longer enter your property, but if you get a craving to visit us, we will build a fire under you that will make steam come out of your trousers. We write this as a warning.

After completing the letter we went with the assigned peasants to the previously mentioned cave and waited until the messenger came up the road with the two noblemen. We held our clubs at the ready, and when they came near to us, we immediately fell out and beat them worse than dried cod until, like us, they fell to the ground and begged for mercy.

At that time I recalled the poetics I had read and, specifically, the genus thumpety-thumpety-thumpety-thum because we had beaten them so frightfully. The messenger didn't know whom he was dealing with, for, to tell the truth, he had perhaps taken the most blows. We threatened to beat him even more fearsomely if he wouldn't swear to us on his honor to deliver our letter into the hands of the captain himself. He promised to do not only this but anything else if only we would spare him more blows because shortly before he had fallen down a hill. With that we gave them permission to run away. We dispersed over the fields, one going this way, the next that. I returned home to the castle with Isidoro, where we spent a goodly amount of time in laughing since this prank had not only begun well, but had also ended fortunately and as we wanted.

Chapter Two. How They Spent Their Time.
Part Two of the Poetics.

He who's able to sit by the stove
Is better off than him who must rove.

It is certainly no small pleasure to catch a cunning bird cunningly; therefore, the reader can readily imagine what joy we felt in our hearts that we had returned our blows and to just those for whom they were originally intended. We would have been twice as happy if we had only known what sort of suspicions the two noblemen had and also the captain after receiving the letter. For, to tell the truth, among all that had transpired in this castle with me and my honest brother Isidoro up till now, there had occurred no merry adventure like this one, at which I had to laugh a thousand times.

On this day Isidoro received a new outfit that was quite unusual in style. He had designed it himself by sketching a model that the tailor had to follow in preparing it. Nevertheless, at the next gathering of nobility he proposed to repeatedly allege it was the newest French fashion and then wager a thousand Taler that not four days would pass in the land before one would get to see a dozen similar ones on young noblemen. In such manner we prepared ourselves because we had received word that in the coming days the nobleman who had exchanged the Ducats would give his promised banquet, at which we were to be the principal guests.

Meanwhile we sought entertainment in hunting, and because a lackey who had formerly been a beater was staying at the castle, we had an opportunity to chase hares because a cold snap occurred and winter was approaching in force. Early in the morning, even before the sun came up, we were on horseback with our greyhounds and riding down one side of the vineyards and up the other. Occasionally a hare appeared near us, occasionally in the distance, but we soon caught up with them with the dogs, even if they were a hundred paces away from the horses. We rode through the peasants' and villagers' cabbages and turnips, and if they said something, even though we had already done enough damage we hit them across the back with our swords so that the dust flew.

When we had enjoyed this fun until noon and the hares had taken to the woods, we returned to the castle and passed the time after dinner with games or cards. Sometimes we also fired pistols at a target, and the noblewoman gladly saw that I was keeping her son company, because he otherwise was accustomed to traveling to the surrounding cities and often gambling away more money in one night than he could win back in a year.

Sometimes I again returned to the books because, having no better way of spending time by the warm stove, I spent it in reading, for, to tell the truth, from such effort I profited more than if I had gone to a seminar a dozen times and listened to their *pro* and *contra*. To my great pleasure I laid eyes on the key which fit the very chest in which two days ago Isidoro had locked the wondrous rules for poetry. Therefore, I opened it and immediately found the book that earlier had so delighted me. I began it again at where I had left off because I couldn't skip a single line at the risk of missing a great pleasure. The rules ran as follows:

After having discussed the four *figuralisimis* sufficiently, we now must of necessity turn to a higher *scientia* that consists of recognizing and measuring the feet in their striding and walking. But feet are of four kinds, among which two are called *directi* and two *indirecti*.

The *directi* are in turn of three types, and the first among them are called *curre cito,* i.e., feet that can run as fast as reindeer, stags, or even pigs' feet, for it is obvious and needs no great proof that swine can run quite fast once they are properly excited.

Because these verses, to speak *originaliter*, are called *curre cito*, they are in a word called currecitian verses and must be read and expressed much more quickly than the priestarian *choral* poetry described earlier, as, for instance:

> Riding and riding and riding to horse:
> The greatest fun in the world, of course.

To properly signal this type it would be necessary to place a rapid *tripla* sign at the start as the *musici* customarily do when they want to indicate a rapid *tempus*. Thus, my honest and well-intentioned advice is that no one should attempt this *genus* who has a slow tongue or quill.

The second of the *directi* types is named and usually called *tardian*, that is, slow and soft, and this type of verse is *e diametro* opposed to the preceding. At no price will I advise anyone to deliver such *genus carmen* quickly but, instead, quite slowly as if one's tongue had been hacked off as, for example:

> Slowly . . . slowly . . . slowly . . . lovely child!

The following verse must be read quickly, for it is currecitian:

> In vain you hasten so quickly and fast.

If one hasn't read these two verses properly and each according to its type and nature, it is necessary that one study them once more and then read them according to the rules.

The third type of these verses is *intelligentian* which are understood without expressing certain words, as *exempli gratia*:

> You think for Ares you can pass,
> Why don't you come and kiss my . . . .

44

There it's obvious that it has to read "ass." For it is the nature of these *intelligentian* verses that one has to understand them even against one's will. I want to give one more example, the better to enlighten the demanding disciple:

> To bowl with you I'd not go out,
> For you are but a stupid . . . .

From the just-cited figure, it is again obvious that this has to be "lout." And in such a manner the patient reader of such *intelligentian* verses will know how to proceed as he desires. I'll give one more example so that the eager disciple will be all the more enlightened.

> With you I do not care to kegle,
> You've got the brains of a salted . . . .

Once again from the figure given it's obvious that it has to be "bagel." And in this manner the patient devotee will know how to continue with such *intelligentian* verses according to his desires and following his own good judgment. However, so that I don't let the time pass idly by and for the sake of better *explication*, I must give one more example, *quia per exempla via brevis est*. Take care, it will turn out nice.

> About you, sir, there's nothing fine,
> You're nothing but a brutish . . . .

Intelligentially it's obvious that it has to be "swine." Some call this *reservationem mentalem poeticam*, and if one views it and under the light, then it is more acceptable than the argument of which some *scholastici* bragged that it is a special theological *stratagema* to be able to neatly trick someone *per reservationem mentalem*.

"What the devil," said Isidoro as he stepped into the room, "are you back at that book again?" Therewith he tore it out of my hands and said he would prefer to have me read any other book in the castle than this one because it was written by one of his cousins to the eternal disgrace of their entire friendship, and earlier in grammar school he had had to rightly suffer on account of this writing since the author had only sought to make fun of the pedants but here and there had delivered stabs that wounded them grievously. It would be better that such a book be kept hidden rather than fall into just anyone's hands, especially since the glorious arts and especially poetry were, in any case, already sufficiently reviled and held by some in ill repute. So it was unnecessary to create vexation and invite the Devil to appear. That's why he wanted to burn the book to ashes. And with that he threw it into the stove. But I've regretted a thousand times not having shoved it into my pocket and taken it away with me incognito.

But that wasn't possible this time, and although I had taken a poker to scrape it out of the fire, Isidoro restrained me long enough for the leaves to gradually catch fire and render the whole pamphlet unusable. To tell the truth, I hadn't lost all that much from this, for, having once seen the concept, it wouldn't be all that hard for me to write thousands of such rules and probably even more amusing ones. I wasn't greatly concerned about what another might think of my work or judge it, however, just as long as through it I could drive away depressing thoughts and reduce my boredom in a manner I personally regarded as the most pleasing.

Chapter Three. Ludwig's Banquet. What Happened to Zendorio During It.

Strong drink can stupefy, no doubt;
Where wine walks in, good sense walks out.

Through a lackey in a blue coat we received the same evening a long letter from Herr Ludwig, who was now determined to arrange the banquet that we had anticipated so outrageously since we intended to amuse ourselves heartily and to a greater degree than ever before. Isidoro provided me with neat and clean white linen, fixed a wig for me, had a bold steed saddled for me, had ammunition and equipment ready for me, and in such fashion we both appeared at the castle to savor the pleasure for which he had waited so long in great desire. Meanwhile at our castle we had staked everything on which of us would swill down the most wine with the expenses going only to Monsieur Ludwig, no matter how much one might win or lose at gambling.

I don't think it necessary to go on at length about that which the reader will be able to judge himself. I mean the absolute courtesy Monsieur Ludwig showed us upon our arrival. He called us his brothers in hell and true gallows-birds if we wouldn't be completely happy at his place and full of high spirits. The room in which he lodged us was hung with ninety-eight pictures of clown's heads and as soon as we entered it, Monsieur Ludwig said, "Brothers, there's a hundred of you here now!" With that he closed the door and left us alone. We had to laugh heartily at the antics of this nice fellow, and when the servant brought up our things, he reported to us how many women and other nobles who had been invited and summoned to this celebration had arrived by horse or in calashes.

As many musicians in the area as were to be found and engaged were brought in and they all began their fiddling at the same time, one in this corner, the next in that one. Indeed, there were even some at the attic windows, likewise playing to the best of their abilities. Monsieur Ludwig had rounded up some forty-two of them, some of whom he placed before the private and secret rooms to play the bergamask for the people relieving themselves in them. He dressed them as satyrs, and they looked so horribly ugly that a pregnant woman could easily have had an accident. Men alternated with women about the table, and it wouldn't have taken much for me to fall in love, if only I had known which one of them I should become entangled with, for the women were all but equal in beauty and manners. They also had the good sense to know how to distinguish between what was intended as teasing or serious. I can't sufficiently describe how congenial and merry the company was, and nothing was more welcome to us than that the old lady had been indisposed and could not be at the feast; therefore, Isidoro could pull out whatever stops he wanted to. The women present were as pleased as they desired, and I believe that at this assemblage easily thirty marriages were broached; how they came out, however, I can't tell you. Some men drank pledges of eternal brotherhood, but scarcely three weeks had passed, so we heard later, until they were dueling tooth and nail with one another. I myself acquired not a few noble drinking companions, but I was preoccupied with the ladies and scarcely heard or understood one word in twenty spoken to me.

This wished-for opportunity gave me cause to decide to enter this evening into a more familiar relationship with a lady, whoever she might be, and thus did I set my sights here and there. An opportunity of this sort doesn't present itself every day, so I deemed it a special precaution to make hay while the sun was shining because a missed opportunity is just as little apt to recur as is time past. Therefore, I thought it advisable to try my luck because through it many a miserable and poor scoundrel has elevated himself. And because I wasn't of the nobility, nor even a sacristan's son — as I had presented myself to Isidoro — but from a family at which the kind reader later will be quite surprised. Nonetheless, I did have personal qualities that many a braggart didn't possess. Indeed, at that time beyond all doubt with my pleasant manner I would have been able to fool many a woman and make her faithful to me, had I not been so amply supplied with wine by Monsieur Ludwig's people that finally I couldn't recognize a cat and probably would have taken a white dog to be a miller's helper.

In such manner I was rendered incompetent for further amusements and, as if in a dream, I heard how merrily they were leaping about in the ballroom next to my chamber. Because I also didn't know what I was doing, I got up and went in my nightshirt into the room, so frightening the women that they ran partly to their rooms, partly down the stairs. Isidoro finally straightened me out and I knew nothing of the affair until he reported to me the next morning that I had wanted to stab and hack everyone to death. He also mentioned that one could see through my shirt in front and back because in my impatience I had torn it to pieces. But the worst thing of all was that in the rear of it there had been a monstrously large yellow stain, at which they had almost laughed themselves sick. The ladies especially asked what kind of crude lout I was. From the words of my brother Isidoro I lost all heart like the man who had sat on a cliff in the middle of the ocean and plunged down with his lyre.

Monsieur Ludwig played even greater jokes on me, for he brought a shirt to my chamber and swore high and low the women had sent him there with it, who in astonishment had so pitied me yesterday and wanted to honor me with a poor breakfast. I don't believe there were as many feathers in my bed as the number of times I turned here and there in impatience, for I found Isidoro hadn't been lying because I saw my shirt torn into a thousand pieces. I also could still somewhat recall having gone into the ballroom, but of how and in what manner I was put into bed I hadn't the slightest knowledge. Soon an entire troop of women came to my chamber door and honored me with some priestarian verses, at which I in bed almost exploded from shame. Thus, I resolved to go surreptitiously to the stalls and ride away without telling anyone.

For this I had no little cause from the great insults and calumnies I had hurled at some cavaliers. For as soon as I came to the stalls, the stable hands who were standing around told me about this. Perhaps from politeness Isidoro had wanted to remain silent about it, but the matter was so offensive to me that I had no desire to remain another quarter of an hour at this castle. Therefore, I mounted my horse and rode away so fast that the dust flew. The quick pace robbed me of my hat, but I didn't look back even once despite cries to me from cavaliers and women; I was no longer listening and looking.

They sent two or three chamberlains after me, but they had all they could do to keep me from wiping my blade on their heads, I was so horribly beside myself. And in order that it not have the appearance I wanted to be a horse thief, I rode home to the castle, dismounted, gave the things to the gatekeeper, and also asked him to tell Herr Isidoro I had been here and wouldn't be seeing him again for some time. I would gladly have given a finger from my hand had I never been to that party, nor set an eye on it. But that was water over the dam, although no one was so greatly disgraced by it as myself. I was not well supplied and thus had to help myself as well as my purse allowed. In such manner I wandered from one parsonage to the next, knowing well that clerics are obliged to help those who come to them with requests.

Chapter Four. Zendorio Finds a Man Hanging from a Tree, Observes Trickery from a Hedge, and Goes to the Castle of Caspia.

Where words no longer will avail,
We've cunning tricks that never fail.

My roaming around the country had lasted a week when, with night approaching, I came to a large oak tree on which a man had hanged himself. In all my life my eyes had never seen so astonishing a sight. I stopped at some distance and viewed the man from bottom to top or, to reverse the common saying, from toes to head. I saw that he was still twitching one leg, and because my road went past the tree, I hastened toward it to come to the aid of the poor creature, since I could only infer from the twitching leg that he wasn't yet dead, but still had some life in him.

Accordingly I drew somewhat closer and when I came to the tree, a fellow in red livery looked out and said, "You there, stay away or I'll burn your hide with my shotgun!" With these words he ducked back into the hollow tree, and I leapt back in no slight consternation since I firmly believed the Evil One was hidden behind it and standing guard over this hanged man. But I had missed the target by a mile, for when I sat down behind a hedge at some distance and peeked through it at the tree, the servant was helping the hanged man down from the branch and the one like the other headed across the field to a village, where they perhaps had their horses waiting in order to ride home on them.

Truly, I didn't know what I was to think or conclude about this masquerade. I had seen that he was hanged and I had also seen that he had then walked across the field alive. I didn't know whether this was a ghost or some other thing. But because night was falling and I wanted to rest my tired limbs, I went to the nearest parsonage because I knew that from there it was no more than an hour to the village in which I was born. The continuing rain and the snow mixed with it had ruined my clothes not a little, and because I was entering my ninth day of wandering from one place to the next, it's easy to guess how I must have looked, especially since I hadn't cleaned my clothes, nor my hair, nor shoes, nor hose, and hadn't washed myself while living in rather desperate circumstances. But I can assure you that in all my life things had never gone so well for me as in the last castle, from where I began to compose and present this my story.

The pastor of this place put me up quite willingly and because earlier he had been acquainted with various professors at the university from which I came, he had a good opportunity to discuss this and that with me because through subsequent reflection the situation of my former circumstances was, as it were, returned to the spit and roasted once again. He gave me a clean bed and provided me with everything most amiably, but I can't tell you how shocked he was when I shared with him my story concerning the hanged man. He could explain it no better than I, so we let the matter drop, however it might have been. But he did tell me that a coach had driven through the village this evening and in it sat a young woman who was crying and wailing uncontrollably.

Concerning this news I had neither many nor great thoughts because I believed it perhaps would have been the companion of the hanged man. For he was very nicely dressed and near him on the ground lay an unusually elegant hat with ostrich plumes, from which I could recognize that it had to be of consequence. With these thoughts I fell asleep and on the following morning continued my road, after the pastor had given me an old coat. He had to hurry off to his sermon and thus on this occasion had no more time to talk with me.

Scarcely had a quarter of an hour passed when it again began to rain frightfully. I took shelter in a haystack now here, now there, and warmed myself as well as I was able to. For the road the pastor had given me a roasted squab, which I ate on until I came to a great house, on the gate to which were nailed many heads of bears, wolves, and other animals. I saw that it had to be a noble home and, because I saw an old women selling fruit beside it, I asked her who lived there. She said that the place had stood empty for more than two years, but now a noble young lady was staying there who had conducted a lawsuit over it and the estate had been declared her inheritance. She knew no more about her other than that she was a fine and pious young lady of good deeds, who gave alms generously and especially to the poor.

The words of the old fruit seller emboldened me to have a go with my pleading at this house, maybe I could come away with half a Taler. Therefore, I knocked and was admitted by a small boy, whom I took to be her page. He asked me what I wanted and if I were a beggar. I said I wasn't a beggar, to be sure, but also not much better than one; therefore, he should take my testimonial to the young lady and say that she should grant me alms because I greatly needed such for my journey. The youth then went upstairs and returned soon, relating that I should be patient for a bit, his mistress was writing a letter, following which I would soon be taken care of.

After a quarter of an hour she herself came out of her room and bade me come up. I was totally stained with dirt and filth, and the reader can well understand what a splendid appearance I must have had at that time. For this reason I hesitated to go up and present myself to her because she was extraordinarily beautiful, the likes of which I had hardly seen in all my days. "Monsieur," she said, "your person is worthy of appearing before me, for, as I see, you are a student. I wish I understood more Latin. Then I would certainly know how to converse more concerning your learning. Through learned people I have come to great good fortune; therefore, I am obliged to help them however I can and may."

Amid continuing conversation, I climbed the stairs, knowing well that she wouldn't eat me, no matter how poorly I was dressed. Then I received her quite politely, and she asked me to come into her room. She was quite alone and, after extinguishing the candle, used to seal her letter. she began by saying, "My dear friend, I've shown you to my room not with any evil intent, but solely to reveal to you a thought that has tormented my conscience not a little.

"You are a student and therefore more learned than the other, common people, whom I have about me daily and from whom I can receive less than no guidance as to what I should imagine or think about an unheard-of incident. Kindly seat yourself in the easy chair and, if you like, be my pleasant guest today, but first I beg you to high heaven not to keep the truth from me, but to give me your candid opinion of an affair I shall relate to you as it was and without great ado.

"Some fifteen miles from here lives a young man of nobility named Faustus, whose family is perhaps the oldest hereabout, and for another thing he is well brought-up and polite in manner and gesture. He spent his youth in Latin schools and subsequently traveled through various countries with noticeable gain, for he speaks their languages properly and consequently is held in good repute by many. Before I moved into this house we lived less than four miles away from one another when I was boarding with my cousin because at the time I was still involved in the lawsuit, which was resolved in my favor as hoped for, so that I now can own my property. But to return to the young noble, it's true that he sought my affection ceaselessly, gave me some presents, and let no occasion pass that he could use for attending me in all ways permissible. But despite all that, it wasn't in my nature to be able to love him or to demonstrate the slightest affection in return.

"He often shed the bitterest tears before me; indeed, he swore solemnly that if I wouldn't love him, he would stab or hang himself, the whole world couldn't save him or keep him from doing that. I was surprised at the senseless love of this elegant man and was secretly annoyed at myself for not being able to love him. My cousin called me a senseless clod a good thousand times, but I couldn't bring myself to say that I loved Faustus.

"Sir, consider how things went for me. Recently a nobleman in our land had a feast; he's called Monsieur Ludwig, is very well-to-do and a man of great humor. I was at the time in that region to settle accounts with the syndic and the lawyer who had pursued my matter so well at court, but they said Faustus had been to them some while ago and provided them such recompense that they were satisfied and pleased. It was a miracle that those people could be satisfied. But Ludwig learned that I had to travel past his castle. Because he also was distantly related to me, he invited me along with Faustus to the meal, where we were extraordinarily delighted by his cleverness.

51

"Now I'll admit to you in confidence that up to that hour I had never fallen in love with any person. But there was one man present, whom a nobleman named Isidoro had brought along. They called him Zendorio, and I fell so in love with this person that I didn't know what I was doing at table. I would have regarded myself as ecstatic if I could have spoken a single word to him. But while still at the table they got him so blind drunk that he was out of his senses and knew nothing of what he was doing.

"Faustus noted well that I was in love with him, for it is certain I couldn't take my eyes off him; although Faustus said he was not of the nobility, but a bourgeois, I must admit that in my eyes he seemed more than noble. Now, observe, sir, what sort of mind Faustus has, for when he saw I was fond of Zendorio, he decided to surreptitiously remove him from his path. But Zendorio may have gotten wind of this and thus mounted his horse and rode off the following morning, when the tumult was just getting started. I was so dismayed by this I told Faustus to his face I couldn't and wouldn't love him at all and, following his announced intentions, he should immediately hang, shoot, or stab himself a thousand times over.

"Monsieur, I would never have believed that my words would have so great an effect on the desperate creature who so utterly loved me. For as I was driving home yesterday and coming to my estate, not far from here I saw him hanging from a tree, from which I am still trembling. I cried with moaning and sighing, for my coachman found nailed to the tree a note in which was written that I was the sole cause of this damnable death. Indeed, even in the maw of hell he would cry out about me for having let him despair and die so pitiably and without mercy for his well-intentioned and proper love." With that she began to cry and begged me to tell her whether she was the cause of this death or not.

"Good miss," I replied to her, "I don't need to reply to your eloquently delivered discourse and treat it point by point, for I myself have not yet learned what love is and what its nature is, although I've read much about it in books. It's true that inclination is always free and doesn't readily let itself be compelled to something, no matter how virtuous that may seem to be. Thus one also finds love depicted as blind by the poets because they love nothing but such a thing that seems to them most useful. In this one gives everyone a free hand and one sees no emotion have a worse outcome than when it is undertaken in ignorance or through compulsion.

"You are as little the cause of Faustus's death as is my riding crop, for it does not follow that I should hang myself if I cannot enjoy that which attracts me. If that were logical, I'd find it hard to believe that a single person would still be alive; rather, they would all have had to hang themselves because no one realizes that to which his inclination has borne him. Thus the fool is himself guilty of his death, and the young lady can be charged with not a Heller of guilt in this. To be sure, the affect of love is one among the greatest emotions a person has to feel as long as he lives, and I know a thousand examples where such fools have caused their own death and in no way improved themselves, but cut themselves off from temporal and eternal salvation.

"My noble young lady is troubling her conscience quite in vain, but you will laugh when I reveal to you what's behind this hanging."

"What!" she said. "Do you know something about it?"

"Certainly," I replied, "Faustus is not dead. Yesterday I walked before the selfsame tree, saw the hat with the ostrich feathers lying on the ground and the man hanging from the tree. I went up to cut him down because he was still twitching one leg, but a lackey in a red coat peered out of the hollow tree and told me to stand back or he would plug my hide so that feathers would fly out of my pants.

"At this I moved on and sat down at some distance behind a hedge, from where I saw with my own eyes every detail of how Faustus, with the help of his servant, climbed down from the tree when it had become quite dark. If I were able, I'd bet a thousand Reichstaler that Faustus is not over twelve miles from here and he'll keep himself in hiding until he hears how you reacted. I don't know what else he could have been trying to do with his hangman's tricks other than to deplorably ruin his reputation before the world and besmirch his family. As for the man whom Isidoro brought along to Monsieur Ludwig's banquet and with whom my noble young lady so fell in love, I am that person, for I am called Zendorio and departed from the castle at that time with great discourtesy, for which I am still quite ashamed."

The noble young lady then stared at me and was ashamed that she had been so open with me in our earlier conversation, but she retracted nothing; rather, she said, "Yes, Monsieur, now I recognize you. You are the very same Zendorio, but tell me, why is your clothing in such a pitiable state? Do you walk around like that on purpose or what kind of accident drives you to such a life?"

"Fairest young lady," I said, "no accident other than a lack of wealth is responsible for my way of living. I was staying with Isidoro as a person whom a fateful adventure brought to his place." And therewith I told her almost the whole story that had happened with Isidoro and me. She was quite astonished and didn't know how to express her joy because in me she had total happiness. This also happened very timely for her because she lived here in such isolation, and thus she made a good thousand resolutions to herself to keep me with her, for I could tell from her expressions that she was head over heels in love with me.

Chapter Five. There He Has Great Happiness, and Thus Reason to Be Sad.

Kind favor many a grave has dug,
The rose's petals kill the bug.

𝔄t this house and with matters as they were, I became aware that love can even strike one who is sleeping if he is lucky. For regardless of my poorly constituted life and disadvantages, this beautiful young lady loved me so that I didn't know whether it was to be called a love of chance or of nature. She immediately ordered a bath to be prepared and when it was ready in the room opposite, I shut myself in and cleaned myself as quickly as time allowed. After this the young lady brought me clothing that had belonged to her cousin, the late owner of this noble estate, so that I could put something on my body and dine with her at noon. Moreover, she hung an elegant bathrobe along with a silk dressing gown on the wall, from which the reader can easily reach the conclusion that things went much better for me in this house than in Isidoro's castle. She even washed my hair and dried it with her own hands and after nothing more was left to do, she withdrew and told me to follow after soon.

Things were such with me at that time I almost didn't know what I should do or not. So good an opportunity was surely not to be thrown away since it doesn't occur every day and scarcely once in a hundred years for even the most fortunate. And to dare such without thinking was not at all advisable because one can easily get burned in a fire of this sort, and earlier at the noble estate in Peltzingen I had had to learn amply that an unanticipated evil tends to fall on the shoulders of one who doesn't hesitate to act without taking any precautions. Thus I had a thousand worries and found in truth that even at such a time man is afflicted by the greatest vagaries which tend to be his most blissful ones.

I dressed and found before me clothes such as I could not deserve through birth, nor earn through my knowledge. Nevertheless, I didn't want to offend this noble and beautiful lady in a situation where it was most urgent for me to cover my naked body. I was in the right place and had the opportunity to put my worries aside, but the preceding reason and one that the reader will soon learn restrained me from taking liberties and caused me to be not a little fearful. Man is so completely subject to vanity that even in his greatest bliss he cannot be satisfied; rather, through his imagination he always retains a fault that irks him. I came into the room where the table was spread and the dishes already served. She asked the young boy to pray, and to her chatelaine she said I had been her preceptor.

There was no lack of even the slightest courtesy she could show me as a noblewoman and our conversation concerned only considerations of how I might remain at her castle without restraint and she might serve me appropriately. It is certain — and only an ignoramus would deny it — that I was sitting in the lap of good fortune at that time, for the lady finally confessed that with her means she wanted to have me ennobled and afterwards take me as her husband. To this end she advanced me a hundred thousand Reichstaler.

After dinner we talked some more about the matter and she took me into her office, where I got to see all the precious and rare things she had inherited from her cousin. The Ducats lay in a special cupboard in a partition of which her rings and other jewels were locked. The remaining money lay in sealed bags that were deposited in iron chests. She also showed me a chest an ell in length that was filled with Reichstaler hammered together so that no one could pull one out with his hand. Apart from her possessions and other ready money, her stalls were full of livestock and the barns full of grain. She had three villages and eighteen to twenty peasants in each. Likewise she was entitled to hunt in two game preserves and to fish in four ponds, from which forty-four hundredweight of carp were sold yearly.

Such was the state of her wealth, and I would have sacrificed a finger from my hand if this estate and opportunity had befallen me in another country or even four hundred miles away; therefore, she found me indifferent to everything and she was puzzled that I was so sad. I sighed frequently and although she asked most urgently about the reason, I didn't want to admit it; instead, I pretended that the great cold I had endured earlier was sitting so poorly with me that I felt an illness was coming on. At this declaration she gave me costly medicine and cared for me in every way possible, from which I had to ascertain with astonishment that this dear child was treating me no differently than a blood brother. Nonetheless I was quite ill at ease about this matter and I could have cried at my fate.

I suffered such a state until the fourth day when she sat down beside me determinedly and brought me to the point where I promised to marry her. "Noble and fairest young lady," I assured her, "your great and rare qualities deserve a cavalier who is to be greatly preferred to my humble self. I'm not rich, not handsome, not clever, not thoughtful and thus know no means of entertaining your loveliness, which gives me good cause to sigh. However, because you are so attracted to me, I am content to please you to the best of my ability. I have to rejoice appropriately at such great good fortune that doesn't come running to everyone. But with a view to my lowly station, I here will swear a solemn oath that for my part I did not make efforts to marry you but felt myself greatly obliged to satisfy your own great desire and most humbly to embrace this great good fortune along with your person and to attend you throughout my entire life as an obedient servant."

Caspia, for such was her name, was greatly pleased at my response, and because in these times it was in any case the custom to conduct quiet and secret weddings without the knowledge and approval of friends and, indeed, even without the consent of the father and mother, she presented me a ring with ten crowns, and in three days she wanted to have some of her best friends summoned here and have the wedding performed.

Now I had risen to a level not attained by one in ten; I didn't know how to feel, for it occurred to me that I could fall again as quickly as I had risen. Had I known things would come so far with me, I would never have been so open, for I thought perhaps thereby I could depart with a good gratuity, but the lady was too greatly in love with me. That was my only misfortune, for luck had wished me all too well.

In the house all manner of preparations and the parson had been sent the text he was to interpret at the ceremony. At this time it happened that a head of livestock collapsed and died. Because it had to be removed quickly from the farm at such a time, someone fetched the knacker,[16] and to my misfortune I was at that very time in the cellar with Caspia, where I was to sample the wine. Just as we emerged the knacker was walking through the house, and when he saw me, he said, "Son, where'd you come from?" I couldn't deny that he was my actual father; therefore, the reader can imagine how shocked I was along with Caspia. I turned white as snow and she fiery red. But the knacker laughed and greeted me with a handshake. I thanked him and gestured to him, but the matter was already too out in the open.

Caspia didn't know whom she had before her, and from derision and shame I hastened away from there as fast as I could. My entire wealth consisted of the ring she had given me upon our engagement and I bartered it away in the next city and took my way toward the Austrian provinces. For a long stretch of the road she called after me to return, from which I could perceive that she loved me anyway, but I didn't look around once. And I believe the knacker must have regretted a thousand times having through his greeting caused himself and me to lose such remarkable good fortune. And this is just why I had been so sad previously, namely, because I feared I might reveal that my father was a knacker not far from this place, something I hadn't yet told Isidoro.

Chapter Six. Gets Away. Demonstrates a Remarkable Return of Love.

The lewd of heart mid scorn do plod,
The pure of soul find peace in God.

Here I must leave to the reader's own imagination what sort of situation developed at the noble house after my departure. Beyond doubt the news about me will have spread far and wide, and Monsieur

---

[16] The knacker was at the very bottom of the social and employment ladders.

Isidoro, Monsieur Ludwig, and some other noblemen will have been heartily ashamed that they had drunk a pledge of brotherhood with a knacker. Indeed, because of it the old noblewoman wouldn't give her son a thing; instead, she reproached him daily or even hourly for having joined company with such a disreputable devil who was hated and derided by almost the whole world. I do not want to speak of the great and painful regret that Caspia will have borne in her heart not only for having presented me to the chatelaine as her former preceptor, but subsequently even regarding and introducing me as her bridegroom.

Alas, what sorts of thoughts will the preacher have had concerning the wedding text? Certainly, the good Caspia will have cried herself almost to death and cursed me a thousand million times as her unlucky star that struck her so unexpectedly and wished me on the gallows. And if one looks at it more closely, she had no poor motivation for this since her first lover, Faustus, wanted to hang himself and the latter one, I, Zendorio, was born a knacker's child. And the worst thing of all in this affair was that in her conscience she was convinced she had engaged and bound herself to me of her own free will and could not blame the inequality of our stations since I had explained to her sufficiently that I was much too lowborn to be her husband.

Someone might say I should have told her of my birth before the engagement so that she might have guarded herself on this cardinal point. But, dear reader, I didn't want to be such a fool as to rob myself of so exquisite a morsel through selfbetrayal, and it was a question whether she wouldn't have taken this excuse much rather as a frivolous argument and unavailing way out, with which I could have made her doubtful about my steadfastness. Then I had truly made a mess of things and was completely resolved to never turn back in all my life, nor to appear in this corner of my fatherland because at the very least her friends would have me roughed up and put out of the way on account of this monstrous affront. And from this the reader should learn what a great presumption is dared by those who, without knowing all the circumstances, fall in love simply from one's appearance and subsequently in some corner in word and deed secretly frame their wedding contract that later bears results of which an entire country knows how to sing and talk. Indeed, I naturally believe people will have read and sung about this prank on all the public lanes to the weekly market days, no matter how much it angered those who were the greatest cause of their own disgrace.

I said before that I was wandering toward Austria to seek my fortune there as well as time and opportunity would allow. Thus, I did not stay long at any spot, for I imagined that Faustus in his exaggerated zeal would quickly pursue me and hack me to pieces on the spot where he met me. But I feared quite in vain because I arrived more than safely at wherever my pleasure had taken me. All the activities of the people were repugnant to me and I wished myself to be long dead and buried.

On the one hand, the love I bore for Caspia still tormented me; on the other, the revelation of my identity shamed me. Therefore, I walked around among the people like a shadow and in consolation wrote for myself all sorts of verses I could think of. If I so desired, the reader would see in several sheets nothing more than some songs I wrote down in my great sadness; for no matter how competent my mind was, the shame of my low and despised birth did not let me soar nor even be concerned with rising to heights, for fear that I might be cast down again with greater troubles than had happened with the engagement. Thus I passed my time as the student helper of a hired employee, whom I don't want to name. Otherwise his peers might believe to injure them I had written that a knacker's son was good enough to serve them.

At that time I again thought back to Veronia and sighed easily a thousand times that I hadn't let myself be killed in the prison rather than having to distress myself about my own birth, which I could do nothing about. From this I saw clearly that every human being has his specific origin, for which he must be tormented as long as he lives. I had neither stolen nor murdered, neither robbed nor set fire to houses, and I also was not otherwise burdened by any major vice, but it pained me beyond compare that through my birth all doors were closed to achieving both honor and happiness.

My master had a wife who was not all too proper. She sought all manner of opportunities to speak with me and made her intentions quite clear. Along with some special displays of favor she gave me money and clothing, but so that her husband noticed nothing of it. Moreover, I was such a closed-mouth person that I would have much sooner let my head be bashed in than reveal the slightest word. But when the affair started to go too far, I revealed myself to her in confidence quite properly and honestly so that she would no longer be deceived and I no further seduced. But the woman didn't ask all too much about whether I might be the son of a knacker or a hangman; instead, she loved me and not my birth, and valued not my origins, but my qualities in which I was sufficiently skilled. At that time I first became quite smart and I must confess that, as it were, I first began to live and recognize in what great ignorance and in what great error we human beings tend to wander around on earth, we who often don't know ourselves and how to avoid our own disgrace.

There were several who customarily visited this woman. and thus I decided to defraud her, to steal her necklaces and run away with them. Therefore, I insinuated myself with her as well as I could and required no effort, but needed only to turn the key and I had the two necklaces to grab that were worth some Marks. Therewith I left before day, and before my departure I broke all the windows in the house, tore up my bed linen, and would have set fire to the house if I had had fire. I was so furious at the whore, who, contrary to all honor and respectability, had attached herself to every lout and hadn't hesitated to keep company willingly with me as the child of a knacker.

The master was not of such great means and power that he could have had me pursued, so I didn't hurry all that much because through taking these necklaces I had not undertaken a theft but a small disciplining from which the bad, wild, lewd woman should learn how it might go for her in the future. She had three or four daughters, but none was any better than she. Finally they all became whores like their mother, and the only difference between them was that the one was an older whore, the other a younger one. The best thing was that I had concealed my name by calling myself Fidrian instead of Zendorio, whereby no one in the whole world could inquire after me if the scoundrels wanted to pin something important on me. But just as they didn't regard whoring as a sin, they didn't deem my deed an evil one, which, in truth, it couldn't be called because through this cunning I had only punished the whore a bit. I wish more such pranks were committed; then so many sluts wouldn't appear at the fairs.

Chapter Seven. Zendorio Becomes Quite Consternated at the Adventure that Isidoro Relates to Him.

> We always err in our delusion;
> He's lucky who avoids confusion.

I made no great fuss about the necklaces; rather, I exchanged them for silver to good advantage at the first opportunity that came to hand. After that I hastened down the banks of the Danube, intent on going to war and seeing if Lady Luck wanted to favor me just as though she had wanted to lift me above the same. To this end I proposed to walk around a bit in the field and to reach a final decision how I might best be helped in my future life. I sat down on the green grass in the shade of a tree when I saw a coach driving up, on which I thought I recognized the coachman. He was the same one who had served with Isidoro at the castle, and when I looked more closely, I saw Isidoro himself sitting in the coach.

At just this point a wheel broke so that they had to halt and, despite my having walked past the coach four times, Isidoro didn't want to recognize me either because my body had wasted away from the intense mourning and incessant melancholy or because I was wearing different clothing. Finally I cleared my throat and called out before me, "Isidoro." As soon as he heard his name called, he looked at me more closely and said, "What the devil! What are you doing here? You son of a bitch, what are you doing? Brother Zendorio, how do I come to see you? See how people run into one another so miraculously." With such words we greeted one another, and because they had to have a new wheel brought from the city, we walked in the meantime in the field and conversed about what had taken place in my absence because I now had been gone half a year.

Initially Isidoro was very surprised at my having run away so woefully from my good fortune, but when I said he would know quite well and, indeed, in full why I had been forced to flee against my will, he burst out laughing and said, "Brother, sit down here for a bit in the grass and I will tell you how you, Caspia, and the knacker were all deceived. Dearest Zendorio, you think you are a knacker's son, and yet your father is a nobleman in our country and of a wealth you can't imagine. After you fled the country, they looked for you everywhere, and some agents are still out to inquire after you by name, but from all appearances you must have changed or altered it because they weren't able to learn a thing about you.

"Your father is a member of the nobility and resides at the place where you think you were conceived by the knacker. He's called Monsieur Pilemann and for all his life he's believed in nothing but the prophesies of gypsies and other vagabonds. At your birth one such tramp prophesied to him that if he would place you in your youth among the peasants who would tell you your father was a knacker, you would be the most fortunate man in the country; indeed, they told him the lie that while still eighteen you would be a general over an entire army and other trash like that. Your father believed the bunglers even more than they asked; therefore, he put you among the peasants while you were still young and they made you believe it so that you have been depressed and tormented by it down to this very moment.

"They sent you off to school thinking this and didn't tell you anything different; thus it happened that from childhood on you have regarded this error as the absolute truth. They further lied to your father that he should not recognize you until you were a monarch; otherwise it could cost him his life. And because he gave no little credence to this foolishness, he cheated both himself and you. I'll skip all that about how you have had to support yourself miserably with the little money he consigned to you, but only through six hands.

"However, at the time six months ago when you made such a fortunate move with Caspia, a cow keeled over, as you well know. Thus your father disguised himself as a knacker and wanted to give you a shock but afterwards an all the greater joy since he had many credible witnesses with him to remove your doubts, but you couldn't wait for the ending. From the bottom of my heart I'm happy that I've run into you in this remote region, and rest assured that I would much rather die than leave you behind. Caspia has sighed a thousand times for you and I still know some songs she wrote in your absence."

Then I had cause and occasion to be truly astonished at Isidoro's narrative. I got up from the ground, looked at the sky, clasped my hands together, leaned my head to one side, sighed, and said, "Brother, is what you say possible and am I to believe your words?"

"I'm not deceiving you and wish you were at home. Then you'd have reason to be astonished."

If I had been pondering things before, now I was even more so. But Isidoro easily persuaded me to rid myself of such foolish thoughts because a person simply erodes his life through despair. He was on a short trip to collect debts. If I would remain at this spot for a week, I should prepare myself in the meantime to ride home with him and order a pair of horses. During such talk the wheel was fixed and Isidoro climbed into the coach after we had agreed we would meet after that time at a certain place and head home together.

Chapter Eight. Caspia is Buried.

For him who thinks repentance is fine,
His life has ended ere its time.

Meanwhile I had thought up all sorts of ways for making this irritating time pass, for it is certain that desiring often turns a moment into an hour. Therefore, I traveled now here, now there because through this means I found a special way of eluding my frequent whims. I built countless castles in the air and found it hard to believe that any great potentate had made so many decisions as I had then in expectation of my future fortune. Only then did I realize what it means to be happy, but, to tell the truth, I couldn't yet be called that because my complete satisfaction was still dependent on the future which tends to be uncertain for human beings. The beauty of Caspia was always in my thoughts, and I could think of nothing but her fairest figure. Thus did I spend all my time on thoughts of love and, from sourness at my still unsatisfactory circumstances, squandered many a pearl on matters I should have put to better use.

During the day I sat down at least twenty times with the maps. Now I was measuring with a pair of compasses, now with the needle, and I was even finding satisfaction in simply viewing the region where my Caspia was staying. It's true I was at that time a proper lovesick fool; therefore I shan't burden the reader with things that usually produce nothing but foolish vanity. Instead, I shall move on to relate the following event.

Some days had passed when Isidoro appeared at the place where we had agreed to meet. He told me maybe thirty funny stories that had occurred with him while he was abroad, and we passed a goodly amount of time with them on our return ride to the castle and Caspia's estate. I likewise depicted for him how amazingly fortune had played with me and how I had survived in the meantime, in which story he likewise found great pleasure.

One evening we turned our horses in at an inn that was only some miles away from Caspia's castle. There we sat down to eat and heard from a traveler that on the preceding day at the estate where Caspia lived a body was being carried from the castle to be laid to rest promptly and interred with great ceremony in the nearest city. From the traveler's remarks we could conclude that it was no person of low estate. Therefore, Isidoro asked him whether he knew or had heard the who the corpse had been or from where it had come. "Monsieur," the stranger replied, "it was a single lady of the nobility named Caspia, who, as people reported, died recently. And because I had to ride past yesterday, I halted until they were done, in consideration of the fact that a traveler moves around in the world for the purpose of noting and remembering all sorts of events, no matter where and how they may occur."

Never in all my life did a blow so pierce my heart as did that when the stranger brought forth such unexpected news that was strong enough to drive all senses from my body. Isidoro's face grew pale as a sheet, from which the stranger could readily infer that he was considerably concerned hearing of these events. Because dismay at an affair awakens a strong desire to learn the truth about it, we remounted our horses, wanting to hasten there and to see what it was with Caspia. We couldn't cast the slightest doubt on the credible words of this upright man, especially since his advanced age and respectability forbade it, and although we didn't like it at all, we found it more than true when we came to a place where someone not long before had preceded us with a team of six. The road went off to the right of our own; on account of this we turned our horses in order to follow the body and get to the bottom of this matter. At that time I began crying and through my tears was unable to see where I was riding, although Isidoro twice reported to me he had seen the corpse traveling ahead. In such a state we hastened ahead and Isidoro had no little compassion with my saddened person, who had to see himself tossed and turned back and forth like a feather in the air.

With effort we finally caught up with them near a high hill where they had halted so that the horses wouldn't be exhausted on the hill. They were taking additional horses from the adjacent farms and thus we had sufficient opportunity to speak with the person who had been charged to oversee things. This was a man of advanced years who was himself saddened by the premature death of this noble Caspia because he regretted nothing so much as the fact that through her the world had lost a considerable measure of bright and prudent wisdom.

From my great suffering I could shed no more tears or at least had so drained myself of them that in the present situation I could only sigh. At that Isidoro took me aside and said, "Brother Zendorio, you are a person of poor persistence if you can't adapt to the most horrible misfortune that may befall you. To awaken the dead women is not allowed to me nor to your sighs. Therefore, it is futile that we torment ourselves with a matter that can no longer be changed. A bit of patience overcomes long misery, and you will be able to console yourself when you reflect that she loved you alone and probably wished on her deathbed that all might go well with you and to your great satisfaction."

After such words from Isidoro we took leave of the overseer, and I no longer knew how to contain myself. No matter how hard Isidoro implored me, I could in no way do as he wished; instead, I decided to follow the body and then starve myself to death because mourning had so taken me over, I no longer hesitated to take my own life. In this way I decided to ride to my father so that I might at least feel some relief from my great grief, because otherwise I fully intended to plunge myself and my horse into a lake, whereby I would have fallen into much greater pain and torment. But Isidoro guarded me well until we arrived at my father's estate, where we were received elegantly.

This day was the first when I became acquainted with my father, and he begged me countless times and even with many tears to forgive him for having drawn down such foul misfortune through his superstition. Alongside me he wept at the sudden demise of the most noble Caspia and told me all kinds of causes that brought her to her death, among which not the least was the extraordinary melancholy that befell her because of my absence. All these stories wounded my heart anew. That's why I retired to a remote room in the castle, where I spent all my time in sighing and moaning. I had left only one sister of fifteen, who had been raised very virtuously. She tried to console me in her childish way and did not know how greatly the loss of something hurts of which one has lost possession as well as the hope therefore.

My father grieved with me and behaved more grievously because of me than I would have believed it possible for him to do. My mother was likewise concerned with freeing me from my frightful suffering, but her arguments were not sufficient to lift from my heart that which had fallen so deeply and lodged itself there. So I locked my room and wept quite alone, without consolation and hope, like the most abandoned creature under the sun.

Meanwhile, Isidoro had gone home again. My father had accompanied him and begged him to visit me as occasion permitted and to see if he could straighten me out because he was very concerned about me. He also firmly believed I was doing harm to myself and that he was the sole cause of all of this. After that they took leave of one another on the road, and upon his return my father consoled me as far as it was proper and possible for him. But the longer it lasted, the more melancholy I became and I learned the basic truth that there is no psyche on earth so happy that it can't be defeated by the circumstances of unrequited love and overcast by the thickest clouds of affliction.

Chapter Nine. Zendorio's Miserable State. He Becomes a Hermit, and What He Encounters in the Wilderness.

The world's with pain and trash replete;
Sit by the fire, you'll feel the heat.

That's the miserable way things were at that time for me, a completely abandoned creature. To be sure, I lacked neither food nor drink and I also had sufficient opportunity to drive out my immoderate melancholy by riding with the greyhounds to our preserve and there dispel my morose hours through hunting, but the incomparable passion of love had so captured me that it completely mastered and conquered any chance desires for pleasure. Finally my father didn't know what was to be done about me. He had called barbers and other doctors to cure my illness, but I accepted their advice no more than their medicines; rather, I decided to run off in secret, to go into a wilderness and there spend the remaining portion of my life.

This region of the country gave no little assistance to my intentions since roundabout there were far and wide enough rugged mountains and jagged cliffs, in and among which I could live well and alone as I intended. Apart from my love for the now dead Caspia, I regarded everything temporal as a mere shadow, indeed, as even less than nothing, and thus I felt no resistance within me that could have pulled me back from my intention, even though the matter itself and the nature of such a life gave sufficient cause to be frightened away. Nevertheless, I could carry it off all the more easily, the greater the satisfaction I was looking for through the desired change.

Four days after I made my resolution I took as much money as I thought such a plan might call for. With the castle tailor I had quietly had a hermit's coat made that was of a rather thick and durable monk's cloth. I put it on in my room, hung a large rosary from my belt, picked up a staff, and, wearing the clerical coat, I walked out of the castle deep at night.

The guard dogs barked at me quite a bit. But because their habitual barking was little heeded and partly, too, because most of the staff had just gone to sleep, I reached the road without being noticed. Earlier I had left a letter in my room, from which my parents could read what sort of life I had taken upon myself and how I was actually resolved to conclude my sad life. In such fashion did I leave the castle at night and entered a detestable wasteland, where perhaps more wild animals lived than humans. I deposited myself between two high boulders on the top of a mountain and made my dwelling out of moss that I tore from the trees. My covering or roof I prepared from large pieces of fallen bark mixed with all sorts of leaves I could find there. Thus was I sitting in a place where neither the sun nor the moon could shine on me, in great misery and boring solitude.

In the beginning it was very hard to live without human company; therefore, I went begging to various remote places and there collected all kinds of food until I became accustomed to digging roots from the ground with my hands. In all my life nothing has been more tedious for me than when I sat there at night so totally alone and abandoned by all human society in my aerie and surveyed my great misery. I heard no clock or bell by which I could measure the time and I can't imagine that any creature in the world has felt as great an annoyance as I did then. Below my mountain there was a large lake, and whenever during the day I perchance saw on it a few fishing boats sailing past or in the distance, this was the greatest joy I had to experience in this desert. Thus, don't judge unfairly that since I am presenting only such matters as are far removed from all amusement through the narration of my mourning, I shall present the kind reader little joy.

But the circumstances described here in great detail are given solely so that one can see what evil a man often subjects himself to when he will not let himself be guided or advised. I had sufficient cause to flee the vanity of this earth and am not to be damned on that account by any man, but when I consider the cause and the beginning of my isolation, I find no great or strong foundation upon which I could have built and sustained the severity of the life I had begun. For it was much more desperation than true resolve that had driven me to choose such a lifestyle that even wild beasts shy away from.

Whenever it rained, I lay down beneath the roof of tree bark so that I might nod off and sleep amid the pleasant murmur of raindrops. I enjoyed this pleasantry rather often and greatly because in these mountains almost every day there were great rainstorms, during which I occasionally read in a book that I had taken with me from the castle as a pastime. Truly, this manner of living would have been most pleasant for me if only I had been delighted enough to forget myself, for the memory of Caspia left me no peace of mind; rather, my thoughts were dispersed in a thousand directions so that finally I didn't know how to counsel myself.

Behold where the human psyche finally ends up when it becomes entangled in itself from well-laid snares. There is no hand skillful enough to untie the knots and Alexander's sword hasn't been honed sufficiently to sever these knots, for I deem no misery to be so great and boundless as that which causes us to become despondent because through it that strength with which a human being is able to console himself is defeated.

"Poor Zendorio," I said to myself, "you're like a wild animal wandering about in the wilderness in search of food and shelter. Misfortune plagued you among men, and lonesomeness torments you among the wild and dumb beasts. You are more deserted than they. You are fighting something through force that they are by nature accustomed to enduring. Be patient and endure your sorrow. Your suffering is not reduced just because you are sad that it can't be lessened. This wilderness keeps your body hidden, but it is not capable of keeping out those hostile thoughts that torment you incessantly. Oh, you, my thoughts! You are those essences that are devouring my flesh before its time, and I am going to be unhappy in you as long as you don't leave me, unfortunate wretch.

"From you and also from you, oh, vain earth, I have had nothing but unending vexation. Wherever I turn, I see nothing but my life as a workshop of affliction in which I must learn and study as long as my difficult days are not ended. Your bitterness, oh disdainful and fleeting Time, is all too familiar to me, and yet I haven't yet been able to reject you because I lack the true foundation of heartfelt devotion through which I might have been able to tear myself free of your bonds. This rude wilderness and this horrible place have a genuine pity for me, and the leaves that sway back and forth on the trees let me know full well how sad they would be about my condition if they were living and could tell me. Oh, how painful you are, how torturous, you tormenting thoughts! Your torture surpasses the horror of the hangman, and the sharpness of your fetters knows no equal. What am I now to do or undertake in the world when I know that the woman in whom I looked for complete satisfaction lies shut in her grave? Why am I to go on living if henceforth I must bury all my hours in that mourning that becomes more threatening to my life the longer it endures? Truly, this melancholy surpasses all the tortures that barbarians have inflicted upon their prisoners."

With such lamenting I wandered back and forth in the wilderness. My hut was damaged now by the wind, now by the rain; that is why I constantly had to make repairs and do work, whereby I was somewhat hindered in dwelling on my quirks. Finally, I saw to my avail a hollow tree in which I could keep myself as well as this place and its situation would permit. I carved a small window in the bark and for the other hole, the entrance, I wove together from osiers a door which I stuffed with tree moss and grass. In such manner I fashioned my new hermitage sparsely yet comfortably enough and desired nothing more than to abide in this miserable state till the end of my life.

One evening when a very heavy rain was falling I found myself in a deep valley beneath my tree home, gathering moss from the trees, with which I wanted to protect my dwelling from frost and cold. The rain grew heavier and heavier; therefore, I hastened up the mountain and closed myself in my cell as well as I could. The pleasant sound of it quite soon caused me to lie down, because I had enough room to do so, and through this means I nodded more and more until I finally began to sleep and had been dreaming for quite a while.

I was unexpectedly awakened from my deep sleep but didn't know at first by what. I rubbed my eyes, looked here and there, but quite soon heard some wolves howling, from which clamor I doubtless had been wakened. After I opened the small window and looked out, I saw not far from me six large wolves beside a stag they had already half devoured. The sight of these animals caused me no little consternation because I didn't know what to do or how to help myself. I fastened the door as well as I could, but from all appearances it was much too weak against so many and large wolves, and running out wasn't at all advisable because I thereby would have stuck myself into their hungry jaws. Because the tree was somewhat narrower above than below, I resolved to move to there, climbed up like a chimney sweep, and poked out a special hole at the top, through which I could continue to observe the wolves.

This retreat served me exceedingly well, for after eating the stag the wolves not only came to my tree, but also tore the door off and apart, when four more joined the original number and raised a frightful howling. With both hands and feet I held myself on high as well as the tree permitted, continued creeping higher, and trembled in fear like a leaf on a tree. After the rain a great wind came that rocked me back and forth in the tree so that I feared the wind might throw me and the tree to the ground, and thus I had a double demise to fear.

The wolves sniffed their noses at me, they leaped and scratched on the tree, and despite my screaming horribly and loudly, they in no way yielded, but continued with their abominable howling in such a way that I completely despaired of life. Up above I knocked out another hole and called for help. But who should have been able to hear me in this wilderness, where I still had seen not one person? Thus, my final decision was to remain in my lair as long as my strength allowed. I tore my hermit's cowl from my head and down among the wolves, which tore it from one another and into little pieces, from which I sensed how they would proceed with my body if it happened into their teeth.

Amid such thoughts I heard a hunting horn and I even believed it was the Evil One because there are examples of people having heard of such hunts by him often and on serious occasions. Thus, the kind reader can see in what sort of fear my heart stood, which gradually came to believe it was being attacked by two enemies. But the hunting horn kept coming closer, and to my great and unhoped-for comfort, I saw coming toward the tree a hunter who gave indications that his limbs were very tired from much wandering about.

He sat down on the ground and four of his helpers came up, to whom he said he had gotten completely lost in the woods. A short time later three more arrived on horseback dressed like the hunters. The wolves that were standing in and around my tree turned around; some stood still, some ran down below. From above I called out of my hole for help, which they immediately provided me by shooting two of them before my tree. The others took flight and at great peril I came down from my tree and offered thanks for their help.

It was soon night, so they built a fire beside the tree and spent the night with me sleeping on the ground. They took turns standing guard and were astonished by the events that I so unexpectedly had faced this evening in the forest. Because I had seen no person or sign thereof in this wasteland, I begged the one standing guard to tell me how they had happened so unexpectedly into this region.

Chapter Ten. Some Hunters are Sent into the Forest by Ludwig.

When fear, bad luck, and fright do strike,
Then someone comes to plug the dike.

"My dear hermit," the hunter said in answer, "it's not without cause that just one hunter in a thousand has been in this area, much less some other person. But our extensive wandering about was caused by a wedding which is supposed to be performed a week from now at a nobleman's castle. We serve a freeholder by the name of Ludwig, at whose castle there's been staying for half a year a beautiful lady named Caspia, who scarcely has an equal in this world. It's not been a year since she entered a secret understanding with a fellow. He was beyond doubt not completely in his right mind, for he regarded himself as the son of a knacker, which he was not, but according to common gossip was raised by his father from childhood on in this belief, whereby he had good and sufficient reason to regard himself as contemptible, although he was in fact descended from an old family of this country. His qualities are known only as commendable, as various members of the nobility have until now reported. From that it seems he must have been a gallant man because after his disappearance Caspia fell into great confusion, from which she was compelled to leave the estate and go to a desolate area where for twelve weeks she led the harsh life of a hermit.

"But it happened by chance that my master was riding around in this wasted area to divide and assign the forest sections when, to his great surprise, he became aware of her in a cave among the stones. He finally brought her out with him and persuaded her to live at his castle and resume her former life. She complied, although under great pressure. But when Monsieur Ludwig learned that her former beloved was nowhere to be found, he persuaded her to the point where she seemed to enter a promise of marriage with a nobleman, although in this there were irregularities that the bridegroom had arranged through money. By name he's called Faustus and is a youth who surpasses all in fame and good qualities. His estates are said to be worth two tons of silver, but despite all that, the young lady is crying day and night because she can't decide to drive the memory of the former man from her heart. All the castle staff pity her and it seems that nothing at all might come of the wedding, for recently a young nobleman by the name of Isidoro, my master's closest friend and brother, came to the castle. He brought word that he had not only encountered the former lover when abroad, but had also brought the latter home with him.

"Now it's astonishing what great confusion developed in this affair, for when Caspia left the castle in dejected spirits and great melancholy, went to the forest, and there started a harsh life, in total secrecy she put her cousin on the estate in her place, signing over to her everything she had earlier owned.

"Her cousin was an extraordinarily nice young lady and one could hardly tell the difference between them. For many a reason she also called herself Caspia but unexpectedly was attacked by a swift illness, because of which she was brought to the grave and recently buried. After her death Monsieur Ludwig, as her next of kin, inherited the estate, but when to his astonishment and contrary to any hope after the story he'd heard he encountered the true Caspia in a mean and harsh forest between jagged cliffs, he conceded the inheritance to her, although she had resolved not to hear another word about it.

"I told you a while ago about Isidoro's return to our castle and also about the happy news he sent to Caspia after his doubts were dispelled, but the young lady regarded it as a phantom consolation meant more to torment her than ease her suffering. At this my master rode with him in the flesh to the estate of the stranger they call Zendorio; however, they returned in great sadness since they could obtain no other information about him save that he had unexpectedly left the palace quite secretly one night and doubtless had gone to some place where he would never be found.

"This news almost broke the heart of the despondent yet still living Caspia, and for a long time she didn't know how she should accept it. In this situation, however, Faustus took advantage of his opportunity, and it seems possible that their engagement to marry might take place quite soon because we were sent out to find some rare and precious game. And that's actually the way and reason we were sent into this abominable wilderness so removed from all humans: otherwise we would not have had the chance to assist you pious and lonely creature and rescue you from a peril in which many an honest fellow has perished."

Chapter Eleven. Zendorio Comes to Ludwig's Castle.

When night is done, there comes the day,
And after storms the sun will play.

The hunter had concluded his words with unusual courtesy after in my heart I had crossed myself many thousands of times since he was reporting things worthy of even greater astonishment than my own. During his narration I sighed any number of times and didn't know how to hide my emotions so completely that the hunter surely noticed this at one point or another. For it is impossible for one truly in love to set his roguery aside completely, no matter how hard he tries to hide it beneath a hypocritical mask.

Thus he asked me why I had sighed again and again during his story and whether I perhaps knew something of this matter. I replied that I didn't know a thing about the event he described, but, instead was rejoicing in my heart that Monsieur Ludwig was still alive, who had been my closest friend among thousands, and I would wish I might still see him before my death if it were possible. The hunter promised to provide me earnest help to this end, then talked about this and that, but I lay down and slept a bit after the fright I had experienced.

They were already blowing their horns when I awoke and found the fire extinguished. The hunter from before asked me to come along as best I could, and with that I hurried with these people this way and that way through the forest with tired feet until after three days and quite exhausted we arrived at Monsieur Ludwig's castle.

They had slaughtered some animals, with which they hastened to the kitchen, because they were concerned about greeting Faustus with a good meal, who had arrived quite splendidly with his people. I was standing in the hunting room, where my escort had lodged me, and saw with great surprise how well he had prepared for his wedding day. His servants shone in the most beautiful livery, but as I was told, Caspia was crying uncontrollably, and Ludwig was busy trying to frustrate the affair as far as possible because he saw that she was not to be moved to return Faustus's love.

Ludwig finally questioned the hunters as to where they had patrolled and finally learned from them that they had brought along a hermit who had sighed about him and longed for him. He laughed and at the news from the hunters came to my room himself, where he addressed me and asked what I did and how I came to know him. I took Monsieur a bit aside and whispered to him, "Monsieur Ludwig, do you no longer know your brother Zendorio?" At this question he turned quickly toward me, ordered the hunters to leave, and said, "Oh, dearest brother under the sun, what wonderful stroke of luck enables me to embrace you here? I greet you, most treasured friend, and rejoice more at your presence than

70

at gold and silver. Dearest brother, what happened to you and how come you're wearing this stylish outfit? The Devil, just look at you! I would have taken you for a hoopoe rather than Zendorio. Do tell me in brief what happened to you, for I'm almost dying of curiosity to learn what your situation is."

With that he led me up eight stone steps where I sat down with him in a small room and told him in detail how and in what manner I had lived up till now and how miserably I had passed the time. Now he was jumping up, now he was sitting down again, so strongly did he react to my story. He clasped his hands, swung them now over his head, now over his stomach, now he hugged me with both arms and pulled a good one on me. "You poor rascal," he said, "you just made it for the wedding. Your beloved had almost scratched her eyes out so that in the end she would have looked like those people thrown on the shore from the ocean without noses, eyes, and ears, which according to the testimony of various authors is said to happen from the various wondrous creatures that dwell in the depths of the watery realm. Your circumstances are painful, but because after surviving the storm you're now standing under the warm sun, you no longer have to despair at such fate that has provided you instead the possibility of doubling your joy. My palace is to regard this day as the most joyful of all, and nothing within my modest means will be held back to honor you. Farewell, I'm going now to Caspia, who has shut herself up all alone in the top story."

After these words honest Ludwig left me and I lay down on a bench because I had not yet rested from the journey. After a quarter of an hour he came down again and I heard him leaping down the stairs. He was immediately at the door and bade me come with him because he had arranged a major prank. He acted almost like Marchetti, the imperial musician. When a German violinist wanted an audition in Vienna, he ran to him and said, "Fast, fast, fast, fast, nice and fast!" That's how it went for me, for I had scarcely risen from the bench when he took me by the arm and dragged me up to Caspia's room. He opened the door and led me in to her most respectfully and then bade farewell, leaving us quite alone together.

Caspia, who was still crying, began to speak with the following words, "Dearest doctor, you have a salve to still one's tears. Because my eyes have become quite raw from them, I beg you to let me have some." I couldn't keep from laughing inwardly that Ludwig couldn't refrain from his foolish didos in this serious matter; he had told Caspia I was a quack who was selling eye medicine. Thus I would have had to laugh, had not sudden joy and great compassion for this innocent child so moved me. "Caspia," I said, "Ludwig is a jokester who makes no distinction between a hermit and a quack. But why are you asking for salve for your eyes? You are affianced and have more reason to rejoice than to cry!"

"Oh, you are quite mistaken, dear hermit," said Caspia. "Ludwig does make jokes, and I'm sorry that he told me you were a doctor, but you have quite falsely concluded that I am engaged, when I don't desire to be so."

With that she started to cry again, but Ludwig opened the room and said, "Brother Zendorio, why are you running on so with her?" Thereupon he pulled the cowl from my head and said to Caspia, "Young lady, don't be frightened and take a good look at this fellow!" With these words he again departed. Caspia almost collapsed from joy when she began to observe me, for she recognized me all too well. I was so moved that I began to cry with her, even though Ludwig was making fun of us outside the door. I kissed her at least a thousand times, and in her overwhelming joy she wanted to display every expression of love and friendship until Ludwig parted us and said, "Now we must put all joking aside; the matter is serious for Faustus must be artfully rejected and the young lady must be yours, Brother Zendorio. The best thing is that you have not yet given your word; otherwise the affair might end up in blood. But let him do what he wants; if he's got any sense, he'll know that it was the wondrous circumstances of luck and not we who took his bride-to-be out of his hands."

Then he discussed the matter with us quite thoroughly and, to get things moving, he had Monsieur Isidoro summoned from the castle, who was almost fatally surprised when he viewed me in my blasphemous hermit's garb. They made short shrift of the business and instructed Caspia in how she was to tell Faustus that he was to swear to her in the presence of certain necessary witnesses that he would not marry her if Zendorio were to appear at the palace within twenty-four hours. However, she would swear to Faustus that she would marry him if Zendorio didn't come within the specified time. Faustus, who neither imagined nor believed anything so little as the presence of Zendorio, declared himself with a solemn oath as Caspia had desired and now presumed he had caught his fish.

Chapter Twelve. Faustus Departs. Zendorio Takes Caspia in Marriage.

Some men grab out in great disdain,
And empty hands are all they gain.

Faustus' oath took place in a great audience of nobles, who were quite surprised at Caspia's sudden decision, especially since she had wanted to have nothing to do with him, much less marry him. But Ludwig and Isidoro had summoned the tailor and had stately garb prepared for me. The morning went past and Faustus was already thinking of a quarter of his gain, despite his not having considered what the evening might bring. So evening approached, and already the fifteenth hour had been counted since the pact had been entered into. The gate was closed, and thus Faustus rejoiced even more that Zendorio would not enter. To this end he bribed the gatekeeper to turn away all strangers, and in such manner he hoped to take the fortress to which he so long had laid siege.

The evening meal was served and Faustus was placed at Caspia's side. She was much stouter of spirit than otherwise, at which Faustus cheerfully congratulated himself in his heart, hoping now to have attained a happy end. Ludwig and Isidoro, who always stuck together like two brothers, brought me with them and quite changed in dress and appearance. At first Faustus took me for a traveling nobleman, and because I was placed below him, he believed me to be anyone but Zendorio.

But when Caspia picked up the first glass, she raised it with the following toast: "Zendorio, your servant offers you this to the health of Faustus." I rose from my chair and Faustus did likewise, much more from consternation than respect. Isidoro and Ludwig then said to Faustus, "Monsieur, the pact is complete. We presume of a cavalier that he will not deny and take back his word, much less his oath. Here sits Zendorio, driven about by a thousand winds of misfortune. He is well worthy of possessing a lady whom Heaven wished to grant to no other, and we are sure that on account of this, Monsieur will display more joy than opposition since his innate courtesy gives promise and assurance of his so judging. Therefore, let us wish luck to him and at the same time to them, who were separated midst endless sighing but now, after surviving so many stormy winds, have safely sailed into their desired port of most delightful pleasure."

Instead of letting himself be subdued by the well-reasoned arguments of the two cavaliers, Faustus knocked over his chair and hastened with his lackey out of the room, mounted up, and rode out of the castle at night with all his people. Hereupon a great jubilation was heard, and the noble party paid not the slightest heed to Faustus's swift and rash departure. People celebrated the whole night, and Caspia could scarcely wait for the coming day when she was married to me with great pomp and circumstance. I shall silently pass over any description of this because such stories avail little or naught and simply arouse a futile longing in him who is not master of his desires.

Book Three.

Chapter One. Nice Happenings at the Wedding. Pilemann's Arrival at the Castle. A Page Goes Bowling. The Greased Climbing Rope.

The world is proud, bold, arrogant,
But at its core it's excrement.

Up till now I have described in lengthy and diffuse stories how down to the present I have encountered some unexpected adventures and consequently been subjected to some misfortunes. From here on my pen will attempt to describe the subsequent circumstances quite clearly. I said earlier this one thing about myself: In writing this history I have no desire to offend anyone; rather, I have attempted to be so gentle that even those who think it describes them will laugh instead of being aroused to any unjustified anger towards me.

This text has also not been undertaken so that one might caricature people, no matter what their station, and present them to the world as a model of all that is evil. No, instead to please them and for their own good one I have depicted the vices so that not the persons who are afflicted with them, but this bad conduct per se is castigated. And what sort of pleasure is it to see one's neighbor mocked when we ourselves don't like to be mocked? But the reader should know that I in no way have excluded myself from this evil when I freely admit that I am the most wicked among all. Or does someone perhaps believe that through this book I have offended him or someone else? Then it must have happened simply from a cause that is known only to him who finds himself offended. And ultimately among so many thousands, who will be able to be just to all? That is as impossible as writing something clean about the unclean because they are like those afflicted with dropsy who convert the best food and drink into water and bring about their decline from things that should be good for their health.

My strange events down to the present have sufficiently instructed the reader how man must wander about always and incessantly amidst great difficulties and what sort of horrible temptations he is subjected to if he doesn't know how to control himself astutely. He has seen how adversely things went for me even in my highest level of bliss, and I was wretched solely because I couldn't perceive my bliss. Now that's no longer necessary and nothing will be more important to me than the story of my subsequent life.

My wedding celebration finally reached its desired conclusion, and when the ball was over, Ludwig stood ready to escort me with two burning torches across the palace courtyard to the room where I was to sleep with Caspia. Accordingly, he went ahead as the marshal and some of the nobility followed after him, then the musicians, and we followed along together in such a merry procession that I could easily scribble six sheets full if I wanted to relate all the wonderful jokes we pulled during this parade. But instead of going to the room as I had thought, Ludwig led us into a great hall where people danced and pranced until it was finally day.

I had no special desire to dance; instead, I drank with Ludwig and Isidoro from a great bottle until I became so drunk that I lost seeing, hearing, and speech, just as I had earlier at his palace. They brought me to bed in such a condition that I didn't even know whether I was a man or a woman. Indeed, I can't even report how and in what manner I got out of my clothes, and on the next day Isidoro said with considerable laughter that during the disrobing I had brought forth and publicly displayed all that I had received from Nature for the continuation of my family.

It was rather dark when I awoke in the bed because I had immediately fallen asleep due to the wine I had poured down myself. Therefore, I turned on my side and caressed Caspia easily a thousand times. I drew her to me and because she was sound asleep, I gradually awakened her. But in such sleep she so held on to the bed with hands and feet that I couldn't move her from the spot, no matter how I tried. I was still under the influence of the wine, so I decided she had little or no desire to do with me as an intoxicated person. In view of that I decided to leave things be and rolled over to sleep it off completely.

When I awoke the second time, the sun was shining onto the bed and into the room. I sat up quickly and when I started to wish a good morning to my Caspia, whom I had embraced with sighs and kisses innumerable times in the night, I was heartily ashamed, for instead of her I found Monsieur Ludwig lying at my side, who had also spent the past night sleeping alongside me.

I immediately leaped out of bed. But as I was putting on my trousers, all the wedding guests rushed me. Along with Caspia they had spent the whole night in dancing and other games found at such events. I can't describe how derisively they laughed at me and teased me about my bedfellow. Ludwig himself produced the greatest laughter when he related in full detail how during the night I had taken him for a tree because I had continually tried to climb him. The women almost split at this remark, and because I saw I couldn't change anything, I contributed my two cents' worth. And in such fashion one after the other tweaked me, and I was greatly ashamed that I had made such a fool of myself with brother Ludwig. But in no way was I to be reproached for having run around while drunk like a senseless person and attempted monkey business enough, for which I was quite well ridiculed by Isidoro and the other guests.

As we were talking thus in the room, a lackey came running in to announce that Monsieur Pilemann, as my father, had arrived at the castle, and because of this they had to cease their making fun of me, which they otherwise scarcely would have done in less than an hour since they needled me during the whole next day. I must confess the truth that I had almost begun to question whether Caspia hadn't also unwittingly made a mistake and lain down with another to my great disadvantage. And although I let none of this show, I did think so all the more and now that it's past I see that at that time I was a right suspicious and complete fool who could attribute to his very best friends a thing that one can't think of without doing great harm to true friendship. And thus I inquired all around where Caspia had slept, and because people at weddings like to appear important or at least be a close friend of the groom, a maid slipped up to me and told me on her honor that Caspia had slept with Frau Ludwig but for less than an hour because the dancing had gone on without a break.

I was sitting on the throne and had to laugh that I could grant the maid so respectable an audience. But such ambassadors merit no better office, and I regret to this day that as recompense for her mission I didn't honor her by letting her wipe my ass, from which the kind reader will readily conclude that from thoughts of love I had forgotten all necessary things and put them to one side.

From joy my father wept gleaming tears and his principal greeting consisted of an apology he offered me for having gullibly believed those frivolous vagrants, the dishonorable gypsies, and letting me be brought up among the peasants in so devilish a delusion. He wanted to make up for this injustice a thousandfold through paternal love and in preference to my sister he wanted to bequeath me beforehand eighteen thousand Ducats. Also he intended to draw his entire will so that I would have no little reason to praise his paternal care after his death. And for my present wedding celebration he brought with him a thousand Ducats and two thousand specie-Ducats that he wanted to have ceded and transferred to me along with giving up an estate to me with all its belongings. Such were the gifts from my father, who was concerned with nothing save keeping me in good spirits.

Frau Ludwig meanwhile was concerned with thinking up a special diversion for the ladies, for on this day various others had arrived from the countryside who wanted to contribute their joy to this celebration. In the castle there was a cook who from boyhood on had traveled about among the Poles as a juggler; he had to spend half the morning performing for us in the dining room. "Brother," Monsieur Ludwig whispered to me, "take some lessons from this cook. They'll serve you splendidly tonight." I had a good laugh at that. And when Frau Ludwig asked what had produced such laughter, I told her of her husband's splendid proposal, but she said I had only made that up and was deceiving her, although it was well-known, and especially by Frau Ludwig, that her husband was an unusual wag who could not only amuse people, but also entertain them splendidly with all sorts of pleasant jokes.

Meanwhile Caspia had almost bumped into the clever juggler, and Ludwig immediately said to her that she would have an encounter with an even nicer acrobat tonight. And because he spoke rather loudly, she was so ashamed that she ran out to the hall and there watched the other young ladies bowling with sand-filled leather balls, for Monsieur Ludwig had offered a gold necklace as a prize. However, he regained it for himself through the following trick:

He had a page of singular countenance with a figure that was quite feminine who possessed a subtle ability for making men amorous toward him, especially those who were incapable of governing themselves through common sense. Thus, he himself dressed him quite alone in his room. He put on him the prettiest crape bonnet he could fine among his wife's clothes. After receiving all such feminine finery, the page had to appear amid the playful bowling party, where Ludwig presented him as one of his cousins. So he had a good opportunity to win the offered prize for himself because the disguised page was the best bowler in the entire castle anyone could find and bring in.

The women were astonished by the unusual dexterity of the new lady and admitted quite freely that they had never seen such skill among one of their kind. "Mamsells," the page said to them, "I've pursued this sport since my youth, for my mother tolerated no other amusement than this one at her palace, and, therefore, you shouldn't be surprised if I topple more pins than you." Then he bowled and scored a strike, and Ludwig mocked all the others for having been so nonplused by his cousin.

Meanwhile there were drinking and board games in the upper room. Some were playing backgammon, others were betting, a third group was playing checkers and a goal-tending game, and the time passed in such merriment that all regarded it as well spent, except for those who had gotten themselves in too deep at cards.

As a safeguard Ludwig had hired a rope-walker who before the evening meal was supposed to descend like a flaming bird from the highest tower of the palace to the courtyard, but because this acrobat feared the fireworks might go wrong as they had with poor Atavan at Regensburg, he begged Isidoro to allow him to dance down without the fire. This was finally granted on the condition that later he would be expected to relate the story of how Atavan had fallen and died in Regensburg. With that he ascended the tower, but the wanton Isidoro had had the rope smeared with human feces, from which the acrobat stank so in his descent that the women had to stuff their nostrils with the napkins, at which Isidoro and Ludwig almost laughed themselves sick.

After this merriment, a bell announced dinner. Monsieur Ludwig asked the women who had won his prize. They told him that this honor belonged to his cousin. At this he had an opportunity to laugh even more loudly since he had tricked them so obviously, which they only first noticed when Ludwig's cousin did not come to the table. The women inquired about her a thousand times, but Monsieur Ludwig excused her under the pretext that she had so exhausted herself from the bowling that she had had to take to her bed. The page had already changed his clothes and was standing at his master's side, they laughed as one about it, and Ludwig pulled outrageous jokes one after the other so that they were half out of their minds. During this the rope-walker came to the table, who was a capital fellow. However, because we had other diversions, he had to keep his story for the morrow.

Chapter Two. Quarreling among the Musicians.

The search for titles knows no remorse
And every ass would be a horse.

As well as the cook had juggled earlier, just as well did he arrange the meal now. The table was set with the rarest dishes that one could encounter anywhere at that time. And just as after love no greater delight can be found than music, to this end from some castles certain people had been ordered, who performed their task with unusual grace. The acrobat could play on the lute and accordingly did double duty, first for the eyes and then for the ears. After this I desired the minstrels change off, at which Caspia nudged me and announced that they must not be called minstrels, but municipal musicians or artists in consideration of their having received such a title from a respectable and wise city council. "But what's the difference" I said in reply, "whether I call them minstrels or city pipers? One title is as good as the next. People say that fellow plays a good violin. If that's all right, then it's all right if I say, 'He's a good musician.' If he plays well, he's a good player; if he fiddles, then he's a fiddler; if it's a violin, then it's a violinist. In sum, on this point I see no reason why minstrel should be a dishonest or disreputable word except that the silly fools don't want to accept it.

"It doesn't hurt the honor or reputation of a city judge if the chief among beggars is also called a judge, and no one is so foolish as to not be able to distinguish them by their stations. So when musicians are gathered together, it's clear which are musicians of a higher degree and, on the other hand, which are of a lower one. Those who serve in choirs in the cities, can read music, and understand other things about what belongs to this subject are the most respectable musicians, for in the words of the Scriptures it says, 'O come, let us sing unto the Lord' and thus one can even argue from Scriptures that they are musicians.

"Respectable musicians of this sort usually live in a city and have various names. In Austria they are called city watchmen as also here and there throughout Bavaria. In the imperial and coastal cities, one calls them the city *musici* and sometimes city pipers. In some, but very few places one calls the string performers Hemmauers. This title appeared in an imperial city where there was a period with a great number of festivals to be given. There was a great need of such people, thus some musicians were fetched from Hemmau twelve miles away. These subsequently settled there and their successors have retained the title Hemmauer down to this day. So this is the philological way and route on which one can arrive at the origin of the Hemmauers.

"In some places the city pipers are called Council *musici* because they are routinely assigned to appear at a certain time at the city hall or near it and sound off with their instruments. That they are called city watchmen in Austria is because on the whole they tend to live in the highest tower in the city and this was so common earlier that even today many cities follow the custom of having their *musici* or pipers play down from the tower."

At the table there was an Irishman who, when he overheard the conversation, said, "Monsieur, you are quite right. The title is of little or no importance at all: Whoever understands his business will be respected by people, no matter how he may be called. And whoever doesn't understand it will be disregarded, no matter how splendid and great a title he has. To pin this point down, there is generally among men a true vanity of wanting to flee the name by which one earns one's bread.

"I truly don't know whether it's better to say musician or city piper. For to get to the bottom of the matter, I can't inappropriately call the guards city pipers by reason of their having to play every quarter of an hour during the night. This happens publicly in the city, and from this follows this incontrovertible conclusion: Whoever pipes in the city is fittingly called a city piper. The guard pipes in the city, ergo, he is rightly to be called a city piper. One person may speak differently about the name, another about its provisions, then I will say that in this discourse it doesn't apply because here we are talking about nothing save the word 'musician' and not about the office and its terms, their application and arrangement. This varies from city to city. It's clear the world's not uniform. Many a pupil has a better native ability than does his teacher, thus many a musician is more artistic than many a city piper — I repeat, many a. Thus many a cantor also composes better than many a Kapellmeister, and from this the musicians will again see that the name doesn't make a matter good where artistry is lacking.

"They tell of the major *musicus* Adam Krüger[17] that once, dressed as a deck hand, he was playing on an organ. The musicians standing around noted well that these were no sailor's chords and, despite his

---

[17] Saxon musician, 1634–1666.

rough exterior appearance, showed him a respect such as no one would have rightly offered a seaman. Thus, whoever wants to be regarded as great must do great things, for there's nothing uglier on earth than wanting to be an artist and not being able to defend oneself against charges of amateurism.

"And what do people really want through their search for titles? I know quite many who on account of this have run around snarling and gnashing their teeth. But that's not to say that everyone is content with the title he received from his superiors; indeed, there are quite many who are not content and seek something more. But I truly don't know what one must call in Latin a person who has to gain his title through begging other than *elemosinarius superlitatis*.[18] That's poor Latin, to be sure, but the profession of such people is not much better. Thus, it won't go well for a poor cause when sound thinking is present.

"Indeed, if I were to learn that they wanted to argue with me on account of my words, I would grant that they were right about everything and greet their artful violinists a thousand times by their title. In Latin art is *ars*, so without great effort I could also call them *ars*-fiddlers[19] if these people are so fancy as to put on airs.

"But just as it is among the great, it's the same among the petty: *nemo sua sorte contentus*.[20] Indeed, I've known a beggar king who proclaimed he was no longer going to drag about in his station, but as soon as possible seek a higher responsibility." Here the Irishman called to the musicians, "All right, you gentleman musicians, make it merry! If you do it right, I'll present you a Ducat."

These words caught their attention no little bit, and thus they began to sing to the accompaniment of their instruments the following song:

> City pipers here, city pipers there,
> We're city pipers beyond compare.
> City pipers there, city pipers here,
> They call us each a brave cavalier.

The Irishman had to laugh at this jest, and I looked around at the fellows. Because Isidoro, who was sitting opposite us, saw well where it was headed, he spoke up and said, "You brothers, sing after me!" Thereupon he sang us the following words that we had to shout after him in the manner with which people tend to greet the new year. The song went so:

> Minstrels here, minstrels there,
> We are minstrels beyond compare.

---

[18] "Beggar from pride."

[19] A common pun on German *Arsch*, "backside, ass."

[20] "No one is content with his kind."

> Minstrels there, minstrels here,
> We're the ones to call cavalier.

To this the scraping fiddlers took exception and sang:

> Minstrels here, minstrels there,
> Minstrel's a word no one can bear,
> Minstrels there, minstrels here,
> We're city pipers year after year.

Following this Isidoro was somewhat offended and sang:

> Minstrels here, minstrels there,
> Why be stupid beyond compare?
> If you minstrels will not be,
> We'll fix you good as you shall see.

When our opponents wanted to start up again, we charged them with overturned benches and chased them out of the room along with their violins and shawms, for what reason did we have amid our joy to quarrel about one single teeny word, from which nothing would be added to or taken from their art? I was so angry at the fellows that in addition I threw a beer mug down from the window at the bass viol. And because some among us learned how to play, we fetched all sorts of instruments, and one person after another played a piece to the table, from which we felt better entertained than by the best music one might find between Novaja Zemlya and the Dead Sea. For roaring music is much more appropriate for merriment than a subtle tickling of the ears that doesn't let a person eat or drink. The latter torments more than it refreshes, for a person ought to hear, taste, and smell at the same time.

To our gain the rope-walker was still there, who delighted us amply with his antics. Then the party really picked up with many draining their glasses and many firing their pistols out the window. The minstrels sent up a lad who was to pick up their recompense. But we chased the lad out just as we had his employers and told him that if they didn't clear out in good time, the lackeys would light their way to the gate with stout clubs.

This gave us further opportunity to talk about the matter, and the Irishman said, "It's true, gentlemen, that local usage plays no little part in this. They're only ashamed of being called minstrels because the title's in bad odor and only those are called that who can be seen and heard in every beer hall or fiddle away at some rural wedding and depart from it with a chunk of bread. And that's why they rightly shy away from it although it's basically a good word per se, and whoever has read *Hercules* knows that it calls Pompeia, the wife of the provincial governor of Padua, that on page sixty-two, line thirty-five. But, as said, the cause is misunderstanding. To give an example: Earlier the word 'tyrant' used to be a splendid and beautiful title used only for great lords, but nowadays it's been turned around and is no slight insult for people who earlier had so boasted about just this title.

"The word 'officer' is used to discredit in the country west of the Enns,[21] and the hangman is usually called that. Who doesn't know and is ignorant of the fact that in Saxony this title is a high trust, for which quite many turn up at the courts with major donations and yet are probably turned away with a handful of Ducats. In some places a one-horse shay[22] is regarded with great suspicion, and in Bavaria one need only to say to a nobleman that a one-horse shay will come tomorrow and he won't stay sitting in his hole, but will soon look for the hole the carpenter left in the wall. On the other hand, in some places that thing is something good for which quite many strive with bribes. The word 'hussy' is a good and old word denoting a house maid who cooks or works in the house, yet if one calls a woman from Nürnberg a hussy, one soon sees catlike claws because she would rather let herself be knocked around than be called a hussy. So it's this way in one place and that way in another, and to please them we could easily have called them city pipers or even royal ones, if they hadn't tried to force the title from us.

"One knows how to treat people, no matter what their estate and profession, but pulling such foolish stunts at a private party on account of such a trifle deserves no better. Don't waste words; just take the fellows by their coat sleeves, throw them out the door, and let them go their way. That settles the matter."

Chapter Three. Conversation at the Table.

Don't call each man as is his due,
For you will hear his names for you.

Meanwhile the women also began to sing, and there was one among them, named Anna, who had learned something about music from a tutor or a Roman cleric. She produced a most excellent tremolo and was adept at coloraturas, from which we concluded that she must have learned to sing very well and that her teacher had been very diligent in his instruction. "Oh, no," Fräulein Anna replied, "you gentlemen are quite wrong, for although I did have a student as my teacher, I didn't learn half as much from him as from our nurse, who was extraordinarily handy with it.

"The one who taught me was an uncommonly nice person. He sang a high tenor and pretended he was a castrato. Thus I was filled with a naughty desire to learn singing from this person because, to tell the

---

[21] That is, Upper Austria, Beer's homeland.

[22] Ger. *Einspänner*, "one-horse shay," could mean "whore" in South Germany.

truth, for all my life I've greatly loved castrati. But instead of teaching me to read music as he should have, he pulled all sorts of teasing jokes, with which he spent and wasted most of the time. We often thought we would laugh ourselves sick at him, the fellow had such a nice sense of humor. Consequently I scarcely learned to sing four notes a week, and the songs he sang for me I would squeak after him until I knew them by heart like the parrot can the Lord's Prayer. Otherwise I might well have learned something from him, but, as said, he conducted his classes with foolish jokes only and at home probably laughed at us, too. Therefore, the little I can do I learned not from him, but from the nurse."

I was surprised at how the nurse happened onto such art, and when Fräulein Anna understood that I desired to find out about it, she begged me for a hearing since she was resolved to tell the whole story. "Monsieur," she said, "It was a nice situation that occurred here. In a city there lived a lady who desired and was willing to do something with music because she had an exceptionally beautiful voice. In the city hall of this place there was a clerk who was perhaps the best musician in the whole city. The lady desired to be taught by this man, but when the good person was with her the first time, he so fell in love with her that he couldn't hide it. The lady finally noted this and not without considerable revulsion . . . ."

"Madam," Isidoro interrupted her, "You're stretching the truth, it pleased her greatly!"

"Oh, truly no," Fräulein Anna replied. "Certainly, she was very angry and said he ought to fall in love with someone of his own kind."

"How precious an answer," Isidoro said to this. "I can already hear that from joy the lady didn't know how she should answer. Otherwise something else would have been appropriate at such an opening."

"Oh, I see," cried Fräulein Anna, "women are certainly so unrefined as to immediately start slapping everyone. In addition, she had to worry about whether the clerk wouldn't have given her a good one in return, for he was a rather clumsy oaf who could have given her a good thumping."

"Damn it," said Isidoro, "is he the kind of fellow who can thump well? In our village I have a couple of old women who are very bad off; if he could show up and give them a couple of good ones, he'd walk away with a good tip."

"For shame!" said Fräulein Anna. "Monsieur Isidoro is quite nasty. I'm through talking."

With that they all began to laugh and it was their decision that a man was a proper fellow after all even though he presumed to love someone of a higher station than himself. Those were slight objections, one person was like another, and coarse people also had coarse emotions and thus gave more pleasure than many a big braggart who imagines he can contribute God knows what to the matter. A lady was nonetheless a person of nobility even if occasionally *recreationis artia* she granted some poor bungler a kiss, which to her was as significant as if her garter broke.

"Indeed," said Monsieur Ludwig, "those are the right ones and I generally regard all noblewomen along with the daughters of the bourgeoisie as proper fools if they think differently. Let none of them imagine she will be honored and loved by a nobleman as much as when she obtains as husband or lover a man of low station. For on the basis of this situation she has reason and opportunity enough to rule over him, to wear the pants, and thus to make a continual slave of him when, on the other hand, she has experienced the complete opposite and often been chewed out, abused, and beaten by her men. My wife herself can bear witness how often I've given her a good thrashing, for things don't always go smoothly in a marriage. A tidbit away from home is no big deal, and I did it solely for the propagation of better love, for I learned from the saying that true love produces quarreling. If I were a woman, I'd fall in love with all my heart with such a low person, secretly run off with him, settle on a gentleman's estate, and spend the rest of my days in peace and joy."

"I'll be damned!" said a noble lady sitting opposite. "That's a fine resolution. If we had all acted like that and run away with scribes, stable hands, students, and boot boys, I would have like to see whom Monsieur Ludwig would have married." All those present laughed at these words, but Monsieur Ludwig escaped by saying he would just as soon marry a peasant woman as a lady of nobility because he had learned one thing before marriage and concluded otherwise about it once there.

"My dear Lady Pockau," — she was of that family — he said to her, "you may say what you want about it and be sarcastic, but it's true. In your youth you make so much of your shabby and lousy affectations and think your glances should be rewarded richly, and it makes no sense that you include students among the common fellows. Oh, dearest Lady Pockau, be assured that there are students who don't concern themselves in the least about higher women than you are. Students aren't fools, they know their situation. High station won't do it by itself; the gallows-birds won't do anything until one donates a few Reichstaler to them *pro labore & studio*, as with doctors after they've cured a sick person. And if what the Latin proverb says about students is true, in this matter generally and this particular case I regard them as the most satisfying in the whole world, for it runs *omne animal post coitum triste, excepto studioso*. If, my lady, you want to know what this means, have it translated by your attendant, who seems to me to be such an *animal* because he's so mightily picky about what I say." At this they all laughed at the student who on this occasion was attending Frau Pockau, but otherwise instructed her children. For joy the acrobat performed a capriole, and Lady Pockau herself was moved to laughter despite Monsieur Ludwig's having gotten at her so.

After this Fräulein Anna was asked by the Irishman and Isidoro to continue and complete her story and to pay no attention to whatever Monsieur Ludwig or someone else might interject. She knew quite well why they were assembled in this place and that they had to be not only merry, but even somewhat coarse, something good friends among themselves would not take wrong. At this Fräulein Anna began anew and spoke as follows:

"The clerk's manner was truly very amusing to observe, for the twerp so ogled the lady that it's impossible to describe it. Instead of music, he babbled something about love to her and listen to how he created an opportunity for such remarks. 'Madam,' he said, 'the tones are differentiated, some are happy, some sad, some in between. The happy ones are for satisfied people, the sad ones for those in love, and the ones in between for those who retain hope, and I belong among the number of the last group because I always live in hope.' Then he would sing to the lady songs that sounded totally sad. Thus the lady had an opportunity to tease him, for she believed he had to not simply hope, but to be in love. He said that was more than true and told her his feelings quite openly.

"At first the lady thought it was a joke, but the clerk laid his hand in her lap, whereby she was compelled to leave him and go to her room. Now at that time our nurse was still a virgin . . . ."

"You can't swear to that, Fräulein Anna," said Ludwig.

"Well," the Fräulein replied, "Whatever she might have been, at that time she still didn't have a husband, but was attending the lady as a chambermaid. The lady complained to her without constraint about everything the clerk had attempted with her from his desire and stupidity. The slut was clever enough to put on the lady's clothes the next day, adorn herself with her usual jewelry, and appeared thus before the clerk, who believed only that she was the lady. Then he began to sing with her and, upon departing, asked her quite politely for forgiveness, promising that he would teach her all the tricks in music. He did so and then the nurse learned splendid tremolos and mannerisms because the lady no longer dared to be in his company.

"When the 'lady' could almost sing, the clerk again brought up the earlier event. In anticipation, the nurse, however, had turned three needles beneath her apron into a convenient instrument against which the clerk's hand charged like a peasant with a bundle of wood against a stone wall. He so pricked his fingers that blood ran down . . . ."

"If she had such an instrument under it, many a person would have come away with pierced fingers."

"The longer you gentlemen tease me, the worse it gets." With that she grew silent and was laughed at even more than before.

"You're a lovely bunch," said Lady Pockau, "and one can hear how you do things."

"Lady Pockau," said Isidoro, "Not one bit different from the clerk," said Isidoro. At that they laughed even more atrociously and then talked about all sorts of things until they arose from the table.

Chapter Four. Atavan's Story.

Good Icarus was so inquiring
That in the sea he was expiring.

I, happy Zendorio, did not know then how I should spend my time in sufficient happiness. Therefore, I proposed all sorts of things, and after the dance was over we agreed, since the weather in any case was very unfriendly and cold, that the whole noble company should appear in the morning in Caspia's room, where with a glass of Veltin wine we wanted to pass the time by telling of all sorts of amusing events. They all agreed, but Ludwig excepted himself, saying that if he had to appear in accordance with their so-concluded resolutions, it ought to be open and permitted to him to include some nastiness, because in any case they had no clown at the castle. The women said however things were, he shouldn't in any case stay away. With that we broke up and went to our beds, each in his fashion.

In the morning we assembled as agreed in Caspia's room, and there she was twitted and teased as I had been yesterday because everyone wanted to know how she had slept on her first night with her husband. After this everyone was given a chair and because the acrobat still had his story left from yesterday, he had to start it so that others would be encouraged to be all the more prepared with their stories. Accordingly, he began and brought forth the following words:

"Most noble ladies and likewise strictest lords and squires! I've been asked by all of you to tell a story I saw with my own eyes, that is, the sad events of the fine doctor and hernia surgeon known as Atavan. This Atavan was a native of Orléans on the Loire and supported himself quite handsomely through his skill. His treatments were so successful that he would have much preferred to repair a hernia than to carve a capon. This reputation earned him high regard from great and small and he was duly honored everywhere.

"In addition to this splendid profession he produced a cure-all that he named Atavan after himself and did a brisk business in it from his booth at the market place because he proclaimed it especially effective against gas pains and other poisonous vapors. In such capacity he also came to Regensburg, where I was staying at the time because of my studies. I regarded it as a sin to miss or skip such acrobatic antics. Whenever I heard boxing or something else nice of which I was a great fan being advertised throughout the city, I left my reading and even my thesis, Suetonius and Horace, lying on the table. For at that time I posed as and felt myself to be a Marx brother,[23] which I was not, and committed thousands of pranks that I won't attempt to describe.

"It happened at this very time that this Atavan at his stand was having it announced through his clown that on the coming New Year's day he intended to descend from the cathedral chapter like a flaming phoenix. But because this place was too holy to approve of such clowning, he found a tower on the square called The Heath. He was advised against this twice, but nonetheless he made arrangements and attached the rope to the upper window of a rather high tower and stretched the other end to a beer hall or the public scales. I judged the horizontal distance to be approximately thirty ells, the vertical to the tower window some sixty span, from which a geometer can figure out how many fathoms the hypotenuse was and thus the whole rope.

"It was on a Sunday evening and the Feast of Epiphany fell on the following day, something I still recall from all the preachers' having railed against it in church. Night and the presence of many thousands of people made the drama more horrible than you can imagine. The weather was somewhat rainy, so the rope was quite wet, something rope-walkers all and I *in specie* regard as a great impediment in such circumstances because it's known that a thousand of them have broken their neck from it.

"I myself was standing among the throng, not far from the corner where the rope was secured and where some fellows dressed as devils were supposed to catch him and save him using bed sheets. Other servants bearing flambeaux walked along the rope and back and forth beneath it and all hoped for a better conclusion than what unfortunately resulted in the performance. We waited for a very long time and very angrily. Finally he screamed down, 'Allumez! Allumez!' I was told that meant 'Light 'em up!' Shortly after these words one saw many rockets rising from him. We were still hoping he would get down safely, but when he had gone perhaps twelve feet in the time it takes to say the Lord's Prayer, the rope began to sway violently. Beneath the large rope he had run a second down to the nearby Golden Cross Inn. A burning bundle of hay was supposed to glide down it and light the pinwheels he had put up around the fountain. But suddenly the poor creature fell down from the rope and remained lying dead as a dormouse where he had fallen. The act had gone so wrong, many people were concerned the rockets might fall on roofs and start fires.

"They had the pinwheels taken down from the fountain and investigated what had caused this horrible event. All the blame was assigned to a grain of sand or a snippet of paper that was in the fuse to the far side which had caused the one side to light earlier and the doctor had been forced to fall away because the weight of the powder was rather great.

---

[23] Ger. *Marx-bruder*, originally a member of a fencing club whose patron saint was St. Mark; by this time an itinerant fencing teacher-performer.

In addition, his arms had been spread apart by a large board that had held the rockets. In tumbling over he had been able to grab the rope with one hand, and if the other hand had been free, he could have come away in one piece. But the fire and the smoke distressed him greatly, and many people say he suffocated in the fumes from the powder.

"You can easily imagine with what horror the people left the square. Very soon thereafter etchings were made and verses written, which the vendors did only for their own profit because a goodly number of such broadsides was sold. Thus the author of such a picture and verses earned the devious thanks of the whole world, which I grant him readily."

"Monsieur Rope-walker," said Ludwig, "you regard your profession with suspicion, as it is in fact not at all reputable. Generally I like such performances but I don't have great respect for the performers themselves. However, don't think I find you odious, for from the story you've told us I can hear that you have studied, from which I have good cause to take you for a student rather than an illusionist."

In reply the juggler said Monsieur Ludwig might take him for whatever he wanted, it behooved him to be his obedient servant in all matters.

Chapter Five. The Juggler Tells His Own Life Story.

If teaching others is your fun,
Why don't you start with number one?

Isidoro had noticed during the acrobat's continuing talking that he was by nature a merry fellow. Thus at several points he begged him to tell his life story, and because the request from the ladies also played its part, he readily let himself be persuaded to do this, and Monsieur Ludwig promised that after he had done so, he would also reveal his own and leave out not the slightest detail about what had occurred with him. With that the rope-walker resumed telling the following:

"Earlier I told a story that was tragic enough about a man who has taken a dangerous step outside his profession, from which he had broken his neck. Now, however, I shall bring to light my amusing biography that scarcely one in a thousand will believe. My birth was not so base, for my father was a city piper in Burgundy, *ergo*, I am just as highborn as anyone. And because in Germany I had seen few towers as high as those where I was born, I had no slight justification for getting into a quarrel with the local nobles about precedence. I think it would have happened, had I not been inclined by nature to a humbleness with which I am especially devoted to the ladies.

"Three years after my birth my mother took me out onto the walk that led around the tower, and because at that hour my father was sounding the eventide call, she told me to listen, assuming I would learn to play the trumpet by ear like the parrot and the Lord's Prayer. I don't know how it happened, but the wind blew my father over in the walkway, for he was such a small and light man that during a time of storm winds my mother had to tie him to the window grill with a handkerchief; otherwise, the storm wind would have blown him out over the peak of the tower, and the foolish people then could have believed someone had carried him off. This time, however, the wind came suddenly and without our expecting it so that he accidentally broke a whole row of my teeth with his trumpet. For this reason I could not be used for the trumpet, for even as a young man I had all sorts of discomfort from my gums. And although my adult teeth grew in later, I was already too old to become a trumpeter; therefore, I decided to continue the studies I had already begun. I went to a school with a teacher who was still single but very fond of the daughter of a comb maker.

"At the time I was a young man of eighteen and only a few years younger than my schoolmaster. As far as his beard was concerned, he had as much as I and at his home he often behaved so foolishly with me that the housemaid scolded us and said, 'Herr Preceptor, don't be such a fool!' We had to swallow such remarks from the maid and I thought if my master can endure it, so can I. When we went too far, she would chase us out of the room with her broomstick, from which one can easily infer, what a pair of *nobile fratrum* we were and, for my part, how diligently I studied.

"The comb maker's daughter almost created the most work for me, for he wrote letters that I later had to make a fair copy of, and he said I should pay close attention to the style because a person could avail himself of it in other situations and matters. He had the habit of always visiting her at night because he was reluctant to go to such a bad place by day, and because he had a respectable job, the daughter believed it would cost him his neck. Butzlia, for such was her name, was already looking forward to the wedding although there had been no thought yet of an engagement. He gave her good hopes of this, and I believe if she had been able to sing, she would also have sung a song of hope as did the clerk whom we considered today. But the preceptor put off that decision from one time to the next and sought nothing other than to deceive her with the pretense of a love headed for marriage.

"The comb maker was an old and feeble man, as was his wife, and for their scant income they had only this only daughter, whom they didn't want to lock up solely so that she might soon get a husband. They knew that my preceptor walked by starlight and visited their daughter at their house almost every evening. But because I had never been with him in the house, they didn't know me at all, no matter how often during the day I had walked past and delivered wanton letters that were the *quinta essencia* of the preceptor's thoughts of love.

"One time it happened that he had to attend a school banquet and he ordered me to attend him there. I pretended I had such a stomach ache I could do nothing about it, at which excuse he only ordered me to remain home and keep myself warm. But I gave the matter a completely different turn: I went to the daughter, proffered her a friendly greeting from the preceptor, and told her without ado that he intended to come alone after eight this evening and in the dark, and she would know what to do.

"Butzlia thanked me quite politely, and, indeed, to tell the truth, the carrion was beautiful enough for a person such as my master, if only she hadn't let him read so long and so often in her book. Two hours later it was I who arrived. I had put on the preceptor's everyday clothes, because he had appeared at his festivities in his Sunday best. And because I was continually near and with him, I didn't need great skill to imitate his voice and gestures. Earlier in delivering the news I had changed my voice from that which I otherwise naturally employ so that my plan went off quite well that no one could have brought off who didn't possess resolve and bold courage.

"In such clothing I walked down the lane in the dark and was seen in the street by many pupils who removed their hats, without doubt because they took me to be their preceptor. Then the order of the day was: Respect, in the name of the Devil. Not long thereafter I came to the comb maker's house, where the daughter, who was standing in the door, quickly led me to a cow stall. Now I also knew where the preceptor explicated his readings and was heartily surprised that they had selected this place for their trysts. But perhaps that happened because the household situation would permit nothing else or because there the preceptor could view his future image in the cows and oxen standing around.

"'Sir,' she said to me when we were seated on the hay, 'I can't stay here long tonight. My father suspects nothing good and my mother is grumpy about everything. We have a room in which we keep all our horn, half of which was stolen from us last evening. Now he's going to keep watch with his apprentices tonight and tomorrow, and if anyone has a desire to climb into it, they'll give him a reception that'll make his back crack. So don't come to me tomorrow, or who knows what misfortune might strike and what the Devil might do.'

"Then I embraced her and kissed her cheeks a thousand times. 'Monsieur,' she said, 'You've never treated me so wildly!' From this I concluded that the pupil had surpassed his teacher. I would have gone even further, had not a cow torn away from her tether, and she was compelled to tie it back up and to call the maid. During this, I quietly headed for home after she in parting had asked me to stay away only tomorrow, but I might come the day after tomorrow, early or late, however it best suited me. With this message I hastened away no better off than I had come and regretted nothing so much as that I hadn't been able to converse with her in a different manner that my preceptor would have been worthy of, had time and opportunity permitted. But I could do nothing more, because that's the way it was. Therefore, I decided to deceive my preceptor so nicely that he'd wish me to go to hell.

"I waited until late in the night for him and meanwhile played a thousand mean jokes on the maid, which I was all too well accustomed to doing. Now I was pulling her by the skirt from her seat by the stove, and when she sat down to nod off, I pulled the stool out from under her ass so that now she was cursing me, now again moved to laughter, the way women in general can be made to be now furious, now laughing. I pulled her shirt up over her head, and although she threatened to tell her master about it, I didn't give a fig about it because the preceptor customarily behaved much worse than I. Thus each had little to reproach the other about, and from this one can easily perceive how pious our children become when one puts them in the charge of such people.

"Amid such games he knocked on the front door. The maid quickly ran down with the candle and it wouldn't have taken much for him to upchuck in her face, he had drunk so much at the school dinner. He staggered from one wall to the other and from them his coat got so snowy white that one would have sworn that he came from the mill and the asses. In all her life the maid had never used as much effort and strength as when she dragged him up the stairs. At every step she stopped and complained to herself mightily about the sustained and hard work to which she was subject in this household.

"'Oh, you besotted thing!' she said to him. 'See what you've done to your ruff! You're more insatiable than a sow that eats and drinks no more than it can but you can't be satisfied with half a bucket of wine. In addition, you so readily join parties and know only too well, as I've often had to hear, that they make fun of you too. They praise you to your face, but behind your back they laugh at you when they see how gullible you are. On top of that, you can't hold your liquor and tomorrow I'll have to wash out and clean your stinking pants. The devil only knows what your shirt will look like. Truly, the laundry women are frequently shocked by it, and those who've chanced to see it at a distance hanging on the line took it for a shooting star. Indeed, the tower guard who can see into the laundry woman's courtyard told me he once saw you walking home at night and fire from brandy was flaring out from your mouth and nostrils.'

"'Urschel,[24] Urschel,' said the preceptor, 'take me up, I'm tight as a tick.'

---

[24] A diminutive of Ursula.

"'I can see that,' Urschel said. 'The boys will learn something lovely from such a wino. You should be ashamed to your very ass for behaving so.' With that, she called to me and I acted as though I hadn't heard since I was standing in a corner a floor above and watching in delight how she tugged him one step up and then one back. Finally she left him lying in his own filth and ran up to fetch me and bring me down, but I lay down in her path. Then she and her candle tumbled over me and the light went out. After that I pulled her by the legs down the stairs where we both rolled over the preceptor, who was screaming alas and alack. The maid took me for a ghost and raised such screaming that the neighbors were awakened. In going back up, I gave the preceptor several good thumps on the head, which he hardly felt in his great stupor. Then I lit the light and asked the maid what she was up to, venturing to play such a horrible trick on my master in the night. But she called me a scoundrel and a thief, for she held me responsible for everything that had happened this time to her and the preceptor. 'You scum,' she said, 'you and your master, one no-good like the other. If my term were up, I wouldn't stay another moment in this house with such coarse and rude people. I've got so much to do that my hands are filthy and bruised and when I want to get some rest, the louts come up, one from the front, the other from behind, and tousle a body like a feather-duster. Oh, just consider that I'm going to find someone who'll knock all that out of you. Do you want to be fools? Then be so in the name of the Devil and spare me your idiotic pranks. The no-goods scarcely look at schoolwork and when they've learned a little from the text book, they straightaway want to be called university students. You are Bacchantes and nothing more. Let the Devil do his work, I'm going to tell the rector. He's not a man to waste a lot of time on such trash; instead, he'll teach you manners so that you'll remember me.'

"I believe the maid would have gone on abusing us for another half hour if I hadn't meanwhile gotten the preceptor to bed in his jacket, pants, and coat. As a joke I tore some holes in the quilt so that he was covered from head to foot with feathers. I trampled his wig and because we had some young hens beneath the stove, I threw it in their coop and wiped it around long enough so that it was nicely powdered. I tossed one shoe behind the bedstead and the other out the window and in the morning I said he had lost one on the road and come home with only one. I tore his ruff into a hundred pieces and pretended he had had an unbelievable fight with the maid on the stairs, for I well knew that when drunk he couldn't think and customarily had no memory of what was done to and with him in such a state.

"Urschel meanwhile was lying in bed, cursing and complaining, and I had to laugh heartily at her chiding, which she pursued quite alone in her room. For it's the usual way of women that they, like biting dogs, growl to themselves and then can't stop when no one's present any more with whom they can quarrel.

92

"The next day no one was more innocent than I. Indeed, the preceptor asked me for advice on what he should do or undertake because early that morning the maid had appeared before his bed and threatened to go the rector and tell him in full detail what sort of dirty tricks we had pulled in the house up to that time. But I just gave her a goblet of Rhenish brandy, and with that arranged peace which wouldn't have been necessary if the preceptor didn't let himself be bossed around so by the maid. But where there's no authority, there's also no fear, and the childish undertaking of a householder will give the servants no little opportunity to speak ill of the matter. Otherwise she would have deserved a good pounding on the hump of her back and to be shown the door the next day. Short of this, however, we had to resort to the brandy, which we had used frequently before. Urschel grew so accustomed to this that she quickly had to invent a reason whenever she felt a desire to drink brandy."

Chapter Six. The Rope-walker Becomes a Bath Attendant, Miraculously Escapes Danger.

Man's love is blind, it knows no class,
It thinks a diamond what's naught but glass.

"As clever as my preceptor thought himself to be otherwise, he did not notice this trick at all although I had clearly made a fool of him. But because he didn't want to believe me, I let the matter drop and for the present told him how the comb maker's daughter twice on the preceding evening had sent word requesting that he show up at her place without fail tomorrow, that is, today, between nine and ten o'clock at night. She would be waiting for him in the room where the horn was stored, where she had something special to discuss with him. On account of this happy news the preceptor leapt out of bed in joy, and even if his head had been twice as aching and throbbing, he wouldn't have noticed it at all. Instead, he was thinking up a thousand ways he might get into the room because he knew full well that the comb maker usually locked the house at all points.

"Because I had delivered the news to him so nicely and politely, he asked me for advice as to what might be the best way to get into the room. I wasted no time and suggested our fire ladder to him, by means of which he could climb up unnoticed and busy himself with Butzlia as he saw fit. He saw that my advice in this was trustworthy and thus he waited for the appointed time. Because I didn't need field glasses to see and feel already how this comedy would end, I arranged all my effects in the meantime so that I could get away in one leap. It went off as planned, for when the appointed hour arrived, the good preceptor took the long ladder beneath his coat, and because it was in any case pitch

93

black, he hoped to get into Butzlia's room all the more easily, which, however, didn't happen and went very badly. He went to the house quite carefully, and I followed behind with a lantern from a desire to watch the outcome. No sooner had he positioned his ladder at the room's window than he was attacked from all sides by armed hands like some prowler and carried off to the guardhouse.

"I, however, quickly packed my knapsack, wore it on my back beneath my coat, and marched ever quietly out of the city gate which was open. Approximately twelve miles away from this place there was a mineral spring and an inn whose owner was a cousin, with whom I stayed for the nonce as a tutor and instructed his two small daughters. And because all sorts of travelers from other places as well as from the aforementioned city met there, I learned quite soon from a citizen that thanks to the Devil, the preceptor had had to marry the comb maker's daughter and pay a twenty Taler fine at the city hall. But he had threatened to twist my neck like that of a goose as soon as he could lay hands on me."

Up to now the rope-walker had been unusually entertaining in relating his biography and, to tell the truth, he had demonstrated a pleasant manner in his narration, in which the ladies took great delight. What was most astonishing of all, an exceedingly beautiful and noble young lady by the name of Kunigunda had fallen in love with him. Her family was neither all that old nor well-known, but she was in good repute everywhere because of her beauty and great wealth. I believe that Isidoro had come to my wedding celebration for no other reason than to make points with her and through this means he could lure an elegant piece of game into his trap, but she had fallen into the rope-walker's net of her own free will. From this we can see how confusedly and contrarily love tends to play within the hearts of men.

But because the company still desired to hear more of his story and especially how he became an entertainer, he continued with approval. "Earlier I've told this noble assembly the first part of my schooling and how I came to my cousin's inn by the mineral spring, where I instructed the two children. I undertook such work more for fun than from need because from childhood on, I had been a great fan of the latest news, of which one heard quite a bit almost daily at that place. And when news from abroad was lacking, one could gather from the chatty maids and the laundry women every hour almost as much as one might need for half a year.

"This manner of living was the most pleasant for me, and I pursued it until at one point a countess arrived to avail herself of a cure there. Her servants said she was doing it on account of her infertility, but they thought she was fertile enough, if only her husband amounted to anything, who had ruined himself through habitual drinking so that they had given up all hope of having an heir. At that time I already played a bit on the harp, and she so loved that instrument that soon it was agreed with my cousin that she would take me along with her and appoint me as her chamberlain. Lord have mercy, how happy I was then! I was leaping in my room higher than the stove over there and preparing myself as well as I could for the upcoming journey.

"Four days later she traveled away from that place and had me sit with her in the coach, where she was so polite to me I could scarcely believe she was serious. After we had gone some hours we came to a very high hill on which there was a dense forest. The road was somewhat stony and difficult to travel; therefore, we alighted from the coach. She walked up the hill with me and ordered me to guide her because she was quite unused to climbing. She told the other lackeys to follow the coach and we were soon parted because they went around the hill while we went over it.

"When we had entered a short way into the forest, she said the following to me: 'Monsieur, there is nothing in the whole world and under the sun I esteem more highly than love, and be assured I didn't hire you on account of the harp, but because of the inclination I felt toward you at first sight. If you want me to go on living, assure me of your presence, and if you want me to love you, assure me of your love for me. From parental compulsion I had to marry a man because he was of considerable wealth and a count. From my birth I have been only a lady of the nobility and have wanted to consent to nothing so little as this detestable marriage if I had not been compelled to do so against my will. If you are resolved to do that which I've asked of you, then assure me of that I demand from you! '

"One can imagine how I must have looked at these words from the lady. I deemed my bliss beyond measure, for I can't sufficiently describe how sorely the beauty of this lady overcame me. I don't believe the Turkish emperor was as happy when he heard of the taking of the fortress at Neuhausel[25] as I was at that time when this beauty opened the way for me herself. Therefore, I said short and sweet, 'Most beautiful creature, whoever wouldn't love you would have to be either more or less than a human being. Such an affection is the greatest pleasure of all in our fleeting days, and by enjoying it one can see what is black or white. My silence will ensue as surely as my constancy since you likewise promised me that you will not indicate by word or gesture to your husband or anyone else that you are fond of me!' With that she embraced me with a kiss as we saw straight ahead of us the coach at the place we were to meet. Then she let the matter drop, and if I wanted to shame myself before the noble ladies, I would tell you in full detail what we did to one another in the coach until we arrived home at the castle, which was not quite twenty-five miles from the mineral spring."

"Ha," said Monsieur Ludwig, "those are pranks, Herr Rope-walker, women like very much to hear them, and the dirtier it gets, the more

---

[25] In Hungary, 1663.

they like to listen. Outwardly they act as composed as the Devil, but inwardly in their hearts they're saying more, more, more."

"Oh, sure," said Fräulein Anna, "in spite of what Monsieur Ludwig says, Herr Rope-walker, I ask you to refrain, but if you want to do Herr Ludwig a favor, then go ahead and tell it. He loves dirty stories more than anything else."

"Look at how virginal Fräulein Anna has become today," Monsieur Ludwig answered. "One certainly doesn't know how she manages to. As soon as she gets her hands on an amorous book, she goes to some private corner, and when it reaches the sexiest parts, she reads them over four or five times and doesn't ask if it's going to get even coarser or more natural. Indeed, she even accompanies it with thoughts that surpass those found in the book, and she won't deny it," he said to her face. "I know women who are surely even worse, and when they read things of that sort, they even wish they were illustrated with etchings or that they could be standing at the door and observing the affair through a peephole. And these are the people one would least suspect it of. But, Herr Rope-walker, do go on and don't hide anything that happened to you at the castle. Later I shall also be quite impartial and not leave out of my story the slightest thing that happened to me."

"It's true," said the rope-walker, "women are human beings and thus not devoid of desires. Indeed, they are fuller of them than many a man who through hard work has freed himself of all voluptuousness. The idle life to which they are subjected infects them with a thousand injurious thoughts, and I think this is the reason some Austrian nobles have their daughters work in the cow stalls and do all sorts of other work with the maids so that they'll have all the less opportunity to pursue their amorous thoughts that are by nature inclined to love-making. But because many don't have the gift of restraint or are locked up too much by their parents so that the cavaliers might not enter, it happens quite often that the stable hands come upon them and make the disgrace four times as great as it would have been. I could cite plenty of examples, but because I'm resolved to present my own tale and not those of others, I shall abstain and continue with my story.

"At the new castle I had new happiness, for the countess could scarcely allow a day to pass without letting me know through a thousand gestures how tied she was to me. I myself regarded her with more than enamored eyes, but there wasn't the slightest opportunity to speak with her alone; thus, you can easily imagine to how great a sorrow I was subjected at that time, from which I fell into no slight depression. But to hide such I knew how to feign certain illnesses that removed me from all suspicion.

"The count was a man of small stature. His trousers were no more than a foot long and thus you can easily judge what a great giant he was, for you had to keep a sharp eye out if you wanted to see him among other people. He had a brother who was an extraordinarily miserly person and, they say, from his great greed he would disguise himself and help the peasants carry manure from the stables in order to be able to earn a Groschen a day. This niggardliness was so abhorred by the other cavaliers that they finally had him locked up and given from all his estates only enough food, drink, and clothing to keep him from dying from hunger or exposure. From this you can see what sort my count was, who was not all too generous although he was not miserly.

"He didn't like to hear my harp at all simply because he had to feed me, for he thought that would be enough to satisfy an artist of my likes. I can't describe how the snot always hung down from his nose; therefore, down to this day I can't interpret it as unjust of the countess and regard its source as a criminal act if she could not be inclined to him through natural impulses. Incidentally, he was quite misshapen, and if people with large noses were king, he might well have won the greatest crown of all.

"He had no experience in any knightly games or other sports because his torso and limbs were completely unsuited and inept for all of them. He was also of such dim intelligence that he could scarcely read properly. His conversation was mostly about his clothes, what sort of material they were made of, and when they had been tailored, how long he had slept earlier, and how once from carelessness he had fallen down a long stone stairway.

"He filled his conversation with such annoying things, and if one spoke to him about unfamiliar matters, he would gape and ask whether there were people in Hispania and whether they also had heads. From this it is plain to see that the countess was wed to a blockhead rather than a man because she didn't have the slightest pleasure from this limp man. What was worst of all, he had allies in the castle, such as his mother and another woman, who kept watch day and night so that the countess wouldn't go astray and look for something that her worn-out husband didn't have. From this she was tormented much worse than had she been sitting in the meanest cell in the fortress at Wildenstein.

"The countess saw clearly that it was impossible to speak to me unless it were through some special plan undertaken in consideration of the continual spying of the old countess, who perhaps knew best how one can cut off the pass. Despite all that she arranged the matter in a totally different fashion, although I didn't know a word about it.

"One evening when I was walking quite alone up and down along the river that ran past the castle, a passing woman told me to follow her quickly because she had something urgent to tell me. I followed her, and when we came among the trees, she said surprisingly that she had been with the countess a week ago and the latter had ordered her to deliver the following news to me:

"First, she ran the bathhouse[26] in the village and formerly had made gold and silver lace in the castle, something that provided her work even to the present. Because of her discretion, the countess loved and valued her in the extreme in that she didn't hide from her the most privy matters. She knew well, and the countess had confided it to her, that the latter loved me with all her heart, and I should be as sure of her, the bathhouse keeper, as of myself that she would not reveal or spread the slightest word about this among the people.

"Not without suffering had the countess had to do without me for so long and thus was having the woman announce how I could get to her alone. Namely, while eating I was to break a glass that was especially valuable. From this the old countess would be moved to get me out of the castle and the young countess would also play a part in this so that I might get away all the sooner. After this I should go to her, the bath-house keeper, and present myself as a bathhouse attendant and seek employment. Once this had happened, the countess wanted to have me brought as a barber to her bathing room to cup her there, and in such a manner we could meet alone, something that was otherwise impossible to bring about.

"You, my patrons, can imagine that this message was much more pleasant for me than a bag of gold, considering that the merits of love far surpass the value of any metals. Therefore, I discussed the matter further with the woman and found her so correct on all points that she readily could be called the model of the most perfect procuress. Because it wasn't advisable to talk a lot in this public place, she left me, and I promised to be at her house by tomorrow at the latest.

"After this I went to my room to nurse my recurring melancholy was rightly astonished at the plan; it was indeed an extreme way to get to the countess. That's why I resolved to break the most beautiful glass in the treasure and run from the castle after the deed.

"The following morning I was called to appear with my harp and I performed so clumsily on it that I knocked down not one, but at least a dozen glasses from the rack. The old countess began to curse and scold at the table, and if the count had known how one should conduct one-self in such situations, beyond all doubt he would have smashed a plate over my head. The young countess also railed at me, and before I knew it, the old woman had already sent a servant to me who terminated my service and moreover threatened me with prison. But in view of the fact that I was a young servant, they left it with my having to vacate my post and the castle as soon as I could. At that, I left, put my knapsack on my back, and when it was nearly night, I turned back on the road, and came to the bathhouse keeper as I had promised her earlier.

---

[26] Such people also performed some of the duties of the barber such as bleed-ing and cupping.

98

"Now I mustn't waste any more time with my story and tell you quickly that on the following day the countess sent a chambermaid to the woman with the announcement that she would like to have herself bled. Therefore, she should send a servant up to the castle who should definitely arrive between four and five, for she wanted to go for a ride afterwards. I was already completely disguised, so instead of my natural hair one saw a nasty red wig I had put on, and because in any case I had scarcely been at the castle five days, I needed no additional skill to hide myself better from the castle staff. Following this I collected the appropriate equipment, pulled my coat about me, and put under my arm the chest with which I wandered toward the castle in long strides and there was led by an old woman into the bathing room, a comfortable facility I had not known of previously.

"After approximately a quarter of an hour she herself arrived and after her came a rather old maid, who was carrying her bath clothes. Immediately adjacent there was a small room in which she dressed and then came into me, where everything was all prepared. She bolted the door firmly, and I was truly astonished at the tenderness of her body, the likes of which I had never seen in all my life. I embraced her with great desire and she kissed me in every way possible. We were about to sit down together when another maid knocked at the bathing room and announced that the old countess was also coming and wanted to have herself bled now.

"You can easily think how this news frightened us since through it all our plans had been completely destroyed. The countess said, 'That's the old carrion who doesn't even trust me to take a single step alone. Alas, if only I were free enough to have hope of running away. No matter how high the castle walls were, I would leap over them and choose to lead my life in a frightful wilderness rather than among these people who were born only to torment me.'

"Scarcely had she spoken these words when the old countess came into the aforementioned small room, got undressed, and was completely astonished that I was shut in quite alone with her daughter-in-law. She asked me my name and where I was from, but I was clever enough to make a fool of the old witch even if she were cleverer than the Devil. With a foreign accent I pretended I had come from Stralsund and on the way had been stripped down to my shirt and robbed by two cutpurses. I also told her how two years ago I had been captured by the Turks and in their prison received a head wound from a Turkish scimitar, as a result of which I sometimes quite unexpectedly fell so unconscious that I couldn't remember a thing for longer than half an hour.

"She was astonished at my story, and I was worried and fearful, for I was quite inexperienced in bleeding and didn't even know how one should apply the lancet and cut into the flesh with it. Finally I did it as well as I could and began with the old woman who began to scream at my violent and merciless slashing. Following my former story, however,

I fell down completely prostrate in the bathing room and acted so well that she could believe nothing other than that the condition I had been afflicted with since the Turkish prison had struck me anew. Therefore, she called to her maid, who had remained with the clothes in the other room, and the latter had to bring all sorts of smelling salts with which they brought me to and sent me home without delay.

"That was the creation of my unexpected fate, without which I could have revealed myself completely. The bathhouse keeper was surprised at my cunning and sent another fellow who was to do the work instead of me. Thus the amorous countess had to let herself be bled against her will. But soon thereafter the bath woman came from the castle and begged me, if I cared for my life, I should be on my way, for the old countess had rather figured things out since a maid had recognized me and that I had been the harp player. She brought me this news on the third day I had been at the bathhouse. Thus I didn't waste much time, and because the countess could not give her money without arousing suspicion, she ordered her to give me three pieces of gold lace to cover expenses on the road. I sold them immediately in the next city, where I came within a whisker of going to prison because there was a cavalier in the house who recognized that they were done in the countess's style. Later to amuse myself I learned rope-walking from an entertainer, and that's why you've erroneously called me a rope-walker, especially since I don't have a broken bone in my body. But I do rope-walking for fun and have till now been sufficiently successful with it and my harp to keep myself fed."

The woman whom they previously had called Lady Pockau thanked him in the name of all for having delivered such excellent and most noteworthy stories from his life. Because it was now her turn, she began with the following:

Chapter Seven. The Story is Graded.

> *Constraint is not what Nature trusts;*
> *You wind the clock too tight, it busts.*

"Before I begin to speak of my own fate I must say what I think of the story of the Herr Rope-walker. First, he did well by not including in his story among all his pranks anything that was either not of purpose nor worthy of note. Secondly, he did poorly in prattling his story so nastily and without cutting."

"Indeed," said the rope-walker, "Madam, I am a Christian and not a Jew, for that reason I did it without cutting."[27]

---

[27] Ger. *Beschneidung*, "cutting, circumcision."

They all laughed, especially Kunigunda, who was mightily pleased that the person with whom she had fallen so completely in love had countered so strongly and quickly. "Whether you are a Christian or a Jew," Lady Pockau continued, "you charged in with a nasty spear . . . ."

"That's a lie," said Monsieur Ludwig. "The old lady intervened; otherwise it easily could have happened."

We laughed even louder about that, but Lady Pockau would not be interrupted but continued and said, "My dear Herr Rope-walker, the countess who loved you is to be praised and to be blamed. She is to be praised . . ." — " . . . for having wanted him," said Ludwig.

Kunigunda said, "For shame, Herr Ludwig, you are so nasty!"

"If you want to keep interrupting me," said Lady Pockau, "I'll give my turn to another."

"As you wish," said Ludwig, "then I'll begin to describe my history, which perhaps will surpass all of yours, so lend me your ears."

"Not at all," said Zendorio, "Brother, let the woman go on!"

"Madam," said Caspia to Lady Pockau, "you are relieved of your story, but do tell us what your opinion of the rope-walker's story is."

"My judgment is this: Those parents who compel their children to marry because of a chance circumstance are acting precipitously. But it is also not to be approved that she fell in love so inappropriately, because it becomes a virtuous spirit to endure misfortune patiently and to march into adverse winds with shoulders erect."

"That's easy for you to say," answered Monsieur Ludwig. "You conceived fourteen children and enjoyed the act more often than there are hairs on my naked dog. You can well say how someone should behave, but you can't demonstrate how one can do it. A young lady is as little a fool as I; the thing has the appetite of a young horse."

At this remark all the women ran out of the room, and Monsieur Ludwig bolted it, knowing well that they wouldn't be able to stay outside long because of the impending severe cold weather. Accordingly, they had to knock, and Monsieur Ludwig's wife told them that he always behaved that way, so they should tolerate him somewhat, for the more they fought it, the filthier the jokes he would launch. "Ha, ha," he called outside after their knocking, "right, you can beg my pardon. I see that you want to hear even worse. Come on in, but first you have to hear how things went for me; then you can go wherever you want to. But Fräulein Anna looks to me as if she's had a tinkle." At that his dearest put her hand over his mouth; otherwise he would have gone on to say something I wouldn't be allowed to record.

After such they all resumed their seat and said that if he was going to be nasty again, they would stick their fingers in their ears. "I thought," he said, "you were going to say 'up your ass.'" At that there was atrocious laughter, and because a bell rang to announce the midday meal, they were all surprised at how quickly the time had passed.

Chapter Eight. Through Love, Carl Heinrich von Zweydig Takes a Wondrous Bath.

He gropes for honey, does the bear,
The bees with stings his death prepare.

At the given signal we were escorted into the dining room by two courtiers, and when the prayer was over, we sat down at the table. The company was somewhat greater this day; therefore, there was high good humor, and only the musicians were lacking, who were doubtless home again. But a lackey who with his lord had ridden through a nearby village two hours earlier reported that he had encountered them in the village bar, where a nobleman had been married to a peasant girl. The lackey's remarks seemed rather suspicious to me so I asked his master, who likewise reported what his servant had said. He also added that the groom was named Faustus, and no one had been able to learn why he had undertaken so serious an act with a peasant girl since the whole country was full of nobility and thus he must have been seriously led astray. Only then did we begin to be truly astonished. I, Isidoro, and Ludwig crossed ourselves, the one in this direction, the other in that, for it is impossible to describe how hard this news struck us. "That's the way it is," said the previous nobleman. "The wedding's over, and from all appearances he'll already be in bed with his bride. It's too bad about so honest a man. I could find in him only unusual courtesy, and as I heard from his servants, he is splendidly provided for. They didn't want to tell me why he married the peasant maid; perhaps their master had forbidden it."

This story ruined our pleasure, for we saw obviously that a horrible madness had seized Faustus since he had undertaken something which either could not last or could be transformed into frightful repentance. For concluding a thoughtless marriage bears no fruit other than shameful regret that is never to be extinguished in one's heart. One thereby blocks the opening to higher promotion, and whoever happens to be ambitious becomes the Devil's pawn.

Then the Irishman said to us, "Monsieurs, one never walks more blindly than on the path of love, where one should employ all caution to avoid going wrong. If one loses his way on it, there's not a person under the sun who knows how to bring him back to the right road. In a marriage one can miss a great amount of happiness, and I believe this single fear of making a wrong choice produces so innumerably many old bachelors. But it's better that Faustus married a peasant girl than wooed a person who was too far above his station as happened with an Italian nobleman who because of this had to give up his life." At this the women asked him to tell the story, and because he acknowledged he was obliged to do so, he told it as follows:

"Gentlemen," he said, "this is the beginning which presents before our eyes the great peril of Carl Heinrich von Zweydig, a German nobleman. He spent his youth among rather bad boys, and it is not to be doubted that from this he was misguided and ruined right from the start. His father passed away while he was still young, and consequently he had all the better opportunity to go his own way, since a mother's gentle care tends to produce nothing but poor obedience in the children. Our Carl led such a life until his fifteenth year, and because Nature had provided him a good head, he had learned rather well and thus was put into a school where he was to prepare himself until he was ready to go to a university. He was an unusually handsome youth, and there wasn't one pupil who wouldn't have felt fortunate in enjoying his company, partly because of his high nobility, partly because of his well-lined purse that his mother was constantly refilling.

"At home he had his own preceptor, but they didn't know they had entrusted a sheep to a wolf, because after a few weeks there came to light pranks, to describe which now time constraints and due revulsion will not tolerate. The preceptor was chased from the house, and to take his place they assigned him a tutor who earlier had familiarized himself with countries through various journeys. But he had the striking flaw of liking to drink to excess, and through this evil he had neglected both himself and his charge more than he could answer for.

"They were sent to Italy to learn the language and other skills, and for this purpose Cremona was chosen, a splendid city and one enjoying at that time special popularity among German nobility. The tutor promised to employ all diligence so that they might return again not only quickly, but also properly trained, to which end he made all sorts of suggestions as to how and in what manner this study and the other skills were to be addressed. With that the two departed, accompanied by a servant, and left behind a weeping mother with a thousand sorrows, who already had a premonition of how things would go with her son.

"After four weeks she received letters from the tutor describing how they had arrived safely by post coach, and thus the sad woman was somewhat satisfied and was most concerned about transmitting letters of credit to her son, from which it can be seen how fond she was of him, since her entire joy was found in pleasing her only son. Meanwhile, however, neither the tutor nor the noble youth had improved himself at all in Italy, for through his gluttony the one fell into disgraceful sloth and the other did nothing but make himself known in the public brothels. Thus, both had at hand the perfect situation for their ruin because they had not suffered the slightest diminution of their money or any other means.

"Julia di Foro, a lady of great beauty and also very high station, who had no match in Cremona, saw our Carl several times riding past her lodgings, because he customarily was at the riding academy at least twice a week. She was a lady of unusual reserve, but also amorous beyond description. She was astonished at the bravery of the German nobleman and finally inquired about his family, which, however, was done so quietly and discretely that neither the tutor nor von Zweydig heard a single word about it.

"One evening, as he arose from the table where he had been the guest of another German, he was hailed by a lackey who delivered a note to him containing the message that within two hours at most he was to appear alone at such and such a palace because one of his fellow countrymen was staying there quite incognito. Carl von Zweydig didn't know it was an unexpected surprise, so he dressed neatly and before an hour had passed appeared at the palace indicated in the note. He asked for the German and since he was still inebriated, a maid led him into a small chamber where he was supposed to wait until she had summoned his compatriot.

"After a quarter of an hour the maid appeared with the so-called German, who was, however, none other than Julia di Foro, the previously mentioned Italian woman. As soon as she entered, the maid departed, and the disguised lady closed the door, began to talk with the nobleman until in astonishment he grasped that she was wearing men's clothing, had left her palace, and in this house was known only by the maid. If he would remain silent about it, it would be up to him to use her body however he liked and chose. If Zweydig had been properly brought up and not so irresponsibly seduced into whoring from earliest childhood, he never would have been overcome by evil desires and ensnared by such a hypocritical whore. He immediately removed his sword and perpetrated horrors with this shameful woman that are better deplored than described. He didn't stop there but continued for some time to satisfy Julia's evil desires because he gave sufficient proof that there could be no one more tight-lipped on earth than he. But in this they both had deceived themselves because they could hide nothing from Him, to whom all thoughts of the heart are known.

"Later they learned from the tutor that he pursued this life for more than eight months under the pretense of speaking with a German who wanted to remain hidden because of an act of murder. And no matter how devoted he had been to gambling, he had put it aside from that hour on and had been melancholy, perhaps for the reason I've already given.

"It happened there was a young baron traveling through Cremona, who was unusually close to our Carl. They spent two or three days in great merriment and there was no honor left that hadn't been shown to the baron. Finally Zweydig accompanied him on horseback, because the foreigner desired to go back again to Germany. When they came to the place where Zweydig had so eagerly pursued his downfall, he confided to the traveler every confidence and reported that in this house he was serving the most beautiful woman in the world and thus had to regard himself as the luckiest man under the sun.

"The baron was astonished and just then they rode before the palace in which Julia di Foro lived with other elevated ladies. At that moment she was standing at the window in the company of some of her playmates, and to disguise her disgraceful deeds she asked who these two cavaliers were. In order for the baron to see that he hadn't been lying, Zweydig bowed low while looking back at the window and the baron simultaneously smiled at the lady, from which Julia concluded she had been betrayed by Zweydig.

"This happened in the early evening and not four hours had passed when Zweydig was once again summoned by the lady and went there quite happy to enjoy his former license and not in the slightest expecting anything evil. He was admitted into the palace quite quickly, but before the gate was closed again, he had received two knife thrusts to his body so that he fell mortally wounded to the ground without having said a single word, where he twitched a bit. This was the outcome of unchaste love that seldom tends to reward one otherwise.

"In this same night Julia had the dead body thrown into the public street, and because it was found before her door, the entire city became not a little suspicious. Finally the tutor found some secret letters, and because they had plotted against him as against his charge, he slipped away silently and brought back nothing save the news of her slain son to the mother, who almost wept her eyes out."

Chapter Nine. Through Love, Philipp Celsi, a Merchant's Clerk, Takes a Wondrous Bath.

> Oh, acting quickly without a plan
> Has brought great grief to many a man.

At such a story some of the women began to cry, and because my beloved was especially affected, the Irishman took the liberty of telling one more that had taken place not long after this one, at which suggestion the ladies were quite content. Then he bowed and began his story:

"The Unfortunate Love of Philipp Celsi,
a Merchant's Clerk
in Paris.

In addition to our daily experience, the following lamentable story shows to what a great yoke lascivious spirits are usually bound and what a great burden they themselves bind onto their backs:

"Philipp Celsi, a Norman, had earned his living since his youth in trade and finally in Paris entered the service of a respected merchant as a bookkeeper. Lady del Phile or, as they called her then, the Princess of Roan, once purchased a piece of silk cloth, during which sale she so fell in love with this Celsi that she completely forgot her high family and sighed constantly for the love of this shop-clerk.

"She soon found a way to make her feelings clear to Celsi, because she ordered that a piece of the same material be brought to her for another dress. The shop owner didn't know the actual cause of this business; therefore, he brought the material himself. The princess was not satisfied with that and sent the merchant away on the pretext that she could negotiate with his clerk twice as well as with him, the owner. The merchant laughed, went away, and sent Celsi in his place to the lodgings of the princess. The latter, however, did not dare to enter; instead, he gave the material to a lackey who was waiting before the room.

"The amorous Phile was quite pleased at this and told the servant to have the clerk appear himself, more in order to be able to reveal her great love to him than to negotiate about the desired cloth. Celsi, who was not so naive at all, was initially indignant at her presumption and apologized for his low station, asked at the same time that she spare his insignificant self since he was born much more to serve her than to love her in such a manner. The princess swore high and low that if he would not agree to this, he would soon experience his death rather than her further mercy. Therefore, he was to swear an oath to her in the present situation that he would let himself be used for her pleasure and would say nothing about their secret affair to anyone, not even his very best friends.

"Celsi didn't know what was best to do here, for he couldn't make up his mind so quickly in this confusing matter. Meanwhile the princess went away and returned with three servants, each with a pistol, who were to gun him down in the room if he didn't wish to consent. When he saw that it was serious and the servants had gradually cocked their pistols, he nodded to the princess, after which she dismissed the lackeys. Celsi then had to swear a solemn oath to her that he would not say a single thing about their secret affair. After this the poor man was forced to all sorts of shameful acts, and no matter how gladly he would have fled from his adversity, he found not a single opportunity at all to depart from his erroneous path because she pressed him so that finally he was completely dominated by her.

"Scipio, as his fellow clerk was called, a person who knew better how to use deceit than figures, stole from his employers at the instigation of some other wicked cutpurses and escaped with a rather large amount after having set fire to the building to prevent his being pursued quickly.

"This act seemed rather arrogant, and because the authorities are allowed to have their suspicions, Celsi was hauled in and people believed he had complete knowledge of the theft and the arson. He offered to take an oath of innocence, but in his chests they found the most beautiful diamond rings and other precious stones, it was assumed that he had acquired such expensive things through the money he'd taken. But

106

these jewels were nothing other than the presents the princess had given him, for he never came away from her with less than a hundred crowns. Because he'd pursued his whoring for over a year, one can imagine what a supply the authorities found, from which they could sufficiently infer that in no way could he have earned such wealth in the time he'd been a bookkeeper.

"They interrogated him in the third degree, and because he felt himself obliged to keep the oath he'd taken to remain silent about their affair, he did not want to come out with the story. Instead, he offered all sorts of explanations from which he made himself all the more suspicious because, as an honest man, he hadn't yet learned how to use subtle lies and deceptions. They took him to the torture chamber, and there from pain he admitted what they hadn't been able to extract from him through persuasion, namely, that he had received all this wealth from the Princess of Roan, the so-called Phile, in a way they would well be able to imagine. He also included the origin and the beginning of the affair as described above. But the worst thing of all for the miserable man was that while he was singing them the truth, the authorities regarded this as a cloak with which he was trying to hide his own guilt. It finally came to the point where he was to be put on the rack again and because he would not change his former story, the torture was continued. None of the judges could imagine that his statement was grounded in the truth because the princess had been regarded in the whole city as a paragon of all purity and maidenly virginity.

"The pain that the miserable man endured so consumed his body that finally he no longer looked like a human being. Even his employer took pity on him and wept quite often at the prison because he could see that Celsi had had to do with the princess. Also, the rings were recognized by various jewelers and it came to the point that people wanted to direct the matter at the princess, who had been enjoying a hunting trip all the while.

"It happened, however, that the guilty clerk was arrested for another theft in Lyon and interrogated physically, during which he confessed among other things that in Paris he had been the sole perpetrator of the crime. The matter came out and before the court which decided to declare Celsi innocent, who had been all but tortured to death. Arrangements were made to interrogate him again concerning the princess in order to understand the matter most surely.

"Phile now had had her fill of the hunt, came to Paris, and sent for her lover, as was her wont, but the procuress soon reported something else to her, for everyone in the whole city was saying that he was to be thrown on the pyre. The princess was extremely frightened, and since nothing can be hidden forever, she learned the situation and she was allowed to read the court papers. She was a very well-to-do person, for which reason there were people concerned with silencing the rabble's talk so that Celsi was garrotted that same evening with a large rope and thus miserably and quite horribly slain.

"From this sad example arises the question whether Celsi had been required to keep his oath or not. And the answer is: No, for he did not swear to endure torture; instead, his pledge had concerned only the *status extra torturam*, which ultimately he would have been able to keep. For another thing, he was in no way obliged *ratione obligationis* because the lady had no right to handicap the poor creature with an oath, and, on the other hand, the authorities had the power to release him from it. Thus this cannot be called an admissible oath when it occurs to strengthen sin and to suppress truth. I shan't speak of the obvious constraint Phile undertook with it. But he was wrong in not having shot himself to death rather than let himself be used for such disgraceful unchastity, *præstat enim honesta mors turpi vitæ*, because a virtuous death is to be much more highly prized than a shameful life."

Chapter Ten. The Ladies' Judgment of This Story.

Whoever quickly makes up his mind
Is a happy son of humankind.

"This story," said Isidoro, "is somewhat melancholy, but, to tell the truth, from it young people can see quite well what danger they subject themselves to when, unthinkingly, they snap at such bait that they often prematurely end their lives. In the opinion of our Irish gentleman it would have been better if Philipp Celsi had let himself be shot to death in the lady's room. But when it reaches that point, things take on a different appearance. Not one in a thousand is fool enough to have himself shot straight off, and in such a situation it's impossible to make up one's mind up quickly. As bold and dashing as the world-famous Wallenstein[28] otherwise was, from great horror he couldn't say a word at the time when he was attacked on the last night of his life at Eger and stabbed to death. Gentlemen, gentlemen, to have to die is hard to swallow, and a quick decision in favor of death is a wee flower that doesn't grow in every garden. But the base-minded Phile must have sucked at a barbarian's breast to have the man garrotted whom she had forced to love her through the fear of death, knowing well that much can be gained through such means.

"One can also see from this the wanton spirit of some women who have to do with people quite inappropriate to their station only in order

---

[28] A. W. E. Wallenstein (1583–1634), brilliant but ambitious leader of Imperial forces in the Thirty Years' War, murdered by fellow officers for disloyalty to the Emperor.

that their vices should remain all the better hidden and think that hiding the same isn't a sin at all.

"Some caress quite young and untrained youths and don't know that thereby they lose not only their own soul, but also that of the young man. As it is regarded by some among us, whoredom is not a bad act, and if this were the appropriate time, I would cite some sad examples that occurred in my homeland just a year ago when a nobleman caught a stable boy with his daughter and immediately hanged him by his neckerchief in the room. But whoever wants to take warning can already see well enough from the Irishman's two stories how evil and miserable it was for both the poor devils. As for Carl Heinrich von Zweydig, the fool got his deserts, for it can't be doubted that even today such superfools appear who think their love invaluable and would even like to have themselves dubbed a knight for it, if only people were fools and erected monuments to fantasts.

"I know one such man in a town who goes now to one woman, now to another, and then the Monsieur talks about nothing but making love, how he can't make love or doesn't want to. But why does he go to such places when people are going to draw the obvious conclusion? He says he can't make love and nevertheless can't stop calling on women. If someone speaks to him of marriage, he acts as though he would have to be begged to, and he believes firmly that the maiden whom he doesn't marry is not in good hands. But according to our general laws he can only take one wife; therefore, one must conclude that in his opinion all the others would have to curl up and die. Ha, ha, I've laughed quite often at these fancies. He does believe firmly that all those who married without asking his advice married poorly, and if you take a good look at his advice, he's scarcely been able to help himself and, at the very least, has no witness to his having helped others.

"He passed through his best years in such a delusion and is now gradually approaching fifty, an age not at all pleasing to the ladies. This mistake is all the uglier because, first, he, the expert on love, committed it himself and, secondly, no means under the sun can be found with which he could remedy it. But what does finally happen to people who imagine that women dream of them? Nothing but the derisive laughter of those people for whom he earlier had wanted to be the teacher. *In fine videtur, cuius toni,*[29] when in tidying up it appears how brashly someone acted in wanting to help others mount a horse and then himself sits upon an ass. Many a man imagines and alleges he won't marry any woman who doesn't have a capital of forty thousand Ducats. But do they think people can obtain money through flattery or shake it down from the trees? Forty thousand Ducats aren't so foolish, and to make the matter all the clearer, please know that the fellow is an artist and fortunate only as long as his employer, the prince, is living. Accordingly, he

---

[29] "In the end, the story comes out."

109

has to paint on the double and go to see where His Magnificence has a post for him.

"He is proud beyond compare and whenever he returns to his homeland, there's no one better than he; instead, he alone is master in everything, so they should see how respected he is at court, where, in truth, his efforts are not as well rewarded as he imagines. He praises other paintings highly, but to himself he always regards his work as the best and cannot hide his own fame. Thus I don't know whether Nature or the love of women so oddly disposed him to sloppily overlook this striking flaw of good conduct when otherwise he regards himself as no mean member of the social structure.

"What good does it do when someone boasts so in his homeland? People know well who he is and thus will show him no greater respect, no matter how much he desires it. I'm a cavalier of hearty good humor and I value such merriment more highly than the highest honor of this land. I'm not afraid to grab beggars in the street and dance around with them, and when I come to my castle, I eat a roasted partridge and am as honorable as I ever was. 'Indeed, you clown,' says many a person, 'that's offensive to the ladies.' But I retort, 'Clown yourself, ladies here, ladies there, do you think I lose anything from that? A woman who loves me pays little or no attention at all, while she who will not love me will be frightened away if I kill only a fly.' A man is by nature nobler than a woman, no matter how noble she may be, and thus women must cherish me and not I them. And what can you do about it if there are weaklings who subject themselves to any pig bristle-dealer's daughter and call her a goddess? I don't have such a scoundrel's spirit and if I did, I'd have myself lashed as long as a limb were left on my body."

"Brother Isidoro," said Monsieur Ludwig, "you speak somewhat bluntly, yet truly. A while ago I was lying ill in that hospital. I spooned, I wooed, I caressed, I charmed, I promised, I swore, *in summa*, I made such a fool of myself that I can't describe it adequately. But since I have a wife on my neck, the fool in me has rather been put to rest; therefore, I say that no person can be properly clever if he hasn't gone a'courting. Therefore," he said to Fräulein Anna and Kunigunda, "get to it right soon so that you'll also be clever one day."

But Fräulein Anna replied that if Monsieur Ludwig were to marry twenty times again, he would remain as he was before, for she had perceived no different intelligence in him after his marriage than he had earlier in his single state. However, she had to admit the longer he talked, the nastier it became. "Indeed," he said, "what I'm talking about you would think about all the more often if I could see your thoughts. I would behold splendid poses almost like those to be found in the garden room on the upper terrace at Schlackewerth."

At these words all those present laughed, and Fräulein Anna would have liked to know why, had she not feared Monsieur Ludwig would give her a nasty answer. And we passed almost three hours in such conversation, and we judged those most fortunate who wisely moderate the emotions of love and are able to be on their guard against all company with women. At that we rose from the table and attended a happy dance, for which the ladies had engaged a fiddler from the village and an itinerant musician, both of whom scraped away miserably enough.

The thoughts, however, that Caspia and I had had concerning Faustus kept tormenting our spirits, for we feared that strange person might have fallen into an unexpected depression because previously he had already hanged himself from a tree and, as it were, cast a premonition of his future state. But Ludwig talked us out of such ideas with sufficient reasons, for he reported that Faustus was a person of unusual caprices who often found his greatest pleasure in something with which another wouldn't even wipe his shoes. On account of this he felt Faustus would get along much better with a peasant maid than with a royal princess from the land of the Grand Mogul. And in order that I might learn the story in full, he promised me to travel there as soon as possible in disguise, whereby we could become thoroughly familiar with his circumstances.

This proposal placated me somewhat, and because this day had been spent merrily and not without moral lessons, I begged Monsieur Ludwig to use the time remaining until dinner by telling his life story, to which he was willing if only the ladies would pay strict attention. At this we brought those who no longer desired to dance into the room, and although Kunigunda adored dancing, she nonetheless followed Isidoro immediately because she gradually had become attracted to him because of his unusual qualities.

Chapter Eleven. Monsieur Ludwig Tells His Life Story.

New wine ferments, that's sure as the sun,
It blows the tap right out of the tun.

When people heard that Monsieur was going to tell the story of his life, the dancing hall was immediately emptied, but the women gave a quite different reason for leaving it when they said the cold compelled them to seek a warm room. This excuse was received without comment, for one doesn't have to be so boorish as to accuse a woman of telling a lie, even when it's a tangible one. Because the room was filled in a moment, they had to bring in chairs from other rooms so that those who hadn't been present that morning for the rope-walker's story could have a seat.

Even my aged father in his old Swedish boots came from curiosity, and I don't believe there was a chambermaid in the whole castle who hadn't hid herself behind the stove or behind the bed, for they knew

Monsieur Ludwig would tell a splendid story if he intended to bring out all the pranks he had pulled since his youth. Then he sat down in a large easy chair, and after the noble party had arranged themselves in a half moon about him, he began:

"Ten, twenty, thirty, forty, fifty, sixty, seventy, eighty, ninety, a hundred, a thousand times I've been amazed at how reputable a person I was in my youth. When I was still a small boy and scarcely removed from my mother's breast — for she nursed me herself and didn't keep some whore with shaved head as my wet nurse, as some are accustomed to do nowadays — when I began with my rascal's pranks with the ravens. We had a hunter who was a person who could shoot whatever he wanted to, for he mixed into his lead bats' hearts as well as young staghorn, which has to be removed at a certain time. From his skill he profited greatly and variously.

"This same hunter brought two live ravens to the castle for me, and I rewarded him for this with a silver spoon I had secretly stolen from the kitchen. Afterwards he helped me dress one raven with all sorts of colored paper and stuff; on his head we placed a rocket with gunpowder and through the nostril we pulled a feather from a peacock's tail, on each end of which we hung a small bell. And when we had completely painted the bird half red and half blue, we lit the rockets above its heads and then let it fly wherever it wanted to.

"Through this I caused a division among the neighboring people, for some took it to be a dragon, others a bird of paradise, and never in their lives had they seen either of the two. Some even regarded it as a flying comet, for we tied about one hundred and fifty feet of string to its tail and from the rocket produced a train of fire, from which the raven began to burn over its whole body. On the end of each wing we likewise hung a bell so that its ringing caused more spectators. In this unheard-of manner we created thousandfold uncertainties among the people, and subsequently it was written in the newspapers far and wide that a burning dragon had been seen in the air, one should repent and be pious, otherwise bad things might happen. Through this means I frightened quite many people away from evil.

"After that my father sent me to a school not too far away from the castle. There I pulled so many tricks I couldn't describe them all in fifteen years, for whenever the school master whipped me for my negligence in reading or writing and called me an ill-bred lout, I put cobbler's wax on the place he sat when he was out, and then if he wasn't watching he often tore his trousers. Occasionally I would break his windows and at night smear his house door with fresh animal manure. I also encouraged my fellow pupils to do such, whom I could counsel much more readily.

"Because, as said, the place was somewhat removed from my father's residence, he had the schoolmaster provide me board for half a year and promised to give him twenty Taler for the board and tuition. But I can swear that within that time I did forty's worth of damages to the schoolmaster, for I peed in all his ink bottles, occasionally also in his drinking glasses and was greatly amused to myself when I saw people drinking from them at table. The broken window panes I ground into a powder and later strewed this in the maids' beds, from which they had sores all over their bodies. When I occasionally ate too many plums or other fruit that caused my stomach to rumble in the night, I crapped in his room and on the next day said I had gotten a stomach ache from his food. He didn't dare punish me because he feared my father might give him a sharp reprimand for not having given me better food for what he was paying him.

"Once the maid called me a lousy tramp and jackanapes, so when she was out, I popped a good handful of dead flies into the stew pot, and when the meal came to the table so unclean, the schoolmaster grew frightfully angry at this and knocked the one maid down one flight of stairs, the other maid up the other. When he sometimes had some red wine from Vigern brought up, which he loved to drink, and while he was out of the room, I would pull some hairs from my head and slip them into his glass, for I knew he could neither eat nor drink anything in which he found even the slightest hair. In this way I got to drink the wine, and he had a new one brought. No sooner had he had his instruments tuned, such as the harpsichord, lute, violin, and clavichord, than I would tear out a string here or there. As if that weren't enough, I slit his jacket, coat, and trousers, and whatever I saw hanging on the wall, I pulled out my pocket knife and abused almost everything that came my way. When the cooper came to repair the cistern, the schoolmaster's wife usually sat on a bench to observe the worker, and when he and his apprentices began pounding, I took a stone and a nail and amid the pounding of the coopers I nailed the schoolmaster's wife to the bench. When she later got up to leave, she either pulled the bench after her or tore a hole in her skirt.

"Whenever strange dogs wandered into the house, I would put a paper around their necks, paint them all over with ink, and then let them go wherever they wanted to. In a word, my conduct was so ill-bred and wild that the schoolmaster finally complained to my father about me. After that I returned home, where I was put under the instruction of a preceptor, against whose great efforts I resisted.

"I picked fleas from dogs and lice from the heads and clothes of beggar boys and collected them in a little wooden box; later I put them into the preceptor's clothes and coat. When he was sitting with us at the table, I can't describe how dreadfully the lice crawled back and forth on his shoulders. My mother often was so revolted at this that she had to leave the table. And because many regarded him as a fleabag, my father dismissed him and I thereby regained my former freedom to go with the hunter wherever I wished, although I scarcely learned enough to write my name properly.

"About an hour from our estate there was a cleric, to whose sermons we drove every Sunday and on holidays. In my youth I probably wished this same pastor would go to Hell a thousand times for having told my father he had committed a great sin in neglecting me so; he then proposed various suggestions as to how I might be helped most expediently. They finally reached an agreement, and I had to board with the pastor and there learn enough Latin to at least make myself qualified for entering a Latin school. In such manner a good portion of my freedom was curtailed, although I did pull a number of pranks on the maids and servants as well as the pastor's clerk.

"We lived next to the church and beside us was the sexton's house, alongside which was a small orchard. And because only a low wall separated it from our building, usually as evening was coming on I was at the spot with a ladder and plucked here and there a pear, apple, plum, or even a peach, whatever I could reach and grab. But once the sexton caught sight of me and gave my head thumps such as I had never seen in all my life.

"His treatment was such that I was resolved to fire a burning rocket into the sexton's house because his attic window was just opposite our own. But I reflected a bit and thought that might threaten us as well as him because his attic was full of unthreshed grain that he had received as tithes from his peasants. Then I seized upon a different means, and because there was a window from our rear building into the church tower, I climbed in secretly and befouled the bell rope over and over with excrement from which the sexton later stained his hands frightfully. Because this prank had gone so well, I thought I'd try another and was going to cut off the bell rope, but the sexton observed me from a corner and beat me so with the knotted end of the rope that I leapt out of the window almost as soon as I had come in."

"Oh," said Fräulein Anna, "that was as it should be. If I knew where to find that sexton, I would like to reward him, and a couple of Taler wouldn't be too much."

"Thanks a lot, my fair Fräulein," said Monsieur Ludwig. "Don't go to any effort; you'll soon hear how it went with the poor rascal. For when I returned full of rage and desire for revenge, I lit the prepared rocket and in a trice hurled it across into the straw. In the time it would take to say the Lord's Prayer, fire was flaring out of the attic window and in the street fearful screaming was heard. I kept running as fast as I could and when I looked back from the countryside, I saw fire rising a good twenty feet into the sky and I can't tell you how greatly I regretted having caused such misery, because I feared the parson's house would likewise catch fire."

Chapter Twelve. Comes to a Cousin's Palace and There Unexpectedly Has Two Charming Adventures.

The asses' trick is nothing new:
The old ones fart, the young ones too.

"This fear gave wings to my feet that I otherwise didn't have, so I hastened quite quickly to our estate but I didn't have the heart to explain why to my father. Instead, I ran to the nearest farm, where I mounted a horse and rode off as quickly as I could. I knew no road or path; therefore, I raced ahead wherever the horse carried me and, as time passed, regretted ever more having served the poor sexton a soup that would occupy him long enough.

"By the setting sun I came to a castle where a cousin lived. From its tower I recognized having once been there with my mother, for the owner of this castle was her blood brother and a rather aged man. At the time I was perhaps fifteen years old and when I came riding into the courtyard, I was greeted by his daughter, who had gone to the kitchen to prepare the meal. She was quite surprised at me, and when I inquired about her father, she told me he and her mother were off at a wedding and wouldn't get back until tomorrow. Meanwhile she asked me to alight, take my horse to the stall, and remain at the castle until her father came back again. I was still filled with the worry and fright that had driven me to this remote castle, which she surely noted in me. I didn't want to talk about it so I told her that I had a message for her father, for whom I would wait.

"With that she led me up a stairway into a small room, where from an oriel I could look out on to the road and see who might enter or leave the castle. Shortly thereafter she sent a maid up to me with a light and an entertaining book that I could leaf through and so pass the time until dinner. Instead, I was worried that soon a bailiff would come and soon thereafter another one would come who would tie me up and take me back. But that didn't happen, no matter how much I feared it.

"When it was almost seven o'clock and dinner was announced, I heard someone riding across the castle bridge. I quickly turned around and saw from the oriel that it was a man who was entirely cloaked. This caused me to take him for now a hangman, now something else because fear depicted him to me in a hundred different guises. Therefore, I locked the room, intending, if it should be a person sent to capture me, to let myself down from the oriel, leap to the bridge, and run into the nearest woods. At this moment the young lady came to my room, unlocked it with a master key that she wore along with others. I turned completely pale and kept asking questions until I confided to her how misfortune had befallen me and out of sheer malice I had set fire to the sexton's house. But someone had now ridden in whom I took to be a

115

bailiff sent to capture me; therefore, I begged her from the bottom of my heart not to reveal that I was present at the castle. Tomorrow before day I would get on the horse and ride off into the countryside. The miss was shocked by my story and not a little alarmed when I told her about the person I had seen riding through the gate. Because I mistakenly believed this person was a bailiff, she made no attempt to change my belief and promised me not to report my presence here to any person who might seek me at the castle. And then she left, saying that she would let me eat alone in this room and then have me shown to a room where I should sleep this night.

"With that she went her way carrying a candle, and shortly thereafter the earlier maid came with a basket and set my place. She brought a boiled hen with parsley and potatoes and a quarter of a roasted suckling pig along with a salad. Amid countless worries and fancies, I ate them in fear and trembling because I didn't know how great was the damage the fire had done. Now I was looking from this window, now from another one to see whether I could catch sight of flames in the sky. But because at that time I didn't understand much about maps, I didn't know in which direction the place lay where I had prepared such nice fireworks. When I had taken care of my slight repast, the same maid that had brought me the food lighted me to a room in which four large beds stood and there she gave me my choice of lying down wherever it seemed best to me. She also brought me a small glass of brandy and a bit of roll. Then I snuffed the light and soon lay down to sleep. Worry is the best instrument for rendering a person wakeful, so it was impossible for me to fall asleep because then I was preoccupied with it like a dog with fleas during the dog days. I turned first one way, then the other, but it was all futile and in vain. Finally something came into the room that I at first took to be a ghost because it opened the door very quietly and crept in with much rustling. I began to bite my quilt and hide myself beneath it when I heard a soft voice I thought I recognized. I stuck my ear out a bit farther and soon became aware that it was my young cousin, who was leading in with her the man who had earlier ridden over the castle bridge while cloaked. They had a lantern with them and couldn't see me or my clothes because I lay hidden in the rearmost bed.

"Then it dawned on me what the score was and why this honest bird had arrived so completely cloaked. I heard and saw almost foolishly well how much my cousin adored him, for they called one another nothing but Honey, Dear Child, Sweetheart, Angel, and such respectable terms, at which I had no little cause to be surprised.

"They both undressed and my cousin asked her lover not to speak so loudly; otherwise they might be heard by her nurse, whose sleeping quarters were beneath the room. After extinguishing the light, they both lay down in bed, and I must admit that out of propriety I won't relate the conversation that to my great annoyance they conducted with one another for a short while. If we were alone, I would go on to tell it, but back there behind the stove and the bed are standing some youngsters, under whose noses one shouldn't rub arcana of this sort or put a burr under their saddles. Like dumb animals they strive to satisfy their carnal desires, and the abomination of a vice does not serve them for reform but much more as a pleasant recollection from which they will ruin themselves and rob themselves of the greater part of their welfare. I had never suspected that my upright cousin was so in love, but now both my eyes were opened, and I can assure you that since then I have encountered few such situations that plunged me into such unheard-of astonishment. I wanted to make myself known at that time, but I was afraid the fellow might kill me, because a person stained with sin does not hesitate to plunge from one vice into another.

"Amid such thoughts I fell asleep and all night long dreamed of nothing but hanging and heads, so that I often awoke and felt for my head to see whether it was still sitting in its old place or not. Finally day came, but I could no longer see anything of the two people except that their bed was quite disheveled. I got up and dressed when my cousin came in and asked me where I had slept last night. I said I had lain here in this bed and had strong and nice dreams, at which her face turned blood red. She went on to ask if I had fallen asleep quickly and whether I hadn't heard someone in the room, but I replied that I hadn't noticed a mouse, much less a person, and why did she want to know such a thing. At this she cheered up a bit, for she believed I hadn't noticed or heard anything of her knavery and then she left. But downstairs in the parlor she gave the maid who had shown me to the wrong room one slap here and another there and fired her on the spot. The maid screamed and said that if she didn't stop hitting her, she would tell everything she knew about her and the musician, at which my cousin grew even angrier and gave her some more blows. Finally I came down myself and parted them safely from one another. But in her anger the maid said things that made me wonder whether I might call my cousin a young lady any longer or not.

"'You nasty fleabag,' the maid said to her, 'you learned from Monsieur Julian how to play that instrument for no other reason than to be able to make love with him all the more freely! Oh, I've seen how he made out with you! Mind your tongue, I'm going to tell your mother everything in full detail, as sure as I'm standing here. I want to see if you have a reason for putting candy and money into his knapsack. May the Devil ride you, you beastly whore, and not some good spirit! '

"'What!' said my cousin. 'You accursed carrion, didn't you fight over a fellow six years ago? Don't you remember how you and your rival went at it with daggers and you superslattern got stabbed in the leg? Ha, you watch your tongue and don't waste any time. I'll have my nose pierced before I let you get away with this. Do you think I don't know how you've been carrying on with the coachman's stable boy? Do you

117

still remember how you stole the plate and sold it to the Jew? Just you wait, I'll teach you a lesson like you've never been taught before! '

"I think they would have gone on arguing if a rattling hadn't re-sounded from the courtyard that restrained them from their present quarreling. My cousin quickly ran out, and I prepared myself to greet my uncle, who, while still in the coach, threatened me with his cane and said what a honest fellow I was and how charmingly I knew how to use fireworks. I was frightened by his words and completely imagined that beyond doubt they were going to hang me, but a lackey poked me in the side and whispered to me that if I gave him something, he would tell me how things stood.

"I promised to donate a silver button from my coat to him if he would tell me how they had heard and how great the damage had been. Then he told me that nothing more than the gable of the sexton's house had burned away and they had heard this because their road to the wedding had borne them by there. And that was the end of it for the nonce. My cousin was very happy to find me at his castle because he had alighted at my parents' place and found my mother crying on my account because she believed I had already ridden on my horse to Nova Zemlya.

"My cousin asked me to come along to his room, where without much ado he told me I shouldn't be afraid on account of the fire; in-stead, I should stay with him today, and tomorrow he would have a ser-vant bring me secretly to our estate. And with that all the fear was gone that had been tormenting me so frightfully and inexpressibly. I stayed at the castle all that day and that night I experienced an adventure even more amazing than the preceding one. I'll thus tell it to you in brief."

Just as Monsieur Ludwig finished those words, dinner was an-nounced. However, because we were all quite curious to hear the story of the second night, word was sent to the kitchen telling the cook to hold things up for a quarter of an hour, and Ludwig continued by saying, "After the arrival of my cousin, his wife went to the kitchen to ask if anyone had been at the castle in her absence, and because most unfor-tunately the just-whipped maid was standing nearest to her, she took the lady to one side and whispered into her ear that the musician Julian had been there and slept with her daughter. 'What?' the wife cried. 'You dishonorable carrion, who are you to spread such stories about my daughter? Oh, may the Devil take you up the chimney, you thunder-and-lightning-witch! Quickly, pack your things and get out of the castle be-fore I have the bailiffs lead you about in chains with an appropriate sign and then throw you in the water. Would anyone believe what this su-perwhore is saying about my daughter? Get out of my sight or I'll run the fireplace fork through your belly, you shameless cow, you flaming whore, you peasants' whore, you Devil's whore!' Amid and between such epithets, the maid ran as fast as she could out of the castle, and my cousin had the clothing she hadn't been able to gather up in her haste sent after her by a boy along with the message that if she were to be seen again at the castle, she would tell her huntsman to shoot her. To tell the truth, I was quite surprised at the precipitous rage of my aunt because otherwise she was a woman of unusual modesty. But not twenty-four hours had passed before I had solved my problem without great effort, and you'll soon hear what the trick was.

"Because it's already time to eat, I'll shorten my story when the material allows. I spent most of the day sneaking up on the maids in the cow shed, attacking them from behind, and tumbling them head over heels with aprons flying. I cut the cows' ropes and was busy as could be doing whatever I could to annoy people. I also undertook something with one of the children's maids that I won't tell because of Fräulein Anna, although the people behind the stove and Fräulein Kunigunda would like to hear it. Therefore, I'll hurry to the principal affair so that we will get to our meal.

"After dinner a lackey led me to a different room, which was built in the traditional style. In it were enough things to furnish a house with spinning wheels, kitchen equipment, saddles, pitchforks, and other junk, so that I would have thought the room was a horse stall rather than a bedroom. I was almost afraid that I was supposed to sleep alone in this room, and so I remained silent until the servant left. I had familiarized myself with the castle and its situation, so I intended to lie down in a safer and cleaner place. I quietly crept down a hall and situated myself in a chamber, next to which I knew my cousin had his bedroom. Between his and mine there was only a whitewashed wooden wall; therefore, I wasn't a fourth as afraid as I had been in the former one and I lay down. After a quarter of an hour, two women came into my cousin's room, and because they had light, I quietly got up to see what they were up to since I took them to be maids. The hollowed-out knotholes served my purpose well, but I was dumbstruck from the first moment at how these two women were caressing and kissing one another.

"From great passion they were about to eat each other up and when they turned toward me, I saw that it was my cousin's wife and her cook. You can imagine what I was able to imagine about this, and I didn't know whether this was the result of love or friendship. 'Monsieur Fido,' my cousin said to the cook, 'be bold enough to get undressed. My husband is sleeping alone in his little room tonight; therefore, don't be worried and let me be responsible if things turn out differently or unexpectedly.' 'Madam,' the cook replied, 'I entrust not only my entire person to yourself and your words, but also my entire wealth. At your behest I shall undress, and I'm probably clever enough to escape the greatest danger. If your husband unexpectedly appears with a light, see to it that you put it out.' 'Oh, no,' said my cousin, 'he believes only that Monsieur is my cook, and I also told him that in his absence I was having the cook sleep with me, at which he was quite satisfied.' While talking so, they both undressed, and I saw with astonishment that beneath her dress the

119

cook was wearing men's clothing and, to be sure, the most beautiful silk trousers.

"That's when I knew what the score was, and after they lay down, Monsieur Fido explained at length how today the clerk had written her a love letter, at which they both laughed so beneath their blanket that it annoyed me. In astonishment, I lay awake all night and thought up a thousand ways of making this disgraceful practice known because never in my life would I have expected to find such devilish and poisonous deceit at this castle. With this in mind, when day had almost begun I quietly got up, made up the bed as well as I knew how, and then took from my pocket my small pistol that I had loaded blank. I stuck the barrel into a hollowed-out knothole and fired away into the room, at which both leaped out of their bed in fright and believed they had been betrayed.

"But I had quickly found my way back into the other room, where I tore the clothes from my body and hastily threw myself into bed after having thrown the pistol into the castle moat, which I was able to do through a window of this room. This shot had awakened quite many of the sleeping and half-dreaming. Soon a scurrying arose in the castle, and some people even thought there were thieves and murderers present. I called some people running past into my room and asked what all the tumult was about. But nobody knew precisely, and I had to bite my bedspread to suppress my laughter; otherwise they might have found me out.

"Monsieur Fido could not get his clothes on before a servant was at their door, and it wouldn't have taken much for him to see the presumed cook standing there in men's trousers, if my cousin hadn't held him up with her unbolting of the door. My male cousin was awakened by the tumult and nothing made me so sorry as the fact that the door hadn't been open. In such manner the affair would have been revealed wondrously but it remained secret since everyone took Monsieur Fido to be a woman and the cook. Beyond all doubt he must have been a young toady whom she could use in this disguise as often as she desired and it was convenient. With that I'll conclude for now, because otherwise the roast pig might get overdone, and I'll tell the rest of it later on." Then we were escorted with two torches into the dining room and, after washing our hands, sat down at the table.

Book Four

Chapter One. The Irishman Sees a Ghost.

Don't always trust what you've believed:
The gullible are soon deceived.

"Truly," said Fräulein Anna, "the life story related by Monsieur Ludwig has a quite odd beginning, and if I had to give an opinion of it, I would have to say without flattery that he proceeded with it politely enough and displayed a greater restraint than is otherwise his wont."

"That's true," said Kunigunda, "but he took a jab at me that I'll repay in good time, and if I weren't so famished now, I'd tell him what I think of him."

"Brother," I said to him, "you'll have to finish tomorrow, but Lady Pockau, what do you think of the story Ludwig's told us?"

"Sir," she said to me, "from it I've seen how youth is more inclined to willfulness than discipline and that revenge is usually planted in our hearts even in early youth. I've also understood quite well that at some castles a lot of whoring and adulteries are pursued and that the people who catch hell are usually those who tell the truth and try to eliminate vice. I've also learned from it that vice often, even usually, betrays and reveals itself, as this story makes clear and obvious when Monsieur Ludwig learns of the daughter's and the mother's pranks without his having any intention or desire to pry into them. From such a story one must also note that fear and worry creep into our spirits in our youth, although they serve only to enlarge the shadow thrown by something actually small and insignificant. One can also see and feel in what great sadness children thrust their parents by running away in ignorance or otherwise help in producing some great suffering. Likewise the concealed musician teaches us that the vices shun the light because they are truly creatures of the darkness. Also, the shot that was fired lets us understand that we should always be on guard against all uncleanliness because we don't know at what moment we will have to die and be gone in a trice. In a word, although Monsieur Ludwig told his story somewhat humorously, it nonetheless has enough substance, and if I weren't like Fräulein Kunigunda and likewise famished, I would tell more that would serve to increase Monsieur Ludwig's fame."

"Damn!" said Ludwig. "Now I finally see what a wonderful fellow I am! Just a minute, because this was all too spiritual for you, tomorrow you'll get to hear a sermon from me that's going to be worldly enough."

"You may do as you wish," said von Pockau, "but people still have an opportunity to learn something from it. Natural affairs are not vile. Such stories are told so that in such situations we should look out for and protect ourselves. Earlier I read in some books a heap of high and great love stories, but those were affairs that were impossible or improbable. Thus the time I spent in reading such texts was ill-spent because it provided no opportunity to apply what was contained in the books. But stories such as Monsieur Ludwig encountered in his youth happen a thousandfold and especially among our kind. Therefore, I regard the latter much more highly than the former because they can happen to us, and we thus have an opportunity to find in them such precepts as we can use profitably and apply to shunning our vices.

"What good is it if one puts a copy of a story before a cobbler and tells him how once someone made a golden shoe, presented it to the mogul, and subsequently became a prince of the realm? Truly, not much differently do some printed stories turn out that are filled with fabricated and boastful deeds that can't be imitated and in reality have taken place only in the minds of their hack authors. For although it pleases the cobbler that one of his colleagues became a prince, he can't possibly duplicate this and if he made such a shoe, he wouldn't know to whom to present it. If he were to give it to a great potentate, it's doubtful he would obtain a meager reward, much less a princedom. Therefore, it is much more necessary to write things that can serve us as a warning for our future life.

"I'll give you an example from my life. When I was still a young chick, I came across a love story about a Turkish empress. I imagined I was the Turkish empress and became so proud and haughty that I rejected many suitors in the firm belief that cavaliers should be sword fighting and tilting as they would around the Turkish empress. What foolishness and how nicely tilted! They finally left me sitting, and I gladly would have given a Ducat to the maid who would have brought me a letter saying that someone was going to ask my mother if he could marry me. I had the miserable love story to thank for that, for with increasing intelligence I learned that I still had to complete a giant leap before I became a Turkish empress, although I had a half moon in my coat of arms. For the Turk was one thing, and my station another. Thus I think it twice as important to hear and read things that are appropriate to our station. And I certainly believe that from such, quite many women have been misled to put aside their usual polite participation in urban life and, through the delusion of being grand ladies, to be overbearing in their spirits and thereby to fall into their own ruination."

"What Lady Pockau is talking about," said the Irishman, "I learned in fact while still a youth. Then I liked to read nothing better than stories about adventures and knightly deeds. And because I read that quite a few such people descend into the bowels of the earth, one evening I put on a suit of armor that I had had the court tailor cut out from paper and sew together. Then I went to a pit alongside our castle that people said went twelve miles into the earth, one of the likes of which is said to exist in Polish Russia. But there I was so frightened by a ghost that for a long time after I lay in bed severely ill. I saw the said ghost at a distance and sitting in a corner a good twelve paces from me and continually spewing fire. I had gone over a hundred yards in the dark corridor and, to tell the truth, I had entered it for no other reason than perhaps some miserable scribbler would sit down with my story and put it into print for posterity so that he could sell it later for a penny or two at every flea market and give it to people to read. But the story had a different ending, for the ghost finally stood up toward me, and I saw standing before me a proper living person whose face was much more frightful to look at than the head of a long-tailed monkey. His eyes were full of fire and about his waist he had a burning wreath and whenever he opened his mouth, a great flame came out.

"My hair was standing straight up, and in my great anxiety I couldn't decide on anything definite until I blacked out and fell down senseless and unable to move and was beneath a great oak tree when I finally came to. It was in the middle of the night and I felt throughout my body that an unusual illness had befallen me. Because I could recognize nothing but the tree, I was afraid to go home since I believed I was not far from the hell where the horrible ghost had frightened me and so tormented me. It seemed to me someone had pulled all the hair from my head, and I thought only that someone had flayed me alive because shuddering had taken over my entire body and made me into a different person. Finally I pulled myself together in the darkness and onto the road, where I came to a shepherd's shelter in which I found two boys of my age who were guarding the animals in the field. I told them what had happened to me this night, but they knew many other stories about the pit that had occurred to people passing by.

"They kept me with them through the rest of the night in which I grew sicker and sicker, and when day approached they sent me home quite ill, where I lay in one spot for fourteen weeks, and no one had greater profit from my adventure than the doctors and apothecaries. My mother then burned all the books that had misled me to such an endeavor, and thus I felt the fruits of those stories that only a magician or an unusual adventurer could imitate. Indeed, I once read that a person who could stand on his head was most fitting to be a knight. Then I began to practice standing on my head so much that finally blood ran out of my mouth."

Fräulein Anna interjected that she had become quite fearful at the mention of the ghost and that if she had seen it like the Irishman, she doubtless would have had to die. "So what if you had died?" said

Ludwig. "Then the dog would crap on your grave!" At this, the whole company began to laugh, and the Fräulein made a rather sour face at him for again starting to make fun of her and behave like a pig. But Ludwig said that if the dog didn't want to, he would do it and even if the grave digger and his wife were present, at which the people laughed even more. And when Fräulein Anna noted that Ludwig wasn't going to change his ways, she also laughed. Later Ludwig compared her to the dog that was carrying meat for the butcher and on his way was attacked by other dogs. When he saw that they had control of the basket, he joined in the eating so that he hadn't exerted himself completely in vain.

Chapter Two. The Rope-walker Goes Courting.

One can't spin his yarn so fine
It can't be seen in bright sunshine.

During and in such conversations our evening meal ended, during which many other stories were told that were based on such themes as tend to inflame the imagination of the reader and to make fools of intelligent people. After the meal people again danced and after that agreed to meet again tomorrow and to complete the agenda with the codicil that on this night no one should revert to invented stories that had never happened, from which the society would be deceived rather than entertained or edified. Ludwig said he wanted to have a horn growing out of his head for every lie or untruthful word he produced, and the others replied that one should not presume that noble persons would do that. In addition, they hoped that no one would suspect that their life stories were so frightfully filthy that they would be moved to revert to such inventions. At this people went to bed, and I lay down with my Caspia beside a bay window that opened onto the palace courtyard.

After almost all lights had been extinguished in the rooms, we heard a lute in the courtyard. And because this instrument is lovely and very pleasant to hear at nighttime, I stood with Caspia at the window, and we were very surprised that the lutenist could play without gloves in this great cold. From this we judged he had to be so hot-blooded either by nature or from the love for women because finally he began to sing the following verses:

> You lips, I've kissed so oft, I send you greeting unfleeting,
> And welcome to you lights, who've torn my heart apart.
> You're welcome, all you flames!
> Within me play your games!

I wrote these verses quickly on my pad by the night light, but while I was doing that with Caspia's help, I forgot the second verse that came out much more nicely. And if it hadn't been so late at night, we doubtless would have let him come up because Caspia especially loved such love songs, of which she had a whole book full written in her own hand. But when we were ready to hear best, the singer ceased, and we didn't know who the fellow must have been because we had never before heard such a voice in the castle.

We again lay down in bed to devote what was left of the night to Morpheus and to look about a bit in the realm of dreams. But in the morning Caspia awoke me because she had heard someone knocking at the door. I opened the door in my nightwear, for I perceived it was my servant whom I had hired only the day before yesterday. And when he had come in, he took me to one side and begged me to forgive him for having disturbed my rest, he had to tell me something he had become aware of in the night.

"Last evening," he said, "when I had gone to bed in my room, the rope-walker arrived with a tall fellow and another who was carrying a lute and could play the same most beautifully. He marched up before Kunigunda's room, where a small girl was standing, who told him to go inside. I know the layout of this castle quite well since earlier and almost from childhood on I plied my trade as tailor here. Because I knew it had a chimney that goes into Kunigunda's room, I hurried up beneath the roof to listen to their conversation. From all appearances they had been talking for a while when I very quietly raised the latticed window that goes into the room. Then to my astonishment I heard the rope-walker tell how he was not such a base fellow such as she took him to be, but was of the nobility and had appeared at this place for no other reason than to make himself beloved among the ladies.

"'The letter,' he said, 'that Monsieur Ludwig sent for an entertainer came into my hands in the village and I surreptitiously opened it. And because in the past out of boredom I learned how to walk the rope, I had a desire to present myself as such and appear here.' To this Kunigunda replied that she was most pleased to hear that, and even if he weren't a nobleman, but the lowest peasant, she would still regard herself as blissful in loving him. To this end he was to appear in a long night robe before her window this evening at the same hour and simply throw a pebble at it so that she would admit him immediately and further demonstrate her affection."

At my window the tailor told me these things with great and unusual surprise. I then said that if he valued his life, he would say nothing of this to anyone and then tell me what else they did with one another. But the tailor knew of no further happenings; instead, he reported that because of the suspicions of his companions, she didn't want to detain him any longer. He said those were his musicians, of whom two or three customarily stayed at his castle. Now he had clothed them as entertainers, just as he himself had had to use such clothing in such a situation in order not to be recognized. And with that the rope-walker had departed, and when Kunigunda asked him his name, he replied he was called Caspar and that the biography he had given yesterday was a rotten lie. She shouldn't believe it; he had had to make one appropriate to his pretended station. Then Kunigunda had praised his delightful fiction and acknowledged that she had seen few people who could equal him. Thus he had left after they had again made certain arrangements that he would appear this evening before her bedroom window at the same time and in a night robe.

To tell the truth, the tailor's story was much nicer to me than if he had mended four pairs of trousers for me. I ordered him once again to keep quiet about the affair, and although my Caspia asked me a thousand times to tell her what the tailor had discussed with me so secretly, I didn't tell her at all and thus I avoided the great number of foolish women who, when they've heard a piece of news or some other secret, run straight out and tell not only their own women, but also all those they meet in the street. People complain that there's so little loyalty and honesty in the world, but what is more lamentable is that there's no longer a Papirius.[30] But one can't deny that silence has become less than durable, whereby great suffering is often caused. How do such useless things concern women? Many a man says: My wife's not a block of stone; she's got to know what's going on in the world too. I say: Indeed, your wife is not a block of stone, but she's also not the fellow to know of a matter that doesn't concern her. Rumor mills only ruin our morals, and if many a person hadn't heard a new bit of gossip, he wouldn't have been made a fool by it.

When the tailor was gone from the room, I had Monsieur Ludwig summoned to me, to whom I confided the whole comedy just as the tailor had told it to me. He almost tore the hair from his head in joy, for he proposed to play a prank on Caspar, the pretended rope-walker, such as never before. He resolved to appear in his night robe before Kunigunda's window that evening, and meanwhile I was to ply Caspar with drink so amply that he would have no opportunity to do his job. And after we had considered everything from front to back, from top to bottom, we parted and awaited the hour.

---

[30] Papirius Fabricius, Roman sage and teacher of Seneca.

126

Chapter Three. Ludwig Relates Wondrous Things. He Boards with a Tailor. How Things Went for the Lady Doctor with Her Bodice.

Our youth is simply knavery's buddy,
It drinks and swills when it should study.

Shortly before it was mentioned that the noble company decided to continue the story already begun. Accordingly, we assembled as agreed in the same room as this morning, and when everyone was settled in his place, Ludwig proceeded to finish his adventures as follows:

"Yesterday," he said, "without great ado I related how I had had a whorish adventure at my uncle's castle, following which I, filled with thoughts, had been led back to my father's estate. After a long sermon he gave me absolution with a good Spanish cane. Nevertheless, my mother interfered in almost all the blows so that not one in ten struck me, and at the time I was smart enough that no better medicine could be thought up for me than to show me the door. Therefore, I waited in a room next to the office until my father's anger had subsided, which usually didn't last all that long, and after a few minutes I emerged from the corner after having shaken the blows from my back like a wet dog does water. And although I felt nothing serious, I acted as though he had broken one of my ribs, something young people know how to do very well, especially in these times. Often after a small bump they raise as great and horrible a cry as though their head had separated from their body as happened with Apele from Gallen.

"I told my mother my heart hurt so much that she began to cry. 'My dearest child,' she said, 'your father kicked you in the side; maybe he ruptured your spleen.' At that she poured out a medicine costing half a Taler, and the whole of me wasn't worth eight Groschen. I had to go to bed quickly, and so that the cold wouldn't shock me, she warmed it for me with a hot water bottle and using all her strength lifted me into it, where I was supposed to sweat a little. She sat before my bed with a flyswatter and cried two handkerchiefs so full of tears that one could have wrung water from them. But I would have liked to laugh secretly beneath the blanket, for I needed only powder and paper to make a new rocket and even could have set our castle on fire.

"After this, my father sought ways and means of having me boarded elsewhere and sent me to a horse trainer, where I was supposed to learn the noble art of equitation. The latter had assembled some eighteen noble youths and roomed them in a separate house, where I again arranged all sorts of discord and pranks. It wasn't enough for me to secretly cut off my comrades' hair while they were sleeping; rather, I ended up cropping the tails of the horses in their stalls and I placed scorpions under their saddles that later stung the horses that swelled greatly and even fell over. For such my father was served with a law suit, and the court's decision obliged him to pay the trainer a hundred Ducats within a year and a day. My father avoided legal wrangling just as the Devil does the Cross; consequently, he didn't contest the sum though some lawyers turned up at his place who said they could argue the matter so that he wouldn't be obliged to pay a Pfennig. But because he had enough experience of the lovely cases of such people or had heard others talk about them, he didn't listen to them; rather, he paid the money before a month had passed. But after his death I found it withdrawn from his will and with great annoyance had to watch it deducted from me as with the sexton's burned-down gable, for which alone forty-two Taler were deducted.

"My own arrogance plunged me into such damages, and my father was again compelled to move me away from the trainer and thus he sent me to a Latin school and told me that if I didn't behave, I would have to become a cobbler without compensation. He gave me a splendid farewell party, at which quite many of my friends were present whom he had perhaps invited only so that they would give me a good warning. I departed with it at this time, after my mother had surreptitiously put into my pocket twelve Reichstaler in a handkerchief.

"I then boarded with a tailor who had worked at our castle when he was a young bachelor. Therefore, my father put me under his authority. But the good tailor would have needed a preceptor himself who would have taught and showed him how to work more diligently and not to drink so much beer so often. This master craftsman showed me more respect than I had previously experienced. He called me 'Young Sir' and gave me my own house key so that I could enter the house whenever and however I liked. From the beginning this gave me the opportunity to have a free hand, and it's quite certain that I was never more dissolute than at this school. The money with which I was supposed to buy my books I drank up in brandy with my fellow pupils, and when I came home blind drunk, the tailor thought I was sick and because he had been ordered to spend money on me for which he would be repaid, he quickly sent to the apothecary and had all sorts of purgatives fetched so that I might preserve my health.

"Finally my father became aware of his mistake and sent me the bound books instead of money, but I was much more clever, for I sold these books for a pittance with which I gambled at cards or dice, which I picked up much more often than a quill. Whenever I could steal a book from someone, I surreptitiously put it in my fly at school and later sold it to a second-hand dealer and drank up the change for as well and as long as it lasted. Surely not one among my fellow pupils can say of me that for as long as I was in the school I paid attention to the instruction or knew my lessons. Because of this, the preceptor always had me kneel behind the stove until I could recite it. But finally I grew too clever for him, for I had my knees painted brown, blue, and red, and I acted as though I had shingles on my legs, whereby I was freed of the punishment and nonetheless did not learn what he had assigned me.

"Whenever an *examen scholasticum* occurred, I would always give two Groschen to another who was regarded as the best in the class, for which he had to make my argument, carmen, oration, chriam, or things like that for me. I must admit that those who read them were often astonished at my erudition. And because my father usually came to the city at that time and attended the examination, it pleased him greatly when he heard me praised by others and he probably tipped the preceptor a couple of Ducats. My mother sent him fifty pounds of flax along with some Westphalian hams. Sometimes she presented him cheese, butter, and linen, so he didn't complain about me. And although he noted it to himself and knew well what would be the best way of helping me, he nevertheless spared me only because of the presents and his fear of offending my parents by punishing me.

"From this evil arose countless others through which I was revitalized in pursuing my blindness. And because idleness is a root of great sins, I fell from one vice into the next until I finally didn't go to school at all, but usually hung out among dissolute people in places of prostitution. But if I want to speak truthfully, there I learned much more than in school, for I learned to flee many vices from their own despicableness and was pointed to a better path by just that which had lead me to them earlier.

"Behold, such fruit and such grain hide beneath a rotting peel, and it is certain that no matter what words are used, no one can describe a vice as it reveals itself in the flesh, and thus its vileness greatly affects the spirit of him who can strip the mask from his emotions and follow virtue. If a person is burned, he avoids the fire all the more, and from this time on there has been no vice I hated and shunned more than whoring, because it is the greatest enemy of all those who seek to be happy of spirit.

"There is no one who studied with me who won't know that I was always ready to have a drink. Therefore I even carried a special bottle in my knapsack and whenever I was thirsty, I would go under the table as though I were looking for blotting-sand, but I did it only so that I could have a good pull on the bottle. Occasionally I let my fellow pupils have a drink and instead of preparing our assignments, we got tight so that we staggered back and forth in school and scattered our writing equipment together with our books across the table.

"I treated the tailor in a pitiable manner. I created all sorts of trouble in the house and when I had to go in the night, I performed on a large stolen rag and threw it out the window. Oh, it was nothing new or unusual when I wiped my bottom on his clothes he had hanging in his room, for I had good and convenient opportunity to do so by means of a window from my chamber into his room.

"Once a lady doctor sent a bodice to him that he had to break his neck to fit because she was supposed to go to a baptism the following day. The master worked as fast as he could and because it was to be taken in only an inch or so, it was ready in the evening. I paid close attention to the spot where he placed the lining for the doctor, and in the night I got up and wiped myself as thoroughly as perhaps the child had been, to whom the doctor would go tomorrow. But I did it only on the inside and, to be sure, on the brown taffeta that lined the bodice entirely, choosing there so that one could tell all the less by the color. The next morning her clerk came to pick it up, and because the tailor packed it hastily, he failed to look at the interior. It was very cold, the clerk hastened off with it under his coat, and the doctor accepted it as it was because she had to buy some armbands that she wanted to wear at the baptism today.

"When the specified hour appeared, she got dressed and the supplicant told her a second time that the other ladies were already assembled in the mother's room and were only waiting for her, then they would bring in the food and dine. The doctor hurried as fast as she could, and because the maids had no mirror in the room, she whipped the one maid out here, the other out there. Now her chair wasn't properly positioned, now her hairpins weren't sitting right, and she could curse so frightfully about something trivial that her husband was frightened; and because she would accept no reproach from him, he had to leave the room. After that she called the maids back and put on the bodice that had been so handsomely perfumed the preceding night. When she now walked down the street in her finery and accompanied by a maid, she imagined how much more brightly she shone than Arabian gold, while within she was lined with nothing but filth. Sheer fantasy, *o vanitatum vanitas!*

"The company rejoiced at her presence, except a few women who were secretly envious of her because of precedence or other matters. The room was heated rather warmly and thus the surprise in the doctor's bodice began to stink frightfully, and no matter how many scented candles they set on the stove, it did no good and the odor grew ever more abominable. They noticed it was coming from the doctor, but no one dared tell her. She noticed it herself and thought at first she had had an accident in her slip and from shame could scarcely eat a bite. Some held their noses, others rubbed balsam on their hands or the sleeves of their jackets because on the latter according to newest claims it was supposed to smell for a whole six months. Those who had no balsam burned the hairs off their hands, but the doctor didn't know what to say or do. Finally she pretended to be having an attack of dizziness and in such manner came home, where she looked now at her shoes, now at her slip, but she could find no sign to indicate she had stepped in something or carelessly let one fly. Finally, when she removed the bodice, the source appeared in all its glory and her maids had as much of it to smell as had all the other guests. Then they knew what had happened, and it wouldn't have taken much for her to have the tailor locked up if only she hadn't been afraid that her disgrace would become known to the whole city and the story might subsequently be sung in the public square."

Chapter Four. Four Students Prepare a Snack at the Tailor's.

Now Luck is fickle, quiet, and sly;
The sow may eat what you do fry.

"When the lady doctor has thus been shamed, I turned to all sorts of heedless pranks, and if someone badgered and pinched my fellow students from that time, they would have to truly acknowledge and admit that there was no one in the whole school then who was superior to me in deviltry.

"Although I had pursued all sorts of mischief in the tailor's quarters, on the other hand I brought him all sorts of gain. He complained quite often about people who dropped into his room unannounced like coarse and rude peasants, and he asked here and there for advice that no one could give him except my quick invention. I told him to remove the doorknob, and consequently all those having business to do in the room had to knock.

"Once while when he was in church, his wife surreptitiously fried a sausage because she thought she was quite alone. While she was preparing it, someone rang the bell with whom she had to talk for a good while downstairs in the house. I stealthily crept out of my chamber and hurled the sausage into the fire so that it dried out completely and burned up. When she put away a roast in her meat box, I opened the lock with a passkey, cut the best meat off the leg, and then gnawed the leg. To prove my innocence, I shut the cat in and it had to have eaten the roast, no matter how little of it she had gotten to eat. This was, to be sure, of no great profit to the tailor, my landlord, but I did direct a lot of work to him from the pupils, from whom he cajoled a couple of Groschen here and there, which we drank up in red brandy in the evening.

"Once the pupils ordered a roasted suckling pig through me. There were four of us, and because they were very scarce and expensive then and occasionally impossible to get, we gave the man six Groschen and intended to consume our meal in my quarters because the others were not so well situated. We also ordered salad and carp. But so that the tailor would have to pay for the meal, I took a handkerchief, dipped it in a saffron sauce and brown medicines, from which it naturally appeared as if someone had treated it as I had the doctor's bodice. Without being observed I stuck it in the belly of the roast pig, and at the table I pretended it was the rag with which we had bound the maid's scratched leg and cursed the tailor and his wife beyond compare, from which I so revolted my messmates that one vomited behind the bench, another behind the stove.

"In such a fashion I came off with the roasted pig *salvo* and *franco*, and the tailor, with whom I discussed it in full detail, knew how to play his part in the comedy so well that it surprised even me. He said that he was heartily sorry and that it was not he, but the maid, the damned gallows whore, who was responsible and had already provided him with several blunders and pranks of the sort. Once her bad and swollen leg was well and healed, he would chase her to the Devil and the Devil's mother, and he had already whipped her for them like some dancing bear. The students were not to regret their money, the two carp were already boiled to a nice blue; with them they should be compensated somewhat. In the future on such occasions he would be in the kitchen himself and keep things in good order so that everything would take place properly and appropriately. My comrades liked this speech and because I did everything to placate them, they finally were satisfied. But they wished many thousands of devils on the maid's back because through her abominable foot rag they had lost an exquisite roasted pig, the likes of which scarcely a single pupil has ever eaten.

"One of them was the son of a wine house owner, and because at home he occasionally had to run down to the cellar, he stole not a little money from his parents by using his fellow students to send wine to various places where we later drank it up. This time it was no different, for on the preceding day we summoned the tailor's wife at a time when he was home. Pretending not to know her, he gave her a good twelve liters from the best barrel and he told his parents that the tailor's wife had paid him a Groschen too much, with which his mother was well pleased because she was among the number who apparently show no hesitation in doing wrong to a neighbor.

"He could do this all the more safely because the cash box for the wine money was in the cellar, and no one could see whether he had thrown anything into it. With such an arrangement, he was of great use to us, for we didn't have a lot of spare change, and had the preceptors known that, they would have sent us packing. But nonetheless we ate our fish and the salad right out of the bowl. We also had the heart to drink to the health of the rector's daughter, who got along splendidly with the pupils and some times kept her father away from the school when we told her there was going to be trouble. The rector also had a son who was in our class. That boy was a rascal, for he stole from his father's study all the arguments we were to work out the next day, whereby we had the opportunity to work them out ahead of time so we went ice skating while the others were sitting there, racking their brains.

132

"Earlier I said something about my lover, how I, namely, pursued the ladies even then and in places for which youth should properly have revulsion. But because I didn't know what I was doing in seeking the sweetest sugar where the strongest poison lay hidden, it bothered me not at all that thus I was learning nothing. These courtings cost me a lot of money, for the poorer the girls were with whom I tended to associate, the more I had to buy for them and provide for their nasty bodies.

"Ha, I've regretted a thousand times having behaved so commonly in my youth with the shameless sluts, and the best of it all is that about five weeks ago an old and hunchbacked beggar woman came up to me in the street and said, 'Herr Ludwig! Herr Ludwig!' I looked at the woman askance and thought, what's wrong with her, and she continued, 'Don't you remember the fair Catharina at all anymore? Have you forgotten her completely? Do you remember how many times you swore an oath to her only so that she should believe you loved her before all others?' I must admit I was completely shocked by the words of this dreadful woman, for I could still recall that at the named school I spooned with a maid whom I called my fair Catharina. Involuntarily I had to remember I had often sworn to her that I loved and treasured her far more highly than the whole world with all its kingdoms, and thus I said to her, 'Yes, I know of that, and how have things been going with my fair Catharina?' 'Oh, Herr Ludwig,' she said, 'take a good look at me, I am she and none other than the one you so often caressed and kissed.'

"The Devil, I thought to myself. What have you done? 'Are you that Catharina?' — 'Yes,' she said, 'it's me.' — 'Get out of my sight,' I answered her, 'or I'll kick you so that you go tumbling over that hill over there, you devilish, disgraceful whore! You misled me in my youth to all sorts of uncleanliness and induced me to neglect my future happiness in my studies.' — 'Oh, Herr Ludwig,' she said, 'In those days you were already so smart that you knew what was good for you. Didn't I beg you hundreds of times to go back to school, your presippers would be angry and all sorts of things like that? But did you do it or did you leave me in peace? Oh, no indeed. The more I protested, the more you pursued me, and at night I couldn't fetch beer or other things home without having you creep in secretly after me. You didn't skip a single opportunity to trick me, and now you regret having gone around with me? Oh, the Devil should have taken you before I ever laid eyes on you, for you are the cause of my complete ruination. Give me a Kreuzer so that I can go on my beggar's way.'

"You can imagine how heartily ashamed I was and to get her out of my sight, I gave her a Groschen, and if I hadn't been in a public street, I would have liked to slap myself, I was so greatly annoyed with myself at having acted so foolishly and attached myself to this witch. Indeed, about six days after that I was told she had been taken in by the officials for witchcraft and that recently she was burned.

"If time permitted, I could cite other examples of what great misfortune and what great vices I fell into in this manner. But I'm certain that you're already aware of what tends to happen in such situations, about which a person would like to wring his hands.

"Then I was attacked by a major and severe illness, and this was actually the cloak for the laziness I was so devoted to the whole time at school. After my recovery and return to the castle, I said that the illness had so robbed me of my memory that I had forgotten everything I had learned so diligently up to that time. I said that after taking to my bed, my books had disappeared and in such a manner I convinced my father that the matter could have been no other way. During the illness I had numerous fantasies and for more than six weeks I talked deliriously because there appeared to me the most fantastic things that could happen under the sun. Because I here still have some time and the opportunity, I want to tell for certain reasons how I actually felt during this illness and how the clever images from my imagination appeared."

Chapter Five. Ludwig's Strange Illness, His Visions, Letters and the Like.

Whoever lets his wits go slack
Will often think that white is black.

"At first it seemed to me that I saw some wagons filled with numbers and hairpins traveling to the fair in Frankfurt, where they intended to walk the tightrope. After that a map wearing a coat came up and presented itself as a shoehorn. Soon afterwards I sat on a birdcage and rode on it over hill and dale, often a good thousand miles in one leap. It seemed natural to me that I had to fetch a pair of freshly baked rolls for my preceptor from Tierra del Fuego. Soon there came four hundred pairs of knitted, torn, and ragged stockings; I mended them with my writing things and as compensation they honored me with an old peruke. I also saw people flying around in the air and dried cod being fished from the ground. I tore my grammar book into a thousand small pieces and then I had the snippets grilled on a spit and ate them as feathers from a turkey. Soon a fireplace fork strung with strings appeared before my bed and I made music with it for longer than four hours in a row. The screws were made from doves' wings and the seat from a beer mug, from which you can conclude what foolish things appeared to me in my illness and at which I still must laugh heartily down to this day.

"Often it seemed to me I was crawling into a flea, and within the flea were sitting moors and Egyptians, and when I was afraid of them and tried to crawl out the back, the flea remained hanging onto my neck and seemed natural to me as though it were a hand basin for washing myself. I often took the stove that heated my room to be a tree from which sausages were growing, and whenever I pulled one down, it turned into a penknife. Often it seemed a whole regiment of skulls were coming into my bed, and it seemed to me that someone was following them, chasing them away from me with a flyswatter. The lady who attended me often said that in all her life she had never heard anyone speak as oddly as I did. Now I asked her who had cut the nose off her fur, now how many weeks a person would have to travel to reach a slipper. Occasionally it seemed to me as though a blacksmith were taking me across the highest mountains on his anvil as if on a sled, and when we were sledding around in the sky, then it seemed to me as though I were sitting on the ocean. Instead of water I saw nothing but duckbills and the islands consisted of nothing but ladies' gloves. The ships seemed to be cast from window lead, and in them there was organ playing you wouldn't believe. I can't find adequate words to tell how I fell and rode into frightful fissures of the world.

"Once it seemed to me as though someone hung a hundred millstones to my feet, with which I traveled in a trice through the earth in a drawer and came into a region where people were making nothing but sword belts. Amid everything nothing seemed more delightful to me than when I thought I saw two oak trees dueling with one another with bagpipes at a fencing exhibition. All those who were watching the fight were later changed into pigs and ate the acorns that the two had knocked off from each other with their wood. It was not unusual for me to jump out of bed and smash the windows because they appeared to me to be crickets flying around that wanted to prick me.

"Often it seemed to me to be raining a mixture of nightcaps and horse shoes, but when they hit the ground, they turned into egg shells. The people who visited me I took to be knapsacks, feather dusters, cows' heads, hazelnuts, quills, stool legs, and cows' tails, so badly had my own senses deceived me. During my illness I was beheaded more than thirty times with a fox tail and broken on the wheel, and I often thought an old woman was giving me a bastinado with her washboard. I could recognize no food by its smell or appearance, but when I was eating soup, it seemed to me as though I were eating hemp and wood shavings, and I took the spoon to be a bathrobe. Occasionally I came to and cried about myself because the longer it lasted, the worse I was getting.

"When things had become quite bad for me and my illness, the wife of the preceptor of my class visited me, the one to whom my mother had given so much flax. She asked me about my condition, for she didn't yet know about the great delirium that had seized me. And because I regarded her in my mind as fire tongs, I said to her, 'Oh, you rusted out bolt of thunder, the Devil has led you before my magnificence, but who bade you speak? Get out of my sight or I'll cut off your head the first ear I can find. Hey, brothers, throw these damned fire tongs into the stove. Oh, you nasty fire tongs, how the soles of my feet hurt! If I only now had a clock so that I could see what day of the week it was. Ha, ha, ha! Just look at how the oranges are tumbling down one after the other! Stand aside, you with the handbasket, go away, go away, fire tongs, go away! All my life I've heard that there's no misfortune in being a soldier, take a look, and what's the turner doing? Good night! Many thanks!'

"My nurse later told me these words and fantasies, and I wrote them down on my tablet as a souvenir when I was again able to use my mind and also the quill. This was something I hadn't completely lacked in my illness, for I wrote a letter to my father, saying that if he didn't want to have me made well, I would accuse him before the Turkish emperor and things of the like. The letter ran thus:

> Father, father, father, I'm writing to you, you father, father, father! I am sick, make me well, or I will accuse you before the *ottomanus ottomani ottomano ottommanansis*, do you hear? I will accuse, *accusare*, accuse you. Now I'm going to take a walk in the field and decorate my royal throne with nut shells, *ornare, ornavisti*. Greetings.
>
> Your devoted *spiritus, spiritus, spiritus, habes habes adieu.*

"Then I sent many other letters not only home but also to other places. I wrote especially to the apothecary in our town, for I regarded him as a cousin and also as a Turk because I imagined completely that I was the King of Peru. This was that letter:

> Mightiest, most powerful, and learned in the arts *patruelismus habet in genitivo patruelismi, participii casus*!
> With this I indicate to you that I have become a king. You already know where, therefore I'm having my trousers mended and cramming my crown into the large mortar, purging it well and good, well and good, well and good. Tell your sister she's going to marry me or I won't become king. Then I'll lay siege to Constantinople and tear the coat off the King of Persia's ass. My slippers are getting quite worn out, you have to get me servants and order drums in which we'll sail to Africa and there collect money from the peasants.
> We'll peddle every tobacco pipe as a telescope and the King of Greece must be our comedian. Then we'll really begin to dance and give the people pills from which they'll have to take to their beds. The innkeeper at the Red Horse will also travel with us, I already have ordered eight thousand wagons of fuses and powder, that's all got to come along.

I'll make up for the wounds I received in Arabia when I tread on the helmet of Alexander the Great. Your sister is much too beautiful, she's got to come along, she's got to come along, she's got to come along. We've sent the flags ahead, now come your boxes of mithridate, after them the snuff and fruit syrups, we'll give them to the peasants who show us the way and betray the enemy. Our troops are already on the ships, see where you get enough trumpeters, three have already died. Friedrich is not yet the kaiser in Japan; otherwise, he would have sent me three regiments. My preceptor at school is giving me four squadrons of foot soldiers. They've got to be used for storming. Arm yourself quickly, I'm ready to move out as soon as I finish breakfast. If you don't show up on time, I'll ride away so that you'll see dust flying. Meanwhile goodbye and send me an aquavit. My Lord Expediter of Mithridate Boxes, I am

> Your most subservient ruler in Peru,
> Jeremias Sebastian Ludwig,
> King in Antissenhofen.

"After my recovery these letters were again read to me, and I was ashamed of my own fantasies because I was told they had been sent around among great and respectable people who were having blood drawn and who were no little amused by them. For it is true that at that time I did indeed feel I was a great and powerful king over twelve thousand men with whom I wanted to lay siege to Constantinople. I thought the curtains were my battle standards and my chamber pot the kettle drum.

"Whenever the nurse came with her bowl of soup, I took her to be a Turkish dignitary who was declaring war on me on behalf of his emperor. My fellow pupils seemed to me to be great squadrons of foot soldiers who perhaps had been sitting around a rather long time in their shirts and pants, and when they brought me greetings from the preceptor, I thought that through them the preceptor was offering me more troops for my impending war. From this it is easy to conclude how great the delusion was that filled me then."

Chapter Six. The Irishman Glosses the Story.

> *The suffering that makes us sad*
> *Can make some other person glad.*

Until now Fräulein Anna had listened to Ludwig's talk with special pleasure and because she wanted to grant him a rest, she addressed the Irishman, saying he should give voice to his well-founded opinion of Ludwig's new story and thereby give Monsieur Ludwig some space to think of that which would follow. To this the Irishman gave a bow and began by saying that he would do so with the permission of the company and at their bidding. Nevertheless, they might forgive him as well as Monsieur Ludwig if he gave it a mixed review.

"Yesterday," he said, "Lady Pockau's judgment of Monsieur Ludwig's story was not bad, and I wish that I could have a better opinion of the continuation of his life story if it weren't for the obvious arrogance of Monsieur Ludwig's conduct at school as was profusely described. First, his father was no slight cause of his evil life, for what does the tailor care about playing the overseer? Such people have to be more concerned about their trade than the welfare of the pupils, and even if they were to bear such responsibility, they are too insignificant to serve as a private tutor for such a creature. Thus, no small mistake was made there.

"Second, the tailor was not a good landlord at all in entrusting a house key to Monsieur Ludwig, for where there's license, the vices are surely not far away, and whoever can pursue them unimpeded is not easily brought back to a proper path. From his story one can also see how children often even in early childhood are misled and spoiled by their mothers and that from such cosseting there appears in the following years a not small but quite noticeable harm. For if children have no fear in their youth, it's clear they'll disregard it when grown up, and thus do some parents create an unending torment for themselves.

"We've also seen well enough what misfortune teachers create among young people when, in anticipation of presents, they spare those in whose names they receive the gifts. Once I also had a preceptor, but the more some parents gave him gifts, the severer he was with that pupil and usually gave him one more slap than he did another who had given him nothing. In such a manner he produced hardworking boys, because no one had reason to hope for his complicity.

"But, regrettably, nowadays there are such greedy and avaricious people. If one doesn't go to them continually with deep pockets and present them bribes almost hourly, they abandon the best part of their effort, they turn their backs on the boys, and 'If they learn something, that's good; if they don't learn anything, that's okay, too.' But their own consciences will preach to them about the grave responsibility they are assuming. Ludwig went on to tell of how the pupils behave in school, which is more than to be pitied, and he surfeited us with how at that time he already began to squire the girls, which, however, he now rues. From this we have to note the frightful blindness of youth with which they besmirch the eyes of reason and often run after something they subsequently regret even with tears.

"He professes that through the detestableness of vice he arrived at self-improvement and understanding of the matter, but what good does it do a person if he makes his house burn down so that he might learn how to put out the fire? Truly, the damage considerably exceeds the gain, and in no way can I see what sort of an advantage is supposed to be hidden in it. However, it occurs frequently that those who associated with all sorts of uncleanliness in their youth are useless for serious matters in their adulthood. Much persuasion will not move them to wed because they are already too deeply rooted in their whoring ways. From this comes their contempt for women, the cold-bloodedness of their emotions, and whatever they do is done solely to deceive people.

"He tells a coarse and ugly story about the lady doctor, and I don't know whether I should find it good or bad. But to please Monsieur Ludwig I shall act as a partisan and say that he has done nothing worthy of punishment. It is known that the devil of pride has occupied almost the whole world and especially women, from which quite a bit of harm arises, especially in Germany. For there each and every bird of prey wants to wear a bodice, gauze bonnets, armbands, roses, necklaces, and no one is responsible for this other than the wide-eyed ladies who don't restrain them, but help to encourage them. Many a maiden who is now attending a countess, baroness, or other lady of nobility wants right away to be general over all the infantry regiments. They think a man should fall on his knees and adore them with bared heads, but afterwards they lie in wait night and day for someone to come and marry them. If it happens, then, whoosh, they've married a stable hand or gotten a cobbler. That's how their great splendor ends up. They know nothing about keeping house, but it is certain the only thing they do know is how to parade their arrogance. Then they carry embroidered skirts on their bodies but not a Taler in their purses. They wear gauze bonnets on the heads and few brains within them, and you may believe assuredly that the greater the decoration is on the outside of women, the less intelligence there is in them, *omnia enim sua ornamenta habent exterius*: They have their decoration only on the outside. They are often like the snails that carry their worldly possessions and house and home with them. They are like the philosopher Plato, who said: *omnium mea mecum porto*: All that I have I carry with me. For this reason one must look out for such pompous people and not fall into their traps, and Monsieur Ludwig behaved right in repaying the doctor so delicately and nobly.

"Now some people think if she's only a doctor, the whole business is all right. But there's more to the dance than a new pair of shoes, and this is about the greatest snare of the Devil in which he usually traps the arrogant, namely, the mania for titles. This is a plague that attacks and ruins almost all men. I myself detect within me that I would like to be more than I am. But the doctor and her bodice made it sufficiently clear how a person can be disgraced in a moment, no matter how hard a person strives for vain honor.

"Monsieur Ludwig also incidentally noted how nicely his fellow pupil could spirit wine out of the cellar, from which we can learn how often parents are taken advantage of and secretly cheated by their children. The cause of this is, first, their lazy and coddling discipline, second, their neglect in supervision, and, third, the poor arrangement with their money. For what business does the cash box have in the cellar?

139

Opportunity makes the thief. And, fourth, the parents are not a little responsible for their misfortune for not punishing the children for their deceptions. Instead, from fear of their becoming known thereby and suspect to other people, they keep it secret unto themselves and in addition give the children money so that they won't tell they stole something. Other parents give their children much too free a rein. Indeed, I know fathers who gambled with their sons when these were still young shits and often argued with them concerning their losses. Then the order is 'Father, lay on!' which sounds beautiful to the ears of a sensible man. Whoever lets his children behave as they wish, must later see them in misfortune which he doesn't want, and there are many examples of children who didn't want to let themselves be trained by their father and subsequently had to let themselves be punished by the hangman.

"From the description of his illness we can observe how strangely the imagination tends to play within the human being, something I could contribute quite a bit to if I weren't hastening to wind up. We have examples where learned people have fallen into the greatest delusions and madness that attacked them for some time. But with Ludwig the fantasies were all the more entertaining, the more amusing he is by nature than other people, for his makeup is of a special kind and far removed from that of many thousands of others. Thus we can believe his visions and fantasies are all the rarer and more unusual, the more uncommon his nature is.

"I also noted that respected people are still amused by letters he composed in his illness. Thus nothing in this world is so miserable and pitiable that certain people won't laugh at it, although they would have all the more reason to regret heartily the state of such a person and fear that they would fare worse, for we are all not yet outside the pale and commonly fall into the errors we have made fun of in others."

Chapter Seven. Ludwig Goes On to Tell What He Did at the University.

> *If everyone in school must stay,*
> *Then who will herd the swine each day?*

"The Irish gentleman's opinion of the matter isn't bad," said Monsieur Ludwig, "although he explained through certain circumstances the nastiness that tended to arise from the story I told. He makes his principal point when he regards the necessity for training children as the best means for being able to improve the world, and thus he appropriately reproaches that license that better serves for ruination than self-improvement. But in this point, as in all matters, it is well to take a middle path, for just as it is a great evil to allow youth free rein, it is also a great tyranny to bind them with too harsh and severe restraints. I'm of the opinion that one should not treat them all too harshly like Otto Hahn, who lived twenty-five miles south of Linz,[31] was accustomed to doing, who found all his pleasure and joy in whipping the children in his charge and in teaching them nothing or very little. For through such fantastic behavior, the youth become afraid to do everything; they are scared out of much good progress, and this fright is a roadblock on the path that leads to the pleasant enjoyment of the arts. Because of a teacher's excessive severity, many a youth throws his book behind the door and prefers to work in the fields rather than at school simply because he's afraid of being whipped continually like a dog, from which many a talent is ruined and destroyed. *Arcus nimium intensus frangitur:* a bow drawn ever tighter will finally snap. And thus among all conditions I regard school as the most artificial, because among a thousand scarcely two are to be found that are proper and above reproach.

"After surviving my severe illness, I was hustled off to a university, and because the place was some hundred and twenty-five miles from my home, I must admit the change of air as well as the unfamiliar region of the place altered and transformed my whole horizon. Winter was gradually coming on, and for this reason snow had closed the gardens and other happy places in which I otherwise would have spent most of my time. Lacking the same, I had to sit down with my book beside the warm stove in my quarters and I openly admit that in this fashion I did more that winter than in all of my prior life.

"Satirical writings and other novels enlightened me most in all matters, and I regarded them as more practical and necessary for human life than logic and all the other abstract courses, since I saw that the scholars were much less in agreement than the satirists who, to a man, found no vice good and attacked the one like the other and, on the other hand, granted balanced praise to the virtues. At the university I freed myself of my former lifestyle. But, to tell the truth, I nonetheless wanted to be back at the earlier school again; and I think it's not at all different with all new students since either the familiarity of the old or the unfamiliarity of their new company is responsible and the cause for this.

"I read through as many German texts as it was possible to get: *Hercules* and *Herculiscum* that a cleric named Bucholtz in Braunschweig is said to have written. *Arcadia, Philander von Sittenwald,* the *Alamodische Hobel-Bank,* Barclai's *Argenis,* the *Rivalry,* all the works of the ingenious Harsdörffer, *Francion, Aramena, Aerumöna,* most of the writings of Erasmus Franciscus, *Onogambo. Clelia, Simplicissimus* in which the entire German or Thirty Years' War is described, *Stratonica, Pastor Fido,* all the parts of *Amadis, Lisimene and Pamilie, Jan Peru, First and Second Parts,* Schweiger's travel description and many more like it, the works of the splendid Jesuit Massenius, those of Baldi, the imagina-

---

[31] The site of Cloister Lambach, where Beer was a pupil and had a teacher by this name.

tive Drexelius, and Bone along with countless small tracts concerning political and theological matters, and in part also from medical books, especially the highly praised and famous Pardus.

"In a word: If I were to cite all the works I read, this day alone would not suffice. But I acknowledge that from them I obtained a better loquacity than I had from twelve months of my professor lecturing me about the structure of an oration. For I found in my readings all sorts of allusions to kings, to emperors, to princes, and to other, ordinary people. I also saw, almost as in a theater, how the world goes around and found it in fact no different from the way books described it. From this I became halfway knowledgeable and I encountered problems I could quickly solve, where others had to carefully grope their way through. And I'll readily take an oath I wouldn't have acquired such cleverness in the classroom.

"Abstract studies aren't suited for me, and now it's far more profitable for me to know how and when one plows the field, sows grain, mows the hay, shakes down the apples, feeds the pigs, delivers calves, cuts wood, runs the household, and does similar useful things as if I were a great scholar. And my barns are much more splendidly filled with grain than with books. Thereby I live much more contentedly in the freedom I've regarded so highly since my youth and I don't want to subject myself ever to the opinions of a philosopher. In all my days I've not learned how to prepare a speech, but I'd gladly appear *ex tempore* with a scholar and perhaps produce more substance than the latter did words. For when I hear scholars speaking of agriculture, they open with an abstract beginning, they start looking for digressions, and, under the pretense of scholarship, use a heap of jargon. They do this only to give themselves time to think and do it so prettily that if someone listened to them for a quarter of an hour, he still wouldn't know what they had said. But I proceed plainly, I grab the subject by the throat, go directly to the point, and say more in a quarter of an hour than they do in eighteen weeks. I've even seen when learned people want to speak about agriculture, they summon peasants and ask them about everything beforehand. Afterwards they boast and are vain about their knowledge of that which in fact they don't practice, and thus they value appearance more than substance. But I don't think like that. For I farm with my peasants, help them sow, plant, graze, cut oats, bring in rye and wheat, thresh, tie and untie sheathes, figure out tithes, arrange for mowers and take them home.

"I pay strict attention to excise taxes, inheritance taxes, property taxes, government taxes, poll taxes, and special taxes so that no one pays too much or too little. I know about all their levies, surtaxes, duties, tolls, and other expenses. I'm familiar with their service for pay, service on demand, service to the church, official service, compulsory service, involuntary service, and emergency service. I know about their quarter-acres, half-acres, whole sections, and half-sections, how long they are and how many rods they measure and what they yield in grain. I know the proper time for planting early rye, late rye, oats, millet, and wheat. I can keep the hops growing very high. I know my way around in hoarfrost, heavy fog, poisonous dew, morning dew, evening dew, St. George's dew, St. Vitus's rain and similar annual occurrences.

"I also know how to plant trees, to graft shoots, and how to protect them and the vegetables from worms. I know how to defend and girdle fruit tree trunks quite nicely with a mixture of wax, cow manure, and dough. Moreover, I'm experienced in animal husbandry. I likewise know horses whether they're kicking, skittish, bucking, or foundered and I don't need to mention fattening cattle and other animals such as chickens, pigeons, ducks, pheasants, turkeys, and the like. And all this benefits my household much more than if I had totally snapped up all of Aristotle's teachings like the bacon from the cabbage.

"Oh, there's nothing foolish about farming; it calls for diligence and much more of it than does philosophy. People regard peasants as simple just because they don't bow and scrape like today's world beaters, but in their profession they are just as much doctors as we are in our sciences. For if the peasant didn't farm, the doctor would get little to eat at his school; therefore, the peasant is to be regarded and esteemed as a *principium* and *causa sine qua non*. We nobles call someone a peasant who may have bad manners or say something crude. But, gentlemen, gentlemen, if some of us were good peasants, there wouldn't be so many bad nobles. Although we think peasants are coarse, they also think of us as crude people, and I'll swear that in many vices we win out over them. And thus I don't know which of the two should be regarded as the better.

"I've talked about all this only so that you can see with what a prize I departed from the house of good learning, namely, the university. Four years later I returned home and now it's been eight years since, following the death of my parents, I married this most exquisite, most powerful, and most gracious mademoiselle."

"It seems to me," his wife responded, "your earlier illness is returning." But Fräulein Anna praised the ending of his story most highly, for she felt that a good householder would not only keep his world in prosperity, but increase its productivity each day. Her father in his time had complained greatly about formal argumentation fashionable then, and she herself would prefer to marry a man who understood farming rather than the law.

"Ha, ha," said Monsieur Ludwig, "I already noticed you'd like to have someone who understood plowing." At that people laughed at Fräulein Anna, and it was just time to go to the midday meal.

143

Chapter Eight. Some Ladies Tell Their Life Stories.

The ladies surely love to chatter,
But they'll grow still if such does matter.

Monsieur Ludwig had told his cook this morning to prepare a new entertainment because they were going to rest a little from telling their stories. In addition, the ladies excused themselves with protests and solemn assurances that they had nothing to relate that wasn't already and sufficiently known. Everyone knew that as women they seldom came among people and thus one could easily understand what heroic stories had occurred in their lives. However, if the cavaliers desired, they acknowledged their obligation and were ready to relate a story they had read, but it would be impossible for them to do anything more.

Monsieur Ludwig and all of us were, to be sure, not satisfied with this excuse. And the Irishman announced that their words were not immediately credible and that, for another thing, when women were in some secret nook, stranger and more notable things tended to happen than to a traveler who has seen half the world. They should stick to the decision they had agreed on. When the ladies saw it could be no other way, they were content so that no one would have cause to say they were too mean to tell what had happened to them in their lives. "Yes, indeed," said Monsieur Ludwig, "you're being very clever in doing this; otherwise we would draw a pretty picture of your lives and imagine things such as no longer can happen to you." With that they sat down at the table, and the cook's clowning was put off until next morning because the women were determined to return after the meal to the former room and begin their adventures.

Words can't describe how eager the entire party was to hear these stories. For this reason they dined twice as swiftly as they would have otherwise, and Monsieur Ludwig was quite eager to play a splendid joke on the rope-walker. Accordingly, they went quickly to the dance hall, and when some brief ballets had been performed, everyone hastened back to the warm room where the ladies had to draw straws to determine who would be the first to speak.

They were nine in number: Fräulein Anna, Fräulein Zusia, Fräulein Leonora, Fräulein Kunigunda, Fräulein Crisis, Lady Ludwig, Lady Pockau, Lady Burundi, and my Caspia. Because they had begun rather early, they hoped all would finish before the evening meal. For they proposed to spend not a quarter of the time on it that the rope-walker and Herr Ludwig had taken. And the Irishman had to promise them to tell his life story during dinner. With that the matter was settled and to the great laughter of the whole party the lot fell to Fräulein Anna, for she had

144

drawn the shortest stick. Therefore, everyone sat down at his designated place, and she began to speak as follows:

"I drew the shortest stick of all and my story will be the shortest of all." But Monsieur Ludwig interjected that if she didn't behave honestly and according to the truth, he would send a spirit to her this night along with a ghost that he could send to anywhere he wanted in the castle. "Yes, yes," said Fräulein Anna, "for my part I'll leave nothing out unless perhaps I've forgotten something." Then she resumed and said, "You all know my family, and I spent my youth in Austria at a castle that is quite familiar to those living around Krems. As a very young person when I was just twelve years old, a baron fell in love with me, but he was the ugliest man I have ever seen. His feet stank so that I often felt I would faint at his side and he wet his bed every night like a child. Whenever he had his boots mended, he would enter it in the house ledger that he was always bringing to our castle just to show my parents what a practical householder I would be getting if I would marry him. I liked his chamberlain much better than him, so I turned him down whenever he asked for my hand.

"After this a young greenhorn turned up who'd recently returned from France. He wanted to love, but didn't know how. Of the French language he knew nothing but *monsieur* and *madame*, which he inserted into everything he said, and when he was telling a story, he would always include that he had been in Paris or say that what he was describing he had seen in Paris. He spent about two hundred Reichstaler on me in one week, and I think he would have spent even more if his tutor hadn't forbidden it, who knew full well nothing would come of it, for the lad was not yet twenty and had scarcely eight hundred Reichstaler at his disposal. He knew only a single bow and he always gave it whenever some boy doffed his hat to him in the street. Finally he wrote me love poems that were so pretty a person would believe that he had been attacked by Monsieur Ludwig's illness. For your amusement I'll recite only one of the letters he addressed to me in verse with assurances of his love. It ran like this:

> Oh Love, oh Love, you great big stone,
> You squeeze my heart right to the bone!
> My spirit starts to fade in me,
> From love I bellow like an ox.
> Whenever I of Anna think
> And offer her ten thousand sighs,
> My heart leaps up beyond compare
> In bed, at table, everywhere.
> Dan Cupid has so conquered me,
> It is a frightful thing to see.
> With his magic sword of love
> He sank my heart deep in the sea.
> The rays of dawn all this while

145

No longer can upon me smile
If Fräulein Anna won't have me.
My heart is beating with a plump.
A savage beast has a better life
Than I, a thrown-out pocketknife.
My torment's grown so very big,
I tear the hair out of my wig,
The which I bought in gay Paree
Right near the market St. Denis.

He wrote a lot of such comical verses to me at the castle, and they served our clerk splendidly for lighting candles. A half year later I accidentally fell in the castle courtyard because it had frozen very smooth. From this fall I had to stay in my room for a good ten weeks, and that's the most interesting event I can remember. I don't care to tell you other pranks that occurred between and among our maids because we don't have any peasant lads among us who could guide themselves accordingly."

Frau Burundi was the second in order and somewhat more ceremonious in her words. She talked of nothing but how she learned to knit, weave, and sew. I grew properly annoyed at that and I don't care to honor her by including her collar-maker's remarks in this book because it's been designed and written by me to amuse its readers.

The third in line was Fräulein Zusia, and in order that she might finish quickly she told the following: "Gentlemen! You know the details of my birth better than I do and there's ample proof I spent my childhood in the field because my father was a colonel over two mounted regiments. In my tenth year I went to a countess who had no match for piety, although physically she was rather weak. She was rather friendly to me, and thus I had good hope of remaining at her castle, had not a frightful matter barred this and parted us from one another.

"Her husband was engaged in adultery with another woman who was the most beautiful one in the whole country. And so that he might get rid of his wife and have the other, he choked his with a horse's reins while she was seated and he later announced she had died of a stroke. But a page who had stood at the door and heard the whole event revealed it in a place where it is most strongly disapproved of. The perpetrator wouldn't have gotten away unpunished if he hadn't thrown a frightening amount of money on the collection plate. He subsequently married his concubine but experienced no success in all his doings, perhaps because he had committed a deed that can scarcely be excused. Shortly thereafter they found the page dead in a forest, from which they concluded he had been killed by a hunter whom the count had hired. This was suspected from the bullet they found in his head and cut out. But the castle finally burned, and the concubine was burned to death along with a child she had conceived in their marriage.

"At that time I wept more in one hour than I would now in ten years, for I can't tell you how good and kind my cousin had been. Her husband hated her extremely simply because she wasn't beautiful and ignored the fact that she was an extremely good housekeeper and had never spoken an angry or unpleasant word to him. Afterwards I went to Hungary and then came here, and that's all I know to tell you about my life."

At this Lady Pockau, who was fourth in order, began by saying: "Fräulein Zusia's story has shown us sufficiently how frivolous desire is not the best guide when it chooses beauty before virtue and thus falls into shameful vice because one sin is usually bound to the next and descends from one evil to a greater one. But just as the count behaved with his first wife, so did a friend of mine with her husband, as you will soon hear.

"My mother died of the fever, and because people thought it seemed to be epidemic, they sent us children away from the palace. My brother, who died in a duel two years ago, and I went to a town, outside of which a cousin had two estates.

"One night we heard a horrible tumult in the house and we could only think that ghosts and spooks were creating it because it was in the middle of the night, but the sole explanation was that the cousin's husband had been attacked in his bed and treacherously slain. The stiletto was still sticking in his breast and my cousin along with her lover, who was said to be a student, were nowhere to be found. Soon afterwards the student was located, captured in a forest, and broken on the wheel, but not a soul was able to find out anything about the woman.

"After that I was boarded with an apothecary, not the one to whom Monsieur Ludwig wrote the nice letter, but one who believed in neither Heaven nor Hell and was constantly concerned with making gold. He had a son taught by a student also named Ludwig, and I perceptibly fell in love with this preceptor and even would have liked to give him a couple of Ducats if he would ever sleep with me, but things didn't turn out that well at that time. But across the way lived a cobbler's helper who quite daringly fell in love with me, and, to tell the truth, I wasn't so disinclined to him. I believe if we had had better opportunity to speak with each other, something might have happened that I wouldn't tell you about. But then things stalled again because he was beaten by students in town and had to move away from fear of being killed.

"That happened in my young days when I didn't know down from up, but when I became a little smarter, an elegant cavalier fell in love with me. I was married to him a year later, for he had to wait that long for me because of my age, and I can't tell you how I looked forward to the wedding the whole year. I even took medicine on healthy days so that I wouldn't get sick and the wedding could come off. This gentleman was shot to death in the war, after which I was married a second time and to a colonel, whom you all knew. But now I'm a widow and forty-two years old."

147

Chapter Nine. Departure from the Castle.
A Ridiculous Deception Involving the
Rope-walker, Kunigunda, Isidoro, and Ludwig.

We often think we're fiddling well
'Til someone says it sounds like hell.

"If you can't produce anything better," said Monsieur Ludwig, "then you can leave your stories at home. I see that you've forgotten too much and left out most everything that could have served as amusement. What good are such tragic stories in a place where we've assembled only for fun? I see quite clearly that a person can't get the truth out of women with even twelve whips because they seek all sorts of ways to hide their personal happenings.

"Oh, how my ghost is going to oppress you tonight! Zusia, Zusia, you're going to feel it the most because you told something I find hard to believe. And because you're all hiding the truth so, it will be very poor entertainment to hear the rest of you because I know better about all your doings than you yourselves. And although you told something funny, it still wasn't true because I know that from childhood on you've never been more than twelve miles away from your place of birth and always had to stay shut in at home. But what I regret most of all is that I didn't make it a condition for all those who haven't traveled much in the world should reveal the thoughts they've borne all their lives concerning love. Then we truly would have had enough to laugh about if you weren't like the first ones in trying to hide almost everything."

The remaining women were quite content with this outcome because they talked as well as canaries do, and because they weren't gifted speakers, they were fearful of saying a lot of foolish things. But what they lacked in oratorical skills they replaced considerably through their pride, and so the one was counterbalanced and negated by the other. Thus the conversation ended for this time. And because most decided to leave the next morning and head for home, Monsieur Ludwig had the peasants told to be ready for the harnessing, and the rest of the evening was spent in gambling, from which Isidoro put more than a hundred Ducats in his purse.

During such gambling the ladies had a different diversion that the Irishman arranged for them with cats. For he was an unusually amusing man and not half as foul-mouthed as Monsieur Ludwig. On account of this the ladies liked to have him around them and gave him all sorts of mementos for his unflagging attendance.

During dinner he was asked to tell his life story as had been agreed. But he excused himself, first, because he wasn't prepared to do so, because up till then he had been busy with the ladies. And, second, it seemed to him to be not such a bad idea if he saved it for the departure in the morning since underway there would be little enough to discuss, and we were quite satisfied with his excuse. And Monsieur Ludwig added that he had a short piece to offer that had occurred to him only a quarter of an hour before. For he was determined to tell everything that was going to happen to Kunigunda this night and to provide the company no little amusement, because he was surely clever enough to carry off the matter so that not even the person who was most ridiculed had a complaint.

With that a deplorable contest arose because it was as much as our farewell party, after which people planned to travel forth. So many toasts were drunk to the health of a good trip, the people soon were hindered and prevented from beginning such with a healthy head, for on the following morning everyone was still deep in the feathers in spite of the bell's having struck eleven from the tower.

I myself didn't know where I was lying and my head was going in such circles that I was seeing double. Thus it seemed to me as though I were lying beside two women and as often as I tried to grab both, I found only the one. Ludwig meanwhile ran around to all the rooms and awoke us from our sleep with great screaming. All his people had to scream behind him and howl like wolves. If someone didn't emerge quickly, they tore off his quilt and sprayed him with water. He was so happy because he thought that during the night he had played a prank on Kunigunda such as the world had never seen. But on the contrary, in his business with Kunigunda he himself was tricked beyond compare. Therefore, I'm going to reveal the story to the reader with no delay.

Above I wrote how the tailor had come to my room and told me what he had heard and understood from the chimney last night and what Kunigunda had said to the ostensible rope-walker. And I subsequently told this story to Ludwig, whom I regarded as the most cunning and cleverest among the cavaliers. And he was so delighted by it that he could hardly wait for night to come because he had decided to make his cunning known since in all his life he had never been handed such an easy opportunity. But that was not the way it went. The tailor had indeed listened at the right chimney, but instead of Kunigunda, Isidoro was lying in the chamber; in the dark he had pretended to be Kunigunda so that he could find out who the rope-walker actually was, for during the latter's narration he had noticed that his story was a complete lie.

I said before that Isidoro had come to the castle only out of love for Zusia and they had already privately discussed with one another how they wanted to trap the rope-walker. Therefore, Zusia switched rooms with Kunigunda and no slight trick was carried off as the kind reader will readily be able to imagine and conclude how the deceived Monsieur Ludwig came running.

In pursuance of our agreement I held the rope-walker up until almost midnight with drinking toasts and I noted quite well that he would like to be with Kunigunda, for he firmly believed she had spoken with him. But I had all the servants present placed before the door, and no matter how much he struggled to get out, I didn't let him away from the spot; rather, I compelled him to remain against his will because I kept drinking toasts to him that he as an honest fellow could not reject.

Meanwhile Ludwig had disguised himself in a fur night dress and arrived at the appointed hour in the room of the presumed Kunigunda which had been opened by the previous maid when the sign was given, and the maid admitted him. With a thousand sighs he threw himself down on Isidoro and kissed him. Believing only that it was the rope-walker, the one deception joined the other. And because Isidoro wanted to disgrace the rope-walker before the whole company, he removed the bed cap from Ludwig so that he could show it tomorrow — that is to-day — and prove to everyone what the presumably honest rope-walker had been doing and planning in the castle.

Ludwig had scarcely come into my room when he told me, still in bed, with special pleasure how he had gotten into Kunigunda's room and hugged and kissed her more than forty thousand times. He had also arranged with her how they would become a pair and depart early this morning. We also finally revealed the adventure to my Caspia, whose astonishment at the cunning knew no bounds. Out of joy Ludwig was jumping over the table and benches and he asked me to get out of bed quickly so that we could celebrate. People quite soon assembled in the former room, and I thought it appropriate if Ludwig would save his story until the departure. And then at the farewells the joke would be all the greater, especially since trouble might arise in the castle because the matter was by nature somewhat ticklish. He finally yielded to my desire, and then breakfast was arranged, at which all sorts of things occurred that I can't report because of all too extensive digressions since I'm determined to produce something relatively pleasant.

Even before the opening of the gate, the peasants had appeared with their horses at the castle. After the harnessing was finished we partly drove in coaches, partly rode on horseback beside one another, and thus we parted from the castle with great rejoicing and many pistol shots.

After open country was reached they drove somewhat slower so that the Irishman's story might be heard. He related in great detail how he had been born on an ocean island and spent his life among barbarians. Later he had come to Trabzon, where as a youth he spent four years in irons and bonds. From there Fortune in the shape of a German noble had brought him to this country, where he had not only studied, but also had military training. He had served three years under the French flag and then reached the state in which he had remained to the present. I have not recorded and presented the Irishman's narrative in his own words because thereby I would have had to wait a rather long time to reach the principal entertainment that came about shortly thereafter. For after the Irishman had stretched his story over almost four miles, we

150

came to a fork in the road where a large inn was located. People thought it quite practical to alight there and warm up as well as have a parting drink. When they had come into the room, they were served much wine as well as some biscuits that are customarily baked in the country.

When Monsieur Ludwig now was about to present the preceding story discreetly, Isidoro spoke up and asked the company what they thought of someone who last night had presumed to address a woman in the castle in a fur night dress and to lie down in bed with her. It's easy to think how this remark appalled the rope-walker and Ludwig even more. But Ludwig, who thought he had picked the safest course, replied that such a person would be as great a dunce as there could be between heaven and earth. At this Isidoro pulled out the purloined sleeping cap, saying he had found it in the castle and asking to whom it belonged. Ludwig asserted that it was his and Lady Ludwig herself said that she had made it for him with her own hands. "Ha, ha, brother," said Isidoro, "are you the worst dunce between heaven and earth? The Devil, what were you thinking about in the bedroom with me? You hugged me and kissed me, didn't you?" In consternation Ludwig didn't know what he should answer or say and the rope-walker was white as chalk. Kunigunda helped them out of their dream in the following way:

"You gentlemen, everyone knows quite well what the deal was. I wouldn't have thought that anyone would have presumed such a thing of me. Monsieur Rope-walker, you behaved frightfully in this matter, and I don't know how Monsieur Ludwig was so prettily detected. I confess I had not a few doubts about the rope-walker's story. For that reason I swapped bedrooms with Herr Isidoro, whither Isidoro had him summoned by a maid, and the rope-walker was so full of honor and respectability he let himself be grandly led astray. Monsieur Isidoro will tell you what he did there."

"He believed," Isidoro said, "I was Kunigunda. He let himself be convinced I loved him, and in this way I learned who he is. He's named Caspar and is of the nobility like us. But as I saw, the following evening Monsieur Ludwig came to my room, hugged me at least forty thousand times, one after the other, and said things to me I don't care to mention." At this Ludwig also erupted and said how he had learned about the matter from me and I through my tailor. I can't tell you how they laughed at the rope-walker and Ludwig. As much as they had laughed at me when I had embraced Ludwig instead of Caspia, they now laughed as much or even more loudly at the present situation.

"Ha," said Ludwig, "never in my life have I been so ridiculed. "Gadzooks, how could I have gone so abysmally wrong! I'll give three hundred Taler for this insult." The entertainer was beside himself. The more fuss they made, the more they were made fun of, and this went on until we finally parted from one another and each traveled on his way.

Chapter Ten. They Come to a Funeral.
A Grave Digger's Frightful Story.

Trash will always interest pique,
A gentle death we do not seek.

Earlier I mentioned several times that Monsieur Ludwig agreed with me to speak to Faustus and inquire about the marriage he made. Although he rode there on the road with me, he thought it advisable that we disguise ourselves and let Caspia travel home to her estate because we would certainly appear there within two days. Therefore, we disguised ourselves in our lackeys' coats and, after saying goodbye to my wife, rode to the village where hearsay reported he was staying with his bride.

For the purpose of this affair we had taken along my old father and decided to present ourselves as his servants on this occasion. Accordingly, he rode ahead and the two of us rode after with his lackeys, just as if we belonged with them. About a half hour later we came to a populous city where we were stopped at the gate because an exalted corpse was to be carried through soon and to the nearby cemetery.

It was an aged matron, and her lord occupied an important office in this city although he was said to have been an idler formerly and the sort of person who offended one's eyesight and had nothing to hold in his hand but a stick. Since, however, he had risen to a high office *omnia cum tempore*, there were in the cortege many citizens and others who appeared to honor him or from other motives. For attending funerals has many reasons: the first and main one is that you have to. *Exempli gratia*: one of our acquaintances or someone from our family dies, then you have to go, whether you want to or not, you simply have to go. The same is true when our good friends or close acquaintances die, then we likewise have to go along even if our thoughts are elsewhere.

The second reason is and is called an official appearance, as when someone receives an office and the city doesn't know it, then he readily escorts the corpse and can through this means easily give the whole city an obvious indication of his rank and precedence. Indeed, one can observe quite precisely how many flatter the funeral arranger and give him a four Groschen piece so that he places them well forward, and this type are the greatest fools.

The third manner of attending the funeral is called the *modus adulandi* or the flattering walk, and here the proverb *dum moritur dives, concurrunt undique cives*[32] applies. This flattering walk is known to all the world and consequently as common as the cobbler's trade. Thus such escort occurs not from proper reverence, but solely from another reason that is quite opposed and contrary to virtue. But since the toadies

---

[32] "When a rich man dies, the citizens come running."

know how to insinuate themselves into all matters, they can't stay away from a funeral.

The fourth reason for performing this task is hypocrisy that leads people to say: Oh what a Christian man! Oh, what a pious man! See how diligently he goes to the funeral; there isn't anyone buried without his presence throughout the year, he's such a Christian man! Hypocrites like to hear such words, and because it has to do with nothing else, they can find a great and dreadful pleasure in this. All these types are reprehensible and invalid because they do not happen or arise from any cause that is without its mask. Burying the dead is a Christian deed, and what belongs to and is understood by burying the dead is to go to the funeral or to escort the corpse to the grave and not to step aside and disappear at the house door or beneath the city gate. My gracious, what sort of an honor would it be if someone invited you to be their guest, seated you at their table, and called for the food to be served, but the cook brought the food only up to the table and then quickly back to the kitchen. Truly, you would think someone was taking you for a great fool. But these people are doing the same thing. You're supposed to walk with the deceased and you don't do it. Many a man says: Wife, I'm going to escort the body. Then he puts on his coat, goes out, and as soon as he's entered his name in the book, he goes back home again without having seen either the coffin or the mourners, and that's supposed to be called going to the funeral.

Indeed, at this great city gate we almost saw ourselves as fools for here a pair took off, there another, and of the fifty couples scarcely ten remained who entered the graveyard.

If you were lying in your coffin and could look out through a small window, I doubtless believe you would be greatly sad of heart that the friendship of those who were so often obliged to you or your family was not greater. Many a person says: I don't like to walk with the body, for the dead man won't walk with me! These words are supposed to be said in jest, but I'll let others who are more knowledgeable say how spiteful they are at heart. *De mortuis & absentibus nil, nisi bene*: Concerning the dead and the absent one is to say nothing but good. But I can't believe this is a good saying because it wasn't known among the blind heathen.

Following the men came the women, who were chattering about current fashions and instead of using the present opportunity to consider and observe death and their future final hour, they had a chat about bedclothes, kitchen equipment, their messengers, nursemaids, and children. One even prated about how many suitors she had this year, another talked about a matter that was just shy of deserving a bastinado. Therefore, I was astonished at the laziness of these blind worldly spirits who didn't want to think about Death until he was standing before the door. Truly, then it's too late. And because we are all greatly concerned about dying, it is necessary that we not abandon or

153

put to one side our thoughts of death. After all the people who belonged to the funeral were through the gate, we rode through it and asked about the best road to reach the village, which was pointed out to us as over two fields away.

On the way my father told a frightening story about a grave digger who eighteen years ago in Magdeburg cut the hearts out of the bodies of the dead, with which he wanted to prepare a powder that made all those who walked across what he had strewn in the road die and thereby he could attain great wealth. "Once it happened that the young son of a respectable man was buried. The arch-scoundrel likewise cut the heart out of his delicate and innocent body, and in that same night the man dreamed how his son came to him and no longer had a breast. He awoke at this vision and told it to his wife, who talked him out of it, telling him it was only a dream that could easily be deceiving him. He should not be confused; her child was buried and in the place where he belonged. Therefore, he should not worry in vain and should go to sleep. He fell asleep, and his son appeared once again as before, at which he awakened anew and sighed dolefully about it. The wife consoled him as before until he finally fell asleep a third time and nonetheless had no rest from his vision. For the third time he was frightened by it so that longingly he waited for day and immediately went to the grave digger, requesting that he might see the grave of his child once more. The grave digger did this, but the father finds the grave altered and disarranged, thus he begs him to disinter the child, he would like to see him again. But the grave digger would not be persuaded, protesting the great fine the authorities might impose on him.

"Finally the father goes to the authorities, who grant him his request and order the grave digger to dig up the child. He did so and the father, totally astonished, saw the child exactly as he had appeared to him in his dream. At this the grave digger was arrested and subsequently under torture confessed everything and other crimes. Among them he admitted that one night he dug up a woman who had died six weeks after delivery and her child that she was holding in her arms. He had started to tear the child from her arms, but the mother had held the child so firmly and strongly and finally opened her eyes. He was so startled by this that he quickly closed the grave and had seen alongside it nothing but eyes that he could not drive from his mind.

Such misdeeds have such an ending, and people of that sort are to be called unfortunate only because they don't learn to recognize their own calamity until the rod is over their head.[33] There are so many thousands of examples that no crime ever goes unpunished. If not here, then there. And yet we see the godless competing for this wreath that hasn't been bound for them yet, and in running after it they fall into the hands

---

[33] In pronouncing a death sentence, a rod was symbolically broken over the convicted person's head.

of the Devil because each of them is of the opinion he'll do it best. As the mirror serves the eyes, so shall the misfortunes of our neighbor serve us, but perverted spirits don't shy away from the pitch black smoke of sin. Thus, it's not surprising that they plunge into eternal flames and often go from temporal death into the eternal one."

Chapter Eleven. Faustus Marries a Peasant Maid. Carander Helps Bring Faustus to His Senses.

Just when you think that all is through,
The dance will often start anew.

In such mournful conversation, which is perhaps the gloomiest in this whole book, we came to the village where, shortly before, Faustus had celebrated his peasant wedding. And in the following I do not intend to burden the reader with doleful stories of that ilk since I don't propose to disturb his thoughts. But I must admit that I included it for the sole reason of having this volume contain stories at which even hearts of stone should take pity. But henceforth I'm resolved to relate adventures that are quite pleasant to read, but not annoying to a person who is mature enough to hold his emotions in check and to distinguish between good and evil. To the best of my memory, up to this point I haven't stung anyone with mocking words from which I might have aroused displeasure toward myself. And doubtless such freedom will be granted to me if I accuse and appropriately rebuke vices and not those who are afflicted with them.

They brought us to the very house where Faustus had married his new wife. Pilemann, my aged father, dismounted and we followed him to the door where Faustus stood smiling and greeted him with a friendly kiss. He called him his dear father and regarded himself as blessed to see him in this isolated place, especially so when he was at the height of happiness with the world, from which we all concluded that he was much happier with his peasant marriage than anyone would have believed.

He led my father into a warm parlor where the bride received him with very polite gestures and caused us no slight surprise with her unexpected manners. My father sat down with him at the table and after he had asked Faustus the cause of his marriage, the latter answered him as follows: "Sir, whoever loves the court hates himself, for those who promise to lift him up will cast him down completely. For this reason I feared remaining at a place where fortune is most fickle. You know that I spent most of my youth abroad and met misfortune every time I fell in love. I find it hard to believe that ever a person was bound by such unhappy fetters as was I. But it was fair to call me a fool for the very reason that I believed no one could be happy save the person who was in love.

"Caspia, who now lies at you son's side, was the only one to whom I would have given my heart. But I saw that conclusion reached on high concerning me was a different one that I could not have gone against. I did not leave Ludwig's castle out of resentment or envy, but the swift consternation at this change robbed me of every courtesy at that time. I resolved that before two days had passed, I would marry a maid who would be most suited for me. After I revealed this decision to Carander, I came here to this village because it enjoyed his special recommendation. I slept a bit after my resolution so that I could say that I had slept on the matter and reached a proper conclusion. After I awoke, I cast eyes on the woman who is now my married wife and who duly lies at my side because I found her full of honor and honesty.

"She is poor and a peasant maid, but what does that mean? She provides me as good and proper pleasure as a women of my station, and she is all the more compliant to me, the higher she deems my family to be above her own. To tell the entire truth, I love her more and more and doubt that I could have loved Caspia with such constancy because I would have had a thousand reasons to be jealous. I grant her to Zendorio with all my heart and wish that if he is as devoted to her as I am to mine with eternal love and kindness, there is no doubt he'll spend his days in greatest pleasure. Peasants' daughters are also not dogs, and I place no value on beauty, nobility, and riches if pleasure is not present.

"I've now put courtly life aside and I want to situate myself at an isolated estate where I can follow my own desires and not the rules of strangers. I have enough money to make a beggar rich so I shall also be able to do the same for my peasant maid. And perhaps my blessing with her will be that much greater, the more certain it is that I didn't marry her simply from desire; instead, I want to show the whole world that I didn't woo her from any deception. The courtly circles can say whatever they want about that, I'll still know that none of them fares as well as I because none of them enjoys such pleasure as I do.

"People have represented my marriage to the whole world as thoughtless. But only those did so who know that the fools believe everything they hear. A member of the petty nobility has certainly married a princess. Why shouldn't the nobility have the freedom to revert and court a peasant maid? When Adam delved and Eva span, who was then a gentleman? As anyone can plainly read, they were not nobles at all. I know well of greater and higher gents than I who have mated with a person of low estate. People say: Birds of a feather flock together. If that concerns our outward activities, it will apply much more to our inner emotions and inclinations.

"Many a person is better served by a piece of bread than a sapphire. My peasant maid pleases me more than an imperial princess from Trabzon or Oriana, with whom Amadis consorted in Prandiflor. Ha, I'm

156

no such weakling and don't believe that I'll regret it, no matter how much others lament and sigh about it, for now it can no longer be changed. Let them do what they want to, if some devil comes he'll be wasting his time because I'm much too sensible. I have no regrets save those deriving from my misdeeds. Indeed, I'd have to be a perfect fool to do so, and nothing delights me more than having others worry more about me and my welfare than I customarily do myself. And even if I had acted wrongly, the matter concerns me alone. But a lot of people don't care to see not being unhappy or showing no sadness about it since I have no cause to. But if I happened to become a beggar, they'd open their mouths so wide in laughter that a person could wash a pair of leather pants in them. But I'll just let the fools laugh as they want to because I desire neither to take away their freedom to do so nor to grow angry about it. I think this the best means for getting the better of their laughter.

"I confess there was one lady in the country whom I would have preferred to marry a thousand times more than Caspia. She is Carander's only daughter and is named Celinda. I traveled more often to honor and please this Celinda than I did to Caspia, but not only did I never get to speak to her alone, but I scarcely even saw her. Her well-known reputation was surely not hidden from you, Pilemann, and thus I admit quite freely that whenever I think of her, my heart is quite moved because through my marriage I have precluded further seeking what has lain in my heart continuously. But don't imagine that thereby I'm expressing regret. Instead, it is intended to make clear just how much in love I have been."

Faustus would have gone on speaking had not unexpectedly a shot been heard before the house which caused him to go to the window. *"Bonus dies*, brother," someone outside called out, and Faustus turned about, reporting that it was Carander, whom he had mentioned earlier. They received him with great courtesy, and Carander expressed his sorrow in elegant and select words for not having been at the wedding, no matter how much he had wanted to be. My father Pilemann had known him for a long time; therefore he sat down with them at the table and asked Faustus whether he regretted having acted so swiftly in so important a matter and having reached a hasty conclusion.

"I can see," Faustus answered, "that the world judges my marriage to be much different from what it is in reality. Herr Carander, let Herr Pilemann present my view to you so that you will see that I never lived in more perfect satisfaction than now. Although nothing in the world can be called perfect, I do wish you could see my contentment. Without doubt you would conclude from it that I am so convinced of this decision that if I weren't yet married, I would do it this instant so that all might see how far removed I am from any thoughtlessness."

"Monsieur," answered Carander, "Your marriage has a far different appearance than you imagine. Therefore, hear me. Then you will have to concede that with my advice I've not overstepped the bounds set by true friendship. You came to my castle full of worries and fancies that according to your own admission had tormented you a thousandfold. I saw what it had to do with, for it was not to be denied that you were seeking my daughter Celinda, whom you attended frequently. I thought you were playing a joke, wanting to marry a peasant maid. But when I saw you were serious, I secretly dressed my daughter in peasant's clothes and sent her here to this house, later gave you deliberate advice to come here, and thus I received word that you slept with my daughter in the belief you were marrying a peasant maid and now have her as your wife."

No sooner had he said this than the disguised Celinda came into the room and embraced her father, and in all my life I've never seen anything as fantastic as this sudden and unexpected transformation. Ludwig himself had never imagined that Faustus would get Celinda in such a manner, and Faustus no longer knew how he should behave.

"Understand," said Carander, "that I've always thought highly of your qualities and had compassion for your great love. Celinda, go dress in the clothes I brought with me and you, my most likeable son-in-law, live with her not as a peasant, but as a lady of the nobility descended from the ancient house of Breitenberg. You two will have ten thousand Ducats as a dowery."

At this Faustus displayed a doubled delight. Still surprised, he embraced Carander with an amiable kiss, who had shown him such friendship in this matter that it would be hard to find its equal in this world. With joy increasing so, we could no longer stay disguised and thus revealed ourselves, at which Faustus was quite astonished. Nothing more could be wished for except that the remaining company could be present. Then in this peasant house there could be as great merriment as there had been at the castle.

Celinda was delighted we were there, and all this day we entertained ourselves quite appropriately by having each side tell what had happened at the castle and at the ostensible peasant wedding. And in this comedy Faustus was much more blissful than I because in this way his wedding had cost him not an eighth of what my expenses had amounted to. For rich people are always charged twice as much, and on such occasions each thinks to his own advantage.

Chapter Twelve. A Man Hangs on the Gallows. They Discuss This. A Pretended Funeral. Isidoro Marries Zusia.

For work performed we get our due,
And he who steals — but why tell you?

On the following morning we set out on our journey, and after we had taken farewell of one another with special compliments, each party went its way. At that time winter began to come on in force. For this reason we had to ride in snow with great annoyance and we lightened our way with all sorts of conversation, especially concerning the strange fate that happened to me and among us. As old and experienced as my father was, he had never heard of such a wondrous transformation. From this we saw that fortune plays with us as with a ball, amazingly throwing us around in the world, now to this place, now to that. Ludwig knew that Isidoro was rather enamored of Zusia. For this reason he wanted to be the intermediary in the matter and bring them together as soon as possible; he also hoped to arrange such entertainments this winter that the neighborhood would have nothing to complain about except the sustained cold.

Amid such conversations we rode past a gallows from which there hung a thief frozen quite rigid. We asked a peasant about the reason for this execution, and he told us the man had stolen some sheep and rams as well as the dried fruit from his neighbor's attic. From this reply we had reason to discuss whether the fellow had been hanged justly or not. And my father said, "No, first, it is contrary to holy law which desires that a thief not be hanged, but return twice that which he stole. If he doesn't have it, one should hire him out for service, and so forth. Although jurists say wrong is not done to him who knows that he must hang for the theft, there's still the question of whether they have sufficient grounds to hang a thief. They reply: It is true the law does not desire it, nor aims to take a life in this case, but *crescentibus delictis crescunt pœnæ*.[34] To this I reply that other sins and vices increase, yet they retain their prescribed punishment. Yes, they'll reply, the punishment for theft is admittedly too mild. To this I say, you shall not judge by the law, but from the law that does not desire that a thief be hanged. There is no argument as to whether the *lex carolina*[35] is more valid than the *lex sacra*.

"They reply to this by saying it's written in the Scriptures that a liar is worse than a thief, but in the end they both will come to the gallows; from this it appears sufficiently, clearly, and obviously that thieves are to

---

[34] As crimes increase, so do the punishments.

[35] The law of Charlemagne, i.e., the laws of the Holy Roman Empire, civil law.

be hanged. I say: No, sir. The Hebrew word does not say gallows; rather, it says they both will come into ruination, for which the translator substituted the word gallows for clearer understanding according to the usage of our time. For it is clear that people hang few or no liars, otherwise there would be more gallows in the world than there are tiles on roofs, and the argument doesn't pertain.

"For my part, I regard whoring as being as bad and serious as theft. For whoever say, 'Thou shalt not steal!' also said 'Thou shalt not commit adultery!'[36] And nevertheless the latter is punished less severely. The answer is that whoring is a less serious crime. But I ask: What is worse, stealing something you can return or stealing something you can't return? If I were the Lord, the whoremasters would hang as well as the thieves. But they say: *non exstat*, it is not commanded. I ask: Where is it commanded that you hang the thief? They say: In the laws of Charlemagne. But what is Charlemagne in the face of Scripture? And thus I concur with Hugo Grotius, because one should proceed carefully in such serious matters and especially with capital crimes."

In this thievish discussion we arrived at my castle, where Caspia, standing at the window, greeted us. Earlier she had sent us fresh horses with which we had been able to proceed more quickly. We had scarcely come into the warm parlor when before the house appeared a messenger who brought a note saying that Isidoro had found his mother gravely ill and she had given up the ghost some three hours later.

To this we sent condolences in a return message and in it wished him good luck on his splendid inheritance. Ludwig added a postscript, asking whether his mother had also willed him Zusia, which doubtless produced a laugh. And thus we had an opportunity to discuss how we were going to spend the spring, because Isidoro was not intent on going around in mourning too long as he made fully clear in his letter that went as follows:

Dear Friends!

I rejoice that you have arrived home with your people in satisfactory condition. I, on the other hand, found my mother in very grave condition as she also died *tres horas* later and is lying in her coffin. Through your pleasing presence you will demonstrate special honor and friendship by appearing here in three days at the latest for the funeral. You know you are obliged to do such for your most loyal and honest friend, who is extremely delighted to return your favors.

I will not wear mourning all too long and will do as our village miller did, who got engaged at the dinner following his wife's funeral. From this you don't have to conclude that I'm not sad; it's only that I can't get the company at your castle out of my head. For I still have to laugh whenever I recall how ardently the deceived Ludwig kissed me. In the present case I'll have to learn in full whether his emotions are so greatly

---

[36] Exodus 20:15,14.

inclined toward me as they were back then in the chamber. *Valete* and do come! The rope-walker, the Irishman, and, *in summa*, all those who were recently together will surely appear.

This letter was somewhat too cheerful for a mourning person, but we knew Isidoro hadn't done it as sacrilege, since his high spirits were only too well-known to us. And it is certain such a person feels more pain at heart, the happier he tries appear. For the harder the stone is, the more fire lies hidden within it; thus, the more cheerfully the heart expresses itself outwardly on such occasions, the more sadness can lie hidden within it. Tears are often false messengers of true sadness, and even if he immediately hired entertainers and bagpipers, it wouldn't be any concern of ours because he was doing what he wanted to and hadn't bet a cent with us concerning his manners. It is to be lamented, however, that the world tends to misinterpret everything.

We then gathered up our mourning clothes and when we arrived at Isidoro's castle all dressed in black, the cavaliers present had a good laugh at us. I can't describe how they made fun of us, for everything that Isidoro had sent to us concerning the death of his mother wasn't true. His motive was simply that he wanted to see us at his wedding. At the castle he had become engaged to Zusia, and his mother had left him his inheritance in her lifetime. Everyone was present who had been at my wedding a few days earlier. Even Faustus appeared along with his beloved and Carander at this pleasant winter festival, where we were entertained in a very elegant and courtly manner.

We reassembled the same city pipers at this castle and for our earlier mistreatment from before we now gave them handsome recompense and conducted ourselves so reservedly and pleasantly that no one could complain of any committed offense. For we knew well that one tends to accomplish little with discord and disagreement; rather, through harmony and unity men, no matter who they are, can be kept in continual peace. And until now I have taken pains and exerted myself to use my quill in such a manner that no one will be offended in the slightest by it. For how does it help a person or what gain does it bring him if he sows his annoyance in publications that are directed at one person or another? In truth, through such he lets it be seen that his mind is implacable and can with quarreling, but if I have cited one vice or another at length, this has happened not in bitterness, but from amusement at those who feel themselves attacked by it.

I have never valued anything on earth more highly than freedom. Therefore, I grant each person the right to interpret this book as he thinks fit because I do not intend to rob him of this jewel that I value so highly. I have made fun of myself in many ways and have included my own circumstances among other stories. Thus I have gone ahead walking in the snow on these winter nights so that when I meet someone here or there, he might want to follow in the path I've beaten. Everything that I've discussed in this book I've offered not as an unassailable

161

argument, but only as certain opinions that I hold of the various things I've spoken of. If someone says there's no elegance of language to be found in it, then please know that it was done over a long period of time and I worked most of it out at nighttime, so it's not surprising that no oratorical splendor is to be found in it. I have sought to teach a person about his life and not his eloquence, a subject in which I have no experience.

The reason for this text did not arise from vain delusion, but from a promise I made that I would describe all the events that happened to me and those associated with me. I have not retracted my word; rather, as far as possible I have tried to describe in brief all the situations I can remember. To be sure, I gladly would have assigned the effort of such writing to the Irishman or someone else, but because they as much compelled me to do it, I have all the better reason to describe the matter as it was.

After Isidoro's wedding was over nothing remarkable happened except that he had a comedy put on that was amusing. The Irishman promised to invite us very soon to his wedding, and after this each went his way to spend the remaining winter at home.

Others sought their amusement in a different way, but I sat down to describe that which has made me so obliged to the people, but especially to Isidoro. Although I intended to make this work somewhat shorter, I could have done so only by throwing out some stories that I can't put aside this time.

Book Five

Chapter One. Zendorio's Housekeeping.

The man who spends more than he owns
Will end up eating naught but bones.

If I again take up my pen and seek to continue the manuscript I've begun, this doesn't happen because I want to detain the kind reader with a great number of unpleasant circumstances, for I am sufficiently familiar with the desires of a reader. In reading such works I hate nothing more than diffuse rambling, from which results no little waste of time and material. However, no one has reason to believe that, like some charlatan or jokester, I am planning to entertain him with silly things, for neither my profession nor any other cause gives me the opportunity. I have always regarded writing much more highly than a profession that might appropriately be called and regarded as every man's fool, for, thank God, I still know well what purpose is served by such foolish ravings and that they tend to bring ruin in their wake.

A well-known heretic said on his death bed: *A utinam non scripsissem*: Oh, had I never set my pen to paper! Doubtless because he had felt in his heart and become aware of the pain that customarily ensues from heretical writings. Oh, how many a man would be a child of bliss in the life eternal if only he had not, in the words of the scholar Guevara, drowned his soul wretchedly in his ink bottle! For, first, an immoral writer not only wastes the time he could have put to better use, but, second, he also misuses the talent granted him, from which something better could have come.

He also smears up the paper and wastes the ink from which and with which something better could have been accomplished and achieved. This threefold damage also affects the printing houses by misusing and disgracing the art of printing which is never sufficiently praised. I shan't mention the futile work and toil that one must have with texts of that sort. From there it is subjected to the eyes of thousands and, unnoticed and under the pretense of acceptability, spread the poison in the hearts of readers who ruin specifically that which is supposed to preserve them from all mistakes, namely, their conscience. Thus the author of such errors becomes guilty of others' sins and often has reason to cry out unto himself: *A utinam non scripsissem*: Would God I had never set pen to paper! As usually tends to happen to such

163

clever fellows who, having sufficiently mocked others, see themselves attacked by the hellish fiend.

But this work has a different intent, and let no one imagine that I have undertaken it so that I might pass the cold and irksome hours of winter. No indeed, but my sole intention was this: to punish vices laughingly and to chastise common failings with a gentle hand. It is true that in the preceding four Books I promised to describe all our happenings, which I've had quite good opportunity to do in the frosty winter nights. But I finished with that much sooner than I had imagined because one event led almost immediately into the next, and thus there was no great need for reflection that tends to be a basic element in other writings. Thus there was also no need for searching through many books like the person who assembles fourteen collections of sermons and from them makes a fifteenth. I have never desired to engage in such pretense and especially not in such a work as this, for I think no person on earth has ever described the life we led. Accordingly it is fitting that after writing the four earlier Books, I continue and describe how the winter passed in and between our activities, for the most pleasant time of the gradually approaching spring and the wondrous fate that sustained us until then admonish me to do so.

I spent the time most pleasantly in listing and writing down our stories. When I grew tired from all the writing, I fetched my two greyhounds that were my joy and entertainment at that time. On my magnificent nag I hunted with them through my preserve, chasing the hares back and forth, and in a short while I had a rather nice bundle of those animals as well as of foxes so that I soon had a handsome winter fur coat from my hunting. Occasionally my wife — back then people weren't such fools that they called their wives their beloved as is the custom nowadays — was visited by various of her peers from the country who drove back and forth in their closed carriages. Almost weekly we received word from Isidoro and Zusia and most of the people who had been at my wedding. Thus in no way did I have cause to complain of great and boring isolation, even though my small castle was off the beaten path. And even if there had been, I had become accustomed to loneliness in the hermitage. I usually sat alone and, having filled a page or two, walked up and down in the room with a glass of wine, which worked better for me than if I had sharpened my quill ten times in a row. Occasionally I visited my father at his castle, where we passed the time either by curling on the pond, if the weather permitted, or playing piquet.

I had twenty to thirty peasants under me, whom I neither tormented nor plagued by so much as a hair, and what should I have taken from them since their previous owner had almost sucked the blood out of them and pulled their skins over their ears. I was deeply sorry for them and established a relationship with them so that they had much more cause to love and praise me than to go their own way. My workers, farm hands, maids, lackeys, and other servants I paid regularly and in full and in no way did I allow my steward or even my clerk to accept kickbacks from the payments and the like or to promote their own causes through them. Thus I won the hearts of many people and, like that Duke of Württemberg, I could duly boast that I would have rested safely in the company of every subject.

I hated hypocrisy like poison, knowing well that from it many thousands of people were hastening to the eternal flames and thus I maintained a Christian state, and not a person can say of me on the basis of truth that I owed one Kreuzer to my subjects from the highest to the lowest. Even if my treasury was small, there was no anxiety and despair in it. In the same way in my business office there was no great misery or poverty. Because I followed the Catholic religion, I gave everything according to merit and little or nothing at all from charity. If I did, it would have to be when I overlooked one or a few Groschen when paying out money or otherwise gave alms that are not generosity, but Christian responsibility.

In such a way I produced hard-working people and prevented much theft that would have occurred, had I not paid properly. For help that is not paid properly or in full will seek every opportunity to assist in hurting you. Thus the maids will take lard, butter, and cheese; the farm hands will take money or neglectfully leave the horses in their stalls to great harm, not feed the livestock at the right time, and who would want to relate all the things that can happen in such circumstances. Truly, they are legion, and just as soon as so poorly paid a servant has an official position, he will cause his master damage and loss because, as the common proverb goes, no office it so small that it can't serve the gallows.

For another thing, I not only had this advantage, but also great praise from all my other people not only for paying all my servants properly and promptly, but also for my thriftiness. For when I saw that a hundred Ducats had been paid into the office and I wanted to plan to have a dinner, I called the steward and asked him if it were feasible to arrange an entertainment and how one might go about it. "Milord," said the steward — for at that time one was not yet allowed to address noblemen as Your Grace, as is done now —, "Our cash box now has six hundred and thirteen Gulden. Milord will scarcely carry off the proposed banquet for less than three hundred Gulden. Well, when these are gone, there'll be three hundred left. These are not sufficient to pay the help. If one wanted credit or a loan for this purpose, it would bring confusion into the bookkeeping, and if one looks at it, there's little advantage for this castle in the proposed entertainment and banquet. Let us put it off until next summer when our income is at the maximum. Then with good reserves one can go forth and be seen without harm and disadvantage."

With such an answer from the steward I saw how necessary it is to maintain proper order. If he had been some base dolt, he quite easily could have brought me into such ruin that even the Devil couldn't rescue me. Here and there in the world there are still such fellows who serve much more to damage the commonweal than to its advantage, paying not a soul, letting themselves be waited on for free, and behaving so crudely and miserably that no one believes or trusts them. But the tears shed on account of the deserved compensation are not simply water, but styli that record in the hearts of God and men the injustice of such people for posterity. One should not bind the mouth of an ox doing the threshing, and how much less that of a man who is doing his best and nonetheless has no hope of enjoying that for which he was hired. Thus an unexpected misfortune befalls many a man for having sinned not of himself, but through the blood and sweat of others.

The better I paid, the greater my fame became; indeed, had I been a soldier and undertaken recruiting, in a short time I would have assembled more soldiers than Westphalians could hams because the money hadn't grown onto my fingers. But finally I became aware that the Devil was riding my steward because he began to pursue his own causes mightily. Instead of paying the hands in ready cash, he gave them certain articles and calculated them at frightfully high prices. For example, he gave the married men salt, candles, wood, butter, cheese, sausages, leather, and the like. But whereas they could have bought a cord of wood for half a Gulden, he deducted a Taler from their yearly wage for such, so, as you can easily guess, the poor devils came out way short and scratched their heads amid alas and alack.

At first I thought the office was profiting, but I not only found that he had pocketed the money left over, but that things were going unhappily in my whole household because I had lost the blessing through which everything is attained and preserved. The servants were sighing unto Heaven and all profitableness at my castle was escaping so that gradually I could feel the obvious punishment. Therefore, I chased the steward to the Devil and the Devil's mother. "You riffraff," I said to him, "Are you in your prosperity supposed to tribulate the people who serve not you, but me? Am I master here or you? Get out of here or I'll have you whipped in addition. Scoundrel, you harass the people as though they were your fools. Get out of my service and go back where you came from, and as punishment for your transgressions, you are to lose all the possessions you own!"

The steward shrugged his shoulders and asserted that I should recall how loyally he had advised and assisted me in various matters. But I said that the latter had totally ruined the former and that now it was quite futile to excuse himself with matters that he had been responsible for in the performance of his office. After that I chased him off, and the poor man and tormentor of people had to eat his bread in considerable misery.

Chapter Two. The Huntsman's Nice Story.

Within an hour there can appear
What's not expected in a year.

Following the common advice, short and sweet was how I dealt with those who went about in my castle offering great and petty rascalities, for I believe that man's greatest happiness is found in this point, namely, in rewarding virtue and in punishing vice without regard of the individual person, no matter what his estate and degrees might be. To be sure, the last was not of great necessity, for my jurisdiction was not at all extensive, and thus I had no unusual special affairs to take care of. But in order that I not tarry too long in my own praise, I'll move on to the telling of the following event.

From my youth on I've been a great devotee of music and had many a delight to enjoy from it when I from time to time came upon a stick fiddle or small flute, which I had learned to play earlier at school. I was also occupied with this diversion when I was busy at my castle with this work, getting it written and subsequently ready for the press.

Once I was walking up and down in the room when I unexpectedly heard a gunshot outside the castle. I put down the small fiddle on which I had just been playing "Three smithies stood beside the forge; their wicked deeds I'll soon disgorge." I opened the window, and ordered my hands to find out about the shot, for it seemed to me it was a deer rifle, with which no one was authorized to hunt in this area — as in all my preserves — save at the risk of losing the same.

Not long afterwards they brought in to me a well-built huntsman, whom to all appearances they had not overpowered, and the one hand said to me that he had been stuck in the deep snow, quite unconscious and still could not recall what had happened. Without boasting I must confess I have always been most sympathetic with suffering or otherwise distressed people, since in such compassion there is no small bit of true Christianity. Because of this the hands had to put him down by the stove for me so that, refreshed by its warmth, he could come to.

My counsel was not fruitless, for the huntsman finally stood up and looked around everywhere in the room as though he had just arrived from the New World. He reached for his dagger and, to tell the truth, I was afraid of this action and believed he was about to attack me because I had had a strange dream last night; therefore, I asked him who he was and where he came from.

"Sir," he gave me in answer, "I truly don't know where I am. Nevertheless I must to the best of my ability thank you subserviently for having me brought to this place and thus being torn from the jaws of ruin."

I said that hadn't happened from good will, but a proper revenge on those who more than deserved it for letting themselves be heard by firing a weapon near the castle, contrary to propriety and law. "You know

167

well," I said to him, "that the preserves are parts of the estates of noble gentlemen. Because you as a huntsman were in violation in a situation where in your capacity you should be on guard and keep criminal trespassers away, you should not be surprised if I not only take away your weapon, but also have you fined several Reichstaler because I value my freedom and my life and desire to do nothing that runs counter to general order and the laws of the land. Did you hear me?"

"I heard you well," answered the huntsman, "and heard more than enough. The statement you directed against me is highly commendable not only for its words, but also for its substance. That the game laws must be enforced is not unknown to me as a huntsman who before now has ridden through many preserves and punished trespassers according to the nature of the matter. And I hope that such will occur with me at this place when I say that I did not fire so that I might frighten the game or drop some other animal. No, rather during a windstorm I accidentally fell into a snowdrift in which I lay so long and threshed about so that finally I was exhausted and no longer knew how I could help myself.

"As I kept rolling down, my weapon fired by itself, perhaps because fortune had ordained that I would be lifted out with the help of other people and thus kept alive. And it is certain that if I had lain another quarter hour stuck in the snow, I would have expired in it and suffocated by now. From this, Your Worship, judge whether I was right or wrong. What do you think?"

"If that's the way the matter was," I said, "then you were not wrong. But I will inquire of my hands about the circumstances of how they found you and how you were in the snow." With that I called them in to me, but each testified in favor of the huntsman because they said he had been found half-dead in the snow and gave no sign of life. This testimony pleased me all the more because I had gotten to see him in a very pitiable state and the dreadful situation of his clothing. Then I had the heat raised and let him dry his clothes because it was quite windy and cold.

After this I got a drink of wine to refresh him and I asked the huntsman to tell me who he was and where he had been traveling to. And since I had requested many people to tell me their life stories, I also asked the huntsman to do this, who proved quite willing. When he had taken a seat on the nearby chair with his back to the stove, he began to relate the following:

"I would give a dozen Taler if I could tell you, sir, who my father or mother was, for then I would be freed of a great worry that not seldom torments and plagues me like a martyrdom. Because I was often called names by boys on account of that, I was in as many fights as there are hairs on my head. I spent my youth with a gardener, before whose door I had been placed, and upon the orders of the authorities, he had had to feed and raise me, although he was reluctant and innocent of the deed and was otherwise a properly Christian and pious man. He was entering his tenth year as a widower when this extraordinary affront was done to him. But I must immediately acknowledge that he didn't make me pay for it in the least; rather, he strove to turn away from the city, outside of which he ran a thriving nursery.

Because of my early age I can hardly remember when he was promoted to a castle where I've remained until the present. I serve the countess there as a court huntsman because she took me in after my stepfather's passing and had me trained in this craft. After learning hunting I served at various castles, but especially at the castle of a well-to-do nobleman near the wild forest. He had a son by the name of Ludwig. With this Ludwig I pursued all sorts of mischief, for I taught him how to dress ravens quite nicely in fire and feathers, and when we let them fly into the sky, a screaming arose in the neighborhood just as if a burning dragon were flying about. With such pranks I spent a while at the castle until the elder daughter fell madly in love with me, and because I didn't know who my father was, I often chatted to her about being of noble birth. Because those in love are already gullible, I easily convinced her with lies so tangible you could grab and hold them with all five fingers. She gave me quite a bit of money and occasionally silver spoons, which I pawned and applied the money to things that could provide Ludwig and me some pleasure. But he was finally sent off to school by his father where he became so accustomed to practicing rascalities that he pulled as many kinds of pranks on the schoolmaster and his wife as he could think of. Quite often he nailed the schoolmaster's wife to the chair she was sitting on, put resin on the schoolmaster's chair, and pulled so many other frivolous stunts that the schoolmaster had to complain about them to his old man and at the same time request him to retrieve his degenerate son.

"In such a manner we were reunited, but soon thereafter I had an accident while tracking deer and had to leave the castle against my will and move to the estate of another nobleman whose wife made love to me splendidly. Between me and this noblewoman so many jokes and adventures occurred, it would take me a full day just to tell them. For she discovered some letters that the daughter of the previous nobleman had written me, and, sir, you can readily imagine how whorish desire rose in her heart. However, she didn't have the slightest reason for this, for, first, I was not her husband and, second, I wasn't drawn to her in any other way than through blind, devilish desire, which usually tends to be followed by trouble.

"Your Worship can imagine how frivolously the wife behaved with regard to herself since out of great love for me she decided to get rid of her husband, who was still a young and elegant cavalier and scarcely fifty years old. This attempt suddenly frightened me so greatly that I sought nothing more than to get away from the place and return to the former castle of the noble maiden who had completely taken over my heart. — I started to say something else.

169

"But during my absence the nobleman had figured things out and was not indifferent because he had caught his daughter reading a letter she had written me. Then he beat her around so with his saber that I believe he wouldn't have stopped if his lady hadn't blocked his last strokes. She greatly loved her children, and that caused a lot of neglect of their welfare. After imparting such discipline and royalties for the writer, he came to me himself and threatened to shoot me on the spot if I didn't get of the castle before evening and disappear. Accordingly I put my knapsack on my back, my hunting horn around me, my rifle on my shoulder, and marched off for the fatherland as fast as I could.

"At that time I was almost drowning in lust and I complained about nothing more than the great misfortune that had captured me at both these castles. But why do I say misfortune! I much rather should have rejoiced at my great good fortune and thanked heaven for extending its merciful hand to cut off this opportunity to fall into a true slough of uncleanliness, from which not one person in a thousand knows how to escape.

"I tried things differently, and at my countess's castle I married a lady's maid, with whom things went partly well, partly poorly, as they generally tend to do in a marriage. But it is certain that I anticipated a thousand times more delight than I subsequently experienced. We both had little to offer, and the Devil himself couldn't have torn the arrogance from her ass. — Sir, forgive me for having to speak so crudely, but it's the truth. — Thus my little money went simply for clothes and I had little or no bread at all at home. I no longer knew what I should do with her, but fortunately in the next year she died of an illness common to all arrogant women since they can't stand it that others are as good as they and their rage forcefully enters their hearts, something to which my wife, too, fell victim.

"I found that, through her passing, considerable worry was lifted from my heart, for, to tell the truth, I didn't love her all that much simply because she was so extremely proud and arrogant, for she constantly called me the son of a whore. And whenever other people called me that, she quarreled with them, saying I was more respectable than they or even a thousand times more respectable. Thus my wife was like heretics who never agree except when they are denying the True Church."

Chapter Three. The Life of Veronia.

The chaste do find discretion's best,
The lewd, of course, must bare their breast.

"From this Your Worship must easily see that I never had peace with my wife except when others were quarreling with me and thus I had to spend my life in constant argument and discord, as long as she was on my back. Indeed, I can't tell you how often I've regretted acting so thoughtlessly and marrying only according to outward appearance, for I thought: Dammit, a lady's maid is no dog; if you'd like to get one, the whole world will know what to sing and say of you. Then I thought: Fool, become a priest, contemplate the contemptible vanities at a monastery, and learn to be pious; it's better for you than if you married a countess. No, I reconsidered, it won't do, cloister life is not a foolish joke, it requires seriousness. Then what are you going to do? Will you become a soldier and let them support you? It's not simply a dangerous trade, but a right miserable one where a person is always running around in distress, torment, want, hunger, exposure, and thirst, in a word, in poverty, and finally forfeits his life behind some fallen fence. If you are discharged, you have to beg or steal: the former is disgraceful, the latter dangerous, thus it's better to stay who you are and try your luck as you find best. Among the countless thousands of human beings you won't find a one, no matter what his estate, condition, or religion may be, who is without worry and toil. When misfortune strikes right away, know that you received life with the condition that you would always be tormented by worries. You'll not be the only person who lifts himself above common annoyances. So get to it!

"*Audentes fortuna juvat, timidosque repellit.*[37] I learned this phrase from Ludwig's preceptor which admirably suited this situation, for when I saw that no person can live or be without worries, I laughed at myself. For the person who plays with fire will get burned on some part of his body, and I believe that among all the people I've met, there won't be one who doesn't always think: Alas, I could have married better, I could have handled the matter this way or that. But, in truth, these are only reproaches from the Devil, who has been a liar and homebreaker from the beginning. Many a person thinks: If only I were this or that, and even if he becomes such, I'll let myself be flayed and lie on a bed of nails if he isn't much unhappier than he was in his former condition. Therefore, it's no slight plague among humankind that no one is content with his estate, and I regard him as happiest who thinks little of rising in life and loves only the honorable estate that will endure in eternity. I didn't draw such ideas out of thin air or an empty bag; instead, they came from another hand into my heart where I weighed them thoroughly and almost hourly — and thus decided to remain alone and to hide myself from women as far as time and opportunity permitted. And although the countess tried to sic another self-centered slut on me, I revealed my reasoning to her and thanked her for her concern. But if she wanted to be so generous and come to my aid with a hundred Ducats, I would acknowledge it as a greater assistance than the proposed marriage. She had to laugh, and so that I might detect her affection, she

---

[37] "Fortune favors the brave and rejects the timid."

slipped me something now and then; through this means she made me so devoted to her that in the end she entrusted me with all her secrets.

"This countess was called Veronia by name and doubtless is more than well-known to Your Worship because her castle lies no farther than forty miles from this place. And although she tied me to her with gratuities, I had to carry out things such that I would certainly have had to pay for with my life, had I been caught. She was a completely amorous woman and I don't believe her equal could be found far and wide. And one needn't tell how she customarily carried on not only with the cavaliers, but also with students, merchants' servants, and, in short, all those who stayed at her castle.

"Earlier I was reading in a small book that described the life of the deposed Queen Christina, but half or most of this text was lies and it is only a frivolous attack from a person who burns with a desire for vengeance against her as can be seen in detail and noted well in how passionate his quill was in depicting her use of her body. I was surprised in reading through this tract that in changing her religion she is said to have simultaneously changed her sexual behavior. But if she didn't change it, why hadn't anyone known anything of this before? I only ask this as a digression, for although shameless and offensive things are to be found in this booklet, my countess behaved even worse, and I was as much as her intermediary who had to deliver her wanton letters, instruct her lovers, and get out of prison those who had been thrown there because of her.

"I frequently performed such services for her at the risk of my own life. I had to free from four chains a student whom the count found with her in the garden and who beyond all doubt would have had to pay with his neck, for the count listens to no excuse, no matter how strongly it is presented, and is harsher in his judgments than the laws demand.

"I likewise helped a baker out of a cellar, into which the count had locked him by himself because he had gotten hold of a letter from him that should have gone to the countess. It ran:

Star of my heaven!

As we agreed, I shall certainly be beneath your balcony this evening. Then I shall act as you desire if you wish to grant me further opportunity. I greatly fear your husband; therefore, I beg you to be very careful and tear this note into a thousand bits.

Such was the text discovered in the baker's letter, from which the count almost exploded into as many bits as the countess should have torn the letter. Accordingly, he locked him in a deep cellar because just at that time a great banquet was going on at the castle, during which he couldn't do anything of great significance to the poor rascal. But the countess didn't hesitate to free the prisoner with my help. For because the cellar was at some remove, I split the door with my hunting knife and sent him out of the castle at night and unrecognizable, having changed his clothes.

"It is not to be denied that Veronia's life was most unpardonable, but another cause must have lain hidden within it. As often as I asked her in confidence about this, she always gave me the answer, she would tell me at the proper time. I can swear that she often kissed me and said, 'Oh, huntsman, huntsman, my dear huntsman! If you only knew how much I love you, you wouldn't be half so cruel to me!' I said in reply, 'Your Grace, I can believe that from your generosity to me.' We were disturbed quite often in such conversations, and she had a better opportunity to be with me because I was showing her how to plant tulips, something I had learned from the gardener and, for another thing, I was married. With odd feelings I often wondered how she so quickly and suddenly attracted despicable and nasty fellows, while on the other hand she hated men who were nicely built, learned, well-traveled, and knowledgeable in foreign languages. She was never attracted to them with any steady or sustained love. And if I asked her why this strange change took place, she answered that this was her nature. The sensible ones were generally somewhat less useful for love than the clumsy and somewhat daring people with whom she could have her pleasure whenever she desired and as it pleased her. "I liked this answer because it is certain that sin calls for foolish ardor much more than a clever mind. And one has to admit that in such doings not a little brutality occurs of which a healthy mind has to be ashamed, no matter how much one is attached to this uncleanliness.

"There's a story about an Italian who once fell in love with a woman from the well-known Orsini family. He was so devoted to her that he could neither rest or sleep. In honor of his beloved he thought up an emblem that has to be drawn in the following fashion. First, he had an eagle drawn that was flying up to the stars. But instead of turning toward the sun, it turned toward the Great Bear and bore the subscript *solem alium non habeo*.[38] With it he wanted to indicate that other than this his beloved he wouldn't love any other figure or beauty more, and even if it were more beautiful and shone more brightly than the sun itself. For my part I regard this emblem as a quite clever and unusual invention of an admirable mind, the likes of which I've heard of seldom or not at all. But if we turn it around and apply it to lascivious spirits, then unfortunately one can't regret enough that they so basely fly past the true sun of the virtues and turn to the ragged scoundrels[39] of the sinful deeds and fall all the deeper into the darkness, the further they let the light of truth go out and disappear from their spirits and hearts.

---

[38] "I have no other sun."

[39] *Bärenhäuter*, lit. "those in / wearing bearskins," thus a continuation of Ergasto's pun.

173

"This countess loved base people, *solum enim alium non habebat*: she had no other sun in her heart, and that's the way it goes with all the people in the world. One finds his pleasure in gold and says in his heart: *solem alium non habeo*. A second loves the creature more than the Creator and says: *solem alium non habeo*. The third seeks his pleasure in cards, but as soon as his lucky star dies, his sun disappears from his purse, that is, his gold, which is often compared to the sun. Many a person seeks delight in the base and transient honors of this world and say to himself: *solem alium non habeo*. Thus, his sun will also descend into the grave with him and let him wait to see where another sun might rise and shine for him. Another takes pleasure in perverting teachings and writings. *Solem aliuim non habebit*: He will have no other sun by which to guide himself and thus will fall into the grave where it's eternally dark along with those he leads about from his leash like blind sheep. And there it will be said of him: *Solem aliuim non habebit*: In all eternity he will have no other sun.

"Forgive me, Your Worship, for adding this digression to my story, which I did solely that you might see how evilly and wrongly those spirits, and especially Countess Veronia, tend to act who have run after a piece of stinking flesh and in so doing have so basely put their own sun of virtue to one side. *Solem aliuim non habuit*: for she didn't want to acknowledge any other sun than this one, by means of which she has created a stench for her own name in posterity whenever someone recalls it. She has, as it were, buried her own bliss with both hands and is hated by those who are capable of distinguishing good from evil.

"Once a nobleman came to the castle who was concerned with various legal matters with our office. His name was Isidoro, and I'm now traveling to him for the reason that we were bound together back then with great friendship. He loved the countess in a forbidden manner, but nonetheless pleasant for the countess of which I was not aware until the poor devil was caught in a forest and, clapped in strong irons, thrown into the prison. At the time the count was deer hunting just as he was accustomed to spending most of his time hunting for game. Therefore, the execution was postponed until his return, and, without any announcement of Isidoro's arrest or his answer to the charges or explanation, papers had already been drawn up that he was to have his head placed between his feet. And beyond all doubt they would have carried it off if I hadn't quietly departed from the hunt and helped this abandoned human being down through the window."

"Monsieur," I interrupted the huntsman, "what I think of your story, I'll say later, but do report to me how you acquired Latin, for I heard you mix in some sentences and phrases that the typical huntsman doesn't use every day."

"That's true," the huntsman replied, "and right at the start of my story I erred in forgetting to report of my schooling, which I, however, don't regard as very necessary. For, first, all my preceptors, of whom I had three, were truly models of pedantry.

"Concerning the first, in whose class I sat for two years in the city where I was laid before the gardener's door, I can't tell anything special because there was so little to him that he would ask us, his charges, about recent news; so we would tell him a whopping lie, and when he found out he had been deceived, he couldn't hold it against us young children. The second one was somewhat more cheerful of spirit but also so lazy that with him I forgot all I had learned from the former one. The third was a sourpuss, for he tolerated no cheerfulness, even if it were inborn. Thus he made us afraid of doing anything, and I believe if I had been with him any longer, he would have beaten me as dry as a codfish because wouldn't stand it at all if I pulled a prank or two.

"He also so pounded my other comrades to pieces that I can swear that in all my life I've never seen any bed clothes that were as clean as the pupil's coats. The most foolish thing of all was that we weren't allowed to make any good jokes in our public plays; instead, although they were written and performed humorously enough, we weren't allowed to improvise as we wanted to, for the preceptor said it would come out as too frivolous. But if somebody defied his order, he had to pay for it for a whole year afterwards and was called a prankster by everyone.

"In such manner I did study a bit, and because my humor could not agree and get along with the preceptors, I said farewell to the books and haven't regretted it a bit, for I've enjoyed delights in the forest that many doctors haven't had in their libraries. I'll let someone else sit with his book; for my part, I'll stride though meadows, forests, fields, I'll climb the mountains, descend into the valleys, look for an animal's spoor, hunt out the foxes, trap foxes and wolves, snare partridges and other birds and likewise hares, and it's a good thing that my former preceptors haven't traveled through my preserve; I surely would have gotten them in my trap."

Chapter Four. The Old Noblewoman Prepares to Die.

Through graying hair and age's plight
Many a trick will come to light.

"You've spoken enough," I said to the huntsman, "and now you'll hear what I think of your story. First, to not know who your father is is a great ignorance. But because this ignorance is so very common these days, it's not an ignorance but an inability to be able to name that which it isn't necessary to know. Let your father be whoever he may; that doesn't concern your character in the slightest. It is sufficient that you are a huntsman, which many hope to be who are honorably born and descended. And on account of that you can keep your dozen Taler in your purse, for it's good that many a person doesn't know who his father is. But it's not good that many a person doesn't want to know his father.

"Through this not wanting to know, many a person imagines himself to be more than he is because in his arrogance he wants to hide the baseness of his origins, something that runs counter to nature. The crow remains a crow even if the birds elect him as their king, and believe for sure that I don't believe in this pretense. But because the world wants to be deceived, it serves it right that it embraces many a whore's child with open arms. From this blindness arose the adage that such children usually have the greatest luck. And I'm of the opinion that this produced a great friendliness, for because you don't know who your father is, it is necessary that all who are fifteen years older than you can be.

"I say this in jest simply to show you I'm not a sourpuss like your three preceptors were. I have pity for the countess and my advice would be this: If the count wants to be rid of his torment, he ought to blow the countess away. It is a question whether the snare or the hare is responsible when he gets caught. If I put it like that, then the snare is responsible. But if I ask whether the snare or the hare is responsible for his ensnaring himself, then the hare is responsible. And that is the condition of your Veronia. She is the snare, the adulterers are the hares, thus neither she nor the adulterers are free of guilt; instead, they come together in one school. But if I were her lord, I would get the snare out of the way so that it couldn't catch or get caught.

"Opportunity makes the thief, and an adulteress is ripe enough to be cut off from the tree of life, for she will only spoil other good fruit who hear of and enjoy her wantonness. Woe to him who brings scandal! In this saying are understood all sorts of abominations from both genders that they sin in their own flesh as well as in other matters such as heresy, discord, and the like. I've heard much more about Veronia than you told me, and Isidoro will report to you in full how I happen to know the countess. If I understood, she told you she preferred coarse people to sensible ones, and that's no great wonder, for I meet people who prefer common leather to Prussian, and most clerks prefer paper to parchment for writing. I'll leave it to you to determine the reason as you see fit. For I can tell that, as a widower, you will be clever enough to know my meaning.

"I've often wondered why this plague has raged so strongly among respectable people and I believe it comes from their believing that in their case such is not be called adultery, but only a flaw in their chaste virtue. And granted that were true, I still don't understand how they could compensate for this flaw. It would have to be that they eliminated this vice entirely, but there's no hope of that as long as they won't believe that this flaw is a frightful and great sin through which one ultimately descends into Hell like a billiard ball into the pocket.

"I wanted to make these few remarks concerning Veronia's life. But among other things, I was particularly delighted by your marriage, and you said truly that a woman's pride tends to bring much ruin in its wake. Many a woman prefers to hunger at home and from that dress herself prettily in her rags. Oh, dreadful folly! The body is adorned without and hungers within. Fool, you hide your need and, in return, make your haughtiness obvious. You don't want people to call you poor and yet you are not rich. But this is no small part of human frailty: the poorer they are, the more they think of themselves.

"Incidentally, you are to be praised for not hesitating to risk your own life so that Isidoro might be rescued. He is my closest friend, and it hasn't been long since he was established as the heir in full of his father's estates. Thus he will display no slight gratitude to you for your diligence, for he's one of the good old Germans and a person who doesn't ignore a service. But above all I'd like to know what your name is."

"Your Worship," the huntsman answered, "you're not asking in vain, and from all appearances this is the strangest bit I've encountered in all my life. The gardener afterwards often told me how he found a note in my diapers that said I was already baptized and called Ergasto by name. I still have the note with me and it is the greatest inheritance I've received from my parents, whoever they may be."

I was quite pleased by Ergasto's answer, and in order that he not learn prematurely of the deception that occurred with Isidoro and me, I withheld my explanation for this time, knowing well that thereby I would have denied Isidoro considerable entertainment since he found his greatest joy under the sun in such mistaken identities. Accordingly I kept Ergasto as my guest, diligently showing him every honor I could that was appropriate for a huntsman but so that he didn't learn that I had lain in the prison instead of Isidoro.

After the meal was ended he bade a friendly farewell and again departed for Isidoro's castle after he had dried his clothes in my chamber and been given his rifle and other equipment. But after he left I had a thousand suspicions, for this was the same huntsman of whom I reported on the first page of these *Winter Nights* and how I was surprised at his great care in freeing me from the prison.

In such strange thoughts I brought the day to an end but I couldn't close an eye that whole night because it was as if I was born under a sign that brought odd revelations with it. And three days passed in such thoughts, when the usual messenger we retained between us brought me the following letter from Isidoro:

Dear Brother!

You're as proper a rascal as can be found between Jacobi and West-phalia. You send me precisely that huntsman who so carefully freed you in the guise of me from prison. And when I straightened him out after his story, he crossed himself a thousand times and said he never would have guessed you could conceal yourself so. It's certain that this winter I've had no more pleasant an adventure, about which we will talk and laugh more in the future.

Now I've fully been made *plenarius heres* of my legacy. And because my mother is gradually approaching death, she has decided to con-clude her will for which occasion I have asked you and Ludwig to please appear. The doctor who arranged my marriage contract will also be present for this act. I regard him as an honest man who won't give anything of mine away. In the meantime enjoy life with your beloved. The huntsman will remain for that long. And because he doesn't have anything to do at his castle except carry Veronia's lascivious letters, he won't leave me this winter, for he shares my sense of humor and pleases me with his conversation. Adieu! I remain

Your eternal friend,
Isidoro

From this letter I saw that the huntsman had arrived at his place and was doubtless frightfully astonished about me. Since Isidoro was asking me for something as important as being a witness, I mounted my sleigh to travel there to engage in winter delights with both Ludwig and Isidoro and also to properly honor the huntsman for his loyal services.

Chapter Five. The Noblewoman Tells a Strange Story Before Her Death.

> *No greater joy is found on earth*
> *Than when two brothers share their mirth.*

The road was rather drifted from the sustained north wind and my servant had his hands full getting me out of snowdrifts until we caught sight of the castle, where I had once asked the gatekeeper for a bite for the road. At that time the red-bearded dunce had turned me away with rude language, but now he stood before the gate, his cap un-der his arm and making a deep bow, and this was the entire army that greeted me before the castle. Ludwig had arrived half an hour earlier with his wife, who was not a little angry that I hadn't brought my wife too, but I excused myself by reason of her having to learn to play the drum since I had hung a rather large one on her, given her twelve les-sons, and she was to perform them all perfectly upon my return.

"You're a comical person," said Frau Ludwig. "Don't you see that Frau Zusia also has one?"

"No," I answered, "this is not just a drum but an army kettledrum, so one would have confused the other in learning." They all laughed heartily, and, embarrassed, Frau Zusia held her apron before her face, whereby every one could see her pregnant body even better; at that people laughed even more atrociously until she hid herself in a chamber.

Because of weakness the old noblewoman was lying in her bed, and as soon as the doctor appeared with a notary, they went to work and because no great difficulties were found, the matter was agreed and settled within an hour. Isidoro presented the doctor a hundred Reichstaler and a silver goblet, the notary fifty Gulden and a chiming clock, and he paid all the outstanding bar bills of the copyist.

With the old woman, however, things grew worse as time passed, and she began to doubt she would live long. As upbeat as Isidoro usually was, his face grew noticeably paler. Zusia likewise was crying by the bed and the castle priest was summoned to do his best for the dying woman. When she revived somewhat from her weakness, however, she asked everyone to leave except for Isidoro and myself because she had always regarded us as her two best friends.

"Dear sir," she said to me, "and dear son! I feel in all my limbs that I am quite close to dying. Because I am now especially oppressed by a matter that I've kept secret for a rather long time, now in my hour of death I must rid myself of it while there is still enough time to tell it properly.

"Thirty-two years have now run past since I went into the field with your late father, my dear husband. At that time he filled the duties of a lieutenant colonel and had the war continued for one more year, he would have become a colonel. But after our side was defeated for the last time at Wittstock, peace soon came, but in flight I became the mother of a child beneath the open sky. The enemy was hacking away behind us, for this reason my husband had to drag me along piteously because he didn't want to part from me at all.

"We finally came to a peasant village and there we had the little boy baptized and named Ergasto. But as we were leaving the village, the enemy were again attacking our people near Felßlingen. Therefore, we had to gallop as fast as we could, and the child doubtless would have suffocated if we had not left him with a schoolmaster with the request to keep this Ergasto with him until it grew safer and we could retrieve him. He took the child and the fifty Ducats included. But when we found our way back, he had been chased away from house and home. From this I found no end to my torment.

"We inquired about him everywhere, but not a person could give us news of the schoolmaster, and that's the way it's remained with Ergasto until this minute. Because of this I beg you, my best friends, to inquire about the matter everywhere you can. I do not know whether the child is still alive or dead. But if he is said to be alive still, treat him like a true brother and get along with one another as is proper and due between one friend and another."

After these remarks she sighed a number of times, but our faces turned fiery red. Because throughout our lives destiny had played so nicely with us, we immediately suspected the huntsman who was named Ergasto. "Gosh," I whispered to Isidoro, "the huntsman might be your brother!"

"It can be," said Isidoro. Here he asked his mother if Ergasto didn't have a mark on his body by which one could recognize him. But she knew of none and sighed even more than before and desired to take leave of all those who were assembled. One after the other went up to the dying woman, and when the huntsman stretched out his hand, both his nose and that of the old woman began to bleed simultaneously. We were not a little astonished at this, and soon we revealed what the noblewoman had confided to us before.

We told the story openly and after we had finished, the priest, who hadn't been in service at the castle for three months yet, sighed. "Dear gentlemen," the cleric said, "now it's time to tell you the matter somewhat more clearly. Three years ago," he went on, "when I was serving in a village outside our land, the schoolmaster died who is to all appearances the one of whom you've now related as having received the child Ergasto.

"He spoke to me in utter confidence and said the child had been consigned to him along with fifty Ducats by an unfamiliar army colonel with the statement that he would retrieve it from him in a few days. But the enemy was in such hot pursuit of him that he scarcely had time to write the child's name on a note and stick it into his diapers. He ran away in the night and reached the town of M**, where he had deposited the child before a gardener's door and continued on his way. The schoolmaster told me this with great remorse and asked me if I could forgive him, for it had not been his desire to abandon the child so basely, but utmost necessity had been the cause that drove him to do such against his will."

The kind reader will easily feel the change that came over the entire party upon hearing this story. For the huntsman Ergasto this news was much nicer and more pleasing than if twelve wolves and eight foxes had fallen into his pit at one time. To be even surer about the matter, he produced the note that he customarily carried with him. From this we could only judge that Ergasto was that very child and thus the brother of Isidoro. Because of this tears of happiness welled from the old woman's eyes at having been able to see her fully-grown son once more before her end. Then the will was changed and although Isidoro came out on a shorter end, it is nonetheless impossible to describe how great a joy he felt at this unexpected change. He kissed Ergasto and the latter him, and amid such joy their aged mother passed away, who three days later was lowered imposingly into the earth.

So did the huntsman emerge from his illusion and from it turned into a nobleman and the son of a whore became the son of an army officer. At this transformation we remained together for almost three weeks and formed among us a new society that we called the Order of Familiars, and during this time the doctor drew up for us the following rules, according to which each member of the order was supposed to live:

First, no one is to be accepted into the order who is under twenty-five.

Second, he is responsible for describing his life story to include things from which the reader is not angered or criticized, but improved in everything.

Third, if someone dies, a gravestone will be donated by the order.

Fourth, if someone commits a significant misdeed, it will be discussed by the assembled order and according to the nature of the matter he will either be suspended for a period or fined a certain sum.

Fifth, the order will always elect two principal members, the one to direct financial matters, the other the administrative ones.

Sixth, everyone is free to withdraw from the order, but only after hosting a banquet and the like.

Seventh, each member is obliged to perform in two plays each year at his own expense and appear in the theater, to which all of the members should and must be invited. The meal at such events would be intrinsic.

They were quite satisfied with these rules and the first to sign were Ludwig von Retz, Isidoro von Zittwig, Ergasto von Zittwig, and I, Zendorio a Zendorio. For because I had told people I was the son of a sexton, I had given myself this title as the kind reader will have learned among other things in the first chapter of Book One. These rules were subsequently signed by my father Pilemann, Faustus, and Carander along with many others.

We then sat down at the table and Ludwig asked me what we had been doing since we last parted from him. Then I related to him our entire trip and how we had oddly learned the truth behind Faustus's wedding and that he hadn't married a peasant's daughter, as was commonly reported, but Carander's only daughter, Celinda, about which I had told them something in earlier letters. *In specie*, however, I told them about the hanged thief and my father's opinion that it was opposed to Holy Law if a man was hanged for theft.

"He is quite right on that point," said Monsieur Ludwig, "for I see in this sentence that the holy commandment is violated that desires that a thief will return twice what he has stolen. Therefore, it is wrong if a person departs from the Law and pursues human statutes. But because we have a person present who can help us best in this matter, we'll let him settle it. Therefore, Herr Doctor, we ask you what your opinion is in this. But you mustn't assert what you've heard others say, but present your decision so that we can see that you have acted impartially and have your own mind, *non enim autoritate sed veritate pugnandum est.*[40]

Chapter Six. The Scribe Gets His Lumps but Goes Elsewhere.

> *Whoever wants to mix with birds*
> *Will find the geese do hiss his words.*

"Gentlemen," answered the doctor, "you desire of me that I not assert what I've heard asserted and in such manner I won't be able to say *quod ego sim animal.*"

"Quite right," answered Ludwig, "I regard this definition as untenable, for I am not an *animal*, but a *creatura ad imaginem Dei creata.* This definition is better and twelve times more exquisite than the old one that let so many propositions pass without closer examination. But judging by it, is it right to hang a thief contrary to the will of the Scriptures?"

"*Domine,*"[41] said the doctor, "where in Scripture is it forbidden that I should have a thief hanged?"

"Ha, Herr Doctor," answered Monsieur Ludwig, "in this case I'll have to give you a lesson. You must know that in the commandment lies the prohibition and in the prohibition lies the commandment. *Exempli gratia*: when it states: Honor thy father and thy mother, that is as much as: Thou shalt not dishonor thy father and thy mother; thus the prohibition lies within the commandment *virtualiter* and *eminenter*, which no rational person will disprove.

"On the other hand, when it states: Thou shalt not kill, that is as much as: Thou shalt let live. Now, doctor, apply these two examples to the commandment in the law by means of which the thief is to be punished and you'll see that the prohibition is in the commandment, that is as much as: He is to be punished in no manner other than that prescribed. For another thing, if you'll excuse me, doctor, are you Catholic or are you Lutheran?"

"Monsieur," said the doctor, "I am Lutheran."

"Well," replied Ludwig, "the Catholics have the authority and right to conduct the other form of Communion, for following your judgment it does not state in the Bible that one may decline the chalice, and I don't see how you can escape unless you admit that the prohibition lies in the commandment."

---

[40] "One should not argue from authorities, but from the truth."

[41] Lat. "master, lord," a term of address for a teacher.

"It is true," said the doctor, "I was quite wrong. Monsieur Ludwig spoke correctly. As far as I'm concerned, they can hang him or have him given a bastinado. I've often argued this matter, but because it was already customary to string thieves from the gallows, neither I nor anyone else could get very far with it. Whoever is a good politician does not deviate from the view of the majority. It he does, he is cursed a thousand times as a heretic, and many a person would prefer to take a different stand if he weren't afraid of destroying his future fortune and forfeiting it completely."

"You've defended yourself quite well," said Ludwig.

During this dialog, I poked Ergasto and told him that this was the selfsame Ludwig for whom he dressed up the ravens so nicely and let them fly away later. He gasped and when the doctor had finished his hangman's remarks, Ergasto addressed Ludwig in the following words: "Monsieur Ludwig, shall we soon make flying ravens again and let the people think they are flying dragons?"

Ludwig was astonished at this, turned away from the doctor, and made a large sign of the Cross. "Well I'll be jiggered," he said, "and you're that huntsman? I wouldn't have guessed it in all my life. Zounds, and you're that same huntsman?"

"Yes," answered Ergasto, I'm the huntsman who was in love with your sister back then, and if I knew where she was, she would be dearer to me now than before."

"Alas, you good man," Ludwig answered, "she went to the dogs long ago." And because Ergasto wanted to hear the story, Ludwig supplied the following information. "The poor thing got a husband with no . . . no noble seat."

"That's nasty," said Zusia. "I see that you haven't changed by even a whisker from how you were at the recent wedding at your castle."

"Nonsense," said Ludwig, "the preacher's not here and moreover you don't understand it right if no one explains it to you beforehand. So, my sister got a husband with no . . . noble seat. He was a right miserable fellow and was constantly drinking in his village tavern with the peasants, thinking that through his familiarity he would win them over. But with this attitude he lost all respect, and the peasants finally made a fool of him. Especially when he was loaded from tobacco and brandy, the peasants became so scurrilous with him that they even drank brotherhood with him. Then my brother nobleman was sitting amid the peasant louts, and at home my sister was crying tears mixed with snot.

"I'm thoroughly annoyed that I can give no better praise to my brother-in-law and if I did, it would be all lies; therefore, it's better I tell the truth as it really was. He was a gambler to be pitied, for if he lost only one Groschen, he would begin to curse and carry on so that the heavens above him and the earth beneath him might have opened up. Finally he even cried like a child when a turkey has stolen its bread and butter, and he had the heart to quarrel and squabble a whole hour on account of a two-Pfennig piece.

"In all his life he never gave a tip but for a clothes that weren't worth a Heller. He wasted a deplorable amount of money. My sister often confided to us in private that if she had given a child an apple or some such, he secretly tore it out of its hands and ate it. In the village tavern he got so drunk that when the innkeeper miscalculated the rent due, my honorable brother-in-law had to give him additional money. In a word, his housekeeping was impossible, and despite my late father's chewing him out a good ten times a week, nothing at all helped. Thus his small estate was ruined, and my sister died at our castle after having no longer lived with him for a year and a half. Their two children also died soon thereafter. Since he left to find amusement, I don't know where he perhaps has helped fill a town moat."

Ergasto was quite saddened at this tale because he saw himself cut off from a hopeful means of joining Ludwig's family. But we soon gave him fresh hope because the whole world is full of such birds, and Monsieur Ludwig still had many noble friends who had studied the *generis feminini*.

During this conversation there arose a great screaming in the palace courtyard, and when we opened the windows, there were two maids who were quarreling and calling each other names in the worst way.

"It's a lie," the first one said, "you did it, you did it."

"What?" said the other. "You stolen cow, you witch's cow, you whore, you did it!"

"You're lying in your teeth," the first one replied, "you shameless brat, you common slut, you dried-up army whore, you did it!"

At this the second screamed, "Oh, you grandmother of all whores' children, you generals' whore, you field whore, you soldiers' whore, you did it!"

The first called at the same time, "You students' whore, you arch whore, you gallows whore, you apprentices' whore, you peasants' whore, you whore of all whores, you thief, you slut, you devil's whore, you did it, you did it, and not any other person!"

"Oh, you stellar whore," the second one screamed quite angrily, I'll throw these keys at your head, you gravedigger's whore, you hangman's whore! Weren't you standing there, you carrion, you frog, you thing on the ground?"

"May the Devil take you!" replied the first. "Come here if you've got the nerve, you actors' whore, you rascals' whore, you whore of all the world!" At that they quickly threw the keys they'd been carrying at their sides at each other's head and finally pulled each other's hair so that their caps and queues fell from their heads. Isidoro ordered his clerk to go down after they had scrapped a bit and make peace with his Spanish cane and tear them apart.

The maids were tumbling so that their dresses and slips went over their heads and they quite often gave us a view of their naked posteriors. But when they finally reached for their knives, the clerk waded into them energetically. "You damned corporals' whore," he said, "who told you to start such a tumult here?" But full of anger and dislike, the maids leaped on the clerk, first tore the collar from his throat, then got the cane out of his hand, and I can't describe how nicely they took care of him. And in such fashion each pulled the next around in the snow like three oxen yoked for plowing.

It almost looked as if the clerk would come off with the most blows; for this reason two other servants came to his help, and when the clerk had emerged, he whipped away as hard as he could, and I believe he would have done so earlier if the two maids hadn't conducted themselves so fiercely in the melee. Now he made up for what he had had to neglect earlier, and he gave them many more blows than they had torn hairs from his head.

"You worthless flaming whores," he said in rage, "now I'll teach you how you should treat people of my likes. Who told you to claw me like that? The Devil will come and fly away with you from the castle. I'm going to give you a proper beating. Didn't the bitches rough me up and scratch me? Do you think you're showing respect in treating a clerk so? Wait, you two devils incarnate, I'll fix you like the Devil and his helpers." Amid more such words, he lashed out with all his strength at the maids, who finally began to scream like cats, for the Spanish cane had already been shattered into little pieces and almost down to the handle. And when for that reason he could no longer flail away, he stuck them in the neck with the remaining stub and grew so tired that he was sweating like a bear that's been baited for a half hour.

In truth, we had to laugh much more at the clerk than at the two maids, who like cats had frightfully disfigured his face and pounded his nose so that it was swollen like a great pear. And the worst thing about it was that the clerk didn't notice that Isidoro had deliberately sent him into danger, because he knew well it would happen no differently to him than it had to several people who earlier had presumed to separate these two maids who were accustomed to brawling.

When the fracas had grown somewhat quieter and each maid was in her place, they were summoned up, and when they appeared, one had to stand on the right side of the room, the other on the left. Isidoro asked them concerning the causes that such an unexpected fight broke out between them.

"Your Worship," said the first one, "the chatelaine came into the kitchen early today. She saw a broken egg lying on the floor. That one there did it," — pointing all five fingers at the woman standing opposite her — "I saw it."

"On my soul, no , sir," said the accused, "she did it."

"Sir, surely believe me," said the first. "She did it."

"If that's true," said the second, "may I disappear. She did it."

"You devil's witches," said Isidoro, "who taught you to swear so? Should you create such an uproar on account of one egg and tear each other's hair? You kitchen rats! Each of you and the chatelaine is no better than the next. Get out of this castle or I'll show you the road so the Devil will fall on you. To fight and curse so for the sake of one egg . . .!" — During such remarks the clerk jumped for joy — "Get out of my sight! And if I see you a quarter hour from now you'll hear a different story. Zusia," he said to his wife, "give them their pay and let the bitches run off to wherever they want to."

Chapter Seven. The Preacher's Discourse on Cursing. Nice Disposition Concerning the Epitaph for the Deceased Noblewoman.

Where oaths and swearing do reside
Good luck and blessings won't abide.

This was the entire farewell address and *oratorio valedictorie* with which the respectable madames had been dismissed at this time. And we had to wonder why such a horrible spectacle had to occur on account of a single egg. But this is the usual nature of women and their innate habit that they can argue for half an hour about a thing that's not worth two words and not be ashamed to deliver a sermon at which they themselves have to laugh when someone shows it to them in broad daylight. Also, the chatelaines are so busy and bossy that they might believe no maid can be clever or diligent without her chatelaine.

"Gentlemen," Zusia said to us, "my chatelaine began this duel between those people on account of the egg. But when she recently broke the honey pot and spilled a glassful of rose water over the sill, she held her tongue firmly and ascribed it all to the poor cat even though I caught her *in flagrante* both times."

"Indeed," said the maid who had hidden at the door and listened, "the chatelaine can raise a great fuss about our having thrown an egg onto the table, but she surely didn't mention that the clerk recently spent half the night in her chamber. I'm sure that's much more to her taste."

With these words she ran down the stairs and among us arose a great laughter at the clerk, who looked as red in the face as the full moon. "That devil's whore," he said, "even goes on to insult me. Wait!" he cried after her, "I'll give you a thumping, you whore, like you've never been thumped before."

"Oh, sure," the maid cried from the stairway, thump the chatelaine instead, she's better accustomed to it than I am."

186

At that the clerk wanted to run after her and even chase her out of the castle. But Isidoro told him to stay because no one has found a better way of treating discharged servants than to close the door behind their butts and let them go their ways.

In order that the two parties have no opportunity to get into each other's hair again, Isidoro sent the clerk into the office to compose an epitaph that he wanted to have carved into his mother's gravestone. Then we talked about various things, but especially about how miserable it was when a householder tolerated cursing and name-calling, and because the chaplain arrived during this conversation, Ergasto inquired of him as follows: "Sir," she said, "What is your opinion of the following story? A brewer once stayed at Veronia's castle who in addition to being a hard worker was a thoroughly pious man. He finally married and the countess gave him in perpetuity the brewery outside the castle. Now he sits there and lives off drink that he brews for all sorts of people who customarily stop at his place. Now the question is: Can the brewer in good conscience allow the peasants and other servants from the castle while drinking in his place to scold, to curse, to utter oaths and other foolishness that is unseemly? Or is he obliged to let his living go and get rid of the cursers? What is your opinion, sir?"

"I shall answer this question briefly," answered the cleric, "for I'm no great windbag who likes to talk about everything and useless trivia. First, the brewer should not allow the cursing of the peasants or whoever they are, but say, 'You peasants, do not curse, or go outside!' And in this way it is my opinion that it's better to suffer hunger in peace than gain a handsome hunk of bread through cursing. For because the brewer is master in his house, by reason of his authority he can punish whoever sins in his house — but understand me, not cardinal sins. For if a cobbler's helper bumps off a miller, the brewer may by no means cut off the head of the cobbler's helper. Thus I am speaking of punishment that is mild and can be applied in good taste.

"For another thing, it's not allowed at all that such a person play the church superintendent and excommunicate the curser. There are quite many cranks of the type who, when the hear the slightest word that runs counter to their pretended piety, sigh, look with eyes averted to Heaven, cross themselves, and carry on so that it often annoys me that the hypocrites can act so completely foolish. Indeed, even a cleric like me doesn't have the power to appear in a tavern and give a sermon, for this isn't the place for such; to do so one would make no great distinction *inter aram & haram*.[42] If you say that in such places, however, one has the best opportunity, then I'll say that's true. But in such a situation a drunken pig is to be punished in a different way, and there are a thousand tricks one can employ in such situations.

---

[42] "between the altar and a pigsty."

"If I were a brewer," the preacher continued, "I would draw up a sign that would clearly state we were not supposed to curse, either to Heaven or here on earth and so forth. If I heard someone cursing, I would put it before him and ask him to read it quickly. If he couldn't read, the person sitting next to him would do it or I would read it myself. If he didn't stop after this, I would throw him out of the house just as I would a mangy sheep from the stall. Never mind the loss of profit. A single curse a person casually allows often causes him to lose more in an hour than he has gained in ten years of hard work. That's my opinion."

On the whole we found this answer not bad, and although others wanted to offer different views, we didn't allow anyone to speak and said let the priest's statement stand. We didn't care if someone else wanted to bring up and interject arguments even if he could and knew enough. At that a good many were quite angry that someone didn't want to believe that they also had studied, especially the doctor, who even opined that he wasn't obliged to applaud the cleric's speech. But we only laughed at him and decided that as soon as he began to meditate, we would show him the door and let him go his learned way. For down to this day I've regarded it as most expedient not to regard anyone as learned who thinks he is learned and not to waste many words with such an ass who wants to stand a clear matter on its head; instead, even if he were right, one shouldn't concede such, and that's that.

Isidoro had been especially delighted by what the cleric had delivered concerning the brewer and he would wish that it were like that everywhere. But people tolerate too much not only in public places; many householders consciously allow things that will weigh most heavily on their hearts on the deathbed.

After this we arose from the table because the cleric had brought some books that Isidoro had ordered earlier through him. After delivering them, he took his leave, and we went to the office to see what sort of good spirits had visited the clerk to help him write the epitaph. And because we didn't want to disturb him in his work, we walked very softly. The clerk must have been possessed by frightfully great ideas, for when still twenty paces from the office we heard him screaming and arguing with himself.

Isidoro and I were somewhat curious. Therefore, we hurried up, but instead of talking to himself as we believed, he was, on the contrary, cursing so that the sky might grow black. "You bastard," he said, "may the Devil take you! Won't you behave? Won't you obey? Listen, you carrion! Am I supposed to push your face into the table? You devilish creature, you worthless road kill, are you going to get better right now? You useless thing, yes, you, I'll show you, you horrid beast!"

We couldn't listen to such wanton words any longer since the others had come up meanwhile and didn't know what was causing the clerk to swear so. Some thought it was a verse; others, however, even believed he had a *spiritum* with him that wouldn't respond. This caused us to tear open the door and in one moment we all were in no doubt because we saw him beat on the table a quill that didn't want to write at all.

"You super scoundrel," Isidoro said to him, "how would it be if I had you whipped like you whipped the maids today? Are you supposed to be such a fool and swear at a thing that can neither see nor hear? Gentlemen," Isidoro went on to say to us, "just take a good look at this lout. He's beating his quill against the table that can feel neither fire nor sword. The fool is punishing an inanimate thing, and I'm surprised that he didn't hang it. To be sure, this great effort doesn't leave him enough time to make his folly obvious to the whole world; otherwise I think he would even put it on the wheel.

"He's supposed to write an epigraph and in so doing he curses worse than a heathen. Those must really be spiritual thoughts! You damned scoundrel, get out of my sight or I'll shatter my cane on you as thoroughly as you shattered yours on the maids today."

During this sustained threat the clerk had more or less cowered, and because he saw no other escape, he took refuge in the nearest toilet, where he bolted himself in and protected himself from Isidoro's anger. "The two maids weren't that clever; otherwise they also would have run to the shithouse."

"Let's leave," said Ludwig. "Who knows what sort of a quill the clerk is sharpening in the toilet? If he's working out his poetry in there, it's going to produce very smelly verses."

The whole company began to laugh at this, and Isidoro took the paper on which the clerk had sketched his ideas for the epitaph. To the extent one could read it, it went as follows:

Causa principalis, causa materialis, causa formalis, causa finalis, from these four causes I must show that the old noblewoman has died. Subsequently I must put: *locum in quo, locum a quo,* and *locum ad quem.* After this comes the *procedere senectutis in genere* and then *in specie.*[43] On this basis the verse must be treated *per logicam: quia homo est animal, ergo homo moritur*[44] is one. *Secundo* and for another: *quia homo est sapiens, ergo sapienter moritur. Tertio* I can give a beautiful reasoning: *quia homo est bipes, ergo etiam moritur bipes*[45] unless one of his legs has been shot off in the war. Therefore, it thankfully appears that that had not happened to the dear noblewoman, so logic was not violated. I can also pose a question and ask: *an mors sit ens rationis physicum* or *positivum in abstractione principii essendi.*[46] Item: whether Hans Sachs did right in personifying death; whether it is *de jure* or *de facto* that the gravedigger in wintertime makes the earth soft

---

[43] "the advance of old age in general . . . in particular."

[44] "Since man is a living being, he will die."

[45] "Since man is a biped, he will die a biped."

[46] "Whether death is a natural being or an abstract concept."

and yielding with warm water so that he and his people can dig all the better. After that come the *causæ subordinatæ*, those are the pallbearers; then the *causa media*, that's the chief mourner, for he walks between two people in the middle; *causæ abstractæ* are the old women because they come last and are far behind the coffin.

Chapter Eight. The Epitaph in forma. Monsieur Caspar Has a Wedding with Kunigunda and What Happened There.

> When fools interpret Holy Writ,
> You'll find more straw than brains in it.

It is easy to conclude what amusement the clerk aroused with this concept. Thus Isidoro was all the more eager to read the following verses that had been prepared according to the preceding outline and ran as follows:

The basic reason, my dear friend,
Just why this lady perished
Was that her life had reached its end.
She got what no one's cherished:
Grim death, that bloke!
For her it is no joke.

The second reason and it's true —
And one that I'm not needing —
That as a mortal 'twas her due,
As you have just been reading.
Her life did fail,
Her face grew pale.

The thirdmost reason I have found
I will no longer from you save:
She died in bed, not on the ground.
Twelve bearers bore her to her grave
Into the ground so deep.
Isidoro her things will keep.

Causa finalis this must be:
She ate not at the end.
I keep this in my phantasy
On which I do depend.
She loved me tenderly,
I was her clerk, you see.

190

The place she told the world farewell
Was just a great big room
Where Death within her spleen did dwell
Without great pain and gloom.
So take my good advice:
She's now in Paradise.

She was of good and noble birth,
A fact well-known by peers.
Her father's armor had great girth
Within the War of Thirty Years.
She's lying there, as you can see,
And I'll not sing: Oh, Glory Be!

But where she now has traveled to
You'll have no trouble guessing
If you do have your wits with you
And haven't lost their blessing.
Gone to bliss without a care,
I think you'll get my old gray mare.

You know how old's her family?
As old as my gray trousers;
Three hundred years ago 'twill be,
They were made by dowsers.
Earthly things she cannot love,
They named me court clerk from above.

In specie she began to wilt
At six times fifteen years.
She was pretty and well-built,
Originally with blond hairs.
These turned white, sir, if you please,
She also had no fleas.

A person's always mortal,
That's why he's got to die.
This saying's known from portal to portal,
It makes so many cry.
Death's no fool, I'll swear,
He walks footbare.

A man has reason, so we hear
And see quite plain in his like
Of good red wine before brown beer,
And riding beats a hike.

With cleverness, they say,
You'll always win the day.

Now everyone has *duo pes*,
In English that's two feet.
This is indeed a *vera res*
Though it may not taste sweet.
That's why he's wont now to expire
With his two feet just like a fire.

No one dies with his two feet
If one's been shot away,
But I don't think I need repeat
That that's just children's play.
Our lady's legs were very fine,
But they were hers and were not mine.

Now one may ask if Johannes Sachs,
That cobbler of renown,
Is worth the waste of candle wax,
Because he did write down
That Death upon a horse does sit.
To hell with him, that's just plain shit.

Isidoro was about to read on and finish the remaining six strophes if Zusia hadn't torn the foolish paper from his hands. "For shame," she said, "the clerk has one nasty mind!"

"Now I see," responded Ludwig, "why he withdrew to the toilet. Isn't that a fool to write such an epitaph for a noblewoman? What devil in hell is going to bring a gravestone here on which someone could carve these stupid remarks? I think many a graveyard would be too small to hold it. Brother," he said to Isidoro, "your clerk is a fool. Set him loose, I'll compose a couple of lines for you myself. What are going to do with that ass? My advice would be that this winter you give the clerk nothing to do but to address certain themes. For through this not only you but everyone who got to read it would have plenty to laugh at. For it is certain that many a learned man cannot deliberately go as far astray as this one did in thinking he was creating something elegant." Isidoro was satisfied and to this end drew up a list of all the subjects about which the clerk was to record his interpretations and inspirations and set them to rhyme.

Then he was summoned from the toilet, and Ludwig asked him who his father was and where he had studied. But in reply he said only that when his mother had become pregnant with him, she mistakenly allied with a poor man, thus he had been compelled to also be poor. As far as his studies were concerned, he ascribed nothing to theory, but everything to practice, following the Latin proverb: *solus & artifices, qui facit*

192

usus erit.[47] He once had stolen a turkey from an innkeeper and later written on the house door: *O mihi præteritum, referat si Jupiter* turkey![48] And this had been the worst prank he had pulled during his difficult life until he learned the clerk's trade and completed his travels as a journeyman. Thus he had become a *licentiatus calami,*[49] that is to say, he had the freedom to temper, cut, and shape a quill large or small, short or long, with or without slit, however it pleased and suited him. And in such fashion he was a *licentiatus calami* and no honest man could enter anything against him unless it were in the toilet or a secret room, from which the king of the night and his people would have to remove it and carry it out.

After all the matters described we took seats in some sleighs for the sake of amusement because our heads were beginning to get silly from the warm air. Accordingly, we drove around the castle courtyard and in the open fields, but without bells. And because quite a few young ladies had assembled from the nearest castles and noblemen's homes for this fun, now and then a man would throw a young lady over the runners and into the snow. But some of the women were clever and put on pants beneath their skirts to preclude protracted observation. Others put large iron heating pans under their skirts so that their bottoms wouldn't be hurt, but when they were thrown over, their furs were so attacked by the fire that after it they were ready for the rag bag. We had such entertainment in our period of mourning, and when the situation allowed, we even brought musicians to the castle, where we had all kinds of fun.

One evening when I was standing with my small flute at a window facing the street and had decided to withdraw, a mounted messenger arrived who brought letters from Caspar, the former rope-walker, announcing that his wedding to Miss Kunigunda had been properly arranged. It was a rather large package which contained nothing but letters to me, Ludwig, and many others. Therefore, we reached a decision in no time at all, and although Isidoro was still in mourning, the cleric granted him sufficient dispensation that he could go with his wife but was in no way permitted to dance. Then we took our places in some coaches to appear at the wedding of the crafty Caspar as we had earlier promised him and we arrived at his castle before two days had passed.

We were shown all possible honors, and because Caspar had pulled such a prank earlier at my wedding by appearing in disguise, we repaid him in the same coin. Isidoro dressed his clerk as a prince and said that he was a young baron from a certain family that had earlier been of great

---

[47] "Only he will become an artist whom practice makes one."

[48] "Oh, if Jupiter would only bring me back the lost turkey" (parody of a Vergil quote).

[49] "Doctor of Misery."

help to Caspar. For this reason he was compelled to be most polite to the disguised clerk, and the clerk had been sufficiently instructed to fit into all situations, even though he was a rather dumb fool.

A week passed before the bride was to arrive, and when we were hoping most surely that she was about to arrive, word came that she had surreptitiously run away and Monsieur Caspar now sat there and didn't know whether he should laugh or cry.

Chapter Nine. Some Pupils Make Pretty Music at the Castle.

Quite often what the great can't do,
A little man will do for you.

It's not a little annoying to a violinist when a string snaps and pops off while he is playing, but it has to be hellishly more so for a bridegroom when his bride disappears just when he thinks he is going to embrace her. And now Monsieur Caspar could counsel himself in both roles since he was a musician and also a bridegroom. He sent his chamberlain accompanied by four servants to chase after his bride and find out about this event. But they neither saw nor heard anything, no matter how often they stopped here and there in the surrounding villages and asked for information. In such a situation they came back, and it wouldn't have taken much for the impatient Caspar to have hung all five of them from the rope we had so smeared with theriac at my wedding. He asked the one who had brought the news a thousand times about the situation, and since he was tormenting himself in vain, Miss Kunigunda revealed herself as the messenger, having disguised herself in such clothes for the fun of it.

If I have ever heard an explosion of laughter, it was the one that resounded at the castle upon this sudden transformation. After that everything went *in floribus*, and it annoys me to describe all the details because I have other things before me that I'll report on before completing this work. People were principally concerned with rounding up merry musicians, but the report of our earlier controversy had made them all so fearful and reluctant that we could find fewer of them than snowballs at the festival of Saint Bartholomew,[50] which is usually called the feast and name day of tailors. Therefore, we took another man from the village who formerly had directed a school where he also instructed the young *in litteris*. He brought along four pupils, who earned their keep musically in the countryside and particularly at the castles of nobles. In a trice they whipped out their violins from under their coats and follow-

---

[50] August 24.

ing them were two with navy trumpets, who strongly resembled tramps.

The two groups faced each other in the hall and performed so artfully that it would have been difficult to find any better in six villages. *Necessitas non habet legem*[51] was the name of the first pupil; the second who played the violin was dubbed *emendemus in melius*;[52] the third they called *solamen miseri socios habuisse malorum*;[53] the fourth had the name *artem que vis terra alit*;[54] and the musician was called *gallus in arbore sedens, gi gi li, gi gi li dicens.*[55] They were shown into the kitchen in this order where codfish and roast hare was put before them. But since they said they had taken a vow not to eat anything from friends, they were treated in a different manner. The two trumpeters, however, we fed separately, and so that they wouldn't spread lice among us, the baker had to shove their clothes into his oven and check to see whether they weren't secretly carrying pistols and stilettos with them. We knew quite well how such fellows tend to deal with people on the road whom they believe they can overpower, for in times like these for many a person they play a sarabande that makes him forget how to move.

Meanwhile all the people had appeared who earlier had shown me this honor at Herr Ludwig's castle along with many others who were devoted to Monsieur Caspar through special friendship and acquaintance. As cold as it was, I had my beloved brought overland by a sleigh, and the Irishman rode on so poor a road that he solemnly swore that he had come within a whisker of suffocating in the wind and snow, had not some peasants come to his help. "Yes," said Monsieur Ludwig, "that's the way it was with my purse; had not the peasants done their best, it and I would have been lost lock, stock, and barrel." Many of the ladies had almost had their noses and ears frozen off, and there wasn't a one there who couldn't have written a description of her trip worth publishing if only she had assumed the effort and written as thoroughly and in such detail as I have.

Despite the cold, however, Ergasto was full of fire and ardor at this reunion and thus laid the foundation for a second marriage, to which we all wanted to help him. I don't mean to criticize the ladies, but it is true, when they noticed I was the broker in this affair, quite a few came to me and surreptitiously asked me to recommend themselves before someone else and fix them up with Ergasto. Although he had no unusual qualities, everyone liked him and the only thing one might desire

---

[51] "Necessity knows no law."

[52] "We'll change it to something better."

[53] "Misery loves company."

[54] "The strength of the earth nourishes art."

[55] "The rooster sitting in a tree, crowing cock-a-doodle-do."

would be that he were a Turk, for thereby he ultimately could have been shared by all of them. I, however, quickly took one pupil aside and taught him the following song:

> An old horse and an old maid
> Don't count for much in any trade.
> I'd happy be, had I a man
> If short or tall
> Or even were he made of flan.
>
> I lie in bed all night so sad,
> For not a man on earth I've had.
> Had I a man, I'd give for him
> A handsome sum,
> But all I hear's *silentium!*
>
> A husband's what has filled my head
> And need just like my daily bread.
> Take me, Ergasto, I can pay,
> I do you beg
> To make my pain all go away.

The pupil had to memorize these three verses quickly while the musician was to compose a melody for them. But the pupil told me that he didn't understand anything about composing. Because of this my plan was foiled and I would have had to abandon it in midcourse if the pupil himself hadn't composed something and given the affair a new life. Since he also played the bass violin, he scratched out on its strings the bass line or the *bassus ad organum*, as the musicians call it. It sufficed perfectly in the emergency, for it's better to have a louse in your cabbage than no meat at all. And thus the pupil was cantor, organist, tenor, and bellows pumper all in one, and if I weren't sparing him on account of his prompt help, I would have also called him a bumpkin.

When he could sing it perfectly, I waited for the night and the time when the marriage of the newlyweds was to be consummated, which I'm not going to describe in order not to make the reader's mouth water. For, although I already promised not to skip the slightest particulars, I surely have permission to ignore that which does nothing more than arouse in the reader a desire of the body, the mere suggestion of which can be harmful. Because in the preceding Books with similar wedding assemblies I have presented the virtues and vices of respectable people, it is not inappropriate that I flatter the common people a little who usually appear and wait on the others.

I would have said many things about the musician and the pupils as well as the trumpeters and made terrible fun of them if I hadn't known that their special weaknesses are world famous and people talk about them and berate them in almost every beer hall. And what would I gain if I were to describe them with every rhetorical figure? For it takes no skill to upbraid a person for his mistakes, but it takes much effort to show one's neighbor how he can improve himself. Whoever beats his ass without showing him the way he's supposed to take is a worse ass than the one he's beating. And this vice sticks to many satirists like a hair will to your quill in that they only scold about vices and reveal the erroneous ways of men without showing or pointing out the path to improvement or impending virtue. I have avoided such castigation like the plague because it does not improve the persons attacked, but only makes their minds defiant; thus from one evil a greater one has arisen and, lacking light, the vices have followed darkness down the path they first entered.

I am no such satirist and much prefer to put the quill to my breast than to paper because in it reside more vices than in all those whom I have attacked with my quill. Through such derision I would also give no small blow to my goal that I have set too simply delight the hearts of people in a time that makes a man's spirits sad and depressed from just observing it. From the basis of what I've said above, there appears clearly and sufficiently what I have tried to do and what I intend to do until the end of this book. Therefore, without great ado I shall get on with the story so that one day I may set aside the subject and my pen, which perhaps has caused the reader even greater impatience than me in the writing of it.

Herr Carander, Faustus, and Celinda came to the castle before the copulation, and the joy was all the greater at the great friendship they bore for us. People were having fun everywhere, and the clerk was honored more than all of us because he sat at the head of the table with the bride and groom. The day passed in this merriment, and when night came on I marched unseen into the castle courtyard with the rehearsed pupil, where from behind a water pump he had to sing the cited song and play the bass to it. No one had gone to bed despite the fact that one could not tarry in the dancing hall because of the severe cold and the clock had struck twelve. Thus great laughter arose in the rooms, and quite a few people came to their windows with lights to see and identify the singer. But we ducked down as well as we could behind the water pump, although a little bit of the bass violin — if there is any little bit about a bass violin — was sticking out.

Ludwig and Isidoro liked the song so well that in their nightshirts they sneaked down to me in the courtyard and so the pupil had to begin again to sing it *da capo*. Some of the women took it as a joke, some found it coarsely amusing, some even found it to be a major insult. Thus every affair finds certain people who will praise it and, on the other hand, those who will defame it. But it struck especially hard the hearts of those who felt it was intended for them. But in order not to come under suspicion, I ordered the pupil to quietly steal away after finishing the song and to keep himself locked in his room. While he was still singing we ran up the stairway and called over to the women who were naming him now a monstrous rascal, now something else.

Chapter Ten. The Clerk Who Had Been the Baron Writes a Wedding Song. Conversation Concerning Domestic Prudence.

Who kisses now but later bites
Is not among this life's delights.

No one, however, found himself more insulted than the musician because, without his approval and prior knowledge, the pupil had presumed to do something at which the ladies were grumbling like Russian bears. Indeed, I believe he would have struck him over the head with the bass violin, leaving him with his head sticking out of it, if I hadn't been the third man in the comedy and somewhat placated the furious man. "Monsieur," I said, "what does it matter whether the pupil learned, composed, and performed the song with or without your approval? Through this nothing in the slightest has been taken away from your honor or reputation. You've become neither wiser nor more foolish from this and have only fallen into an unnecessary rage.

"You cannot take from the pupil that which he can do, and I am responsible for making him my chamberlain, and thus he is more than you or the trumpeters. He offered not the slightest insult to the ladies, but for me and all the cavaliers present, he performed a service that you were not capable of performing. Otherwise we would not have been so senseless as to go to you and ask you for something that we had not judged by your capabilities. With this we wish you a good night, sleep well, and tomorrow I shall bring a glass of wine to you." After such words I went to bed. But on the following morning when I awoke from my sleep, the trumpeters were already having a grand time. They played some old tunes about the Swedish mortar, and the money they requested as a gratuity they drank up in brandy. Although they didn't have a Groschen in their purse, they were happier than I and had their hats on the back of their heads like bagpipers about to play a tune.

This morning the groom and the bride were splendidly teased. But Caspar just laughed at me, saying that in a long time he had encountered no caper like that with me and Ludwig. But when at noon we revealed the deception with the clerk, he was heartily ashamed that he had shown all possible courtesies to the man. Therewith laughter again broke out, and in one moment the clerk was deposed from all the respect and honors he had had until now. Isidoro ordered him to compose a song in honor of the bridal couple. He worked this out within a quarter of an hour and brought his draft to the table before dinner was half over.

We don't enjoy a splendid state
If we don't have a wife.
Without such we grow desperate
And stay so throughout life.
To live in celibacy
Is truly not right good,
For there it's bad to be
And rarely as it should.

You monks are much too blind
To see how poor's your life!
You'll sleep with cold behind
Until you take a wife.
And wedded life's no sin, you'll find.
Each man will this assert:
It's best to feel the skin
That's 'neath a woman's skirt.

I do confess and without strife
That in my need for woman's love,
If I declined to take a wife,
Into the grave they would me shove.
Therefore I'll love but one,
I wish that here she sat!
So I should pick my hon
Quite soon, and all of that.

The ladies, who didn't know Latin,[56] had this explained mostly by the pupils because they didn't trust Ludwig's translation or those of the other learned noblemen. For they knew that occasionally we had been too German and had been joking with them in many matters. Thus, this day, too, came to an end, and as night fell, we climbed into the waiting sleighs and rode about with flambeaux, a stunning sight. Many of the women were deliberately thrown into the snow so that people could see what they had been bragging about all their lives, and in such manner we also ended this entertainment. Afterwards we spent three straight weeks at the castle that were not much other than lost.

During this time we had consumed so much in Monsieur Caspar's dining room that there was almost nothing left in his pantry. Finally some pigs were used that he intended to use to pay those who had catered his wedding or performed some other service. Not everyone was happy about this. Thus he was accosted almost hourly by those who had provided wine, beer, meat, and other things. After these three weeks scarcely two days passed before there was such a pile of letters demanding payment that he was quite annoyed. "Brother," he said to

---

[56] The original has half its lines in Latin.

me, "upon my word as an honest man, the people who need it least are the ones who have me besieged most often. You know the white-haired nobleman who lives on the other side of the forest and who has no wife or child and so much money at his disposal that you couldn't count it. Nevertheless he constantly has my sleeve tugged like some beggar's cloak. Now I know debts must be paid, but I can't tell you how much this incessant dunning annoys me. Earlier he promised to help me out with a hundred Taler. But now because of a handful of change he won't let me sleep or rest; instead, he wants to be paid come hell or high water, and you saw yourself today that his servant, as all impolite louts do, publicly dunned me before all of you and made the matter as urgent as if his master's whole welfare depended on it. I would gladly pay it, on my word as an honest man, if I were able to. I wouldn't know where to find six Taler of ready cash if I didn't have my wife's money at hand which I'm not going to disturb. What annoys me most is that he wants to be my good brother and won't loan me eight or ten Taler. Every person needs his possessions, but as a favor to a friend, I'd give the shirt off my back and wait until he was ready."

"Fool," I said to him, "why are you depressed about that? I'll advance you a thousand Taler and not expect payment as long as you can't pay. Good brothers are sometimes poor friends. When drinking every one of them can do great things, but when they are actually supposed to help, they are lame and limp. That you trust such people! You regard many a person as a best friend who is such least of all. Everyone can pitch woo to that which is another's, but when it concerns his own purse, then it's *altum silentium*, that is: hold your tongue.

"My good friend," I went on, "you're not yet a courtier, for otherwise you would know that nothing is more necessary for peace of mind than to never trust anyone wholeheartedly. Indeed, you mustn't believe everything from me, for herein lies the understanding of satisfaction that eludes so many because they have relied or still rely too much on others. To be sure, one person is born to help the other, and in such an act one person is the other's god. But they abandon this majesty as often as Jupiter did when making love to humans. Thus angels of salvation easily turn into devils of torment who later harass much more than they helped. If you want to live in peace, see to it that you pay all your debts the sooner, the quicker., for thereby you lift from your heart a great stone that otherwise will eat away many years off your life and swallow them like a sponge. It is better to suffer need than to borrow, for a paid-for piece of bread tastes better than a roast bought with borrowed money that I can't repay. For another thing, don't give anything away in vain and do not be too hospitable, for as long as you keep treating, you're a good fellow, but if you fall into poverty, not one person will respect you any more. Indeed, not only your best friends, but also your brothers and sisters will despise you and make fun of you wherever possible. Thus hang on to what's yours because you don't know when bad times are coming. That's why it's better for you to be prepared for an emergency than to not want to face it until it's present. A soldier who trains in armor before the battle is all the more composed in the fray."

"Truly," Monsieur Caspar said to me, "that's what I'll do. Your admonitions are more valuable than all the conversations we've had with one another since my wedding. I know several examples where such men, after losing all credit, are laughed at and made fun of not only by their earlier friends, but also their former servants and help. Whoever provides himself with water beforehand can all the better extinguish the fire when it breaks out. Here I recall what happened to a famous emperor. When he first lay with his bride, he said to her: *tota es formosa*, you are quite shapely. Then he marched away and drove his enemies out of his land. After this glorious victory he returned home but found his empress in the throes of a high fever. Her previous figure was so consumed by this high fever that he almost didn't recognize her any more. Therefore, he said to her: *periis facies tua*; my dear, he wanted to say, your figure is quite gone, it is perished and lost.

"It's just that way with many good friends. At first glance you can say to them: *totus est formosus*: my dear friend, you are quite upright, quite trusting, quite friendly and loving. That lasts a while and if perhaps a small war intervenes, the fair figure changes into an ugly fever illness and then it's: *facies tua periit*: my friend, your figure, that is your uprightness, your honesty, your brotherly love is gone, your help has disappeared, *facies tua periit*, you are no longer the German of old. And this is one more of the plagues that man is subjected to here on earth since human activity turns the wheel on a wagon where all the parts are now on the bottom, now on the top, now at one side, and thus a human being is nothing but an insignificant ball with which fortune plays until the yarn breaks."

During this conversation we heard the sleigh horses being harnessed; therefore, everyone prepared for departure. Before we parted I begged Monsieur Caspar to confide in me whether the story of his life he had told at my wedding actually had happened or whether it was the product of his imagination. Then he said in reply that it had actually happened to a young student who had taken flight because of it and had spent fourteen weeks at this his castle and then gone on his way. This was satisfying news to me, for, to tell the truth, I had had a thousand fancies about the story he had told then.

Chapter Eleven. The Nice Revelation of the Story about the Countess in the Bath and Whom She Actually Met. A Much Too Severe Judge Receives a Very Strange Answer from a Whore.

One person goes and wins the fight,
Another bears the honors bright.

When we departed from the castle, the sun was already climbing somewhat higher and the boys were gradually ceasing to ruin their shoes through sliding on the ice. The Irishman escorted us, and although we had believed we would soon be appearing at his wedding, it all was still wide open because his affection for his beloved had rather frozen up this winter. As far as one could tell from him, he had put such an intention completely aside, for he was resolved to become a Capuchin monk or even play the hermit. He said that as his permanent residence he had selected a place near his small castle where not a person would get to see him. He wanted to make the castle a way station for traveling people and in the meantime a long and protracted pilgrimage.

With such conversation we parted from one another. Isidoro could not stop being surprised at the Irishman's sudden decision because he had been a happy spirit all his life and always thought highly of true ladies. After we parted I stayed with my beloved for three more days at Isidoro's, and there various released soldiers who had appeared with their discharges before his gate had to tell us their life stories, which I could make into a book by itself. After this I and my wife took leave of Isidoro for the time being and were in somewhat of a hurry because otherwise I certainly would have had to have my sleigh loaded onto a wagon and myself and it driven overland, for it was thawing everywhere. And so I arrived home while there was still time.

As soon as I alighted, the clerk said to me that a student was waiting for me who desired to speak a few words with me. I had him brought in, but his request was for nothing but a little travel money that he badly needed in a season such as this. What pleased me most was that he spoke Latin extremely well and to all appearances had a singular mind. He announced among other things that formerly he had enjoyed great favor among the nobility and had stayed with one who was named Caspar. He also wanted to travel to his place this time and to apply for some position. From this I noted that he was the student from whom Monsieur Caspar had borrowed the story he had told and thus I had an all the greater desire to hear him speak about the affair as the principal, to which he readily agreed. Thus at my request he began the following recitation:

"Monsieur, fortune drives me about like a ship on the sea . . . ." (Here he told the story word for word as the rope-walker had in Chapter Five of Book Three.) " . . . And when I was about to sell the silver lace, I was put into prison and locked up tight by the cavalier who recognized it." (This story refers to the conclusion of Chapter Six in Book Three.) "In this prison," the student went on, "I came to recognize to what frightful danger lascivious spirits tend to subject themselves, for I was regarded as a thief, which, however, I was not. If I wanted to be out of danger, I had to admit of necessity how things stood with the lace. For because I no longer had any favors from the countess to hope for, I didn't want to lose my life so disgracefully on account of her, for it is certain that they would have strung me up from the shiny gallows without mercy and compassion. Therefore, I made it short and sweet, caring little how it might turn out. The matter was taken under judgement, and soon thereafter they brought into my prison a whore who had created quite a lot of friendship because she had made quite a few men relatives.[57] This disgraceful slut was jailed opposite me, and thus I obviously saw into what respectable company the odious addiction to fornication tends to lead a person.

"I sighed quite painfully about my misfortune and wished I had never laid eyes on the countess. Soon the confined whore was examined by the judge who was still young and harsh. She admitted many capers she had committed outside the city. But because he didn't know how to catch any big fish with that, he forced quite many things out of her that had taken place in the city and among its citizens.

"After a long list of the miscreants he didn't let up, however, but was even harsher with her than before. When she saw that she could conceal nothing, she gave him this answer: 'Your Honor. Because you want to know everything right, I must in truth confess and withhold none of the evil I have committed. Therefore, listen well and record it accurately in your book. The first person who slept with me and used me as a whore, that was your father when he was still a clerk in ** and **.' — 'What,' said the judge, 'my father?' — 'Yes,' answered the whore, 'Judge, that's the way it was, your father was the first man who slept with me.' I can't tell you how ashamed the judge was in the presence of those sitting at the table as notaries. And because the girl was ready to swear an oath about it, the judge declared she was mad and out of her mind, let her go, and said if she uttered a single word about this to the citizenry, he would have her thrown on a pyre.

"At that time I became aware of how the emotions can affect a judge who is not always in control of himself, and in this confusion I had the best opportunity of freeing myself from my fetters and secretly slipping out of the prison. Accordingly, I climbed out the window quite clandestinely at night and was up and away until I reached the castle of the aforementioned Caspar, who kept me safe for fourteen weeks. Then

---

[57] In German slang men known to be sleeping with the same woman are referred to as *Schwäger*, "brothers-in-law."

dressed as a craftsman's apprentice, I ventured among the people again although I avoided by a good margin the city where I had been captured. But everywhere people told me how the count had had his wife whipped terribly on account of me and the bathhouse woman chased out of her village for having dared engage in such procuring.

"The poor countess died from her pains soon thereafter, and the count can't find a bride, no matter how hard he tries. But, as gossip has it, he again wants to take a lady of the nobility who doesn't have much to offer, and this is finally going to happen, for women don't like to be alone. And although many a woman thinks she's smart enough, there aren't many of them capable of giving themselves the best advice, especially in a matter that removes their virginal status. But she'll end up worse than the judge with his examination of the whore."

The student's story surprised me not a little. What struck me as especially odd was that the countess could love him because he was rather coarse and uncouth. Thus I thought of Ergasto, who had related to me on this very spot that Veronia had much preferred to deal with crude people than intelligent ones, whereby she simply disgraced herself and was talked about by everyone. The student also mentioned various other pranks he had undertaken with the maids and other women when he was a pupil, but as I've written earlier, I will not use such disgraceful deeds to excite those who read such books not so that they might avoid vice, but solely that the might pursue it intently.

Chapter Twelve. Against His Will a Student Passes His *examen rigorosum*[58] in the Open Field.

> *The major thieves just run away,*
> *The little ones are made to pay.*

Here I revealed my thinking to the student and sent him with a letter of recommendation to Caspar, who could best assist him with his plans and probably would be able to help him get a parish. He thanked me for my gratuity, but things went weirdly for the poor devil.

On his way he came to a castle where on that same day a preceptor had committed horribly insolent acts. First, this man had gotten tight as a tick and subsequently smashed all the windows in the castle because the nobleman hadn't given him a Pfennig in pay for half a year. The preceptor played this game for a good hour and had so cursed and defamed his absent master that the rafters might have bent. Finally he had even presumed to beat the noblewoman with his cane and threatened her if she wouldn't pay him the money due, he was resolved to take a candle

---

[58] "rigorous examination," i. e., orals.

and set fire to the castle. The lady was so shocked by such a threat that she gave him the money and wished a thousand times that her lord would come home soon. When the preceptor received the money he vanished with it and stole things from the castle worth more than twenty Taler. This happened around noon, and when the nobleman came home in the evening, he heard the news in great rage. He immediately remounted with his groom to run after the fellow and catch him.

Now misfortune struck the very student who shortly before had told me his story in such detail. And because he strongly resembled the nobleman's preceptor, the nobleman in fury whipped him about the road for real and called him a son of a . . . time and again. Whatever the student thought at the time, the reader can note how he felt when, without cause, he was unexpectedly attacked with such hospitality. At first he took the nobleman to be one of the soldiers who commonly rob travelers. For this reason he hopped about in his cloak so that from a distance one easily could have taken him for a windmill. Finally the nobleman's eyes were opened, and when he recognized his mistake, he set the student on his groom's horse and promised to promote him because of this unintentional whipping as soon as possible. Thus, against his will the student was thrashed into a master of arts, for in the following week he made him the preacher in the village, and the student could properly boast that he had passed his *examen rigorosum* quite well.

I thought I'd laugh myself sick at this incident that the student wrote down for me in a letter with many nice details. I would record it here word for word if only the material that I intend to use in the following Book Six didn't restrain me from doing so. For what do you gain from such letters other than wasting your time and learning less than nothing? I'm not writing this book for a peasant who's better off if he knows how to clean the dirt off his plowshare than how to skillfully solve the complications of this treatise and memorize them; rather, I've written it for the kinds of minds that are capable of framing a letter themselves from the student's circumstances and of knowing in advance what the letter directed to me must have been like.

And what's the purpose of filling story books with things that only cause aggravation? And although this person or that may find some pleasure in them, for most people this is a heedless discursiveness that diverts one from the main goal and arises from the author's vain desire to be a great writer and to show that he has also gone to school and stuck his nose into books. For another thing, it's also no small madness to describe in such writings the ceremonies of the cavaliers and ladies and other people of quality and the pompous prattle accompanying their politenesses. For even though I may be recording language that is in vogue at court when I write, to another person it may be regarded as not good or at least unusual. If certain reasons didn't hold me back, I would here list a whole catalog of things that have been used in various books to the great annoyance of the readers.

But the reason for such works consists solely in the vain arrogance of egotism because most people think it a great imprudence if in even the briefest text they didn't display all their knowledge and learning, all their *locos communes* and quotes from Ancient authors and other writers, all their imagined and affected courtliness, all their elegant phrases and the like and thus make them known to the world. But I, on the contrary, have decided on something far different because I will not rave on at great length to please you or anyone else since I'm dealing in subject matter and not words. Thus, the subject matter is not to be filled with words, but the words with subject matter, for words waste a lot of time that should be constrained by the subject matter.

So in this book, too, I have kept things short and introduced no dialogs that are conducted in jargon or just go on too long. Long plays are simply tiresome, no matter how pleasing their subject is per se, for I didn't care to think up various conversations, by means of which I intended to adorn my writing. No, truly not; instead, I've stuck with the words and phrases used by our group back then because I regard them as neither too literate nor too simple and thus suitable for everyone.

On the other hand, let the reader be assured that at the instigation of the many subjects treated here I would have ventured to work out a grand Hercules, if I hadn't known that the most pleasing books are those that can be read through in three or four days in idle relaxation.

Thus it is my intention to continue on and report how things ended up for Countess Veronia because I know that not having given some news about this would be unpleasant for the person who in any case likes to ruminate about matters of love. But please let no woman imagine that in depicting Veronia's crude adultery I have insulted the honor of any woman, for any such intention has been far removed from my pen, which desires nothing more than that it be looked upon with favor by the womenfolk. Truly I am not of the great lovers or foolish gallants who use most of their time idly, since they think of nothing but their own folly and often trifle away their eternal welfare and walk all over it for the sake of a piece of stinking flesh.

I would much rather do hurt to myself than print a matter about so high a lady, who, however, can not truthfully be called high because through her own promiscuity, she lost her nobility and sank far beneath the common class when she did not hesitate to ignore the means by which nobility prospers, namely, chaste virtue, and to desecrate her body through many thousands of whorish deeds. I hope that this text is brought before her eyes, and then, convinced by her own conscience, she would have to admit that not a fourth of her misconduct has been described in it, whereby I, as author of this story, have done her a great favor. But although I don't want to be merciful to such a person or have the reputation of showing favor to one who is depraved, I shall lay to one side the worst of her secret love practices only so that not a single innocent spirit be aroused by them, nor that a thousand poisonous snakes emerge through my opening of a fetid slough, nor that my good intention produce an evil end.

Book Six.

Chapter One. What Kind of Miser Crispan Was.

The miser only gold does chase
And dies, like Judas, in disgrace.

At the castle with which my father endowed me upon my wedding I ordered a farmer to keep a good eye on the household as well as the water and grazing rights that brought me considerable rent every year. And I must confess that quite often during the writing of this book I rode here and there and pursued many thousands of whims and crazy ideas while on the road.

Sometimes on such a trip I was whistling some cavalry songs, and because my groom was from Steiermark, he had to tell me underway how the girls in his village tended to behave and how many of them he had slept with in his life. Then I heard how this twit in the same circumstances had enjoyed better luck than many a nobleman and was all the more fortunate because the favors done for him hadn't cost half as much as for someone of my station, since frequently many a poor wretch has almost made himself a beggar from spending on the whores and ends up wondering how it happened.

"I was brought up in Graz not far from the main fortress," said my groom, "and because of an old serfdom the nobleman had the right to take the peasants and other children born there into his service without payment. Oh, sir," he continued, "this nobleman was a miser, but I don't know whether he's still alive or not. But if he's dead, then he was a miser who had few equals in all the world. I had the misfortune of having to serve him in my youth, and because he was much too niggardly, the peasants in the village had to chip in and have a livery made for me. Whenever I came into the tavern and the peasants were drunk, one of them would pound me on the head and then another one would, so I was almost pounded deaf in my youth, and hence the nobleman likewise whipped me when I didn't respond to him quickly enough.

"Ha, I often laughed myself blue in the face when the nobleman received letters, for he saved them up until he had quite enough of them lying in a copper pan to melt the sealing wax from them with which he sealed other letters. From this you can clearly see what a frightfully greedy devil possessed the nobleman. I'd have to be lying like the worst scoundrel if I said I received one drop of beer the whole year except when his cousin gave me a small glass, two of which he always used to empty at mealtime. But however clumsily and foolishly I behaved with my master, he hit me only with his hand. He didn't have the heart to use his whip because he was afraid of wearing it out on me, and then he would have had to lay out four Groschen for a new one.

"He kept only one single horse and inquired everywhere in the countryside whether someone or another wanted to use it for a day or two. That person had to give him two Gulden and provide a tip for the peasant that accompanied it, for which he also charged, and thus he earned any number of Groschen and Pfennige with his horse. He often scratched his head when he saw the maids feeding the hens. But he gathered the eggs from the stalls himself though he didn't have the heart to eat one; instead, he had them taken to the weekly market and sold for a good sum. Once he counted out a good fifty into a peasant girl's basket, but on her way she stumbled over a rock and broke them all on the road. He had all her clothes taken from her and kept them until she had compensated him for the fifty eggs.

"It is certain that no human being ever suffered greater toothaches than he did. And nevertheless money was so dear to him that he would have died from pain before he laid out the measliest Heller for drops. Once when he was having a new roof put on and was one worker short, he sent to the preacher and asked him to fill out. All his windows were covered with paper, and I can swear that at the castle they were my sole concern because when one became spotted, I had to tear it down and paste up a new one. Thus the nobleman could install and maintain all his windowpanes with a half bushel of flour. I can't tell you how the ladies and others criticized and scolded when they were assaulted by a summer storm and compelled to turn in there. Otherwise probably not a person would have come to his place except for a few who wanted to amuse themselves at his lifestyle and discovered an even greater parsimony in the castle than people had said earlier.

"I still think that he was terribly in love, and as maladroit as I usually am, I still could note all his tricks because he was rather clumsy in his stinginess. In no way did he dare to marry due to great fear of losing too much thereby. For he said quite often, he would have to cry his eyes out if he ever had an heir. And he busied himself with such meannesses without cease and had to let himself be mocked and laughed at not only by his peers, but also by base people and even by his peasants.

"He once came to a wedding not as a guest, but as a disguised observer because he had heard that it would be extremely elegant. This wedding took place at a castle, and I had to walk across the fields with him because he was dressed as a schoolmaster in an outfit he had inherited from his great-great-great-great-great-great-grandfather. For his family tree had borne such fine branches that I hardly believe that someone would have given a Batzen for the lot of them. We arrived at the noble wedding when people had begun to dance. And because I was soon

209

recognized because of my livery, the gentlemen asked me what my parsimonious master was up to and whether he was still skinning lice for their pelts.

"'The Devil,' one of them said to me, 'it's too bad you're being raised at this arch-cheapskate's. The scoundrel isn't worthy of bearing a noble name because he deserves to be named commander of all the cheapskates. That shit-ass should be mortified at displaying such avarice that the whole world talks about it and laughs at it. As soon as possible I'm going to publish a book about the thoughtless skinflint that should frighten him. I believe the Devil himself is riding him, and if I could just once lay hands on him in a convenient place, I'd beat his avaricious hide to shreds so that he would remember a proper nobleman.'

"All this the nobleman said in the presence of my master, whom he didn't recognize because of the disguise. At this my master began to tremble and shake because he believed the wedding guest would take him by the throat. But as luck would have it, a new dance was struck up, whereby the nobleman was prevented from continuing to sing the praise of my master that he otherwise would not have spared him. For he had a very insolent mouth and chattered away like a spinning-wheel, although in this matter he had shown little understanding. For what did it concern him that my nobleman had been miserly? He had lost nothing and gained nothing thereby, and also had become neither more clever nor more foolish.

"'Indeed,' said my master as we were leaving the dance floor, 'Jost, my dear Jost, that's got to be a mother . . . who cursed me so. If only I had had my right clothes on! I would have shown the lout to be a coward. It's just as well he didn't recognize me. Oh, how cleverly I'm going to get even with him! Today I'll have four peasants observe the road. I know him, I know him, oh, I know him! He's one respectable bird, a braggart, nothing more. He thinks he's a big deal and can't do anything. Whenever he comes into company, he behaves like a fool. And when he's supposed to pay nine Pfennig for a tankard of beer, the pulls out a whole handful of money so people will see that he too is also well off. But at home his wife goes hungry, and I've heard that he sends his two servants to his villages to steal chickens from the peasants. Oh, that chicken thief! The Devil take him and his wealth! That's a scoundrel, that's a mother . . .! He calls me a skinflint, up yours, skinflint yourself!

"'If I could fence, oh, how I'd slash him about his chops so that his dainty teeth would pop out! Oh, what a fool I am for not knowing how to wrestle. Damn, how I'd throw him to the ground so that his kneecaps would have to shatter! Oh, Jost, oh Jost, if only you had punched him in the face and run away quickly! You're a miserable bastard!' But I thought: 'Master, because you didn't do it, you're one too!' — 'Oh, that gallows bird,' he went on, 'how he attacked my honor. Oh, if my late father had known this, it would have pained him greatly. But enough, enough, I can borrow, if not today, then tomorrow. Who knows how this business will come off. The Devil probably sent me to that wedding and not a guardian angel. I've been to a wedding, but never again. I'm so furious I could tear my hair out!'

"My master covered the road to his castle with such foolish conversation with himself, and I had to laugh at his fancy plans. When we came to the castle, he immediately sent four peasants to the road where the nobleman who had insulted him earlier had to ride by. 'You peasants,' my master said to them, 'if you do your job and go at it stoutly, I'll reward you with a Groschen's worth of beer and let you bowl for an hour on my alley without paying.' The nobleman's uncommon generosity made the peasants mightily brave; they picked up their flails and went off to the road after the nobleman had had a pint of beer drawn for each of them to give them heart.

Chapter Two. He Has a Nobleman Beaten and Is Visited by Some Ladies. Their Compliments Before the Gate. A Strange Duel.

Like in the forest when you shout,
An echo's all that will come out.

"These emissaries fulfilled their assignment quite well and perhaps delivered more blows than the nobleman ordered them to. My master couldn't have been happier when he became aware that some appeared before him splattered with blood. He leapt with joy like a goat, and they were to tell him every detail of how the beaten man had behaved or what he had said. But they couldn't tell him anything other than that they had thrown him off his horse, swung their flails across his back, and beaten his horse to death. 'Yes,' one of them said, 'we thrashed him like a frog, and if some people hadn't come to his help, we would have beaten him as dead as a doornail. But to our good luck we escaped into some underbrush and they couldn't ride after us although they did fire two shots at us.'

"During this conversation a coach came to the castle filled with women who had been at the wedding and heard that at his place lived as tight a skinflint as could be found anywhere. That's why they had come, more for fun than for any other reason, to visit the nobleman, my master, so they could see with their own eyes this phenomenon.

They arrived at the castle's gate just as I was walking with him beneath two linden trees. Because he hadn't changed out of his schoolmaster's garb they didn't recognize him and asked, instead, whether the mangey cur, the nobleman Kratzfilz,[59] were at home. 'Yes,' he said, 'he's at home and waiting for a coach full of infamous whores. If you're them,

---

[59] Another of many German words for 'miser.'

211

you can drive on in.' From this they recognized that it was he himself; they ordered the coachman to turn around and told him to his face that in all their lives they had neither seen nor heard of so nasty a lout and total boor as he was. 'Look,' he said, 'you all can kiss me you know where, you filthy douche bags!' — 'Oh, you tightwad,' a lady called from the coach, 'you aren't worthy of having a louse bite you!' Herewith they drove off quickly and called him a pinchpenny and he called them superwhores in return. Thus they kept bestowing honorary titles on one another for as long as they could hear.

"'Look at those proud wagtails,' he said to me, 'how quick they are to fight. I think the Devil wants to aggravate me. Oh, they won't get me with their derision by far! And who knows who'll bury the other, dogs also eat meat. Fools, foolish pranks! Oh, you carrion, you scullery maids, you flea-bitten witches! You've had time to drive away, otherwise I'd set your tightwad to music, you sluts! No sooner are you given a pair of gloves than you start prancing around, you rich fools! Oh, that the Devil would drown you in your curses! Did I deserve that from you? If you're brave enough, come back! I showed that gallows' bird today what the score was. If I knew who you were, I'd have you nasty devils so thrashed that your miser would be jumping out of your eyes and noses, you stinking bags! The fools go around bragging, but if you lift their skirts, they're wearing ragged slips! Yes, the Devil would have to be riding me if I were to marry a woman of the nobility! No, no, I know full well that there are other people out there and perhaps much better than you, you bedsores!

"'Those flaming whores called me a cheap mangey dog and, what's worse, a tightwad too! Oh, you mangey curs yourselves, you're mangey curs and not I! You don't know yet what a virtue thrift is, you wanton people. Look, look, they called me a tightwad; oh, that God knows who would scratch your asses, you nasty birds! If only I had a sword four miles long, I'd hack you to pieces like little beets!'

"In such conversation, which he again was conducting with himself, he sent me to his cousin so that she wouldn't fix anything to eat, because he was preoccupied by frightful anger and disgust. And when I told her the reason, how things had gone for him on the dance floor and before the castle gate, she was not greatly surprised because she knew well how despicably the common people customarily talked about his household. 'My dear Jost,' she said to me, 'My cousin's bungling is too well-known. When you've really found it out, you'll be able to believe it better than I could tell you. I've already settled my accounts; if it concerns me, I don't ask any questions.'

"I didn't know what she was trying to tell me, but later I learned the explanation all too well, so I'll have to tell you in proper order how prettily things went at the castle. The nobleman who had been so fearfully attacked by the four peasants at the instigation of the cheap miser had finally learned the truth of the matter and because he had certain proof of it, he sent my master the following letter:

> An affronted nobleman wishes every misfortune that can occur under the sun to descend on the head of the archscoundrel Crispan. Herewith prepare yourself for a fight or you shall see your castle and the village in flame within two hours. What your schoolmaster didn't teach you with his whip, I shall teach you with my sword, and the thick skin your parsimony has given you I'm going to pull over your head with my own hands, you archrascal of all rascals! I will not rest until I've perforated your body with a thousand wounds. Then the ravens will eat you up beneath the sky and I will have your domicile plowed under as was the custom earlier with Troy, in case your knowledge extends beyond your village. Now do what is appropriate, I will be before your gate in half an hour.

"A lackey brought this letter and as soon as he had delivered it, he took his leave, reporting that his master was inflamed with great rage and would appear as soon as possible on his gray. After this report he left, and because of this challenge my master was so fearful that he couldn't make up his mind what he should do in this case."

Chapter Three. Jost Tells His Life Story. Ludwig and Isidoro Try Out a Thieves' Trick.

Sometimes we only say we're friends,
Our hearts will tell us who offends.

"From that time on I haven't seen anything as funny in all my life. For poor Crispan grew more distraught, the longer it went on, and he even sent to the preacher for advice as to whether he might or might not enter into such a frightful and dangerous fight in good conscience. But most unfortunately the preacher was not at home because he had had to call on a dropsy patient who was about to begin his final trip. For this reason he turned to another means by deciding to summon all the peasants in the village, of whom there were maybe no more than six. But right then it was in the time for sowing, so they were all busy with their horses in the fields, something that hadn't occurred to Crispan in his great fright. He asked now himself, now his cousin for practical advice, and I wasn't able to give him any sure advice here even though I wished with all my heart that one day I'd be free of my aggravating and base service. In such circumstances the village tavernkeeper came to the castle, wanting to buy some straw to spread in his new barn. But, master, although he was rather devoted to greed, for this time Crispan let the business go and asked him rather about a practical means of escaping his impending danger. The tavernkeeper was a clever bird and had trafficked in intrigues all his life to an indescribable degree. He knew quite well that Crispan had no courage; for this reason he made the danger twice as great.

"'Dear sir,' he said to the nobleman, 'you sure picked the right man. There's no more skillful fencer in the whole country, and you haven't yet eaten as many roast chickens as he has impaled stout fellows on his sword. Truly, I wouldn't give a thousand Taler to be in your place now, for I fear you might come away with a wound that will make you forget how to stand up.'

"'I believe that quite well,' said the nobleman, 'but is there no advice to be found for me?' — 'Sir,' answered the tavernkeeper, 'for now there's nothing better for you than to hang yourself before your gate in a sling like I have at home. For your opponent will not only feel great pangs of conscience at your action, but in view of that turn around and ride back where he came from. However, your castle help and I will keen and mourn before the gate, and in this way you can avert the danger with a smile on your face.'

"'That's not a bad suggestion,' said the nobleman, who with folded hands begged the innkeeper to just take care of the matter and bring the sling because the challenger would arrive in a quarter of an hour. At that the tavernkeeper took off at breakneck speed for the tavern and brought back the sling, which was sewn together from good sole leather. He put this on over the nobleman's underclothes and all of us carried him on a ladder to the castle gate, where the tavernkeeper blackened his face with walnut dye that made it appear as though blood had been cut off completely. It was astonishing what pretty lessons the innkeeper gave the nobleman on how to pose naturally, how to hang his head and look like one hanged. It almost seemed as if the innkeeper either had been hanged once or at least would still be hanged, for he arranged the nobleman so skillfully that we ourselves finally would have doubted whether he was living if he hadn't asked at various times if the challenger was riding up or not. He kept calling, 'Is he there? Is he there yet?'

"From this we readily concluded that fear was tormenting him greatly, for he begged us to stand by him loyally in this danger; then he wouldn't look at his four Groschen piece, but give it to us willingly. After this admonition the nobleman galloped toward the castle with two lackeys, and before the gate we broke into a horrible howling like dogs and wolves. The tavernkeeper ran his head into the wall again and again as though he were mad and crazed. We did other amazing things of this sort, and the challenger and his servants stopped in astonishment when he gradually was able to see why we were playing such a woeful and pitiable game.

"'You poor people,' he said to us, 'who is the hanged person?' — 'Oh, dear sir,' said the tavernkeeper with a great sigh, 'our nobleman!' Then he again ran against the wall quite convincingly, and the others asked the nobleman for advice about what they should do with the hanged man. 'You needn't be sad' he answered, 'about a man who ruled you only with disgrace and dishonor. In him you lost not a member of the nobility, but a boor such as the world has never seen. Four days ago he had me waylaid on the road by four peasants who not only left me unconscious in the ditch, but also ruined my best horse. Your master committed such knavery and deserved no better death. And in revenge I'm going to send this bullet into his body, even if I were to fall into the greatest misfortune for doing so.' With such words he drew his pistol and cocked the hammer.

"When the suspended Crispan caught sight of this, he called from the sling and cried for mercy. The challenger said, 'What! Is it customary at this castle that the dead speak?' The innkeeper saw that his plan had failed, so he took flight towards his home, and we soon followed after, with one person hiding here in the castle, another there. But when the challenger had stumbled onto the deception, he so whipped Crispan, who could neither move nor defend himself in the sling, that the latter's pants were noticeably gilded.

"During such action the clerk and the cousin in the castle had packed everything in a trunk and stolen most of the silver along with the money. And because I saw my best advantage in times like this, I too quietly ran away, and the others stole whatever they could get their hands on. In such fashion not a person remained behind who could have helped him from the sling except the tavernkeeper, who hauled him down half dead and took him back to his house. How it went from there I can't report, for I came to an old noblewoman in a small one-story castle who took me in only because I was already wearing livery. From this I could easily figure out that I would remain in service only as long as it didn't tear apart or fall to pieces."

This tale that my groom Jost had related to me with special amusement rather delighted me since I learned from it that strange things frequently happen not only to me and my coterie, but also to other people, only that we don't always know it or know the people who have often had a greater adventure than we ourselves. Because my groom's unusual circumstances were pleasing to hear, I wanted to hear how things had gone for him with the old noblewoman, but without our noticing it, we had drawn so near to the manor that I no longer had enough time to give ear to his words. Therefore, I told him a few precepts he should derive from his story, such as, what a frightful, wild beast greed is. And with that we rode into the dairy farm.

The farmer was quite glad that I had come in person, for he had already prepared to ride toward me and indicate what a great danger they had survived last night. "It's fortunate that Your Worship has arrived," he said to me, "for yesterday a thief came into the sheep stall, whom we caught and have locked in the cellar in two chains." — "Ha, ha," I said, "we'll have to pluck this thieving bird! Tell me, is it a soldier or who is the thief?" — "We don't know," answered the farmer, "but it took all we could do until he surrendered. There was another man with him, who ran away and kept laughing so that we could hear it from across the field."

I thought I had to take a look at the thief right away, and from the appearance of the matter, have him arrested; therefore, I went into the cellar, and when the farmer opened the door, the confined man said to me, "Brother, you must have time that you come yourself." At these words I leapt back, for it was Monsieur Ludwig, and it was impossible for me to keep from whipping the farmer and his helpers around the cellar no small bit. But Ludwig told me to restrain myself, saying that they had done their job and had not treated him inappropriately. But a poltergeist had frightened him terribly in the night. Then they freed him immediately and I embraced him joyfully. But he no longer could stop laughing.

Then we went into a private room where he told me how he heard I at one time stayed at this farm. "And," he went on to say, "because at that time I had a discharged soldier with me who liked to talk about various tricks, I had Isidoro brought over to my place because I knew he was a special devotee of such doings. The cavalryman told us a great many things about how one could cleverly steal, and among other things he said that if you had torn a hole in a sheep stall and wanted to know whether the shepherd or peasant was inside standing by the hole and watching, you should poke in your hat on your sword or a stick. If it was true that someone was watching, he would strike out and you could take off for where you had come from. But if you didn't detect any blow, that was a sign that no one was in the stall watching the sheep.

"Now I have to admit that this thieves' trick tickled me no end. I thought day and night of rehearsing this trick and putting it to work. Because I quite soon chose the situation of this very estate for doing this, I came quite late yesterday with Isidoro across the field and when we found the house already closed up, we dismounted at your sheep stall with no other intention than to perform the trick learned from the cavalryman and to give you some amusement. With the axe he had brought along Isidoro knocked a large hole in the wall and I stuck my hat in a dozen times but wasn't aware that anyone inside was watching. And there wasn't anyone inside. When I had crawled in and was about to hand out the sheep and rams to Isidoro, the twit closed the hole and shortly thereafter the farmer caught me in the middle of the stall, and I can't tell you how I knocked around with his people before they cast me in chains. That's what happened, and I'll give the farmer a tip for having been so alert and catching me."

I laughed more at this story than at any other contained in this book that lets you see that you must always be on guard against all crime. For in such circumstances even the most innocent are in danger, and those who mean best come away with the most blows. But what surprised me most of all was that Isidoro had abandoned him and had taken flight like a thief. For this reason we wrote him a letter, and on the third day thereafter he showed up at our place and we had our usual jokes with one another. Ludwig promised to put the whole story into a comedy as soon as possible and to have it performed at his castle. After that for a solid week we had fun and passed the time in every way you could think of. Because Ergasto also would be married very soon to a foreign noblewoman at Isidoro's castle, everyone was prepared to be properly high-spirited at this meeting. In the meantime I spent my time with dirty jokes and shot the breeze with him at the mill because he was a grand master and old hand at such.

Chapter Four. Jost Comes to an Old Noblewoman. How Things Went for Him with Her Daughter.

> *What people do in younger years*
> *Right often later reappears.*

After their farewell I remained at the estate for some days, during which time I instructed the farmer in how he should arrange the cow and pig stalls for the coming spring as well as the manure heaps. And because I did see that doing the work alone at this farm seemed somewhat too difficult for him, I decided to look around for a competent steward who was to supervise things and keep my accounts. After such instructions, I rode back again with Jost. And because I desired to hear how things had gone with the old noblewoman, he continued his earlier story, saying:

"I told Your Worship all about how my miserly master, my first one, was whipped in the sling and how some of us, particularly myself, got away from the castle."

"Yes," I said, "I heard all that from you. So go on and tell me how things went with the old biddy, namely the old noblewoman."

"Well," said the groom, "stick with me. Earlier I said she accepted me on account of my livery and thus kept me as long as it hung on my body. But after half a year she chased me off, during which time I learned a few things. She had a daughter who was rather blasé."

"What does that mean," I said to him, "blasé?"

"That's as much as saying," he said, "that she didn't stoutly defend her honor, for she spooned magnificently, and because I was a simple lad, I had to deliver all sorts of love notes for her. An old nobleman who lived not far across the fields was her most ardent admirer. But the girl led him around by the nose and tricked him out of many presents, which she later gave to a schoolmaster's son who played the organ in the church. The latter was eighteen years old and gradually developed

217

an interest in girls when she gave him every opportunity to exercise a free hand. But purely from jealousy about this, the clerk was so hateful and contrary to the young man that he reported all sorts of pranks by him to the old noblewoman so that she might chase him out of the village. The girl told the young man about this and he told the schoolmaster. The clerk and the schoolmaster got into a quarrel about this and from there into fisticuffs since they often attacked one another like rabid dogs and knocked over tables and benches in their scuffling. The brewer at the castle was still a bachelor and perhaps thought about the girl more often than the brewery. And because she was frivolous enough for such practices, she might have fallen for him if the huntsman hadn't entered the game. And I can swear that she lay down in bed with me quite often, especially when her mother was bedridden with gallstones, an affliction that attacked her rather often. For at such times the old housekeeper Ursula had to stay with her, and so the girl pretended she was afraid of being alone. But she forbade me to say anything about it to her mother or any other person."

"Jost," I said, "what did you do then when you were lying beside the girl?"

"Ha," he answered, "what should I have done? At that time I knew quite little or nothing at all about such business. But I still know well that she kissed me for half an hour at a stretch and grabbed my body as though she wanted to pick lice from me. But I was such a young toad I didn't know whether she meant ill or well with me. 'My dear child,' she said, 'you are much too fine for a peasant lad. I wish you were bigger, you'd quickly be the castellan and later my husband.'"

"Jost," I said, "that was a good offer."

"Yes, sir," he answered, "but nothing came of it. Otherwise I'd be better off than I am now."

"Jost," I said, "what was the daughter called?"

"Sir, she was called Veronia and later even became a countess, but I haven't seen her since my youth."

From this explanation I was jolted to realize that this very woman was the Veronia of whom the kind reader has already heard quite a bit. Therefore, I let him continue, for I had known she began her disreputable life when quite young although I had never heard her antics described. "Jost," I said, "go on! Good Jost, go on! How did it continue with Veronia? Did she truly like you?"

"Oh, sir," he replied, "definitely."

"How old was she then?"

"Thirteen," he answered.

"How old were you?" I went on to ask.

"I was scarcely eight years old," Jost replied, "but I did like it when she stroked me now and then. And when she had lain with me, on the next day she gave me a lot of nun's farts,[60] of which I ate so many I almost could have crapped an abbess."

"Ow, nasty," I said to him, "you're really a coarse lout."

"Yes, sir," he answered with smiling face, "but nevertheless they tasted great. But once I got tight as a tick on good wine she gave me before we lay down and I truly don't know what she did with me that night. But on the following morning I became aware that I had soiled and stained the bed all over for I had lost control in both front and rear. So that the matter remained hidden, the daughter surreptitiously stuck the sheets in the privy and quickly took another pair from the closet because she carried with her the keys to all the chests and boxes in the castle.

"I can't tell you how many suitors she had. For she became more beautiful, the older she got until finally she became an elegant wife, which happened four weeks before the old noblewoman chased me off because she could no longer use me for anything. She gave me no more than three Groschen for travel money; that's why I cried bitterly on the road because I had not thought she would dismiss me so meanly. Oh, I thought, if only Veronia hadn't moved away so soon! She would surely have granted me a beautiful Ducat, but now it's too late. If I knew where she was, I'd go straight to her. What am I supposed to do now? I have no money, I have no clothes, I have no service, and I may not return home. Indeed, I thought, you have to go where the road takes you, be it up hill or down dale. I traveled for a good while in such a state. When I was hungry, I begged a meal from a peasant, but if it was in a city, I found other means.

"Nothing surprised me more than when I once came into a town and was begging through a window to a noblewoman. She had me brought to her and then asked me everything, who my father was, what was my mother's name, how old they were, where I had served, who had had the livery made for me, and things like that. And when I had informed her that my father was named Martin and my mother was called Anna, they were over fifty, and the like, she became interested in examining me further, what I had done at the castles, and hadn't there been beautiful young ladies there. At this I related to her how I had carried on with Veronia or, much rather, how she had with me. That pleased her extremely, and because she assumed I was rather innocent, she asked me a lot more, whether I hadn't done this and that and tried such and the like. From that I've concluded down to this day that the ladies must be quite interested in knowing about such foolishness, even though I can't see how they profit from it."

'Yes, my dear Jost," I said to him, "you are a fool. They much prefer to hear such things than having you tell them a whopper made up from all the stories in the world. For such intimacies are exciting to hear, as-

---

[60] The French *pet de nonne*, a sweet fritter.

suming they can hear them in private and in quiet. But in public they'll run away from such stories as if the Devil were chasing them. I know many of them, my dear Jost, who like to read nothing better than where it gets a little nasty. To be sure, they say: The Devil, isn't that one nasty book! But they think: Oh, if it would only get better, if it would only get better! And in discussing imperfect chastity, this is a frailty that all humans must admit to.

"My dear Jost, why do you think Veronia took you into her bed and the other noblewoman examined you in such detail? Oh, they knew full well that you were a simple devil who didn't know up from down. If you go out now into the entire world, you'll never again have such an opportunity solely because you are no longer so simple. For some people believe that hiding their sins is the same as not sinning, and because no one is more tight-lipped than a simple person, no one has greater luck with the ladies than do the fools. But I'm talking about those who burn with desires like uncontrollable wild mares and find their greatest pleasure in backstairs affairs and also don't shy away from seducing an innocent youth, pouring their whorish poison into young hearts. But, Jost, what happened then?"

"Your Worship," he said, "things went very foolishly. When I thought I would never get anywhere, I came to a glassworks in the forest. There I worked beside the cooling chamber, but it didn't last all that long. When I broke some glasses, the master chased me away although I was extremely loathe to leave the place because it was so nice and warm in the winter, and not far away lived a hermit who visited us almost every day.

"After I left the glassworks I ran to the hermit Bernhard, for whom I had to collect bread in the villages. He put a long Capuchin cape about my body so that only my head was sticking out at the top. On my back hung a sewn-on sack into which the peasant women threw cheese, bread, dried apples, pears, and dried pears; occasionally they also gave me money. But some called me the hermit's bastard boy and chased me away from their doors with big clubs. With such begging I roamed around in the villages until my sack was full enough. Then I went back to the cell, where Brother Bernhard had collected quite a bit of such food. He taught me some nice prayers, and I have him to thank for being able to read. In all my life I've never lived so tranquilly and I've often regretted that I didn't remain with him for the rest of my days. He was a thoroughly pious man, and I cannot say in truth that I ever heard him say a senseless word. When I told him that the people called me his bastard boy, he said, 'That's the way of the world; they regard that which is best as the worst and usually that which is worst as the best.'

"He fasted three days a week and prayed on his knees six hours a day. But one day I came begging to a cleric's manse, and he had my cape with the food sack removed, for he said an idle life served for nothing other than to make people lazy and keep them from work. But to tell the truth, the hermit Bernhard was ten times more pious than the cleric, no matter what the latter imagined about the hermit's life. Instead of my previous devotions, I was assigned to work in the stalls, and there in a short time I learned more about cursing from the hands than I had earlier about praying from the hermit. I spent three whole weeks shoveling out manure, and I can't tell you how full of lice I got.

"Our housekeeper wasn't fit for the Devil. For she couldn't stand it if we rested for fifteen minutes after hard work; instead, she cursed us time and again whenever she saw us standing idle in the stalls or elsewhere. When the stall work was done and the horses fed, I had to carry wood with the hands or pound cod in the woodshed, and I can't tell you how the housekeeper nagged us. If we didn't remove our hats quickly in her presence, she said, 'You assheads, you gallows bait! Don't you know how to treat a great mistress? Do you louts have to be so impolite and let me walk by you without a display of respect? Oh, you clumsy dolts! Someone ought to lay your oxheads before your feet! The Devil should come down on your heads. You're to start paying respect to me or things are going to change around here!' And she threw such words at us almost daily, for she seldom ended a speech to us without mixing in several varieties of scoundrels."

Chapter Five. Jost Comes to a Young Nobleman. The Life They Led Together.

Now every person does fear work,
That's why Lord Pongratz it does shirk.

"My dear Jost," I replied to him, "in my youth I read that little people are most accustomed to puffing themselves up and that people who have little to do usually think up positions for themselves that might break the back of an ass. Your housekeeper, or whatever the whore called herself, is also to be included in this number because she demanded such great respect from you as base people. *Laudari a non laudatis, vituperium est*, say the Latinists. Now, my dear Jost, I must put that into German for you, and it means that praise and honor that we receive from someone who is not praiseworthy or has little or no honor is simply not to be called an honor, but instead a disgrace and unfitting. Accordingly, all those are perfect fools and fantasts who want to be honored when they themselves possess little or no honor. How can someone give me something that he himself doesn't have? It's as impossible as were I to say, 'Jost, make me into a doctor since you are a fool.'"

"It's true, Your Worship," Jost said, "that I'm not too learned. But all the same, the housekeeper acted so coarse that even the peasants could notice it."

"But listen, Jost," I said to him, "wasn't she sleeping with the priest, and don't you know anything about that?"

"Sir," he answered, "on my honor I know nothing about that. But I heard not long after I ran away that everywhere she was being proclaimed a priest's whore."

"Fool," I said to him, "people say a lot that's not true."

"For sure," answered Jost, "for they also said of me that I was a pious young man, yet I was an archscoundrel in the flesh, for listen to how it went with me:

"I finally ran away from the manse and intended to visit old Brother Bernhard and tell him how I had spent these three months and had to eat many a small piece of bread. But on the road I met a student who was headed for the university. He was wearing a purple riding coat and because he was on horseback, he had large French boots on, for perhaps along with good German rectitude he had already worn out his German ones. On his left arm he carried a Spanish cane on a silver chain, and at first I thought he was a doodle dandy because he was carrying a cane while mounted. His hat billowed with white ostrich feathers, and when he talked to me he mixed in much French and said if I didn't want to move along with him like a good fellow, he would fix me up dandy. Because I thought he wanted to give me some candy, I said, 'Oh, sir, give me a hat full.' But he drew his pistol out of its holster. Only then did I notice what he meant, and thus I walked on behind him.

"When we continued on, he came with his horse to a ditch where it took him a whole half hour before he got across. Then I thought: Well, Jost, don't just stand there, get going, and it's every man for himself. So I took my hat under my arm and took off, for I well knew that he couldn't catch me if he took as long to jump back as to jump over. 'Oh, you rascal!' he called after me. But I thought to myself: Rascal, schmascal, anyone who can't jump that ditch is a rascal. Accordingly, I hastened to the nearest thicket and there I lay on the ground and watched the student until I could no longer see him."

From this tale I had enough information from Jost that Isidoro had been that student; he had earlier told me his story in private and made mention of having run into a peasant lad on the road. Because we now were near my castle, I bade him continue his story and tell me in brief what had happened to him later. "Afterwards," said Jost, "I moved on and herded sheep in the field for a peasant. But one day two wolves came upon the herd, and out of fear I and my dogs ran away. The wolves tore apart easily eighteen wethers. Then I had to run away once again, for I feared the peasant might kill me because he was a wanton rogue who had shot quite many of the prince's hares, game, and swine.

"After that I came to a sexton in a small village. There I had to ring the bell for morning, noon, and evening prayers. But one day someone so smeared the rope with stinking excrement that I had whole lumps of it on my hands. It was a young nobleman who was playing a dirty trick

on the sexton. But when he came a second time and wanted to lubri-
cate the rope again with the same medicine, we beat him with knotted
ropes around so in the bell tower that instead of smearing the rope, he
might have done so to his trousers. 'You gallows bird,' the sexton said to
him, 'who taught you to put such a mithridate on my bell rope? Doctors
like you don't cure any disease.' Then he took the stuff the young nobleman had brought with him and smeared it all over his face so that he
looked like one of the people who run around on Shrove Tuesday."

From Jost's story I noticed quite precisely that it was the same story
the honorable brother Ludwig had recently included in his life story. For
I could remember that he then set fire to the sexton's house, climbed
out, and got away, on which point Jost's story and his agreed. "What
happened then," I said to him, "and what sort of turn did your story
take?"

"After this prank I wasn't too sure I should remain in the village, for I
often saw something sitting in the graveyard or even sometimes in the
ossuary. But especially when someone was about to die, there was usually an omen in our room. And when I rang for prayers that same evening, there was a rumbling in the church that made my hair stand on end.
The sexton paid me better than all my previous masters. I also left his
service more honorably, and he gave me a good Reichstaler for the road
but was arrested soon after my departure, for at night he had removed
rings from the fingers of the just buried and taken their clothes, usually
performing this stunt alone. I covertly watched him one night from the
garret window where I usually slept. But I didn't want to say anything;
instead, I sought ways and means for my getting away without hurt and
detriment.

"I don't know how luck has so often struck me. I again came to a
young nobleman who wasn't of the best sort, however. He gave me
only three Gulden for a year's wages and he paid me them by here four
Groschen and there three Kreuzer, now half a Batzen, now a Zweier,
and this usually happened when he had gambled and won half a Taler
or three Fünfzehner. My principal duty consisted in having to scratch his
back every night and picking lice out of his hair. He had only one pair of
shoes and whenever he had them repaired, I had to lend him mine in
the meantime, so I stayed by the stove and had to cast bullets and shot
with which he shot hares. For he passed his time in such idleness, and
when his old father said he ought to sit down with a book and read
something instead of roaming around in the woods, he laughed at him
and said his rifle was much dearer to him than twenty books, however
well written they might be. He often cursed at being so poor and
wished he were a merchant's son instead so that he could have a better
wardrobe. He took many silver buttons off his white-haired father's
coats and bought powder and lead with the money he got for them.
Sometimes we snared the neighboring peasants' pigeons and had them
roasted in secret.

"Once he was invited to a wedding and if his cousin who lived not far away on the other side of the forest hadn't loaned him a few Taler, he would have been compelled to stay away. I traveled with him and in order that I might appear honorably at this assembly, the old noblewoman had to loan me her servant's livery. But his shoes were so worn-out that my good German soles were walking on the ground. The brim of my hat likewise hung down like the wings of a crippled goose, and my shirt hadn't been washed in a good sixteen weeks.

"In such an outfit we walked two miles to the wedding. And because he had never or very seldom been among people, I would have been more courtly than he if only I had been a little better dressed. 'Jost,' he said to me on the way, 'the Devil take you, how properly I'm going to stuff myself! Ha, ha, I'm looking forward to that with all my heart! You mustn't stand far from me, I'll slip you many a piece of roasted food to keep for me for the way back, and I'll tell you what you're supposed to eat. Just shove a bunch of rolls in your pants or wherever. I don't want anyone to notice. I'm a mother . . . if I wouldn't like to get my hands on a silver goblet. But if you were adroit enough to bag one, I'd be all the happier.'

"'Sir,' I said, 'they might catch me and beat on my fingers. If you want to steal, go ahead and steal; then at least I'll have the advantage that I won't be hanged.' — 'Nonsense,' he said, 'who's talking about hanging? You just have to get loaded. Then you can say it happened while you were drunk. Someone who's drunk is halfway regarded as innocent in any case.' — 'No, sir' I said, 'know that it won't happen. I might steal when I was drunk, but they would hang me sober. All I'd gain from that would be sleeping it off. Dammit, sir, it won't do, they might run you and me off.'

"'Oh, you fearful weenie,' the young lord said, 'have you gotten so old you can't snitch? — 'Sir,' I said to him, 'you're a nobleman and you're not ashamed of stealing?' — 'Aha!' he replied. 'That's a skill not mastered by every dunce like you. With a single snatch I'll pocket enough to last me half a year for hunting and bringing game into the kitchen. You mustn't think at all that they hang someone because he has stolen,' he continued. 'Oh, you mustn't believe that; instead, thieves are hanged because they're clumsy and steal so that people notice it. Those whose thefts are not noticed won't be hanged for as long as they live; their cleverness and cunning caution leave them scot-free of the gallows. Oh, yes! At festivities I've expedited many a silver spoon into my pack and later the poor servants and common people who were serving must have done it. And I'd be a dyed-in-the-wool scoundrel if at a wedding I didn't pocket at least as much as it cost me. Didn't I deserve it for the effort of getting drunk and sweating so while dancing? Oh, don't try to tell people they're to eat and drink for nothing and then also give a present. Oh, Jost, my dear Jost, you just haven't gone to the right school yet. Stealing is no small stunt, it takes quite a bit of brains and it requires greater imagination and reflection than does the most perfect oration. Because of that just pay attention. What'll you bet, we return home in four days richer than when we set out?'"

Chapter Six. Pongratz Behaves Nicely at a Wedding. Pockets Nothing but Goblets and Silver Plates. And How It Continued with His Whore.

The one for whom you do great favors
Will often ill reward your labors.

"Well, I thought, the matter will go all right; if the nobleman steals, the nobleman will hang. I couldn't care less. In such conversation we came to the market village where the wedding was to be held. From afar we heard the trumpets and so we followed the tooting until we reached the house where all varieties of pipers, musicians, and village fiddlers were present, who were supposed to fiddle the noble wedding party into the church. My young lord was received quite politely by the bridegroom. Had he known, however, what we were talking about on the road, he would have sung him a requiem that would have brought the house down.

"While the wedding was going on, along with some other nobles my young lord got dressed in a small room because I carried for him in my satchel all the clothes he had borrowed from his old cousin. Oh, how happy he was to be among such pleasant company! His companions were not a whisker better than he, and it seemed to me the bridegroom would have poor profit from these honest fellows. For one said he had come to the wedding for no other reason than to initiate a duel. The next wanted to outrage the women. The third wanted to see how he could make the bridegroom a cuckold, and my master intended to shove whatever he could reach into his bag and take it away with him. You honest chaps, I thought to myself, might well have stayed at home, and if I knew that I was to have such guests at my wedding, I would buy kindling and burn the scoundrels before they even put their coats on.

"But that's the way it was on this occasion. The wedding party came out of the church, and after they sat down at table I can't describe how cruelly and frightfully the four nobles carried on. They had dined for scarcely half an hour when the first one began his duel, for he poured a glass of wine into the face of a person for whom he had borne an old grudge. At this plates and bowls were thrown around the room, the two began wrestling, and while everyone was defending himself and watching the fighting, my young lord shoved a large goblet in his pocket, two silver plates into his trousers, and a saltcellar into his coat pocket. He gave them to me to keep, and when we were going home, he laughed at me for having been so simple and timid. 'You fool,' he said, 'I spent the time nicely. I believe I got this gear at a place where no one will talk. It's worth at least twelve Ducats. From that I can buy enough powder and lead for all winter and some shoes, too.' When we came home, he forbade me to say a word about it to his father; instead, he went with me surreptitiously to the attic. There between stone walls he built a great fire, over which he melted the stolen goods. He sent me to a town with the melted silver where I sold it for a Taler an ounce, and I brought him back twenty-three Taler in a handkerchief.

"He was called Pongratz and for more than half a year he secretly kept a whore in his room, about whom no one in the castle knew anything except me and him. Everything she produced in a large crock to satisfy her bodily needs I had to carry from the room, and Pongratz promised to give me a Taler a month for performing this service. But whenever he put the money in my hand, twenty-nine Kaisergroschen were missing, otherwise it was a full Taler. Once the old man was making an inspection and when he entered Pongratz's room, he found the whore sitting completely naked on the chest because she happened to be examining herself for fleas. At the time Monsieur Pongratz had taken his rifle into the forest again and thus couldn't attend the drama that was being played at the castle with the whore. For with his cane the old nobleman chased her naked and undressed down the stairs, and it was all she could do to escape the servants who were supposed to have caught her. I can't describe how she ran across the fields in her torn nightshirt to where earlier she had rented a room from an old lady who very soon would be going to a poorhouse. The men did pursue her to this house, but when they learned that she was Pongratz's whore, they kept it to themselves and told the old man she had leaped into the water and would have been washed down the flume.

"'That flaming whore,' the old man said to us, 'presumes to go into my son's room and there pick off her fleas? I think the Devil and his mother led her into there. If I knew Pongratz had any knowledge of this, I'd whistle him a ditty that wouldn't sound so pretty.' When Pongratz came home and the old man asked him if he had any knowledge of the woman in his room looking for fleas. Before Pongratz had reached the castle, I had told him everything. Thus he could plan his moves all the better and he said, 'What! My father found a woman in my room!' — 'Indeed,' the old man said, 'I not only saw her in it, but also picking off fleas.' — 'Oh, the disgraceful witch!' said Pongratz. 'It was surely a thief who was not looking for fleas, but for certain passkeys to break into the castle. Father, if you will permit me, I'll set out after her with my servant Jost and if I meet her on the road or anywhere, I'll put a bullet in her hide so that she'll forget flea-picking for the rest of her life.'

"'No, no,' said the old man, 'just never mind, my son, she's already received her just reward. The whore threw herself into the water where she'll soon get rid of her fleas. Aren't they vile creatures? In broad daylight they enter the castle and behave so basely it's frightening.' After that Pongratz did everything possible to placate his father. But the following week a small child was found before the castle gate, at which the old man almost tore the hair from his head, for he gradually figured out the deception and regretted a thousand times that he hadn't had the whore locked up better.

"The son tried to excuse himself, pretending the child perhaps belonged to a stable hand. But a note was enclosed in which Pongratz was named as the father. And because for this reason life would change for him at the castle, he listened to reason, and I went off to war with him. Approximately a year later he was shot in a skirmish while on patrol, and I sneaked off with his two horses because he had promised to give me travel expenses after his death.

"I brought the news to his father, who was not too saddened by it, because he had to keep the child with him and have it brought up. 'The rascal,' he said to me, 'didn't deserve anything better, and that's the way it ultimately goes for all disobedient children who, contrary to their parents' desires, engage in all sorts of mischief and chase after whores.' After he had made many repulsive comments about his son, he asked me if I had brought his weapon or his clothes. But I assured him I had given money for his burial, for which reason I had taken the horses as my property. 'What,' he said, 'the horses as your property? The Devil take you, you'll have to leave me one, nothing can help you from doing so! Just be quick about it, leave one here. And with the other you can ride off to whatever gallows you want. Who knows whether you weren't the culprit yourself and gunned down my son Pongratz for the nag!' When I heard the foolish father saying such things about me, I remounted my steed and took the other horse's rein in my hand so that I rode off again as swiftly as I had come there. In the next village I sold them to a speculator who formerly had been a court manager in Franckenberg. And with this money I acquired clean clothes and for many years worked for various peasants with whom I had my ups and downs, just like usually with the weather."

Up to this point Jost had told me a good part of his life and beyond all doubt he would have gone on if we hadn't arrived at the castle quite soon. He was kept from doing so because he had to unsaddle the horses and with a stableman ride them to the horse-pond. It's true that fortune had treated him somewhat roughly and dragged him around in the world like many another. Nothing surprised me more than his having served Veronia in his youth. That's why not one in a thousand knows who is another's friend and relative. The example of Pongratz and his whore is pitiful enough, and such vice tends to follow when one gives too free a rein to young people, from which their parents often bring the bitterest misery down on their own heads. But there's nothing I'd like more to know than what sort of conscience the whores have who tend to stay completely hidden for quite a long time in castles and other houses and knowingly let themselves be dragged about so despicably in mortal sin. Ultimately, however, fear and trembling seizes them and they don't even take time to collect their clothes. And although Pongratz's whore did not throw herself into the water or drown according to the men's statement, I am nonetheless certain that she will not have died a much better death unless she acknowledged her sins in time and turned away from her wrongful path. Whores can get along for a good while, but ultimately ruin follows. And even though it's not felt noticeably, it's nonetheless strong enough, but wakeful conscience thrusts nothing but fiery tongs into the whoremasters' hearts, and, convinced of their deliberate uncleanliness, they become the hangmen of their own bodies.

Amid these thoughts, Jost unsaddled the horses and I told my Caspia the odd thing that had happened to the honest Ludwig in the sheep's stall at our estate, at which she slapped her thighs at least twenty times in laughter. She was happy that Ludwig, who otherwise always treated others roughly, had himself been made the fool.

Chapter Seven. The Fashionable Tailor Brings Hay and Straw to the Castle instead of Wedding Clothes. A Peasant Hand Falls in Love with Zendorio's Cook.

Go watch the rich, you really must,
They reach for gold and find but dust.

While they were so surprised at that, I took my fiddle and played the song "Thirteen Tailors Could Stand the Gaff, They Ate a Deer in an Hour and a Half." After that I attempted a fantasy, for it is certain that in this isolation I sought no better diversion than through music, which I had studied in my youth and over time I had learned how to sight-read. An organist lived not far from my castle in a small town. I gave him a few bushels of my winter grain. In return he had to come out to my place every Wednesday and teach me a little about composing. I didn't write "a little" without purpose, for he himself didn't know so very much. Otherwise, he could have taught me even more.

I had a great parchment, to be sure, but the pieces I wrote on it were very small, for I composed nothing but trumpet tunes that a shawm piper had to perform at our gatherings. From time to time I also wrote verses and various songs that I don't want to record here simply in order that this work not become too diffuse and that the reader's pleasure not be inhibited.

Some tend to think that a house isn't well built unless there's a line or two of verse written on it. But, to tell the truth, although I've worked out a countless number of all sorts of such songs and so got through some boring times, especially irksome winter nights; in fact I'm basically no great lover of poesy because one's imagination is never more blanketed with lies than when one writes verses. I didn't want to keep this reason from the reader so that he might think that perhaps I had sloppily overlooked it or was so exquisite and delicate with my works like some other fools of our present day who will publish nothing unless someone counts out a Taler on the counter for every letter of the alphabet. But people will put something else in their purse, and I'm of a totally different opinion in this matter because I have a head on my shoulders and am guided by other people as little as the French are by Swabian fashion.

Accordingly, I played merrily on my fiddle until dinner was ready. Upon my return Caspia had put a capon on the spit and boiled a carp blue, because I greatly enjoyed that fish. And while I was sitting alone with my thoughts and had decided to write a comedy with Pickelhering[61] in it, I heard some sleigh bells jingling from the road. They drew nearer and nearer. Thus I assumed they would pass the castle because the main road of our country ran past it. But when they came up, they stopped and inquired if there weren't an inn here where they could spend the night. I called down from the window that, indeed, I had no inn but if they would be content to spend this night in my modest castle, I would be pleased to enjoy their company. The person in charge of the two sleds wanted to drive on when I again asked him to stay, to which he finally consented but with the condition that I would forgive him his rudeness and not go to any trouble for them. But thereby I gave myself a splendid treat because I prefer to converse with no one more than those who travel up and down through the country. Indeed, I can say in good conscience that no beggar can safely pass by my castle who hasn't had to tell me his whole life story word for word.

I finally went down and learned quite quickly who the newly arrived Monsieur was. "Sir," he said to me, "Pardon my crudeness. The night and the cold attacked me simultaneously. I've already traveled twenty-five miles today and am afraid it might hurt my horses if I were to ride any longer into the night, even though I have no time to spare in delaying my necessary trip. I am a couturier from a neighboring region and have to deliver some wedding gowns to castle Wildenstein, where a person by the name of Ergasto is to be married quite soon. The four who are sitting in the rear sleigh are my chief apprentices who will have to work at the wedding. And thus you are informed about our company. I hope it will not offend you."

"Monsieur," I said to the new couturier, "I've learned enough from your declaration. Let your chief apprentices walk in with you. To be sure, I'll not treat them fashionably but I can assure you that you they shall be my very welcome guests." Therewith I led them into the living room, where they were surprised by its elegance. They asked my people

---

[61] The standard slapstick prankster in farces of the German Baroque.

who I was. But I had already ordered them to say that I was a tawer. Therefore, the only answer they received was that I was such an artisan. In support of this I had some goatskins and other hides hung here and there in the entryway, and thus the tailors readily believed what my people had told them about my profession.

The chests which held the wedding clothes I had taken to my upper room. But while we were eating, I told Jost that he should open them in secret, take out the clothes, put them in the cabinet behind the desk, and fill the chests with hay and straw instead. Jost did his tasks in a satisfactory manner, and I performed a pleasant service for the couturier, his assessor, and his apprentices with my capon and the carp. The leader talked most of all among the group, but said almost nothing about his trade; instead, he talked about great matters of state, which surprised me. But these were nothing but things that traveled up and down in the country in newspapers and were hidden from no one except those who couldn't read or had no ears. I said, "Sir, I'm a common artisan and don't know a word about these things all year long. I eat my chunk of bread in peace and let the warring parties charge, set off bombs, fire their field-pieces and howitzers, establish bridgeheads, set troops across a river, attack the baggage train, and so forth. Therefore, such things are of little use to me because I am only disturbed by them and yet don't have a Pfennig's worth of interest in them. This I regard as the greatest knowledge and the most necessary message of all: To live piously and to die blissfully."

"Yes, yes," said the tailor, "my dear tawer, it's true that's most important. Meanwhile, though, a person also has to know what's going on in the world. You have to do this and not omit that; to live on earth and know nothing about it is crude ignorance. And don't you think," he went on to me, "if the war should move into our country and the armies came to occupy this region that I would have many clothes to make and you many hides to prepare? Oh, no one knows where this person or that can make his fortune. I've done favors for many a person, especially the shopkeepers. For whoever had the most miserable goods, I'd send the most people to him and say that he'd received new goods and French ones, the likes of which were not to be found far and wide. In such manner I got many an embarrassing piece of junk out of the store, and I had my certain profit that couldn't rightly be denied me as the pusher of the clothes."

I liked the tailor's conversation all right, but his trickery didn't please me so I drank his health repeatedly and got him and his people drunk. In such condition they went to rest and early in the morning wanted to know what the bill was. But I said that no one was permitted to pay for anything in this tawer's house and that I regarded it as a special kindness to my craft that I was honored by being visited by a couturier and enjoying his splendid conversation, which I, for my part, would know how to repay him through my insignificant services.

With such a compliment I sent the tailor and his company off, and he drove away merrily with his sleigh bells, believing only that he had slept that night at the home of a tawer. And because my groom had to show them the way until they had passed through the hills, he brought back word that they had been surprised by nothing more than my splendid wealth. Meanwhile I had gone through the wedding clothes piece by piece and wanted to know nothing so much as why Ergasto had planned to proceed so quietly in this important deed, since as companions and good friends we previously had promised not to hide the slightest thing from one another. But as I later learned, he had kept it secret only so that he could summon us all the more unexpectedly and thus provide an unexpected joy, at which one is usually merriest. For the more unexpected the joy, the more delightful its pleasure, but it was all the more amusing to me for having given it such a merry beginning.

I thought at least a full day about what Isidoro and his brother Ergasto would say about my prank and about how the couturier would react upon opening the chests of clothes. But I had to wait for the story to develop in the coming days, during which I once again composed all kinds of songs and later set them to music. I also had my special fun with catching sparrows or *Spatzen,* as they are called in Austria, that frequently appeared on my manure pile. In part I shot them with clay bullets, in part I spread lime on the branches and such. Despite assembling rather a lot of them, I was never so tight and cheap that I would have had them roasted and given to my help, which meanness was practiced by many other of my peers in the country and in towns who not only gave their people sparrows to eat but even slain crows as wild pigeons.

Oh, no, I've not been such a cheapskate in all my life and, if the weather is good, I won't become one in a long time, for what does a person have to enjoy on earth other than life? Truly nothing. Therefore, it's a special vanity to save and scrimp until you go to the grave since you won't even be happy or full from the means you've gained because misers always think: Today my possessions are going to disappear, tomorrow they'll disappear, the day after tomorrow they'll disappear, and so forth without end. No, I've not let such shoddy thoughts enter my heart. I let my help enjoy my means and small wealth generously, and I seldom ate a roast without having one prepared for them too. Starlings, indeed! It sufficed me to spend my time catching them. Why should I go on to try to gain a profit by having them served to the poor servants? They work much more than I do; for that reason I find it unfair that an idle person should be treated better than a worker. And on this point I received no small praise from my people. They also worked half again as much, and I clearly detected their industrious hands in the increase in livestock, in the fertility of the fields, and in the flourishing of many other things.

Two days after the couturier had taken leave of me, a peasant from the village came to me, saying he had secretly fallen in love with my cook. If I wanted to be so kind and be helpful to him in the marriage, he wouldn't deny me a dozen Taler. I told him that his intention was not bad, but to be praised, especially because he had brought the matter to the right place and informed me as her employer at the outset. "You can apply your money to your fields," I told him, "for I'm no scoundrel who busies himself with such pettiness on account of such a matter. But have you already spoken with my cook?" — "Your Worship," said the man in love, "I've not talked to her but otherwise I've gone around with her." — "How did go around with her then?" — "I danced with her a couple of times." — "Indeed," I said, "you didn't go around with her, but danced around with her." With that he told me the occasion when he had gotten to see her, and because I liked the fool, I had my wife and the cook come up. I explained to them how, driven by a special love, this good friend had brought me a proposal of marriage and, to be sure, on account of the cook. If she were of a similar mind concerning this and would exchange marriage vows with him, it should be considered and acted on accordingly. I and my wife for our part said we would let nothing lack that might serve for their good and their being accepted and many other things like that.

"What?" said the cook. "I'm supposed to marry a peasant lout! That will never happen! He can keep his courtship of me; if no one else shows up, he can stay away too. I don't believe I've even spoken one word to him, and he presumes to court me? Oh, what disgraceful rashness! I see the fellow is a fool or at least has sunstroke. No, no, I don't want to marry yet!" With that she ran out of the room.

Chapter Eight. The Cook Would Prefer the Clerk.

Cookie's heart does beat much warmer
For the clerk than for the farmer.

After her departure the suitor stood there as though someone had slapped him, and it surprised me that the cook thought so much of herself and didn't want to marry a peasant. "Dear friend," I told him, "your suit is off to a poor start, but winds that rise quietly have a greater effect on later ones. A citadel is not taken in one quick storming, so you have to see how you arrange the affair so that you emerge victorious. How well off are you?"

"Your Worship," he answered, "in ready cash I have two hundred good and hard Reichstaler."

"Ha," I said, "for the cook one hard one is good enough." At that my wife also ran off, and I remained alone standing with the farmer, who began to smile a little. "What else do you have?" I said to him.

"In addition," he replied, "I have four hundred bushels of winter barley and nine acres of land. That's my entire wealth, and if the cook won't take me, I'll simply have to see how things are in someone else's house."

"If you're that wealthy, you're a fool for not chasing bravely after the whores, whereby you'd probably remain single and not be nailed down by keeping a house."

"No, sir," he said, "fornication is forbidden. I'd rather have a wife than a whore. No one wins anything from whoring, and our neighbor's Chris has often said that if he hadn't chased after the whores so, he'd now be richer by a hundred Gulden."

"My dear fellow," I said to the peasant, "on this point you're much more blessed than many a braggart who is obviously lacking in understanding of this vice. But I've heard that otherwise you're not so physically fit, for people say that earlier you had been cut and thus had very little ability to satisfy a woman."

"Oh, sir," said the farmer, "how is that possible! Who said such a thing? I think people are fools or on their way to becoming so. That'll be the day — cut! A fool's joke. I'd like to straighten the cook out about that if she would only take me otherwise."

"No," I said, "you may do what you want to; I can't compel anyone to do that. If the cook wants you, you'll get the cook; If she doesn't want you, you won't."

"Sir," said the peasant, "a fool could have said that to me. That's why I'm asking you for advice how I could get the cook to church and have her as my wife. Didn't you hear me? I'll give you twelve Taler, sir, twelve Taler, twelve Taler."

With these words he struck the floor with his staff, and because the cook believed I was calling, she came up and asked what I wanted. "Nothing else," I said, "than to have you make up your mind how this honest person is to regard you. Take a few days, then I'll speak to you again and receive your answer, whether or not anything is to come of it."

"Oh, sir," said the cook, "I can't bring myself to marrying a peasant. If you wanted to help me get a clerk or the schoolmaster in our village, then I'd soon tell you what I was thinking." Meanwhile the peasant fellow had departed, shaking his head and muttering some words to himself.

"The Devil has deceived you," I said to the cook, "if you won't take that honest fellow. You fools would like to have someone in fashionable clothing, and when you get him, then you often scarcely have bread to eat. What's wrong with the fellow? He's a nice figure of a man and he's already a farmer, so he's no fool. He can probably get a wife anywhere, but you'll not quickly find a man that pleases you. Oh, my dear cook, you're a long way from that! Believe for sure that you'll find such an opportunity won't be standing before your door every day and playing you a dance on the zither. No one has regretted courting when young if it was done properly. And do you think you're going to accomplish so much with a clerk? Cook, cook, you are so wrong! You'll lick your chops one day to catch so good and young a peasant fellow.

"You simpletons act so arrogantly with one another and if it gets that far, you're up to your necks in misery and torment. You think and imagine you're snagging a big deal with the schoolmaster. But what are you going to do with the stupid fool? He can't do anything and understands nothing, and when I recently had him as a guest, he even peed in his pants when I had toasted him with only a couple of glasses of wine.

"He has an angry and obstinate head, likes to gamble, and gets into quarrels oftener than he prays. If I were to tell you what sort of a reputation he has among those with whom he grew up, you would laugh at him rather than love him. People dirty-mouth him everywhere, and no mater how people attack him, he doesn't defend or better himself. From this you can conclude that he doesn't think much of himself. Not a person in the whole village can say that in all his life he displayed a courtesy to anyone. Instead, he insults all the people and is a toady beyond compare. He exists only from my largesse, and if I dismissed him, you'd have to go begging with him and have used up your chance. So make a decision soon. I shall neither compel you nor turn you away from your plans for the clerk or the schoolmaster. But there's not much to either of the two. My advice to you would be that you take the farmer; if he stinks of manure, he also stinks of money, which you don't find just everywhere nowadays. Many a woman prefers to marry a soldier rather than a peasant, but when he's discharged, she'll come to the peasant's door with two children on her back and begging for a piece of bread. Whoever can marry into a steady income is sufficiently blessed in these times, and such opportunities truly don't come knocking every day. What do you think, Sophia?"

"Your Worship," she answered, "you know and are quite aware that I've spent all my days and most of my time among young noblewomen, and if I were to marry a farmer from the country, God forbid, how they would laugh at me, those who knew me before or spooned with me. Your Worship, they would clap their hands over their heads and say, 'Just look at this! Sophia, Herr Zendorio's cook has married a peasant. This and that person wasn't good enough for her and now she's become a cowherd.' Your Worship, don't you agree that would give me a splendid bellyache?"

"Foolishness," I said, "if your bridegroom doesn't give you more to worry your belly about than does the talk of your acquaintances, then the matter's already settled. Well, you're just monkeys and fools. Through your marriage you are seeking your own happiness. If you find it, you've got it, and it doesn't make any difference what people say or think. What good is it for you if you marry the schoolmaster and have to go begging with him? Even if his position is of higher repute than that of a peasant, the subsequent misery is all the greater. I regard it as much better to be able to afford a piece of bread in a low station than to have to suffer great hunger in a high one. Sophia, Sophia! You don't yet know what goes on in the world. People's talk has nothing to do with anything. If they say, 'How awful, Sophia's married a peasant,' and you're eating a good roast, that's better than their saying, 'Oh, Sophia did well to marry the clerk,' and your having to eat sauerkraut. My dear Sophia, you do see, don't you, that people's opinions are of no importance?"

"Your Worship," Sophia said, "you may soon get a strange decision from me. Does the fellow have any money?"

"His wealth," I said, "is not as bad as you probably imagine. Along with a good bit of money he's got a lot of grain stored and in addition has expectations of inheriting his father's farm. A happy home doesn't consist of having ample means, but of getting along with little and working your way up. He has two hundred Taler in cash and much grain in his barn. That's what he's earned up till now from his labor, and his father will give him a wedding gift of at least fifty Gulden. On top of that he has arable land from which you'll have enough bread to eat throughout the year. Compared to that, many a great boaster has to scrape together here and there the money for his weekly bread. Let others say whatever they want, when you're your own woman, you'll have little need of being guided by others. Many a person will laugh at your station who is, however, happy if you invite him as a guest and put a meal before him that he often could not pay for.

"I'm a cavalier of sufficient means and, as such, could have been a minister at a court long since. But the satisfaction I find in humility fittingly keeps me away from a glory that consists of fleeting vanity. You see that I have a cheap violin in my hand and am not half as burdened by it with crucial worries as if I were holding a scepter instead. This fiddle is for me, but the scepter is for other people and requires great effort to be used intelligently. You are, to be sure, only a cook and no two stations above that of a peasant. And when I note where you came from, I don't see what reason you have to refuse this fellow, for your mother was a poor linen weaver. Therefore, regard where you came from and not the ladies with whom you've stayed and worked for. Moreover, you're not among the most beautiful, and it's only a question of a few years before you'll be full of wrinkles. And whenever you look into the mirror, to your annoyance you'll regret having so woefully let the opportunity to marry go past."

"Sir," the maid said to me, "I will think about it. What Your Worship presented is probably the basic truth; I'll see how it goes, but I'll take four weeks to think it over." Accordingly, I had the peasant summoned, and he was quite satisfied with the decision. With my permission he had free access to the castle so that he could get better acquainted with the cook and she with him.

235

Chapter Nine. Zendorio Receives a Letter Concerning the Couturier and Appears at Ergasto's Wedding.

Many a man will swear an oath,
He wasn't here or there or both.

I had gotten that far with the wedding of these two people when unexpectedly a letter was delivered to me from Wildenstein castle. Recognizing Isidoro's handwriting, I opened it all the more eagerly because of the increasing desire to receive some news concerning the couturier and his load of hay and straw. The letter consisted of the following lines:

Very beloved brother!

From all appearances the couturier, Master Jonas, was treated splendidly by you as the rich tawer. And if I'm not wrong, you're also the person who filled his clothes chests with hay and straw. For when he saw your portrait hanging on the wall, he offered to swear an oath before me and my brother Ergasto that this person and no other was the tawer at whose house he had stayed and who had treated him so prettily. You can never believe how the tailor carried on when he found such unexpected material instead of the wedding clothes, and it would have taken very little for him to start crying. For this reason send the clothes here at this opportunity and you are also invited for next Tuesday, for my brother has decided to wed a foreigner by the name of Sylvia and is now concerned with bringing her here. *Cetera textus habet.* Forgive me for writing so poorly. I'm busy with a play that's to be performed at the wedding festivities.

Wildenstein, St. Edward's Day[62]

I read this letter a good twenty times in a row and jumped around the room in delight at the tailor's having identified me through the portrait. And because the wedding was so near, I took the clothes with me. But this time Caspia had to stay at home because the hour for her giving birth was drawing quite near. Along with my boy I took no one with me other than the honest Jost, who had to tell me more en route of how he had spent his life. But since this narrative contained little other than all sorts of changes of employment, I shall expend little paper on an unnecessary report; instead, I'll tell how things went at the castle in Wildenstein.

The tailor clapped his hands over his head in joy when he saw me drive into the castle. "Welcome, Herr Tawer," some cavaliers screamed down from the balcony whom I couldn't recognize due to my rapid gait. But after I had climbed down, I saw beside Monsieur Ludwig the worthy Herr Caspar and Faustus standing in the corridor, who asked me how

---

[62] The eighteenth of March.

many dozens of goat and calf hides I had prepared with my Caspia. I had to laugh at such a question, and the tailor immediately came to the sleigh to pick up his clothes and we almost had a bit of comedy with one another.

Then Ergasto arrived with his beloved along with six sleighs of foreign cavaliers and ladies. And I wouldn't have enough room on twelve sheets of paper to tell all that transpired among us on his arrival. But I previously stated that I didn't intend to record simply compliments that were paid, but only things that pertain to the story.

In the evening we were hosted very splendidly, and on the following day the wedding was performed, after which a splendid banquet was held. With the foreign ladies there was extraordinarily little of beauty or praiseworthiness unless one had to note that haughtiness tends to generate its own reputation. In truth, I wouldn't know what other qualities to attribute to them. Many of them didn't favor us with a single word; we knew what was up, we could tell they wanted to be begged for such. But we left them and their delusion sitting on their posteriors, and no one was in the least concerned about their grandeur except perhaps the simple peasant boys who had to wait on the table. For they said that in all their lives they had never seen an ass wagged back and forth like these dolls were doing. On this occasion, however, dinner was not protracted, for because Isidoro wanted to have a play performed, people hurried through the meal and the toasts were saved for another time because it wouldn't do at all if someone quite drunk wanted to watch a play or some other show. People arose from the table and the women put the desserts in their bags to eat during the play or to throw at the gentlemen's necks, from which the reader can judge that the men were sitting in front on this occasion.

Chapter Ten. The Merry Comedy There and Other Things.

*The person who won't speak his mind
Is often thought a fool, you'll find.*

The reader shouldn't be surprised that I broke off the preceding chapter so short, for with everyone hurrying to the event, I couldn't properly hang around in it any longer. Amid a flourish of trumpets and kettledrums, the whole party was led into a large paneled room where the theater was erected. Isidoro had assembled the best actors he could find from the various schools in the surrounding villages. The theater itself consisted mostly of curtains and tapestries mounted on boards. Thus it is easy to conclude that there was very poor machinery and little use made of it.

Elevated benches had been arranged facing the theater and when the wedding guests had taken their places, an artificial dove came down over the theater and quite brightly and clearly called the words *The Enamored Austrian*, for Isidoro had done quite a bit with mathematics and it was nothing new for him to enclose certain words in a wooden instrument and to release them at a certain time.

It almost looked like someone wanted to serve a splendid dish in a clay bowl, I mean as if a splendid performance were to be given in this shabby theater. For this reason everyone paid strict attention despite someone's having spread a lot of sneezing powder on the benches to distract the audience, but before they noticed it, there began

Actus primus. Scena prima.
Jorgias and Rutilio.

JORGIAS.   I truly don't know what I'm supposed to do or how I'm going to reach a conclusion for my love. I'm pressed from the right by my lack of wealth, and from the left by the contempt that all women show me. But a philosopher lives here who is a mighty doctor. In his robes he knows more than all the windmills in the Spanish Netherlands. He mixes into everything like a sow you drive into the field for the first time in spring, and from that they tell him he's a *Magister* in it. His name is Rutilio. Therefore, I'll ask him for advice and see what's his opinion concerning my love. Look, here he comes like I hoped.

RUTILIO.   That man is a churl! The rascal wants to assert that Erfurt in Thüringen is not a city and he says *simpliciter*: Erfurt is a village, an Imperial village, the largest village in Germany. Oh, the scoundrel! He had time to run out of the auditorium and away from me; otherwise I would have given the devil arguments that would have made his nose bleed. Oh, you rascal!

JORGIAS.   Good day, Herr doctor!

RUTILIO.   Can you imagine his logic: *Omne id, quod est pagus, non est civitas. Erfurdium est pagus, ergo non est civitas.*[63] Oh, you ass! You impertinent boor, you and your argument!

JORGIAS.   Herr Doctor, how's it going to turn out with my love?

RUTILIO.   I wish you had to go to the gallows with your argument. The fool cannot distinguish *inter esse politicum & inter esse physicum*. Oh, you insolent boor! *Alia enim est intentio entis politici, alia entis physici.*[64]

---

[63] Everything that's a village is not a city. Erfurt is a village, ergo it is not a city.

[64] Political existence is one thing, physical existence is another.

JORGIAS.	Herr Rutilio, are you listening to me? I want to speak a word with you.
RUTILIO.	Oh, if I could only give that rogue a slap! *Erfurdium enim considero aut physice, aut politice; si considero physice est civitas, si politice est pagus imperii.*[65] That settles the matter.
JORGIAS.	What do I have to do with Erfurt! Just tell me if my beloved will be faithful to me!
RUTILIO.	*Secundo* I will answer thus: *Ubi non habitant rustici, ibi non est pagus. Erfurdii non habitant rustici, ergo Erfurdium non est pagus.*[66] The matter is as plain as the sun in the sky.
JORGIAS.	Don't let me stand here for nothing.
RUTILIO.	Well, what do you want?
JORGIAS.	Herr Doctor, how do you advise me? Should I continue in my love for the tailor's daughter or not?
RUTILIO.	*Tertio* I will say thus: *quod vulgariter vocatur civitas, illud est civitas; Erfurdium vulgo vocatur civitas, ergo Erfurdium est civitas.*[67] Who wants to crack that nut for me?
JORGIAS.	What, crack a nut? Crack a nut? Just listen to one word.
RUTILIO.	You knave, should you and your logic say that *esse physicum* is a moral discipline? Then I would argue: *esse tuum, est esse physicum, ergo tu es homo moralis, quod est absurdum.*[68]
JORGIAS.	Herr Rutilio, listen to me!
UTILIO.	I hear you, but that ass, the Herr Superintendent, he wants to outargue me that Erfurt is not a city. Sooner than affirming that Erfurt is a village, I would say: *quod forma et figura differant sunt realitate intrinsica, quod etiam est absurdum.*
JORGIAS.	Herr Rutilio, you're having philosophical fantasies. What am I to do with my beloved?

---

[65] I can view Erfurt in a natural way or in a political way: if I view it in a natural way, it is a city; if I view it in a political way, then it is an Imperial village.

[66] Where no peasants live is not a village. No peasants live in Erfurt, ergo Erfurt is not a village.

[67] What is usually called a city is a city. Erfurt is usually called a city, ergo Erfurt is a city.

[68] Your existence is a natural one, ergo you are a moral person, which is absurd.

RUTILIO.   And what's worst of all, the gallows bird asserts *quod per esse intentionis intelligantur realitates animi? Quod est contra rationem.*[69]

JORGIAS.   Herr Rutilio, help me with your advice just this one time.

RUTILIO.   *Si enim esse intentionis spectat realitates animi, sequitur, quod cantus ist esse intentionis, quod est absurdissimum.*[70]

JORGIAS.   Should I leave now?

RUTILIO.   *Insuper* the rascal says: *qualitates rationis sunt coadæquatæ species intentionis, quod est risibile.*

JORGIAS.   Herr Rutilio, I believe everything you say, but do tell me how I am to conduct myself in my new love.

RUTILIO.   Yes, yes, there's no other way: *notio prima est qualitas rationis, ergo notio prima est species intentionis, non est credibile,* it's impossible.

JORGIAS.   Did the Devil give you your arguments?

RUTILIO.   Oh, the boor, the coarse boor presumes to ask me: *quid est musica?* Fool, music is an art for those who can't do it and a science to those who can. *Res est clarissima.*

JORGIAS.   I think he'll end up foolishly today from arguing.

RUTILIO.   *Omne enim, quod scio, non scio, ut artem, sed ut scientiam.* That is the basic principle.

JORGIAS.   Herr Rutilio, Herr Rutilio!

RUTILIO.   What do I have to do with you? *Scientia est effectus artis, ergo quod per artem didicimus, hoc necessario scimus.*

(Exits.)

Actus primus. Scena secunda.
Strabo, a philosopher, Jorgias.

STRABO.   I'm looking for the honest Rutilio to talk with him about how he judged the subject I presented to my students today. But whom do I see here?

---

[69] That form and figure are different in their inner reality. That is contrary to reason.

[70] This and the remaining Latin passages in this scene are further mockery of scholastic logic.

JORGIAS. Sir, I am Jorgias, the enamored Austrian, and I wanted to get advice from Rutilio, but he's halfway crazy today and won't answer about my concern.

STRABO. What? Rutilio crazy? Do you presume to speak so rudely of one of my equals? I swear I won't forget you to the gods, but make your impudent mouth known in all the schools.

JORGIAS. What? Are you also a scholar?

STRABO. To be sure, and indeed a perfect scholar, without equal in all the world.

JORGIAS. Sir, I've come here . . . .

STRABO. You must not say, 'I have come here,' but 'It seems to me I've come here.'

JORGIAS. And thus I beg you . . .

STRABO. You mustn't say, 'I beg you,' but 'It seems to me I beg you.'

JORGIAS. . . . because I am the most enamored human being.

STRABO. You're not a person, but an ass, *id probo sequentibus: asinus habet duas aures, tu habes duas aures, ergo es asinus.*

JORGIAS. Herr Philosopher, whoever has two ears like I is also an ass. You also have two ears, ergo you're also an ass like I.

STRABO. What are you saying, you scoundrel?

JORGIAS. You're a rascal!

STRABO. I'll report it to the judge that you called me a rascal.

JORGIAS. Sir, you mustn't say, 'I'll report it to the judge,' but 'It seems to me that I'll report it to the judge.' And also not that I called you a rascal, but that it seems to you that I called you a rascal.

They wanted to continue their conversation but, as luck would have it, the theater collapsed about them and not a few people were injured so that this merry and amusing event could not be brought to the desired conclusion, no matter how much that was desired by people who had formerly acted at schools. But against his will Isidoro had to leave it at that because some of the main characters had received facial injuries from the falling wall and thus large bandages had to be applied.

For this reason they postponed the event to another time, for Isidoro reported that two more philosophers were in it who would try their arguments on Pickelhering. The cavaliers were somewhat placated by that, and meanwhile the ladies were busy getting the dancing started, after which they were once again hosted most magnificently.

Chapter Eleven. The End of Veronia's Life.

Taking poison chokes the heart,
Vice does pain and grief impart.

Along with this story, on the dance floor we enjoyed splendid fun with the fencers, who travel back and forth in the country and usually post their fencing shows on the town halls. There were quite a few Marx brothers and Vitus fencers,[71] and so they had to knock one another around in the castle courtyard for three days in a row as well as they had learned it from their master. The white-headed baker was the best with the pole, and the man in black dealt many good thumps to the head. Brother Hans was not bad at all on the side of the Vitus fencers. But from time to time he would get a generous swat across his leather pants from a wooden sword so that I have to laugh whenever I recall what an artful pose he struck at that time. As two Marx brothers of long standing, Brother Ludwig and I were sitting together, and I asked him what he thought of the earlier comedy and the fencing. He replied that although he hadn't seen the play, he recalled that he had once read such a work in French by Molière.

In it not only were the philosophers given their due, but also made fun of with wonderful fantasies. "For it's not a little mad," he said, "to be so consumed by a philosophical argument that one forgets all human company and often doesn't hear what another person is saying. With the second philosopher we have to see that earlier there were a number of such foolish types who believed that no one could truly say that this and that had happened; instead, they thought it much better if one would say: it seems to me it happened. But from this philosophizing it later happened that if one of the philosophers was whipped on a public street or elsewhere, the judge couldn't render a certain decision, for if the whipped philosopher complained immediately to the judge and said it seemed to him that he had been whipped, befouled, and properly pushed around by this person or that, the judge said, 'If it only seems to you and you can't report the incident with certainty, then I can't hand you my judgment.' That's what I think from our recent short event and it annoys me that the walls collapsed so soon. Otherwise we would have heard more nice things, for Isidoro diligently studies his books. But what's even more, he has a very quick mind and can produce a work from which you have enough to learn and to laugh.

---

[71] Adherents of fencing styles originating with fencing societies that had Sts. Mark and Vitus as their respective patron saints.

"As far as the fencers are concerned, I do like their way and style of fencing, but I'm not inclined to the people themselves. For their profession is among the most miserable and, indeed, the first of all in the world that might be done away with. The people harm their bodies only to make people laugh for a poor reward. I don't think there's another profession under the sun from which one can learn nothing at all. Rope-walking is ultimately good exercise. Jugglers need a subtle magic of the eyes. A street quack in the end helps those who believe firmly in the things he gives out, no matter how bad or worthless his medicaments may be. People who display animals, eat fire, swallow swords, and the like let us understand what unbelievable things can be done and how Nature has placed so many an unusual animal in all places on earth. Compared to them, I don't know what I should think about the fancy fencers. But I do know well that those watching are often greater fools than the fencers themselves because when the show is over, you see a great many of them attack one another and push each other around and beat one another. The fellows travel from one city to the next, and because they don't lead a proper Christian life, they seldom die as Christians. It would be better if they were to fight their own profession."

During his talk which he larded with many examples, the show ended after the two parties had given each other a good thrashing and pounded their heads. Afterwards Isidoro led us back into the large dance hall, where we were summoned to dinner by the ringing of a bell. At the table all manner of things again were discussed, but especially love, the most pleasing topic of all to the ladies. On the next day we gunned down some three hundred and thirty foxes, and after them we chased two wild boars, after which entertainment we all took leave.

I was most desirous of getting home, for I received word that my Caspia would become the mother of a child quite soon, and the cavaliers told me with one voice that they would be its godfathers. At that promise I and many others departed from the castle, and because Monsieur Ludwig had to visit a debtor on that road, he rode beside me twenty some miles. En route I told him my Jost's story of what had transpired with him and Veronia, asking incidentally whether he had heard any news of her since.

"Dearest brother," Monsieur Ludwig answered, "now it's been demonstrated what kind of end such a life will find, namely one in horror. Approximately three weeks ago she ran off with a gallant. In disguise, her husband followed the thief and caught him in a small town outside the country where he couldn't keep himself from whipping out a concealed pistol and with two bullets taking the life of the man who defiled his marriage. He would have shown her mercy if she had asked him for forgiveness, but in her rage and fright they couldn't understand one another. Thus she was horribly stabbed by her husband with an Italian dagger and people assure me she had more than eighteen wounds in her breast.

"Such dramas ordinarily come to such an end, and one can wish that the abominably punished Veronia traveled to an even greater torment in the hour when she died and into the slough where such spirits burn in eternal suffering."

Chapter Twelve. The Irishman Becomes a Hermit. He Talks about the Vanity of This World.

The fools will chase both power and glory,
For clever men they're not the story.

He would have gone on talking if he hadn't been prevented by the clear ringing of a bell, and because it came from a deep valley to our left, we turned our horses and looked down. There stood an old ruined cloister, out of which we saw a young monk walking with a large sack over his shoulder. We initially regarded him as a member of a convent who was to go begging in the surrounding area for bread for the others living in the cloister. So we held up until he climbed up to us. Ludwig addressed him and although he spoke to him cordially, the man walked past us as if immersed in deep thoughts and didn't look around. "Brother," Ludwig went on to say, "are you an ass or are you a human being?"

"Sir," the man said, "whether you regard me as an ass or as a human being, I still belong in your company."

From this answer we both understood that it was the good Irishman, who earlier had resolved to spend the rest of his life removed from the world in total isolation. Ludwig now grabbed him by his beggar's sack, and in great astonishment the Irishman crossed himself because he had so unexpectedly stumbled on us and we on him. He told us his present circumstances, how things had gone for him as a hermit in this valley, and that apart from him only one old hermit was living down there, with whom he usually spent all his time. "I've banned the world from my heart long since," he said to us, "for in the end it provides nothing but painful aggravation and can't find consolation in fighting this. I have renounced all high honors and will fight for nothing more than the basest humility for as long as I shall live. I am opposed with all my heart to the desires of the flesh and the secret arts of the Evil One, for they murder the soul and later can torment it much more than they delighted it previously. I disdain all the wealth of the entire world and regard no treasure as lasting save that which men collect in Heaven. I regard vain reputation and the empty praise of men as of no worth and miserable because many a person, delighted by temporal praise, hastens toward shame and disgrace. I damn all pride and arrogance because they are a rope that binds many thousands of souls and leads to the place where the arrogant spirit burns and roasts in eternity. I condemn disgraceful greed and reach instead for the generous hand of Heaven that usually gives generously to the needy.

"I cast out all vengeance and from the bottom of my heart forgive all those who surreptitiously or openly, wittingly or unwittingly, within or without our country have attacked or insulted my honor or anything else, and in like manner ask all to forgive me whom I have hurt or insulted. I condemn the vices *in toto*, from which the blinded earth hastens toward infinite torment. I hate them, I flee them and damn them. All worldly vanity runs counter to my spirit, and I wish that I were already buried and resting in the womb of my mother, the earth. Farewell, my former estates, farewell, my former friends, I have parted from you and will not come back. I love solitude more than your company, for thereby I flee no small opportunity to sin.

"I hate a lot of words, for solitude teaches me to pay attention to myself and to speak of only those things that can never pass away. Blessed is he who knows you, oh vain earth, and who doesn't love you! Even more blessed he who flees you! You talk a lot, but demonstrate very little in fact; you promise your servants a good wage, but in the end you pay them with the sword. No, no, I will say good night to you, for I already cling to those riches, than which no greater can be found."

With these words the Irishman in his brown cowl made a small bow and went on his way. Ludwig praised his good intentions and said that in him the world had lost an unusual model of courtliness. "His lifestyle," he said, "is Christian enough, but in truth not valid for all men. To be sure, when we look at the end of this earth and its glory, it is not meaningless that thereby we often are quite moved inwardly and encouraged to a new and purer lifestyle. The Irishman did the right thing, and I believe his satisfaction with his life far surpasses ours, because contentment of the spirit far transcends delights of the flesh. I would have liked it if Nature had implanted such a spirit within me so that I might stay in an unknown desert or a great forest like the Irishman and like you earlier. But I find myself both inwardly and outwardly unskilled and unsuited for this work.

"What good is it to us if we parade around in total bliss on this orb and do great things to make our names grand and immortal thereby! Truly, it is but a delusion that hurts no one more than him who relies on it too much. Not without cause did the Irishman say farewell to desires of the flesh, for it is certain and undeniable that through this sinful and lamentable pestilence many thousands of human beings are plunged into the eternal abyss. And what do we ultimately accomplish through our voluptuousness other than through it we dig our own graves in which we often inter our temporal and eternal well-being? Oh, the Irishman has done well in this deed, and his intention to remove himself from the world will lead him to Heaven if he diligently and unceasingly pursues the work he has begun.

"What does it help us humans that we invade countries in war, lay waste to them, even bring them under our dominion? Many a person fights and defeats his outer enemy and nonetheless permits himself to be so cravenly conquered by his inner and invisible foe, who often can be driven back and away by a single pious thought. What did the miserable Veronia gain through her wantonness? Her desire was brief, her pleasure imperfect, her delight sinful, her marriage stained, her life shortened, and, what I don't want to believe, her soul perhaps lost forever! Carnal depravity bears such fruits, and she did enjoy it because she never acknowledged the sin in which she was so frightfully lost." These words were the last Ludwig spoke to me on the road because shortly thereafter he rode into the above-mentioned village where he had business with his debt collection. With that I took leave of him and rode straight home with Jost, where I now found a young heir.

Chapter Thirteen. The Cook Cheats on the Peasant.

Bucephalus, the bards recount,
Would only let one rider mount.

At that time I surely enjoyed the greatest joy under the sun, and since the opportunity fitted so well, I married my virginal cook to the peasant fellow, who suited her better, the longer they knew each other. But three months later the fellow had a frightful problem because now this young nobleman, now that one came into his house in his absence. The lover who came almost daily was named Finis and the peasant Opus; thus one easily could have said: *Finis coronat opus.*[72] But finally I took the cook in hand, and after she had confessed to me a long list of those who had helped her pass the time, I made clear to her her disgraceful deeds and the added misfortune that customarily follows such a vile life. "Do you think," I said to her, "that this dance will go on forever? Oh, my dear cook, whoever dances to this fiddle will soon see its strings snap. Do you think people don't know about your sneaky tricks? With tear-filled eyes your husband complained to me about how you were cheating on him. You ought to be heartily ashamed. Did you learn such a thing from me or my wife? Did your parents teach you such a trade, or where did you dig up such whorish tricks? Now, you whore, you're standing there pale and shocked, but how will it go for you when you've died and have to face a severer judge than me? Your heart is beating and pounding in your body like a weaver at his loom, isn't it? Why do you associate with such fools who are simply leading you to your ruin? Do you think I don't have the power and authority to have you led

---

[72] "The finish puts a crown on the work," a pun on *corona*, "crown," and *cornus*, "horn," the traditional mark of the cuckold.

around publicly in stocks or have the time counted out on your back with a rod? I've said this to you for the last time and properly warned you. Abandon such business or you'll experience the bastinado."

Then her husband came to me in the small room and said, "I heard from the door, Your Worship, that you gave my wife a good reprimand, and, on my word, you were right to do so. Sir, I can't complain enough of how she cheated and tricked me. Now I find her in the field, now in the garden with some cut-rate Romeo, but with Your Worship's permission, if another one comes into the house, I'll fix him up so good that he'll think about sneaking in windows all his life. From all that traffic I can barely cut a bale of hay. Recently I chased one across the field with my scythe and gave my neighbors plenty to laugh about. Therefore, Your Worship, I beg you to give me some good advice so that she'll have a while to think about it."

"See," I went on to her, "what an honorable minx you are?" Then I called my wife, who added her three cents' worth and spoke to the cook in such a way that she finally began to cry and her husband began to plead for her. "Well," I said, "if you want to intercede for your wife, we'll forget the matter." With that they departed and the cook swore to me and my wife that she would change from her whorish life and keep better house. But when they had gone down before the gate, the wife grabbed her husband by his hair and scratched his face much worse than the two maids had the clerk's. But I took my bird-shot pistol and shot at the whore's bodice until she ran away and left her husband behind, up to his ears in the muck.

"Yes," I said to my wife, "when such poison comes between married people, there's no medicine strong enough to remove the affliction. I know well that our clerk was the sole onset of all this uncleanliness. But very soon I'm going to pull that quill from behind his ear so that he knows it's been properly pulled. And so that he has no opportunity to go out, I'm going to lock up his jacket, pants, and coat. That way he'll have to write and conduct his tedious matters sitting in his bed. I noticed quite a while ago what inkwell he was dipping his pen into, but I'll turn the tables on him just like when Isidoro and I were given a beating at the estate in Peltzingen."

"To be sure," said my wife, "adultery is a great and ugly sin. Better to have the fellow chased out of the house than knowingly allow such arrogance. The schoolmaster is also not in the clear. My advice would be to have them both yoked in the pillory and whipped until they got a new skin, for they'll do no good in their old ones. Since you earlier pretended to be a tawer, it would be rather appropriate now if you gave their hides a good tanning and chased them out of the village."

Chapter Fourteen. Jost Gets Married. Frightful Tumult at the Castle. The Irishman Brings Them onto a Proper Path. Therewith This Entire Book Proceeds to Its Conclusion.

Worldly pleasures bring elation,
But good for him who seeks salvation.

Then my Jost came up the stairs and since I had few mercenaries standing guard with halberds and spears before my chamber, he came right in. "Sir," he said, "I've changed my mind. If it's all right with you and your wife, I want to marry the small cowherd and she wants to marry me. Therefore, I beg you not to withhold your good will and because I've worked for you for a good while loyally and diligently, give me good advice on how I can conclude the matter best."

"Yes," I said, "you and she alone and no other people, that's the best plan."

Jost smirked at this answer and kept spinning his leather cap around in his hand like a cat's tail. "Sir," he said, "that would certainly be the best deal, and I agree to it."

"You nasty ass," my wife said, "that's one beautiful proposal!" With that she hastened away.

But I gave Jost good advice and said, "How will you feed yourself with your Trudy?"

"Sir," he replied, "I'll simply have to work diligently as you well know. You don't save much when you're single, and when you go to a dance, your money evaporates into beer and music so that it eats at your heart. So I also think the girl is also good enough herself."

"Yes, yes," I said, "I also believes she's good enough herself, but how do you think she'll look from the rear?"

"Sir," he said, "you just can't leave your teasing, but when do you think we could get married?"

"Indeed," I said, "if the bride doesn't run away, whenever you want."

"Ha," he said, "I'll get her good and interested, you won't grow old waiting."

"Well," I said, "if you're serious, then think it over properly, my dear Jost. You don't jump into marriage like into your boots. Whoever wants to strike it lucky must have his eyes wide open." When I said this, Jost opened his eyes wide like a cat that wants to start a fight with a guard dog. I had to laugh at his simplicity. And because not much could be improved or worsened about his marriage since he would have to do as well as he could in any case, I immediately summoned the little cowherd as his future bride and said to her, "The very honorable and virtuous Monsieur Jost here present, a loyal worker who diligently curries the horses and shovels out the manure as, respectively, my stall inspector and farm reformer, has delivered to me a knightly, properly styled, and splendidly conceived oration and proposed to marry you and to select and choose your person as his loyal married spouse and housewife. If you want to have him, say yes, but nice and loud so people can hear it."

Then the girl screamed so loudly and clearly that it resonated in the fiddles and instruments hanging around. Then they both had to join paws, and I and my wife made arrangements for the wedding, at which all those were to appear at whose castles I earlier had been happy and merry. Accordingly, she prepared a good menu, and I wrote the following letter to all my acquaintances, but especially to Ludwig:

Now it's my turn to invite you and all of my good acquaintances to my small castle and, to be sure, to celebrate the wedding of His Highly Noble Worship, the Honorable and Resolute Herr Jost, who has assented to a enter marital union with the Most Honorable and Virtuous Mademoiselle Trudy, my small cowherd. To carry this off is not well possible without your presence; therefore, please grant me the honor and diversion of being able to make you happy at my place. Meanwhile think about some merry prank we can play on the bridegroom. I don't care to invite the argumentative doctor. The fool thinks a lot of himself and believes that whoever won't argue with him is a fool. If your wife wished to do me the favor of helping my wife cook, I would appreciate it. She would have to be here, however, next week. I'll let you worry about the musicians. I had so much hell to pay with the recent musicians, pipers, and such fools that I almost want to have nothing more to do with such fools. Meanwhile take care of yourself. The wedding day is set for the twentieth of this month. You'll know how to behave accordingly and provide yourself with ammunition for drinking toasts. *Vale!*

Your more than trusting Zendorio

When the note was delivered, I received the following answer:

Dear friend of my heart! Your note was delivered to me quite properly by our ordinary postmaster. I wish a thousand happinesses to the bridegroom on his bedding-down. He's a simpleton, honest in his words and diligent in his work; beyond all doubt he'll make a nice and very patient cuckold. You write about musicians that you don't want to have anything to do with them. My advice would be that we write to a Latin school for four or five pupils, they'll make enough noise for us, and when we get them loaded, we'll have more to laugh about them than about twelve fools. They'll also be content with a Taler, where one can scarcely get rid of the other fools for eight. They also won't put as much roast, cakes, and cookies in their bags. But now pay attention that you don't put the gambling table too near to the wedding party;

otherwise their lice will crawl on our clothes. Farewell, my wife will certainly come, your wife can rely on that.

With return greetings, your Ludwig

I received such and similar answers from almost all of those whom I had invited to this wedding. Jost meanwhile was busy having himself made new trousers of sheepskin and he bought the bride a green and crimson skirt. That was the entire wedding finery for both parties. For although the rascal had a hundred and fifty Gülden in hard cash, he now began to scrimp, perhaps because he had been brought up by the strange nobleman Crispan. A week later one after another arrived at my estate, and I was happy to have company to make me properly happy. For what is better for a person on earth than a merry and cheerful time? A lot of money just creates worries and great estates demand great supervision. But an amusing hour sweetens all labor and a good drink of wine is the best medicine for all cares and fantasies.

My little castle was situated not far from the Rhine. For that reason my cellar, although not large at all, was full of exquisite Bacherach wine. That's why we said, "Our dear old wine from Bacherach makes us glad and tight as a clock. Oh, noble old Rinkauer, you ever-precious wine, you make the peasants glower; for them you're much too fine." In such manner we got an early start on the jubilation in my house. I provided everything that could be eaten or drunk. Then Ludwig drove up with five students in my coach. "Behold," he said to me, "I bring my five sons of the Muses. But I don't know who their mother was. This one," he said, pointing at the one with the bass viol, "is from Purmesquick, where they drill the little holes; he'll make more fun for you than a half dozen bagpipers." Jost then arrived to greet his wedding guests. "Jost," said Ludwig, "how many fools are there here?"

"Let's see," said Jost, looking at the students, "I'm one by myself and there's five of you, and people already know what you are."

At this there was great laughter and Ludwig asked, "Jost, what am I then?"

"Sir," he said, "you're the biggest one!" Therewith he hurried into the courtyard, and Ludwig threw his traveling cap at his back.

I can't tell you how thereafter we horsed around the whole night, riding chairs and benches back and forth in the house, up one stairs and down the other, we danced in our shirts and hopped about with all sorts of instruments in the courtyard. Jost had to be present for everything, and thus we had enough to laugh about with all the holes he had in his shirt. Because at that time there also was a big fair in the town near me, all sorts of entertainers came there, not the least among whom were the Italians who peddled beautiful curios and toys. Because most of those had to ride by my castle, I rounded up some of the Italians who had to demonstrate their curios and toys all at the same time. And then we and the ladies, who were present in goodly number, couldn't stop laughing when the young men were all screaming frightfully at the same time and singing about their *bella Catharina*. Amid this tumult the five students with violins had to contribute their bit, to which we nobles blew on our hunting horns. The village shepherd also had to add his horn, and to anyone else who didn't have an instrument, I gave a key; whistling and grating were mixed together like in a stamping mill. Soon we were climbing in the fireplace and calling out the hours from the window until finally the day of the wedding arrived.

We were just as merry at this wedding as we had been at the others. Against his will, the priest had to give us permission to horse around. We placed Jost and his bride at the head of the table and above them a Latin inscription that read: *locus supremus inter nos supremum stultum capit.*[73] "Sir," said Jost to the pupil with the bass viol, "what does that mean in German?"

"If the cook is good you'll eat in class, and if you doubt it, kiss my ass!"

"Yes, yes," said Jost, "Herr Ludwig wrote it out, he's occasionally right coarse and joking, we mustn't hold it against him."

"Sure," said the pupil, "one can't hold anything against the nobility, one has to laugh at whatever they do and even if they say, 'You know where you can kiss me!'"

"You're telling the truth," said Jost.

At this great laughter arose because some people had observed and paid close attention to their conversation. Therefore, we place the bass player with us at the table so that we could enjoy his conversation all the better. He then quietly proposed how one could play a good joke on the bridegroom and arranged that someone took the bottom out of the wedding bed and placed a tub full of fresh water under it. After that he had a clean sheet spread over it as if the bed had been freshly made and the pillows and the quilt tacked onto it. When in the evening the bridegroom wanted to go to bed with his bride, he and the bride put on a great and protracted show. Neither wanted to be the first in bed, and through surreptitiously bored holes we observed this exchange of courtesies. After much arguing they finally agreed that they would climb in together, but — Gadzooks! — how they fell into the water. They had enough to do to stand up again and get themselves untangled from the sheet. "Rascal, thief, scoundrel," said Jost, "gallows birds prepared this bath for me. I hope your fingers contort, you rascal and your tub of water." At that we hastened in the darkness into the room, put out the light, and splashed water on the bridegroom and his bride. Some threw water in every direction, and thus we ruined our good clothes until we finally broke the bed to pieces and threw Jost's and his bride's wedding clothes out of the window.

---

[73] "The chief fool among us takes the highest seat."

When Jost saw that he could do nothing about it, he finally submitted patiently to it, changed his attitude, and went along with it better than anyone else. Then we brought him down again with us, and the students made him in his shirt a *magister philosophiæ*, for which the bass-playing rogue acted the clown. Others brought the bride down and because they were both dripping wet, we tied them together by their shirttails and chased them both back up the stairs to a different room.

Nothing was nicer than a student who fell in love with Magdalena, Frau Ludwig's sister. Because the latter was a cunning lady, she told the student he should surreptitiously steal away from his comrades and clandestinely climb up the chimney behind the fireplace, where she would come to him after everyone was asleep. The chap believed her words as though they were a rule of grammar. Thus he stole away and climbed up as well as he could. But meanwhile she revealed her plan. The bass player brought coals under the chimney and pretended he wanted to roast some sausages. Through the smoke he choked the enamored monkey so that he finally fell down quite unconscious. He had his head between his legs so that one could take him to be much more a bagpipe than a human being. The laughter of those standing around was so great that one could scarcely see how he managed to leap out of the fire.

Then we began our earlier music again, and so that the ladies wouldn't be forgotten, danced with some until they had grown sleepy, then we really began to horse around. We poured wine not only in our gullets, but over our heads. As soon as a glass was emptied, someone hurled it down into the road and fired off a pistol or a carbine. Finally I rounded up all the rattles in the village, we started up a clamor that might have deafened someone. Since almost all the glasses were smashed, we drank from other vessels such as lead shakers, slippers, tin cans, powder horns, pisspots, from which one person vomited under the table, the next out of the window. Only then did we have the greatest fun when the students were drunk. For then they began to argue and finally assault one another, so that we had enough to do to hold them off. In such drunkenness and tumult we carried first one here, another there, one to the hay mow, one to the dovecote, and the third we stuck into the oven. *Summa summarum,* we played the game until day came on, until one person fell here, the next there, full of wine and tumult, not knowing whether it was day or night.

I was awakened by a blow and when I awoke in the house where I had lain with others of the nobility on the straw and looked up with half-opened eyes. I saw a monk standing over us with a long sack over his shoulder, who had pounded on the pantry with his staff. "What is this?" he said. "Am I among men or cattle? Do I find reason here or have I come to senseless people who are out of their minds? Oh, Zendorio, oh, Ludwig, oh, Caspar, oh, Isidoro, oh, Ergasto, and you other good friends, how did you happen into this debauchery? Is that making proper use of Heaven's gifts? Where is your reason? Where is your light? Where is your good example? Do you call that improving your life? Do you call that spending your life blissfully and peacefully? Oh, arise from the grave to life, awake from sin unto virtue, open your eyes to that which is good and improve yourselves." Finally one after the other woke up, and when we got a good look at the monk, it was the Irishman, who begged his way up and down through the country.

I can't sufficiently describe how shocked we were at this, for formerly we hadn't been so approving of his lifestyle, and thus he had a good opportunity to nicely rub our mistakes under our noses at this time. "Oh, brothers," he went on to say, "I haven't come here to chastise you but to admonish you so that you will wake up not only from your sleep, but also in your spirits. Cast off these infamous hellish guises of temporal lust and strive much rather to serve Heaven in sustained repentance. What does it help you to spend your life in such a state that you always have to fear eternal death? True bliss does not exist in possessing great means, but in knowing how to use them in Christian modesty. I do indeed wear a coarse coat on my body, but also an inviolate conscience in my heart that is the most precious jewel in human existence.

"Hope for this, strive for this which, if you have gained it, will be of purpose to grant you true bliss, that is, eternal life. How do you profit in condemning your bodies in revelry and continual partying? Thereby you not only bury yourselves before your time, but in addition do harm to the salvation of your souls. Set a new course and change your lives not to please me, but yourselves, for the world is dying in its sins. Therefore, abandon them so that you will not have to die along with it."

With these words he departed, and "What?" said Ludwig, "wasn't that our Irishman?"

"Yes it was," I said, "and what he said was more than true."

"I feel all his comments in my conscience," said Ludwig.

"And I," said Caspar, "am full of repentance."

"Therefore," I said, "let us arise from our excess and follow a different path to strive for our eternal salvation."

With that we arose and also woke the others, and because the hermit still lay in our thoughts, each hastened his way homeward with the firm resolve of bettering the life he had led until now and spend it in a manner pleasing to God. So that after all our transient earthly trifles and fleeting vanity we might ultimately arrive at the triumph of our immortal eternity, where proper tranquility and lasting peace without deceit, contentment without want, love without hate, accord without discord, life without death, and all sufficient bliss will blossom and prosper without cease and end.

253

A Brief Report to the Reader

Since this text has found some approval among readers who usually look for the substance in such works, to concede to their desire the translator offers to prepare and submit for printing *German Summer Tales* very soon. Meanwhile he commends himself to the reader's continuing friendship and, because he is a human being, begs that he might be forgiven human mistakes. *vale.*

ADX-7492